MOB NEMESIS

Former FBI Special Agent in Charge

JOE GRIFFIN

with Don DeNevi

MOB NEMESIS

How the FBI Crippled Organized Crime

Prometheus Books

59 John Glenn Drive
Amherst, New York 14228-2197

Published 2002 by Prometheus Books

Inquiries should be addressed to
Prometheus Books
59 John Glenn Drive
Amherst, New York 14228–2197
VOICE: 716–691–0133, ext. 207
FAX: 716–564–2711
WWW.PROMETHEUSBOOKS.COM

06 05 04 03 02   5 4 3 2 1

Library of Congress Cataloging-in-Publication Data

Griffin, Joe, 1939–
    Mob nemesis : how the FBI crippled organized crime / Joe Griffin with Don DeNevi.
        p. cm.
    Includes bibliographical references (p.) and index.
    ISBN 1–57392–919–0 (alk. paper)
    1. Mafia—United States. 2. Organized crime investigation, United States.
3. United States. Federal Bureau of Investigation.—Officials and employees—Biography.
4. Police—United States—Biography. I. DeNevi, Don, 1937– II. Title.

HV6446 .G83 2002
364.1'06'0973—dc21   2001048719

Printed in the United States of America on acid-free paper

To my wife, Sandy, and to my children, Joe, Chris, Kevin, Shawn, and Jennie,
all of whom I love dearly.
To the street agents of the FBI,
who make the FBI the best investigative agency in the world.
They are responsible for the successes that I discuss in this book.

J.E.G.

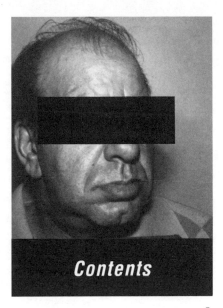

Contents

8 CONTENTS

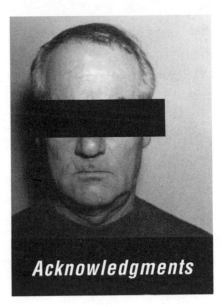

Acknowledgments

I would like to thank my wife, Sandy, for the support and encouragement she gave me for this project. Without her help I would not have been able to even begin this book. She spent weeks organizing and cataloging the extensive public records, personal records, and news reports that I used to refresh my memory for the writing of this book. I would also like to thank Dean Winslow, Dave Drab, John Sommer, Tom Thurston, and Barbara Bartus, who spent many hours of their free time gathering some of the public records and documents that I have used to round out this book.

I would like to thank the supervisors and agents who were assigned to the Cleveland organized-crime squad (the 9 Squad) and to the surveillance squad (the SAM Squad). They were completely dedicated to the FBI and to their mission. They were magnificent in the trenches fighting against the Cleveland La Cosa Nostra family. They were courageous and they never flinched.

I would also like to acknowledge U.S. Department of Justice Strike

Force Attorneys John Tarrant, Bob Stewart, Donna Cogeni Fitzsimmons, Abe Poretz, John Sopko, Virginia Junewicz, and Greg English; U.S. Attorneys Ken Schroeder and Pat McLaughlin; and Cuyahoga County Prosecutors Ed Walsh, Carmen Marino, and Tom Buford. They skillfully presented these cases in both federal and state courts and they eventually won our battles. The war against the Mob is not yet over, but mortal wounds have been delivered to some of the crime families and more are to come.

My special thanks also go to Bill Baker, Pat McLaughlin, Wilson Funhouser, Damon Dunn, and Meg French, who assisted me in editing this book.

Finally, a note to Don DeNevi, a college professor who now teaches the condemned on death row at San Quentin State Prison. I am indebted to you for learning about my work while you were researching your behavioral science unit book at the FBI Academy in Quantico, Virginia. Thank you for your persuasion, your patience, and above all for encouraging me to tell my story in my own way.

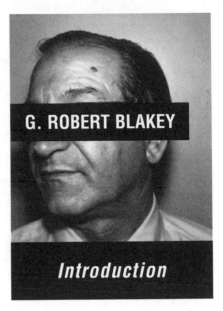

G. ROBERT BLAKEY

Introduction

Americans have a new love affair—with "organized crime." The flirtation began years ago with the *Godfather* movies, two of which won Oscars and two of which are among the highest-grossing films of all time. Indeed, Mario Puzo's 1969 best-seller, *The Godfather*, on which the movies were based, still remains in print in paperback. That love affair today, however, is largely focused on Tony Soprano and his dysfunctional blood family and his equally dysfunctional, but bloody, Mob family. Soprano, a fictional Mob boss from suburban New Jersey, is featured on *The Sopranos*, an HBO series dealing with the problems of his two families: one composed of hoodlums; the other, of teenagers. Indeed, it is sometimes difficult to tell which gives him more trouble. The popularity of the series is everywhere evident; restaurateurs and movie house owners are reported to welcome the end of the series each season, and the return to these establishments on Sunday night of their hopelessly addicted TV viewers.

Fascination with crime is, of course, not new. Literature took up the romantic or heroic criminal long ago. The birth of the novel as a literary form in the sixteenth century was soon accompanied by the birth of the *picaro*, the merry rogue, the deceitful and dishonorable but not malicious hero or heroine who charmed and thieved his or her way through life, as in Henry Fielding's *Tom Jones* (1749) or Daniel Defoe's *Moll Flanders* (1722).

Nevertheless, this public focus on organized crime is problematic, particularly when it only looks at romanticized fiction in film or books, for those engaged in organized crime are seldom engaging. All too often, they are little more than sadistic cowards, as Joe Griffin's gripping book, *Mob Nemesis*, so aptly shows. Indeed, Griffin's book is an excellent antidote to the misconceptions found in popular fiction—film, books, or TV series. For that reason alone, it ought to be widely read.

The public focus on only one part of "organized crime"—the Mob— is also deeply troubling. The concept of organized crime is surely not exhausted by the Mob, as those of a variety of ethnic backgrounds are found in organized crime. Mob informant Joseph Valachi put it well to Sen. John L. McClellan in his 1963 Senate testimony: "I'm not talking about Italians, I'm talking about criminals." One troubling danger in focusing on only the Mob is that public consciousness tends, mistakenly, to equate organized crime with the Mob. And when law enforcement success in breaking it up is credibly reported, as Griffin's book does so well, the public may be misled into thinking that the "problem" of organized crime is "solved." It is not. Organized crime—like other kinds of crime— can be curtailed; it cannot be "solved." To be sure, "a" crime—say, a murder—may be "solved." But as long as fallen human nature remains unregenerated, murder will be with us. Cain killed Abel at the beginning of time; in all likelihood, brother will be killing brother until the end of time. The job of law enforcement is, in fact, a lot like battlefield surgery: it is always bloody, difficult, and dangerous, but it is nevertheless necessary, and it will not be rendered obsolete any time soon. The problem of organized crime is, therefore, increasingly being curtailed by sophisticated law enforcement efforts at the federal level and in some local areas, but it is not being solved.

Familiarity with the literature on organized crime also quickly shows that the phrase is used in various contexts with varying meanings; the phrase does not have a single or fixed definition. Like Humpty Dumpty's language, it can mean whatever the speaker chooses to make it mean, and it has meant many things to many people. It can be used, for example, to refer to the crimes committed by organized criminal groups—gambling, narcotics, loan-sharking, theft and fencing, and the like. Here, a difference of opinion some-times exists. How sophisticated should a criminal group become before it is called "organized crime"? What about professional thieves? What about white-collar crime? The Report of the National Conference on Organized Crime in 1975 broadly defined "organized crime" as "any group of individ-uals whose primary activity involved violating criminal laws to seek illegal profits and power by engaging in racketeering activities and, when appro-priate, engaging in intricate financial manipulations." The report of the Pres-ident's Commission on Crime and Administration of Justice in 1967 more narrowly defined "organized crime" and limited it to underworld groups that are sufficiently sophisticated that they regularly employ techniques of violence and corruption to achieve their other criminal ends. The commis-sion also observed that "white-collar" crime "is now commonly used to des-ignate those occupational crimes committed in the course of their work by persons of high status and social repute." On the other hand, a case can be made that the misuse of legitimate organizations by the so-called white-collar offender is often little different from the running of illegal organiza-tions in the underworld—excepting, of course, the direct use of violence to achieve illegal ends—though white-collar crime, say, pollution, can and many times does indirectly cause as many deaths as organized crime causes directly. But that is an argument for another day. Typically, white-collar crime and ad hoc groups such as youth gangs, pickpocket rings, or even professional criminals who come together for one or more "scores" are excluded from the category organized crime by most law enforcement officials and scholars.

Among groups that can plausibly claim the dubious title of "organized crime," other useful distinctions may be helpfully drawn. A distinction may be drawn between enterprises, syndicates, and ventures. Some, too, would probably not apply the label of "organized crime" to each of these groups; they would restrict it to syndicates.

An organized crime *enterprise* is a criminal group that provides illicit goods or services on a regular basis. An example would be a narcotics wholesaler and his cutting crew. Thus, it is a criminal firm or business organization.

An organized crime *syndicate*, on the other hand, is a criminal group that regulates relations between various enterprises; it may be metropolitan, regional, national, or international in scope; and it may be concerned with only one field of endeavor—say, drugs—or with a broad range of illicit activities. A syndicate is, therefore, a criminal cartel or business organization; it fixes prices for illicit goods and services, allocates illicit markets and territories, acts as a criminal legislature and court, sets criminal policy, settles disputes, levies "taxes," and offers protection from both rival groups and legal prosecution.

A *venture* is a criminal episode regularly engaged in by a particular group of criminals; it may be the hijacking of a truck or the robbery of a bank. It is a manifestation of organized crime only when its members have ties to a syndicate, which gives them access to superior resources, including capital, skilled labor, or outlets for stolen property.

In 1951 the Kefauver Committee in the Senate, after the first comprehensive look at organized crime of the United States, declared that a nationwide crime syndicate known as the Mafia operated in many large cities and that its leaders usually controlled the most lucrative rackets in their cities. Unfortunately, the committee's use of the word "Mafia" was not discriminating. In fact, "Mafia" is a word of uncertain origins and multiple meanings. An 1868 dictionary defines it as a neologism denoting "bravado," while another of 1876 defines it as of Piedmontese origin, the equivalent of "gang," the popular sense in use even today, such as when those around former President Jimmy Carter were referred to as the "Georgia Mafia." Nevertheless, it is principally used today in reference to two separate but not always distinguished criminal organizations, one in Sicily and one in the United States.

In Sicily, the organization is ancient but its origins are not clearly determined. It is composed of groups called *cosche*, a corruption of the word for "artichoke." The *cosche*, or groups, control various licit or illicit areas or activities on the island; the groups also form close ties to politicians for protection and patronage. Each group is headed by a *capo*; the familiar term *don* is merely a name of *rispetto*, or respect; it does not mean "head" or "chief." Some *cosche* are more powerful than others. To become even more powerful, the various *cosche* come together to form *consorteria*, or a loose alliance, which together make up the *amico degli amici*, or "friends of ours"; the *onorato societá*, or "honored society" of Sicily; or, in short, what we call the "Mafia."

In the United States, the early Mafia must first be distinguished from the Black Hand, or *Mano Negro*. The Black Hand was not a group or organization, but a technique in the 1900s of extortion centered solely in Italian immigrant communities, that is, of sending a Black Hand, signifying death, if extortion money was not paid; no convincing evidence has ever been produced that these extortionate activities extended to the larger community in the United States. The *Union Siciliana* must also be distinguished from the Mafia, though it was widely infiltrated by gangsters; it was a legitimate fraternal organization, which was chartered by Illinois in 1895 and, after 1910, it was supervised by the state's Department of Insurance. It was not, as such, a criminal organization, and it ought not be confused with the Mafia. The American Mafia or La Cosa Nostra, the focus of *Mob Nemesis*, was formed in 1931 in New York City by the leaders of a series of criminal groups in New York and in other major urban areas. It was not then, and it is not now, a foreign branch of a Sicilian organization; it is, and was, fully American in character, even though a number of its early members were members of the Sicilian Mafia who fled from Sicily because of law enforcement pressure brought to bear on them in the 1920s by the Fascist dictatorship of Benito Mussolini. Indeed, when several of its leaders, who happened to be born in Italy but were nevertheless raised in the United States, were deported to Italy by the federal government following the Kefauver Committee's investigation in the 1950s, Italian law enforcement authorities rightly complained that American gangsters were being foisted off on them and that they were Americanizing Italian organized crime. It is the story of the rise and fall of the American Mafia that is so vividly told by Griffin in *Mob Nemesis*. It is a story well worth telling and reading.

The Mafia's made membership in the United States in 1963 was approximately 5,000. Twenty-five hundred of these were in five families in New

York City; 300 or more were in Chicago, the other major city of widespread organized crime activity, under one family. Cleveland, the center of Griffin's book, was smaller; it had 150 members grouped into one family. The Mafia at that time was composed of twenty-four *borgate*, or families, each headed by a *capo*. The *suttocapo*, or "underboss," was the second in command; the families also had a *consigliere*, or "counselor." The families were subdivided into *regime*, or "crews," headed by *caporegime*, or "captains." Not equal in wealth, power, or status, the various Mafia families were under the general jurisdiction of the *commissione*, or "Commission." In 1963 it included the bosses of four of the five families in New York City and the bosses of the families in Buffalo, Philadelphia, Detroit, and Chicago. Members were known as *soldati*, or "soldiers" or "wise guys." The soldiers were the individuals who, along with their nonmember associates, engaged in the illegal activities of organized crime: gambling, narcotics, loan-sharking, hijacking, labor racketeering, and the rest. They were also those who engaged in the legal activities of organized crime: garbage disposal, restaurants and bars, vending machines, produce, trucking, and garment manufacturing.

The higher-ups in the organization, the bosses and other leaders, stayed out of the day-to-day dirty work of organized crime. This they left to the soldiers, insulating themselves from most street-level techniques of law enforcement investigation: physical surveillance, questioning, serving search warrants, and making low-level arrests. As *Mob Nemesis* shows, penetration of this insulation requires sophisticated techniques, such as wiretaps and bugs, and the careful turning of insiders to be witnesses.

The organization is known to outsiders as the "Mafia." To insiders it is known as La Cosa Nostra or "this thing of ours." It is also known by a wide variety of other names—in Buffalo, "the Arm"; in Chicago, "the Outfit." Composed of Sicilians or Italians, its members formed numerous alliances with others. In Chicago, for example, from Alphonse "Al" Capone, who died in 1947, to Anthony "Tony" Accardo, who died in 1992, men such as John "Jake" Guzik, a Polish Jew, and Llewellyn "Murray" Humphries, a Welschman, played key roles in the organization. In short, no ethnic group has had a monopoly on organized crime in the United States.

Recognition of the common ethnic tie of the members of the Mafia is essential to understanding its structure, as described above. Nevertheless, some are rightly concerned that the identification of the Mafia's ethnic character reflects unfairly on Italian Americans in general. Indeed, U.S. Representative Marge Roukema from Ridgewood, New Jersey, is sponsoring a resolution in Congress condemning the entertainment industry's negative portrayal of Italian Americans generally, but particularly in *The Sopranos*. She aptly observes: "If this kind of ethnic profiling were being directed at African Americans or Hispanics, they would have been marching in the streets." This false implication was eloquently refuted by one of the nation's outstanding experts on organized crime, Sgt. Ralph Salerno of the New York City Police Department. When an Italian American racketeer complained to him, "Why does it have to be one of your own kind that hurts you?" Sergeant Salerno answered, "I'm not your kind and your not my kind. My manners, morals, and mores are not yours. The only thing we have in common is that we both spring from an Italian heritage and culture—and you are the traitor to that heritage and culture which I am proud to be part of."

Today, La Cosa Nostra is but a remnant of the 1963 organization. Membership is down to 1,150. Seven hundred fifty of these are in New York City, where its five families are shells of their former selves; only 40 to 50 members are in Chicago, where its seven crews are down to three. The Cleveland family is virtually destroyed. The causes are various—death, old age, the rise of rival groups, and changes in economic and social life; but the most significant is law enforcement pressure, as Griffin shows in *Mob Nemesis*. That pressure has stemmed from lawful wiretaps and bugs, turning key insider witnesses, criminal prosecutions, and civil suits—using, in particular, the federal Racketeer Influenced and Corrupt Organizations statute, which authorizes long prison terms, the forfeiture of ill-gotten gains, and civil suits used to break the hold of the Mob on labor unions. In fact, most families of the Mob are today little more than street gangs. The National Commission, fearful of FBI surveillance, has not met in ten years. La Cosa Nostra no longer has any special edge in an underworld teeming with Asians, Russians, and South Americans. In short, the sun has not set, but it is twilight for the Mob.

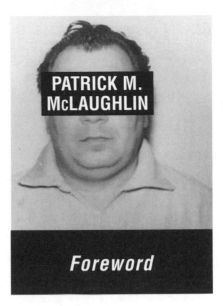

PATRICK M. McLAUGHLIN

Foreword

The Mafia, La Cosa Nostra, the Mob, the Brotherhood, traditional organized crime: All names associated with a criminal element portrayed by such American classics as *The Untouchables*, *The Godfather*, and now *The Sopranos*. If your image of mobsters is that of glamorous, rough but teddy-bear-like loveable fellows, read this book!

Joe Griffin, a man who knows about the Mob, brings us back to reality. This book could only be written by a man who labored in the trenches of law enforcement's war on organized crime spanning several decades. During a thirty-one year career with the FBI Joe Griffin so labored, and the story he tells will leave you shocked by the brutality and violence enhanced by a wealth of photographs accumulated over his three-decade tour of duty. If you want the uncut, real-life version of law enforcement's war on La Cosa Nostra, unfiltered through Hollywood's cameras—read this book!

From his humble West Virginia beginnings, Joe takes us on a journey through his FBI career with a focus on his interest in and unique contributions to the efforts by the Department of Justice to recognize, challenge, and largely dismantle Mafia families throughout the United States. A recognized expert in traditional organized crime, Joe Griffin earned a stellar reputation within the ranks of law enforcement officers and prosecutors for his personal contributions to those efforts. Joe's assignments included Chicago; Buffalo; FBI headquarters; Louisville, Kentucky; and Cleveland. A piece of Joe's tale, the demise of the Cleveland La Cosa Nostra family, is well known to me, as we met during the years I served as the United States Attorney for the Northern District of Ohio (1984–1988).

This real-life story is a tribute not only to Joe Griffin but to the thousands of FBI and other federal law enforcement agents, along with their state and local counterparts, who risk life, limb, and the pursuit of their personal and family relationships to protect society from those who would do us harm. This work also pays tribute to the dedication and commitment of the Department of Justice prosecutors and their state and county colleagues in molding the investigator's work product into successful prosecutions and, through the sentencing judges, into long prison terms. Those sentences played a key role in convicted Mob bosses violating the Omerta —a Sicilian code of silence—and cooperating with the Department of Justice in the prosecution of entire Mob families and ongoing criminal enterprises. As you will see in the experience of Angelo Lonardo, ultimately the acting boss of the Cleveland La Cosa Nostra family, the journey to become the highest-ranking La Cosa Nostra figure to break the code and turn on the Mob comes with a unique insight into bureaucratic bungling, shortsightedness, and turf battles.

The men and women on the front line of the war against organized crime not only inflict casualties, but sustain them. While celebrating the successes achieved by the systematic dismantling of entire Mob families in several major cities, this book speaks to the toll inflicted on the agents who man the front line. Joe Griffin is no exception and he pulls no punches in addressing not only the good, but the bad and the ugly as well.

This work presents a detailed, gripping story that dives into the cold, dark, and dirty waters of the Mafia with horrifying glimpses of gratuitous violence. Notwithstanding the obvious successes of the agents and prosecutors in taking out La Cosa Nostra families and their criminal enterprises, must we remain vigilant? Does society need protection from mobsters, both real and "wannabes," and their schemes, scams, and violent tendencies? The answer: Read This Book! You will never again see a movie, TV show, or a fluff piece on the Mafia without filtering those accounts through the unforgettable experiences of the Department of Justice and those working with them, as told by a point man in the war against the Mob. Joe Griffin—clerk, special agent, Sicilian language specialist, assistant special agent in charge, special agent in charge, recipient of the FBI Medal of Valor—and now storyteller extraordinaire. Read, and enjoy, this book!

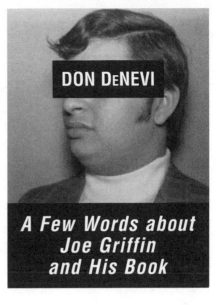

A Few Words about
Joe Griffin
and His Book

The very personal, very detailed story that follows is quite unlike any previous memoir on organized crime in America. Rather than the self-righteous recollections and confessions of yet another professional assassin–turned-snitch, or the glorified imaginary fiction of mafia dons, *Mob Nemesis: How the FBI Crippled Organized Crime* is the battle chronicle of a tough special agent's thirty-one-year crusade against "worthy adversaries," those cunning, highly intelligent criminals of Italian descent who preside over multimillion-dollar empires they call La Cosa Nostra.

FBI Medal of Valor recipient Joe Griffin's perspectives on organized crime in the Upper Ohio Valley—the structures of the crime families; their shifting alliances; the feuds, scams, and far-reaching connections—are unique. Placed in chronological order, those insights contribute to a rare anecdotal history. As the FBI's former special agent in charge of the Cleveland office, Griffin documents the New York–Ohio Mobs' evolution, from Stefano Magaddino's arrival in the United States to the rise of his subordinates and the vendettas of retribution that followed.

The nemesis came to know his deadly adversaries better than they, the Mob figures, knew themselves. Griffin's story is also the record of one man's dedication (*obsession* might be the better term) to succeed where all others failed. A pleasant man of somewhat scholarly appearance and obvious personal dignity, a jovial and social man who nevertheless maintains reserve in relationships, Griffin was born a natural tactician who loves to character analyze. When it came to face-to-face meetings with Mob leaders themselves, he knew instinctively what to say and do. His daring in dealing with them was the result of an absolute reliance on instinct and judgment, which has served him well in many tight situations, as well as in the death struggles he faced. He was willing to take considerable risk, especially when it involved himself, although his actions were carefully weighed and minutely planned.

In October of 1964, when he was one of three newly arrived agents assigned to Buffalo's recently established organized-crime squad—one of the nation's first—the Magaddinos were free to do what they pleased. They were semipublic figures, apparently immune to prosecution. Today, twelve years after he retired from the FBI as its senior field commander, Griffin has good reason to smile. Magaddino, one of the founders of La Cosa Nostra, was destroyed and died in disgrace. His successors in the 1970s are imprisoned or dead. The Cleveland La Cosa Nostra family has been destroyed. The boss of this family was convicted and decided to break Omerta and talk. He was "flipped" and is in the Federal Witness Security Program (commonly referred to as the "witness protection program"), after having testified against the La Cosa Nostra Commission (the leaders in New York City) and the leaders of the Chicago, Milwaukee, and Kansas City La Cosa Nostra families. They have all been convicted and most are in prison or dead. As one of the chief strategists of these major victories, Joe Griffin savors the triumphs with more than customary relish.

He writes: "We did something that, at times, we thought we'd never live to see. We lopped off the heads of some of the biggest crime bosses our nation has ever seen. Nailing them was worth the years of hard work we put into our investigative operations. Maybe our efforts were not the coup de grâce in all cases, but it was a mortal wound that's going to bleed them until they're all gone."

Revealing new anecdotal material and fresh observations about traditional Mob lore, Griffin's motherlode of original material is presented within the loose chronology of his evolution from neophyte Mob watcher to one of the country's leading authorities on organized crime. Thanks to this story, we see the Buffalo and Cleveland Mobs undergo a fundamental transformation over the years—once Omerta, or the code of silence, was broken. Now, in Buffalo, Cleveland, and many other cities, with many of the "made" men either in jail or dead, non–La Cosa Nostra "associates" are assuming positions of greater access and influence. But they don't have the disciplined organization that formerly was La Cosa Nostra, so the new breed will be more vulnerable.

And, again thanks to Joe, career criminals are portrayed not as jaded drudges packaged in overly familiar fictional clichés, but as they really are: greedy, cowardly, coldly rational inhabitants of a private, secret world known as La Cosa Nostra. Their loyalty is to power, greed, and corruption, not to their personal families or to their country. It is the ways of their world that we outsiders find so incomprehensible.

As for the reader, the no–nonsense, deliberate text that follows is reminiscent of any one of the several thousand debriefings Joe prepared during his thirty-one years of service in the FBI. All the better for you to feel authentically included wholly within his actions. Eloquence and rhetorical skill have no place in describing systematic murder.

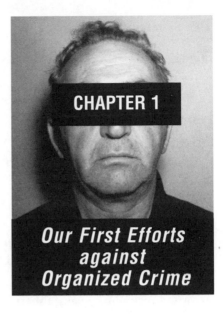

CHAPTER 1

Our First Efforts against Organized Crime

Meyer Lansky was once overheard on a hidden FBI microphone stating, "We're bigger than U.S. Steel." He was right. Organized crime is more profitable than probably all of the top Fortune 100 companies put together. Consider the figures: in 1945, nearly $500 million; in 1965, $40 billion; in 1985, $100 billion. And today, considering the enormous drug trade revenues, who knows?

But as the great and gentlemanly Estes Kefauver, former chairman of the Senate Crime Investigating Committee, told the nation in April of 1951, "In the earlier and more violent days of rum-running and hijacking, the big-city gangs thrived on murder and other crimes of violence. As the years went by, and the mobsters became more sophisticated and experienced, they realized that killings were not only bad business but bad public relations, that 'in union there is strength.' Gradually they got together; they toned down the violence; and, astounding as it seems, began reaching more or less peaceful agreements on division of territory and 'spheres of influence.'" In later years, when massive violence broke out, we were able to use this to our advantage, as you will see.

THE MAFIA AND THE CAMORRA

In the beginning, there were principally two organized-crime groups that came to the United States from Europe, the Sicilian Mafia and the Camorra, which was Neapolitan. Around 1890 members of these gangs began infiltrating the immigrant population coming into the United States and they settled in those communities located in our major port cities, such as New York, New Orleans, Buffalo, Chicago, Cleveland, and Detroit. Their first victims were their fellow new arrivals to America. Protection rackets were established by these gangs, and these operations soon collectively became known as the "Black Hand." In the late 1800s the Mafia was first successful outside the immigrant communities when it began using the extortion technique against fishermen and cargo shippers at the New York docks. They eventually took over the docks and, to an extent, they are still there. However, it wasn't until Prohibition in the mid-1920s that these gangs really gained a foothold throughout America. During Prohibition, the gangs became rich and powerful. This caused gang wars over territories and resulted in tremendous violence in New York and Chicago. According to legend, one night in April 1931 the turf battles between the Mafia and Camorra families resulted in hundreds of Mob murders throughout the United States. This night became known as the "Night of the Sicilian Vespers." To stem the violence, which was costing the gangs to lose tremendous amounts of illegal revenue, something had to be done.

On April 15, 1931, Giuseppe Masseria, who was then the "boss of all bosses," (*capo di tutti capi*) was shot to death in a Coney Island, New York, restaurant. He was succeeded as family head by Salvatore "Charlie Lucky" Luciana. The new "boss of all bosses" became Salvatore Maranzano.

LA COSA NOSTRA

Masseria's death signified the end of the gang war between the Camorra and the Mafia. Several weeks after Masseria's death, all of the Mafia and Camorra bosses met in Chicago and agreed to form a new organization,

La Cosa Nostra (LCN), which translates as "this thing of ours" or "our thing." At that juncture, Maranzano and Luciana created the Commission, which was a body that was to rule over the twenty-four La Cosa Nostra families that remained. La Cosa Nostra became something totally unique to North America. Regional designations were dropped and most of the families took the names of their original founders.

More important were organizational shakeups at this time. Luciana took over the Masseria (formerly Camorra) family, with Frank Costello becoming his underboss. Vito Genovese became the boss of what became known as the Genovese family. Joseph Profaci retained control of the Villabate group that became the Profaci family. When Joseph Profaci died of natural causes on June 6, 1962, he was ultimately succeeded by Joseph Colombo and this family became known as the Colombo family. Philip Mangano became boss of the Mineo (former Mafia) family, which later became known as the Carlo Gambino family. Gaetano Gagliano became boss of the Reina (former Mafia) family, which later would be known as the Thomas Lucchese family. Joseph Bonanno became underboss in the Maranzano (former Mafia) family, which today is known as the Bonanno family. Stefano Magaddino became boss of the Buffalo (former Mafia) family, which became the Magaddino family. Frank Milano became boss of the Cleveland family. Al Capone was then the reigning boss of the Chicago (formerly Camorra) family.

On September 10, 1931, Salvatore Maranzano, the successor to Joe Masseria as "boss of all bosses," was shot and stabbed to death in his Manhattan office building by four members of Meyer Lansky's Jewish Mob who were posing as police officers. Lansky's assistance rendered him an important nonmember of LCN for the remainder of his life. Lansky could not be inducted into LCN because he was not of Italian or Sicilian descent. However, he became the most important nonmember in LCN history.

LCN families are said to be organized like a Roman legion. Each "family" has a boss, an underboss (suttocapo), a counselor (consigliere), soldiers (buttons, members, made guys), and internal squads of members (dicinas or crews) were formed that were headed by a capodecina (capo, street boss, captain). This term translates as "boss of ten." I find it interesting that

FBI offices are organized the same way. Each FBI office has a special agent in charge (boss) who reports directly to the FBI director. The second in command is the assistant special agent in charge (underboss). Each office has a principal lawyer (consigliere) who is called the principal legal advisor, and the office is divided into specialized squads (crews or dicinas) headed by a squad supervisor (capo).

To become a member of LCN, the prospect must be 100 percent Italian or Sicilian, he must be sponsored by a current LCN member, and he must be tested, usually by committing a Mob killing, or "hit." A ritual, consisting of a prick of the finger and the taking of an oath to remain loyal to the "family" over the member's own personal family and country, was established. Once a man becomes an LCN member, his only exit is death. A code of Omerta was established and it was forbidden on pain of death to talk about LCN with anyone who was not a known member or to mess with another member's wife or girlfriend. A method was devised to identify members to each other: When a member introduces another member to a second member, he is introduced as "a friend of ours." If a nonmember is introduced to an LCN member by another LCN member, the nonmember is described as "a friend of mine."

The original National Commission was comprised of the bosses of the five New York LCN families and the bosses of the Philadelphia, Buffalo, Chicago, Cleveland, Detroit, and New Orleans families. This has varied over the years. Today, due to recent turmoil caused by the incarceration of most commission members, the Chicago family boss represents the Chicago family and all LCN families west of the Mississippi on the Commission. The bosses of the Genovese and Gambino families now represent the New York families on the Commission.

With this consolidation of power, their crimes became organized and their criminal businesses were henceforth referred to by law enforcement as "organized crime."

LAW ENFORCEMENT AND THE MOB

When I entered the Federal Bureau of Investigation in 1957, only a handful of law enforcement people and elected officials were insisting that organized crime was a growing threat to the safety and security of the United States. It wasn't until the early 1950s that congressional investigators began in earnest to dig up details about Mob businesses. It wasn't until years later, in the 1960s and 1970s, that they passed laws that could be used effectively against organized crime.

The FBI didn't become actively engaged in the war against organized crime until the Mob was exposed in the infamous Apalachin raid, which occurred on November 10, 1957. In fact, other agencies won our federal government's early victories against organized crime. You'd be shocked to realize how many people still believe *The Untouchables* were agents of the FBI. They were actually agents of the Alcohol, Tobacco, and Firearms Division (ATF) and the Internal Revenue Service (IRS). They sent Al Capone to prison because he violated alcohol and income tax laws.

FBI Director J. Edgar Hoover took over a scandal-plagued Department of Justice bureau of investigation in 1924 and personally built it into what is regarded today as the greatest law enforcement agency in the world. He established the FBI Laboratory and the FBI Identification Division. He founded the FBI Academy—the "West Point of law enforcement"—in Quantico, Virginia, where thousands of police officers from over the world are trained under the FBI National Academy (FBINA) program. He brought law enforcement into the twentieth century and dedicated his life to the FBI. But with regard to organized crime, he, other national law enforcement leaders, and the Department of Justice dropped the ball.

As late as 1957, more than a half decade after the Kefauver Committee's startling revelations, Hoover believed and publicly stated that there was "no proof of the existence of a national syndicate, or organized crime network." But as he focused his attention on the legitimate Soviet communist threat in America and reactive crimes such as interstate car theft, bank robberies, and occasional kidnapings, organized crime became stronger and FBI field agents were increasingly providing his office with important intelligence information on the nation's growing organized-crime problem. But Hoover was not alone in not recognizing the growing threat and existence of a national organized-crime organization. William Hundley, the chief of the newly extablished Organized Crime Section of the Department of Justice in the early 1960s, is quoted in Peter Maas's book *The Valachi Papers* as saying, "Before Valachi came along, we had no concrete evidence that anything like this actually existed. In the past we've heard that so-and-so was a syndicate man, and that was about all. Frankly, I always thought a lot of it was hogwash."

Then, in late 1957, three dramatic events occurred that changed the face of organized crime in America forever. First, from October 10 to 14, 1957, the American LCN leadership, led by Joseph Bonanno and the Magaddinos of Buffalo, met with Sicilian Mafia Boss Don Giuseppe Genco Russo, Salvatore "Charlie Lucky" Luciana (Lucky Luciano), and other Sicilian Mafia leaders at the Grand Hotel des Palmes in Palermo, Sicily. The purpose of this four-day meeting was to initiate and formulate plans for the Sicilian Mafia, with the active cooperation of the American LCN, to expand its heroin-smuggling operations to North America. Second, based on orders from Vito Genovese and Thomas Lucchese, Albert "The Mad Hatter" Anastasia was murdered in a barbershop chair at the New York Park Sheraton Hotel on October 25, 1957, clearing the way for Vito Genovese to assume the throne of the Vincent Mangano crime family. Anastasia certainly had the killing coming. This lunatic awaited execution for murder in Sing Sing's death house during 1921 and 1922, until his henchmen were able to kill several witnesses. He eventually won a new trial and he was ultimately freed. Later, he took delight in bossing "Murder, Incorporated," a gang of murderous psychopaths responsible for at least thirty executions and corpse dismemberments on behalf of other crime families.

Finally, after the assassination of Anastasia, Genovese needed to hold a national Mob convention of all the top LCN family bosses to explain and justify the Anastasia hit, to carve up Anastasia's empire, and to sanctify Genovese as "boss of all bosses." Genovese also had to explain and confirm the new LCN relationship with the Sicilian Mafia in the heroin-smuggling operation in North America. Three weeks after the Anastasia hit, on

November 14, 1957, a summit of all the nation's Mob leaders was held in the hamlet of Apalachin, New York.

APALACHIN

All the mobsters who mattered in North America were invited to Apalachin by Genovese and Buffalo LCN boss Stefano Magaddino. But Genovese wanted to have the "congress" convene in Chicago, which offered a central locality as well as the usual protective coloring and camouflage of a big city. Stefano disagreed. Why not have the meeting at the Apalachin home of one of his most trusted LCN associates, Joe Barbara? The rural setting, he argued, would be ideal to escape any possible sophisticated police surveillance. These were "farmer" cops who didn't know or care about organized crime. Furthermore, the peaceful ranch setting with its cows and crops would help soothe any frayed feelings left over from Anastasia's unexpected demise. Genovese reluctantly agreed. When he learned he was to be the host, Barbara sent his son out to make hotel and motel reservations for some one hundred men in the surrounding area. "Give our friends the best you got. Price don't matter," the son told one of the hotel clerks. A special shipment of some four hundred pounds of prime beef tenderloin was ordered from the Armour company outlet in nearby Binghamton and block motel reservations were made at many of the area hotels and motels.

So on that notorious Saturday morning, these LCN big shots and their bodyguards poured into Apalachin at the same time in their black limousines. On duty that morning, New York State Police Sgt. Edgar D. Crosswell, an eighteen-year veteran in this hamlet of 481 citizens, couldn't believe his eyes as he stood by watching the flotilla of shiny new cars pass down the road to Barbara's ranch house.

Working with only a handful of local police, he quickly assembled a roadblock near the Barbara residence. As the meeting was taking place in the gigantic and elaborately finished basement, the outside lookouts saw the police and quickly spread the word that the police were about to raid the place. Panic broke out among the approximately 120 mobsters and it was now everyone for himself. Bodyguards and chauffeurs were stunned to see their bosses tossing away wallets, guns, and identification as they climbed over fences, hid in the fields and barns, and tracked across the open countryside to the nearby woods. During the raid, sixty-six of the gangsters were arrested. Many, including Stefano Magaddino, escaped through the woods.

Later, at the station house, Crosswell asked the arrestees, "What are you all doing here?"

"We heard Joe was sick and come to see him," they repeated one after another. "It just happens we all come at the same time."

"That's right," Barbara confirmed, "I had a heart attack eight months ago and they all came to see me."

Suffice to say, it was impossible for even the unbelieving Hoover not to realize that this was a major crime conclave.

On the Monday following the Mob's Apalachin disaster, Hoover ordered that the FBI launch a major effort to fully identify the nation's Mob leaders and to develop intelligence information about who the hoods were and what they were doing. The "sleeping giant" had finally awakened. "Top Hood" squads were immediately and quietly formed in New York, Buffalo, Chicago, Cleveland, and the other major cities where the Apalachin attendees lived. These squads identified the meeting places and, with the concurrence of U.S. Attorney General Herbert Brownell, FBI agents secretly placed hidden microphones in these locations to eavesdrop on the meetings. This is when we in the FBI first heard the term "La Cosa Nostra." Once the leaders, members, and criminal associates were identified, they were placed under close surveillance and we began attempting to make cases against them.

We had an another major break in September 1962. Joseph Valachi was in the Atlanta federal prison on narcotics charges when he learned that his LCN boss, Vito Genovese, who was also now imprisoned there on heroin-smuggling charges, had put out a "contract" on his life. Valachi, an LCN member for more than three decades, was now ready to talk. When the FBI learned of Valachi's possible cooperation, he was moved from the federal prison to a "safe house" for his protection and Hoover dispatched James P. Flynn, a top New York FBI agent, to handle the Valachi debriefing. Over the next year, Valachi confirmed what we had been hearing on the FBI microphones for the past four years. His details were breathtaking. He revealed the deepest secrets of La Cosa Nostra.

On September 27, 1963, this second major Mob defector,* who certainly never intended to become a full-fledged informer, testified in the caucus room of the Old Senate Office Building in Washington, D.C. In intimate detail, he described the structure of organized crime to Arkansas senator John L. McClellan's Permanent Subcommittee on Investigations— as well as to all America and the world—the framework, power bases, secret oaths and codes, and identities of the members of La Cosa Nostra. This was the first time the American public heard about La Cosa Nostra. In answering hundreds of questions and suspicions raised by Apalachin, Valachi's testimony in essence marked the beginning of the FBI's public assault against the Mob. All of a sudden, organized crime was here, and the giant was on the move.

The chain-smoking, gravel-voiced Valachi identified twenty-four LCN crime families either by location or by the name of one of the earlier "bosses." In Western New York (Buffalo, Niagara Falls, and Rochester), Toronto, Northern Ohio, Cleveland, and the Ohio Valley, as in other sites of LCN headquarters cities, the crime stories were virtually the same: murder, narcotics, labor racketeering, gambling, loan-sharking, public corruption, pornography, and extortion. After Valachi's stunning testimony, irrefutable evidence began to accumulate showing how these criminal LCN activities invaded the economic infrastructure of each of these vital hubs, threatening the integrity of each city's governing process, escalating taxes, increasing the costs of goods and services to the consuming public, and jeopardizing the personal safety of our people.

---

*The first informant to reveal the secrets of the Italian Camorra and the Sicilian Mafia was Tony Notaro from Springfield, Massachusetts, in May and June of 1916. Part of the treasure trove of information he provided concerned the initiation ceremonies of each criminal group. These ancient rites had never before been known to law enforcement.

The machinations, financial and otherwise, of organized crime were of such gargantuan proportions that to untangle them at first was virtually impossible. But after Apalachin, the FBI became totally engaged in the war against LCN—and these efforts continue to this day.

THE BATTLE BEGINS

In the 1960s and 1970s, after we publicly entered the battle, the FBI was constantly attacked as being anti-Italian because of our efforts to break La Cosa Nostra. Hoover was very sensitive to criticism, and this may have been one of the reasons he did not want to publicly go after the Mob until we could definitely establish that LCN existed. I recall numerous occasions in the 1960s and 1970s in which defense attorneys attacked me personally with this charge when I was on the witness stand testifying against Mob leaders. Some of the public bought this outlandish rubbish. My memory of this was jarred when I read an important article by Jay Maeder in the New York *Daily News* on October 27, 1998, headlined "Stairway to Heaven—Joe Colombo's Great Civil Rights Crusade, 1971."

> At this point every other aggrieved special-interest group in the firmament was gloaming onto the emerging politics of victimization, a dodge that quite usefully absolved everybody of everything. It occurred in the spring of 1970 to 47-year-old Joseph Colombo, boss of what had once been the Profaci crime family and was by now the Colombo crime family, that perhaps he might grab a piece of this action himself. The Mafia. La Cosa Nostra. What the hell was it with all that stuff? Why, there was no such thing as the Mafia. It was just something the FBI had made up. It was just a dirty slur against all the good, honest, hardworking Italian-American people, that's what it was. Joe Colombo wasn't going to stand for it.
>
> How come everybody the FBI arrested had Italian names? Therefore, all Italians were mobsters, was that it? Was that what the FBI was imputing? This was like arguing that all Italians were New York mayors, since Fiorello LaGuardia had been one once, but legions of pols immediately rushed in to join the crusade all the same. "Stigmatizing an entire

ethnic group!" roared Bronx Rep. Mario Biaggi. "A psychological burden on all of us!" The FBI couldn't believe its ears. Mobsters were complaining now that they were being discriminated against?

The freshly minted Italian–American Civil Rights League got to work in April, coincidentally just minutes after one of Colombo's three sons, 23-year-old Joseph Jr., was charged with melting down coins for resale as silver ingots. Suddenly there were hundreds of picketers outside FBI headquarters at Third Ave. and 69th St., protesting the federal persecution of all Italians everywhere. This extraordinary spectacle went on for weeks. Neighborhood residents finally went to court to demand some peace and quiet.

Now, all at once, the league was chartering chapters all over the Northeast. On June 29, nearly 100,000 people rallied in Columbus Circle to hear chest-thumping speeches from Biaggi, longshoreman boss Tony Scotto and hoodlum Vincent Gigante's priest brother Louis. Shortly, U.S. Attorney General John Mitchell deemed it enlightened to ban such words as "Mafia" from Justice Department communications: "There is nothing to be gained by using these terms," Mitchell ordered, "except to give gratuitous offense" to "many good Americans of Italian–American descent."

In Albany, Gov. Nelson Rockefeller directed the state police to amend its vocabulary as well. Ford Motor Co. chief Lee Iacocca pledged that the offending words would no longer be heard on the Ford-sponsored TV series "The FBI." Producers of the forthcoming film "The Godfather" agreed to drop them from the script. In November, 5,000 guests at a black-tie league event at the Felt Forum ponied up a half million dollars in contributions as Frank Sinatra, Jerry Vale, Connie Francis and Vic Damone entertained.

Joe Colombo had discovered something. In 1970s America, all you had to do was cry out Ethnic bias! and everybody around you would cave in on the spot.

It was really quite brilliant. Considering that Joe Colombo was, after all, a Mafia boss.

And not even much of one at that. Joe's fellow bosses just rolled their eyes. Hands-down the most featherweight boss the mob had ever known, Joe had spent his life running craps games until fortune beckoned in the early '60s, when Joe Bonanno handed him a contract to whack Carlo Gambino and the up-and-coming Colombo realized it was in his better interests to tip off his target instead and then accept his gratitude after Bonanno was deposed. Just a cheesy little bust-out guy, that's all Colombo had ever been, and now his new patron Gambino was throwing him a whole family. Nobody could believe it.

And now, for God's sake, he was also the loudest and most headline-happy boss the mob had ever known (this was before John Gotti). Like so many populist demagogues before him, Joe Colombo was finding that he quite enjoyed the attention. On the night of March 22, 1971, he threw himself a testimonial banquet, and more than 1,400 supporters assembled at the Huntington Town House in Huntington, L.I., to hail him as "the guiding spirit of Italian-American unity" and to salute him for "restoring dignity, pride and recognition to every Italian."

Comic Tom Poston emceed. Enzo Stuarti sang. "We are building a stairway to heaven!" the feted Colombo cried out. "Peace and brotherhood, that is all I seek! There is a conspiracy against all Italian-Americans!" As it happened, he was due in court the next day on a perjury matter. "My conscience is clear!" he bellowed. The silver-ingot case against Joe Jr., meanwhile, had recently collapsed, by reason of a key witness' abrupt inability to remember anything about anything.

Through the spring the juggernaut noisily rolled on under the stewardship of 26-year-old Anthony Colombo, who liked to denounce "self-loathing Italians" such as state Sen. John Marchi, who regularly informed the public that the league was plainly nothing but a con. "Italian-Americans have been had," Marchi sighed.

Anthony also sued WCBS-TV for $1 million for reporting that he was a "reputed Mafia chief." Quite a glib fellow, he suffered only one small embarrassment, when the federals seized what they said were loansharking records and he angrily replied that in fact they were lists of benefit-ticket buyers, then had to try to explain why an anti-defamation group would identify one of those individuals as "Johnny the Wop."

In May, the Colombos announced they were joining forces with Rabbi Meir Kahane and the Jewish Defense League, and that they would all be fellow freedom fighters together.

John Marchi was not the only New York Italian deeply troubled by the league. Another was Don Carlo Gambino, who was becoming increasingly unhappy with his one-time protege Joe Colombo. What was Don Carlo supposed to do with a crime boss who kept holding press conferences?

On Monday morning the 28th of June, there were just 3,000 supporters at the second annual unity rally in Columbus Circle, but it was early yet. Presiding over events, Joe Colombo at 11:15 a.m. was striking poses for photographers when one of them pulled a gun and pumped three slugs point-blank into his head and neck, whereupon he himself was instantly gunned down by other parties who then instantly vanished.

Mob war, cops agreed. The dead shooter was one Jerome Johnson, a black ex-con presumably linked to the recently disimprisoned Crazy Joey Gallo. Everybody knew Crazy Joe had been openly plotting to move in on the Colombo Brooklyn rackets with his newly built black army. This was something Carlo Gambino could easily have stopped if he'd felt like intervening.

Anthony Colombo, for one, found this law-enforcement theory distasteful, since its premise was that there were no rival Italian crime families in the first place and was therefore defamatory to Italian-Americans. His own position was that his grievously wounded father had been cut down by shadowy historical forces, like President John F. Kennedy had been. "They need patsies," he suggested darkly.

"The CIA has done this before," nodded the Rev. Louis Gigante. Comatose Joseph Colombo lingered on for several more years. So did the Italian-American Civil Rights League, under new management, the younger Colombos having promptly abandoned the group after the shooting.

Crazy Joey Gallo was rubbed out in Little Italy in April 1972.

The three Colombo sons pleaded guilty in 1986 to federal racketeering charges and went to prison. "I have not admitted that I am a member of organized crime," Anthony Colombo declared.

A NEW ERA

But those of us FBI agents who arrived in Buffalo and Cleveland in the early 1960s and 1970s went to work. In a way, we sort of ushered in a new era. Neil J. Welch became special agent in charge of the Buffalo FBI office in the mid-1960s and immediately placed special emphasis on organized crime. He established a special surveillance squad to attack LCN. Up to that point, specialized surveillance squads were only used against foreign counterintelligence targets. Because of these efforts, we were able to take out the top LCN bosses in Buffalo during the 1960s.

Later, beginning when Clarence M. Kelly became FBI director, the entire FBI followed Buffalo's lead and switched local FBI priorities from investigating car thieves and bank robberies to attacking organized crime and drugs. Although there were major setbacks, the losses were primarily in the courtroom and not on the streets. With this new emphasis on organized crime, during the 1970s and 1980s we accomplished what was previously thought to be impossible. The entire LCN family in Cleveland was destroyed, and each of the National Commission members was convicted and imprisoned for one hundred years. Most of the national family bosses and underbosses were successfully prosecuted.

We worked hard to build a rapport and solid working relationships with city, county, and state police departments, where shaky relationships had existed before. In addition, we connected with local media, who found us more cooperative and accessible than ever before and who assisted in exposing this cancer on our society. And more important, we brought new administrative strategies, management skills, and procedures to battling the mobs.

Although not one among us considered himself or herself anything special, each had this fierce determination—an absolute and utter commitment to rid the American people of the ruthless and fanatical gang rulers and their guttersnipes.

One final point. Before completing this story of Mob busting in Western New York and Ohio, you will have been introduced to more than one hundred Italian and Italian American names, almost all of which rhyme in one way or another with murder and all of its peripheral criminal activities. The thousands of other Italian American men and women I know in the communities of Buffalo, Cleveland, Chicago, New York, and Washington, D.C.—in church and in college, in law enforcement circles, and in small and big businesses—were embarrassed and ashamed of their infinitesimal, ethnically related "cousins." Where the mobsters numbered in the low hundreds, the decent, generous, hardworking, law-abiding, good people of Italian and Sicilian descent are in the millions. They helped build our cities and communities while the criminals tried to destroy them. They hated the mobsters more than we did because it was names like Masseria, Magaddino, Bonanno, Giancana, Maranzano, Luciana, Scalish, Nardi, and Licavoli that brought great shame to a great people. When they spoke of life, these others spoke of death. Where they were devoted fathers and mothers, determined to keep their children from lives of crime, the others taught that easy money came from the streets, regardless if it meant death sooner or later.

Many brave men and women have fought against the evil forces of organized crime. Many have devoted their careers and, in some cases, their lives to battling this societal menace. Many of them will be mentioned in this book. It is this single-minded dedication that brought down some of the most powerful Mafia families in the nation.

I am proud to have been a soldier in this war. This is my story.

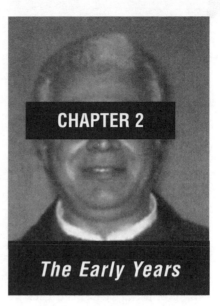

CHAPTER 2

The Early Years

Over the years, family, friends, and colleagues have asked why I became an FBI agent. Was joining the bureau the result of a youngster's dream or the matter of a simple law enforcement ambition? After much reflection during my thirty-one-year career, I've come to the conclusion that it all boiled down to a matter of lucky circumstances. I don't remember ever having this ambition at an early age. As a kid, I listened to the radio shows about the FBI, such as *The FBI in Peace and War*, and I greatly respected the FBI, but I didn't dream of being an agent. I wanted to be a fighter pilot.

During the first twelve years of my life, growing up in Weston, West Virginia, I attended Catholic grammar school and high school. I wanted to go to Georgetown University. Financially, we barely made ends meet. Dad abandoned us when I was ten, never to be seen or heard from again until I located him about twenty years later in San Francisco.

We didn't have a lot of money. I was the oldest of three boys. Mom worked as a bank teller and I worked part-time starting in the sixth grade, beginning at Montgomery Ward as a stock boy. I don't even remember having a discussion with my mother about going on to college, but somewhere along the line I developed the ambition to attend Georgetown. I figured I could work for the government in Washington and attend

Georgetown at night. A little research revealed that the FBI was the best federal agency in the government. So, during the last semester of my senior high school year, I sent an application to the FBI in Washington, D.C., applying for admission at Georgetown at the same time.

During the summer of 1957, less than a few weeks after my graduation, the FBI began my background investigation and in August I received an appointment to start as a grade 2 clerk with the FBI in Washington. The starting salary—$1,850 per year. My mom, my brothers, and I were really excited with this appointment. In fact, to this day, I recall arriving at Washington's Union Station after my overnight train trip from West Virginia. Dressed in my well-worn suit, checkered shirt, and tie, I proudly asked a uniformed cop where FBI headquarters was located. Although he politely pointed the way, I glanced back as I walked away and saw him looking at me as if I were some country bumpkin who just come in from the hills— which, of course, is exactly what I was.

As instructed, I immediately reported to the Personnel Section at FBI headquarters. That morning and afternoon were spent filling out forms and going through the time-tested bureau indoctrination procedures. The staff really looked after the young kids like myself arriving in Washington for the first time. For many of us, the capital was the first big city we had ever seen. Secretaries provided us with a list of FBI-approved apartment developments and rooming houses.

The following morning, I was assigned to the Identification Division in what is called the Technical Section. Thousands of arrest fingerprints arrive here each day from police departments across the nation. These fingerprint cards need to be searched against the millions of fingerprints on file to positively identify the person arrested and to verify that the person is not a wanted fugitive. After attending fingerprint training for two months, I became a qualified fingerprint examiner.

During that period, I enrolled in evening classes at Georgetown University and began attending classes at the business school, which was then part of the Foreign Service Institute. I went to night school and worked as a fingerprint examiner during the day. After about six months, I applied to be a tour guide at FBI headquarters and was accepted.

The FBI tour was and still is the most popular tour in Washington. Our tour guide training lasted several weeks. In addition to having a lot of fun, we learned everything about the FBI from the time Attorney General Harlan Fisk Stone appointed J. Edgar Hoover as director of the Bureau of Investigation in 1924 to the most recent public FBI cases, from John Dillinger to the most recent "Top Ten Fugitives." I enjoyed the interchange with the public, as well as the eager excitement of the little kids when I told them stories about the bureau. The highlight of the tour was a shooting demonstration performed at the basement FBI range by one of the expert firearms instructors from the FBI Academy in Quantico. I was impressed by the enthusiasm and strong public support for the FBI that was expressed by these tourists. At this point, I decided that I was going to be an FBI agent.

After arriving at 9:00 each morning and heading directly to the Identification Division, where I examined fingerprints for about an hour, I normally walked over to the main Justice Building where I would begin giving tours to the public. In 1958 only those young men who wanted to become FBI agents and were attending college were allowed to serve as guides and the tour jobs were highly coveted.

I first saw J. Edgar Hoover shortly after I began giving the FBI tours. One day I was in an elevator going to the first-floor tour office after having completed a tour in the FBI Laboratory. The elevator stopped on the seventh floor and, lo and behold, the famous J. Edgar Hoover and his assistant, Clyde Tolson, came aboard. I was thrilled when they both smiled at me and said, "Good morning, young man." I returned the greeting and did not say anything further. Several floors below, the elevator door opened and a young, pimply faced clerk started to bring a file cart into the elevator. Hoover immediately asked the kid, "Are you going to bring that into this public passenger elevator?" (This was forbidden; the file carts had to be moved on the freight elevators for security reasons.) The kid looked at Hoover and Tolson and obviously did not recognize them. He turned to Hoover and replied, with some obvious irritation, "What the hell do you think I am going to do, buddy, tie a rope around it and drag it up the steps?" The kid brought the cart into the elevator and proceeded to the second floor of the Justice Building, where he exited the elevator in an area occupied by both the FBI and attorneys from the Department of Justice. Hoover and Tolson were fuming and I could hardly suppress my laughter at the incident. I learned that an investigation was immediately undertaken to identify this clerk, but to no avail. Shortly thereafter, identification badges were issued for the first time to all FBI employees in the Washington, D.C., offices, who were henceforth ordered to wear these on the front of their suits.

During my first two years in Washington, I made friendships that would last my entire career and beyond. Such friendships included Dick Schwein, who twenty years later would became one of my assistants in Cleveland and later a superb special agent in charge of the San Juan, Puerto Rico, and El Paso, Texas, FBI offices; and Bill Gavin, who became one of my closest friends. Bill, who years later would serve as the assistant director in charge of the New York FBI office, was assigned to the FBI Laboratory as an examiner in the Serology Section, where evidence containing body fluids is examined. Bill is one of the most humorous guys I know. Bill's desk in Serology faced the half-wall-to-ceiling windows where the public was allowed to pause and observe his unit during the tour. His desk was flush with the window. One morning, my tour group was crowded in the hall in front of Bill's desk and I began giving my normal lecture about how the FBI scientist was conducting a very important examination on the body fluid evidence in order to determine the blood type. Bill was holding a beaker labeled in bold letters "BLOOD," which was filled with a red liquid. As the thirty-odd kids and several teachers watched him in admiration, Bill slowly lifted his serious face from the comparison microscope, grabbed the labeled beaker and gulped down the red liquid. Snarling, he turned to us and looked up. Bill had long fangs protruding from the sides of his mouth. I laughed, and the kids and teachers—with the exception of one—started laughing hysterically. That one prim-and-proper exception didn't think this was funny and, upon returning home, she wrote a scathing letter to J. Edgar Hoover complaining about our clowning around. Fortunately for us, the letter did not mention any specific names, otherwise we would have suffered the director's legendary wrath.

Ultimately, three other FBI employees—also Georgetown students—and I located an apartment on MacArthur Boulevard near Georgetown. We all were enrolled in night classes at Georgetown while working for the bureau during the day. Meanwhile, I learned that the FBI had a baseball team manned mainly by agents from the FBI Washington Field Office, and that clerks were also invited to try out for the team. In fact, Steve Bock, the star pitcher, was then a clerk. Because I had played varsity football and baseball in high school, I decided to try out for the squad the next spring. And, fortunately, I was good enough to make the team. We were in a semi-professional league and the team was the pride of the FBI. Hoover even attended some of our games, which were against other federal agencies and corporations in the metropolitan areas of Maryland and Virginia.

Being in the FBI was a great life. I loved taking tours in the morning and playing baseball in the afternoon, and relished taking the streetcar at night to Georgetown, where I was carrying between eighteen and twenty-one hours of study per semester. Unfortunately, there wasn't much time for many social activities. My take-home pay was a little less than $150 every two weeks, which barely got me by. Shortly after my second baseball season began, the bureau transferred an agent from the Philadelphia office to the Washington field office to play first base (my position). This guy had once played in the majors, so it was little wonder that I was benched.

THE MOVE TO CHICAGO

In the latter part of 1959, midway through my junior year, the officials at Georgetown changed the rules relating to night students. I was disappointed to learn that the university would no longer allow night students to carry twenty-one hours (four or more classes) and work full-time. Student loans were also beginning to really mount up. I began to look at other options, since I was also getting impatient to complete college and get on with my life. A college degree was required to be an FBI agent and my ultimate goal was to become an agent; however, I didn't mind considering a detour if that was required. I learned of the Air Force Aviation Cadet

Program, which paid the college tuition of qualified candidates who agreed to five years active duty as an officer/pilot. I immediately applied for this program and passed the academic and mental aspects of the test, but I ultimately was disqualified because of my vision. With few other options available, I decided to transfer from Georgetown to a school I could attend full-time. I checked around and found that Chicago had two universities, Loyola and DePaul, that would accept every credit hour I had earned at Georgetown. I requested a transfer to the Chicago FBI office.

In early 1960 I arrived in the Chicago field office as a clerical or support employee and was placed in charge of the night shift. I replaced Ed Hegarty on this shift. Ed, who would ultimately become one of my closest friends and later the special agent in charge of the Chicago FBI office, was leaving Chicago to attend new agents training at Quantico, Virginia.

After being accepted as an undergraduate at DePaul University, I was very fortunate to meet three great guys: Bob Moore, George Griffin (no relation), and Paul Marum. They were three single rookie agents who sublet a penthouse apartment at the Piccadilly Hotel located in Hyde Park on the South Side of Chicago. They told me they needed a fourth roommate and I jumped at it. Each of us paid sixty dollars a month and we all thought we had lavish quarters. Not only was the entire apartment richly paneled, with chandeliers everywhere, but also each of us had our own gigantic bedroom and bathroom. There was a paneled living room, a formal dinning room with high crystal chandeliers, a full kitchen, and maid quarters. Needless to say, we enjoyed some great parties there. Some of the Chicago White Sox stayed at the hotel, as well as the Chicago-based American Airlines stewardesses. Several of the players and stewardesses would occasionally attend the "bureau" parties—I remember meeting Nellie Fox, who was then a star second baseman for the White Sox. Although it was a great time, I spent most of my time studying and working. I went to school at DePaul five days a week during the day and worked the evening shift at the FBI from four P.M. to midnight. I'd usually get home about 1:00 A.M. and do my studying, and then repeat the process the next morning.

At the time, the Chicago FBI office had one organized-crime squad that worked exclusively on gathering intelligence about what we were learning was La Cosa Nostra. The boss of the Chicago LCN family was believed to be Anthony "Joe Batters" Accardo, who would later be replaced by Sam Giancana. The Chicago agents had secretly placed hidden microphones in many of Giancana hangouts, including the Armory Lounge and a downtown tailor shop. One of my assignments was to prepare and encode the daily teletypes to FBI headquarters summarizing the information developed by informants and the results of the technical coverage we had on the Chicago Mob leaders. I enjoyed typing these communications and sending them by teletype on a daily basis to Mr. Hoover's office because I was learning so much. Every evening after I shut the switchboard down at 7:30 P.M., I walked back to the "hole," a highly secure and sensitive part of the office where the code machines were maintained and the microphones were monitored. On occasion, when a large number of Mob meetings were taking place at multiple locations at the same time, I was assigned to monitor the mikes.

This was the most fascinating part of my job and I loved it! On nights when important Mob meetings were taking place, I gladly worked into the early hours of the morning. It wasn't long before I realized the tremendous power that organized crime had over our society and the terrible, murderous nature of the men who were members of LCN. Listening to them night after night, I came to the conclusion that virtually all of them were total bums, through and through: little men who preyed upon the weak and powerless. Their vision of themselves was propelled by glorifying works of Mob fiction, not by reality. Most were stupid, arrogant bullies who ruled only by virtue of their guns. They were governed by greed and the lust for power. Most of them were disloyal to their personal families and, of course, none of them were loyal to their country. You would be as amazed as I was at their normal, daily conversations. When most of us casually talk about baseball, politics, or the news, their normal conversation with each other related to ripping someone off, stealing something, taking violent action against someone, or conspiring to engage in some other illegal act. This was their small talk.

During the next couple of years, after witnessing firsthand the planning of truck hijackings, the discussions of gangland murders and other acts of violence, the corruption of police and other public officials, as well as their other sadistic activities, I came to the full realization that they were the scum of the earth—monsters. Slowly, I developed a real hatred of LCN, which has properly been termed a "cancer in our society." Soon, an intense desire grew in me to join the battle against organized crime. That resolve has never wavered and remains to this day.

One evening, I heard Sam Giancana describe how he had committed multiple murders. Not surprisingly, he was always armed to the teeth and always accompanied by others when he got tough. This was typical. I recall him discussing a particularly heinous crime—the murder of William "Action" Jackson, a loan shark who was suspected by Giancana of being an FBI informant, although he was not. Giancana laughed at how he had grabbed Jackson off the street, hung him on a meat hook, and tortured him by inserting an electric cattle prod into his penis and anus. According to Giancana, Jackson was kept alive for three days during the ordeal. Giancana talked about this almost gleefully.

Interestingly enough, several years later I encountered Giancana in Hot Springs, Arkansas, when I was assigned as a special agent in the Little Rock FBI field office. On that occasion, several of us were conducting a surveillance of Giancana during one of his frequent trips to meet with Phyllis McGuire of the McGuire Sisters singing group. The McGuire Sisters were appearing at the Vapors Club, which was an illegal casino/nightclub that openly operated in Hot Springs as if it were located in the middle of Las Vegas. While driving Phyllis in a flashy yellow Cadillac convertible out of the Vapors Club parking lot onto Park Avenue, Giancana noticed one of the surveillance agents who was sitting on a nearby park bench. Giancana stopped the car, lifted his hand, and gave the agent the "middle finger salute." Before Giancana could drive away, the agent trotted over to the car, grabbed Giancana by his shirt and physically lifted him out of the car seat. With Phyllis screaming, the agent quietly told Giancana to apologize or he was going kick his ass. Giancana turned white and muttered, "Sorry," before he was placed back in the car. Yeah, Sam was a real tough guy. The Vapors Club continued to operate, despite frequent raids by the FBI and the Arkansas State Police, until 1967, when Gov. Winthrop Rockefeller directed that all of the gaming tables and slot machines be destroyed.

Through my fraternity at DePaul, I met Sean M. McWeeney. He was also a struggling student and he was looking for a job. I recruited him to join the FBI as a night clerk. He joined my shift and we began working closely together and became lifetime friends. Sean also developed a personal dislike for these dishonorable men of La Cosa Nostra. Later, after a tour as a U.S. naval officer, Sean came back into the FBI as a special agent. He would later supervise the Colombo LCN Squad in New York, and ultimately become chief of the FBI Organized Crime Section in Washington.

Overhearing these LCN guys, I noticed how petty and disloyal they were even to each other. This caused me to realize that the concept of their Omerta, or code of silence, was probably baloney and that these men could be turned against each other when facing long prison terms. They were not invincible by any means. They could be turned, or "flipped" as we say in the FBI. Events would prove me right.

Getting back to my college days at Chicago, I first submitted my application to be an FBI agent during the last semester of my senior year. At the time, James H. Storm was the special agent in charge (SAC) in Chicago. He interviewed me for the special agent position and I was rejected as being too young. I must admit that I was still pretty green. I was trying to get them to make an exception to the age requirement. I was just twenty-two years old and the age requirement was then twenty-five.

In Chicago I learned one lesson that I never forgot during my thirty-one-year career, especially during the ten years that I was an SAC. The lesson was that an FBI night clerk can get into anything anywhere in the office. No bit of information or desk is immune, even the SAC's desk. After Storm turned down my agent application, I "bagged" my personnel file from Storm's office and determined that Storm had written on the interview report form, "Griffin will complete his college work and have 5 years of Bureau employment by September, 1962. He transferred to Chicago in June, 1960 in order to accelerate his scholastic achievements and become qualified for consideration as a Special Agent applicant at the earliest possible time. He is 22 and looks no older. He gives the impression of being rather short, although he is 5'10½". He was not completely at ease during the interview, but when he finally relaxed he had a contagious smile. He seems intelligent and alert and has made good school marks even while working full time for the Bureau." Storm recommended that I be turned down because I was immature and looked too young.

Me, immature? He didn't know the half of it. I learned that Storm wrote a weekly "brownnose letter" to Hoover. Every Friday afternoon he brought the letter in a sealed envelope to the mail room and asked Sean or me to put in the Bureau Mail destined for FBI headquarters. One night, I got a look at his file of Hoover letters in his desk and discovered that they were all of a "kiss ass" variety. To generally paraphrase most of them: " Mr. Hoover, you are so wonderful, we are so lucky that you are the director, you and God are on the same level." Naturally, I started copying these letters and sending them anonymously throughout the office. The mischief caught on. Storm was not a popular SAC. Some agents began throwing paper clips into Storm's office every morning as they were walking down the outside hall, which drove Storm crazy. In fact, the paper clip tossing got so bad that Storm began hiding under his desk in the morning, trying to catch the culprit.

One evening around 7:45 P.M., I was temporarily filling in at the radio room when Ralph Hill, one of the agents assigned to the Organized Crime Squad came on the air and went "in-service" by stating, "This is the Green Hornet and I'm 10-8" (meaning going "in service"). I knew Ralph's voice. I laughed and said, "10-4," logging him in-service. Storm happened to be walking by, heard Ralph's transmission, and rushed into the radio room. He grabbed the mike from my hand and said, "This is the SAC, will the agent who just went into service identifying himself as the Green Hornet please give your correct credential number." Ralph didn't miss a beat, replying, "I may be green, but I'm not that green!" Storm "stormed" out of the office.

Fortunately, several months later, SAC Marlin Johnson replaced Jim Storm in the nick of time. If he hadn't, I'm certain that my sophomoric activities would have gotten me fired. Marlin gave me another interview, after which he recommended me for the next new agent's class. I finished my senior year at DePaul in the 1962 winter semester and, even before the graduation ceremony, I was appointed an FBI special agent and was off to

Quantico. During the Chicago years, I met my wife, Janet, who was a stenographer in the FBI office. We were married in June 1962, and by the time I went to Quantico she was pregnant with our first son, Joe. She remained in Chicago while I reported to the FBI Academy to begin my career as an FBI agent.

NEW AGENTS' TRAINING

At that time, the training at the FBI Academy in Quantico lasted fourteen weeks. The entire academy, which preceded the current academy built in 1972, was located in an old brick building on the marine base grounds. Everything was very cramped. We spent ten weeks at the Justice Department building in Washington and four at Quantico, where we received physical training, defensive tactics, and firearms training. The weeks in Washington were devoted to studying federal law, rules of evidence, accounting, crime scene forensics, and investigative techniques.

In Washington, we were required to rent quarters either in bureau-approved rooming houses or apartment buildings since there was not enough space for us at Quantico during the fourteen-week training period. Three other new agents and I were able to secure rooms in a brownstone behind the U.S. Supreme Court building on Capitol Hill, which was owned by an very attractive older woman. At least she appeared to me to be older—I was a "kid," barely twenty-three, so my perspective was questionable—she was probably forty years of age. Agnes (not her real name) was a divorcée who dated one of the bureau officials we saw every day at FBI headquarters. We were basically naive: all four of us were convinced that she was a spy reporting our off-duty activities to J. Edgar Hoover, maybe even to him personally. I recall one Saturday evening when I stayed there over the weekend. She called up to me and asked that I go down and check the front door; and she said she had heard something at the door. My room was on the third floor. As I jogged down the steps, she stepped out of her bedroom on the second-floor landing, wearing a thin negligee with no bottom and smiling seductively up at me. This was fulfilling one of my fantasies, but I was convinced it also was Hoover's first major test of my morality. I just passed her by, checked the door, came back up, and said there was nobody at the door. Then I returned to my room. I guess I passed Hoover's morality test, but I certainly flunked hers.

As I recall, we spent the first eight weeks in Washington, the next two weeks in Quantico, and then we returned to Washington for two more weeks, where we worked actual bank robbery and fugitive cases with agents from the FBI's Washington field office. The final two weeks before graduation we spent back in Quantico for our firearms, defensive tactics, and academics tests. This was a crucial period, but all twenty-five members of our class passed.

Toward the end of our training, we received transfer orders to our first office. I was assigned to the FBI office in Little Rock, Arkansas.

On our last day in Washington, our class was granted the usual audience with Director J. Edgar Hoover in his lavish office. On the day before the meeting with Hoover, Assistant Director Joe Casper, who was in charge of the FBI Training Division, appeared in our class and lectured us at length as to how we should conduct ourselves in Mr. Hoover's presence. For example, we had to give Hoover a firm handshake, making sure our palms were not sweating, state our names and where we had been assigned, and get briskly in and out of the director's office. Casper said that we must wear blue suits and black shoes. Well, I only had one suit, which was brown, and brown shoes. So I came in the next day with my brown suit and brown shoes. I was promptly called out into the hall by Mr. Casper. Casper told me to see Sy Tullai, the agent in charge of our training class. Sy was a wonderful person who had an outstanding FBI career as an expert on Russian espionage. He really looked after the new agents. I went to see Sy and he asked me what size shoes I wore. I told him I took a 10-D. He said that Casper had instructed him to swap shoes with me. I said, "Sy, but these shoes go with this suit. I'm wearing a brown suit." And he said, "But this is what Casper wants." So, I then switched shoes with Sy. I put his black shoes on and although I broke the rules of fashion, I guess I filled half the bill for Mr. Casper.

Another humorous incident occurred in this first introduction to Hoover. Bill Bromly, a former Philadelphia police lieutenant, was a member of my new agents class. He was a little older than most of us, and a bit of a class clown. Prior to entering Hoover's office, we were lined up alphabetically and entered the office "briskly." When it was Bromly's turn to meet the director, he said, "Mr. Hoover, I'm Mike Cassidy," which was the name of the agent standing right behind Bromly. Sy and Casper, who were standing beside Hoover and Associate Director Clyde Tolson, turned white. They knew who Bromly and Cassidy were. Fortunately, Mike Cassidy was very quick, displaying the poise of a good agent. Mike stepped up to Hoover and said, of course, "Mr. Hoover, my name is Bill Bromly." Then everything was cool. After we finished the meeting with Mr. Hoover, no one said a word about this incident. Casper did not say anything, nor did Sy, because I'm sure they were fearful that if it came out that this had happened the whole class would probably be in trouble, as well as the two of them. I'm sure Hoover did not appreciate jokes from new FBI agents.

We were instructed that at 5:00 P.M. on the last day of training, a Friday, new FBI agents must immediately depart Washington—that very day. It was forbidden to hang around Washington over the weekend because the bureau training officials were always fearful that the new FBI agents were going to get into some kind of trouble that would rub off on them, the FBI, and Hoover. So that Friday evening I flew to Little Rock and reported in the following Monday to my new SAC.

MY FIRST ASSIGNMENT

One of the strictest rules agents learned during training school was that FBI agents were not allowed to drink coffee during work hours. It was strictly forbidden. In fact, they told us "horror" stories about agents caught drinking in coffee shops who were fired on the spot for slacking off on their responsibilities. This type of scare tactic was a common thread I detected at FBI headquarters that continued until Hoover's death in May 1972.

When I reported to Little Rock, I went into the office of the SAC and introduced myself to his secretary. She told me to meet my new boss, SAC Roy K. Moore, across the street at a small coffee shop. I laughed and said,

"I certainly will." I subsequently learned that Roy K. Moore was a legend who was considered the best SAC in the FBI. I went over to the coffee shop and met Moore. He was sitting at a table with several veteran agents who were supervisors in the office. He asked me to join them and after introductions, he told me that I was going to be assigned to his squad working bank robberies and fugitive cases. I could not have been happier. Most of the agents assigned to Little Rock were also first-office agents, with the exception of the supervisory staff and some old-timers who were assigned to the small satellite offices located in other parts of the state, which are called Resident Agencies (RAs).

As Little Rock first-office agents we were pretty much on our own because of the experience level in the office at the time. My initial caseload consisted of fifty cases, half of them interstate stolen car cases, and half of them federal fugitive matters. They were not complicated, but fun to work and good training material. I was really fortunate to have the opportunity to work for Moore. At that time, when a case of major national import occurred, Hoover frequently called on Moore to go out as the on-scene SAC to organize and supervise the investigation. In my later years, when I was an SAC, I tried to emulate him and several of the other great SACs I later worked for: Neil Welch and Dick Ash, in Buffalo; Jim Ingram, in Washington; and Roy McKinnon and Stan Czarnecki, in Cleveland.

Early in my career as an FBI agent, I learned that to be a good agent you have to be smart and hardworking, but you also need good luck. I recall one interesting experience that occurred in my first month at Little Rock. The case involved a fugitive by the name of Oscar Warten. He was from Little Rock, but had been arrested for armed robbery in Kansas and was incarcerated in the Wichita county jail. Warten escaped, stole a car, and, several days later, returned to his hometown driving this stolen automobile. Warten was spotted by a couple of deputy sheriffs on the outskirts of Little Rock. They gave chase and he ultimately jumped out of the auto and ran into the woods of a large federal forest reservation. A massive manhunt was quickly organized and, because he was an interstate fugitive, the FBI joined the fray. We participated in this gigantic manhunt with the Arkansas State Police and county police agencies. Armed prisoners, who were called "trustees," from the Arkansas State Prison had their trained bloodhounds leading each search party. On the second day of the manhunt, Warten was found hiding in the woods and was arrested. A day or so later, as he was being returned to Kansas by two sheriff's deputies, he overpowered the officers just across the Kansas border, stripped them, and left them shackled with their own handcuffs by the roadside. Warten made a U-turn with the patrol car and headed back to Little Rock. Within an hour, we got the word and headed out to the interstate. Several hours later, we were advised by radio that Warten had been observed by sheriff's deputies driving the patrol car back toward Little Rock. They gave chase, and he drove the car off the highway and escaped back into the same woods, the same forest preserve in which he had been caught several days before. Phase two of the manhunt began. Roy Moore called us on the air and said, "Let's head back out to the woods. We're looking for Warten again. He's escaped again." We joined the deputies and Arkansas State Police. Before long, there must have been five hundred officers involved in the manhunt. We established the outer perimeter, which was several miles outside of where Warten had entered the forest. Teams began fanning out from the escape point. The bloodhounds reported with the trustees several hours later and they joined the manhunt. We planned to work twelve hours on and twelve hours off until the subject was located. On the third day of the manhunt, about 3:00 on Sunday morning, a lead was called into the command post from a citizen who lived about thirty miles outside of the outer perimeter of the search area. This man had observed someone suspicious in his backyard. Moore assigned me and another agent, Dick Miller, to proceed to that location and check out the complaint. We were the newest agents, so we were given the lower-priority leads. Of course, this was the lowest type of lead priority possible. The location was well out of the area where Warten had last been seen, but Dick and I were happy to get the assignment and we proceeded as directed. We drove in separate cars through this densely wooded area toward where the sighting had occurred. After only a few minutes, we reached a bend and saw a guy standing by the side of the road trying to hitch a ride with us. The road was really winding so we went around the next bend where we both stopped and I yelled out to Dick, "Hey, that's our guy. That's Warten." So, we U-turned and came back with both cars, and pulled in on either side of the guy with our guns drawn. Of course, it was Oscar Warten. He had just come out of the woods and was trying to get out of the area. He had in his belt two loaded .38 Colt revolvers, both taken from the officers he had overcome. Dick and I handcuffed Warten and shoved him into the back of my FBI Plymouth, and Dick climbed in with him. We left Dick's car parked by the side of the road. I began the drive back to the search area, calling into my bureau radio microphone, "This is Unit 32 Little Rock. We have the subject in custody." I got no response and I called a second time and a third time. Then, finally, somebody got on the air and asked, "Do you have Warten?" I said, "Yes, we do." When we arrived back at the command post and we could see police and FBI cars parked with their blue lights flashing as far as the eye could see, on both sides of the rural road. All the officers came to our car to see the trophy, Oscar Warten, and Dick and I stood proudly by the car. I said to myself, "Well, this job may not be as difficult as I've been led to believe." This is when I first discovered that luck has a lot to do with being a successful FBI agent—timing, luck, and a lot of hard work. But luck is a part of it.

On the following Monday, Moore called Dick and I into his office and told us he was going to appear on a morning television show that day and asked us to accompany him to explain to the public how we had located and arrested Warten. This was a very interesting and enjoyable experience. I learned from Moore a basic premise in FBI leadership, which I always tried to follow later in my career: When an agent performs excellent work, it is most important to give the agent personal credit for what he or she has done—publicly, if possible. This is so important for morale and for the agent's family, which often suffers because of the many times the agent must be away from his or her family.

During the new agents class, we were given a language aptitude test. I apparently scored well on the test. After I had been in the Little Rock office for about eight months, Moore called me into his office and told me that FBI headquarters had asked him to determine if I was interested in attending the U.S. Army Language School in Monterey, California, to study Russian or Chinese. After thinking about it for a half second—and because of my interest in investigating organized crime—I told him that I didn't want to study Russian or Chinese, but I'd be very interested in studying the Italian-Sicilian language. I knew that the U.S. Army Language School, at the request of the FBI, had just initiated Italian-Sicilian language training classes exclusively for FBI agents. My friend Ed Hegarty was then attending the first such class. Moore immediately told me that he would recommend me for the Italian-Sicilian training.

MISSISSIPPI

In the fall of 1963 the White Knights of the Klu Klux Klan began a campaign of terror against Mississippi's black citizens. Civil rights leader Medgar Evers was gunned down in the driveway of his Jackson, Mississippi, home by an avowed racist. A series of terrible, racially motivated church bombings began in Mississippi that were obviously the work of the Ku Klux Klan. Because of Moore's extensive experience running special investigations, Hoover ordered that Moore proceed immediately to Mississippi to organize and supervise this investigation, which was now designated an FBI special investigation. Moore took all of the experienced Little Rock agents with him to assist him in the cases. Moore was later joined by Joe Sullivan, another outstanding SAC who was one of Hoover's "go-to" guys. The first-office agents remained in Arkansas, continuing the regular investigative work of the Little Rock FBI office, and some of us were later ordered to Mississippi to join up with Moore. Fortunately, I was one of those agents. For the short month that I worked in Mississippi, I learned firsthand from the "master" how to run an "FBI special."

There were a number of different bombings, all believed to have been conducted by members of the Ku Klux Klan. Moore set up the operation much as a gifted general would conduct a military campaign. He set up a squad for each bombing, and on each of these squads, coordinators were named and specific agents were assigned to handle every aspect of the investigation: gathering and cataloguing the physical evidence at the crime scene, conducting overt investigation such as witness interviews, and conducting interviews of Klan members and associates to gather intelligence concerning the Klan. This last aspect, the Klan interviews, was most important—this is where potential informants were identified and targeted for development. Everyone knew his job and we all went about it in a very orderly fashion. In the evenings, usually about 9:00, Moore would call a conference and the coordinators of each part of the investigation would bring everyone up to date on all aspects of each investigation. As we proceeded, this became a war with the Klan.

The Klan was routinely picking the locks of the bureau cars and putting rattlesnakes under the front seats of the cars. Our tactics were tough and aggressive. The job was to not only solve the crimes that had already occurred, but to infiltrate the Klan in order to prevent future bombings and murders. Tactics such as "lockstep" surveillance were used to interfere with the Klan activities. We established a program to interview all of the known Klan members in order to develop informants in the organization. We would occasionally start rumors to cause discord among the Klan members. These same tactics would later be used in the beginning of our war with LCN.

After only a short time in Mississippi, Moore called me into his office and advised that I was being ordered to the U.S. Army Language School in Monterey to study Italian-Sicilian. I was elated, since this would guarantee that I would be working on organized crime. I returned to Little Rock and began to bring my one hundred or so cases up to date so that my replacement could take them over.

Moore remained in Mississippi and, with Hoover in attendance, he later opened the first FBI field office in Mississippi at Jackson. Moore and Sullivan and, later, Neil Welch and Jim Ingram, conducted the massive investigation of the 1964 murders of three civil rights workers, Andrew Goodman, James Chaney, and Michael Schwerner. If you have read the book or seen the motion picture *Mississippi Burning*, from my experience there, I would say that you have seen a very accurate depiction of how these investigations were conducted. The investigation was thorough, tough, and aggressive. As a result, the Klan was totally infiltrated and the bombings and murders were solved. The Klan was destroyed. Moore remained as SAC in Jackson until his retirement in 1975. After a long and successful career, Ingram retired as an FBI assistant director in 1982 and returned to Mississippi as the director of public safety. Welch would later become the assistant director of the FBI in New York.

On November 22, 1963, President John F. Kennedy was assassinated in Dallas, our neighboring field division. At that time, the FBI had what was called the "Security Index." This index had been established many years before with the concurrence of various succeeding U.S. attorneys general. The index contained the names of all persons known to the FBI who could be considered possible threats in the event of a national security emergency. Among others, the index contained the names of all known Ku Klux Klan members. The Little Rock office was instructed to immediately determine the location of all Security Index members in our territory. I was given several names to check, including the top Klan "klucker" in Arkansas. I proceeded to his modest and unpainted house, walked up the loose cinderblocks that served as his front steps, and knocked on the door. His wife answered the door and she was weeping. After I identified myself and told her that I needed to see her husband, she invited me in. I was shocked to see her husband, the "top klucker," and their children watching the TV coverage of the assassination. They were all in tears, like most of America. I couldn't believe that a leader of the Klan would be mourning as we were. From my experience in Mississippi and Arkansas, I knew just how stupid and ignorant these Klan members were. This mourning was inconsistent with their beliefs, but this man must have had some humanity in him. I later told one of the agents remaining in Little Rock that he should take a shot at this guy to make him an informant. I don't know if he ever did.

SICILIAN LANGUAGE SCHOOL

In December 1993, right after the tragic events in Dallas, my wife and our young son, Joe, drove in our little Ford Falcon convertible to Monterey, where I began to study Italian and Sicilian at the U.S. Army Language

School. I talked to Ed Hegarty, who had just completed his class. He had been sent to Philadelphia and was assigned to the specialized "Top Hood" squad. Ed gave me a briefing on the course and I learned what to expect.

As you know, after the infamous Apalachin crime conference, the FBI put on a full-court press to gather intelligence on the organized crime group that we later learned was called La Cosa Nostra. The FBI had been caught flat-footed with the Apalachin disclosures. The FBI needed to quickly determine who was involved in this massive organized-crime conspiracy. We needed to identify the leaders, members, and associates and to determine how they were organized. We needed to determine details of their activities and how we could go after this group.

In 1957, under the National Security Act of 1947, the FBI had the authority to place hidden listening devices (microphones) in the meeting places of American communist leaders and their Soviet masters based on the knowledge that the American Communist Party was being financed by the Soviet Union. There was no authority to use these microphones in criminal cases. After Apalachin, it became apparent that organized crime did have an adverse effect on our national security. With the concurrence of successive attorneys general, beginning with Attorney General Herbert Brownell and ending with Ramsey Clark, Hoover determined that organized crime represented a national security threat to the United States and that microphones could be used against them. The Mob's tentacles were even then believed to stretch across national borders. As a matter of fact, some of those mobsters arrested at Apalachin were from Canada, South America, and Sicily. Right after Apalachin, Hoover sent directions to FBI offices in Albany, Boston, Buffalo, Chicago, Dallas, Detroit, Las Vegas, Los Angeles, Newark, New Haven, New Orleans, New York, Miami, and Tampa, instructing them to identify the meeting places of these organized-crime leaders and to secure "technical coverage" of these locations for the purpose of gathering intelligence information. The meeting locations were identified and hidden microphones were installed through surreptitious entry, which was also authorized under the National Security Act. Unfortunately, the Warren Court would later rule that these hidden microphones were not legal and could not be used in court.

During this initial technical intelligence-gathering activity, which began in November 1957 and ended on July 12, 1965, the FBI was also conducting extensive physical surveillance of LCN leaders and covering their social functions, such as weddings and funerals, to gather intelligence concerning the structure of La Cosa Nostra. You may wonder why we covered the weddings and funerals. It is amazing what we learned at these functions. You could pretty much determine what rank a man held in the organization by observing his body language and how these individuals interacted with each other.

When the microphones were activated, it was determined that many LCN leaders only spoke the Italian or Sicilian dialect. Initially the translation of these conversations was done by a Sicilian-born Catholic priest who was a Washington-area FBI contract worker and several Italian or Sicilian American agents whose parents were native Italians or Sicilians who taught them the language as children. However, because of the volume of translation work and the need to conduct interviews in Italian and Sicilian, it eventually became essential that additional agents be trained in these languages.

The U.S. Army Language School recruited a native Sicilian professor, Nino Maltaggio,* to head up this program in the Italian Department. He came to the United States in 1963 and established the Sicilian language program. Nino was a marvelous person and a great professor. He hated the Sicilian Mafia and was totally dedicated to teaching us the language, which is not a written language. In addition to teaching us the Italian language and the Sicilian dialect, he also exposed us to the wonderful history of Italy and Sicily, and to the great culture of the wonderful Italian and Sicilian people. I came away from this experience with deep respect and admiration for them, and this increased my disrespect for those that would hide behind their heritage, the members of La Cosa Nostra.

The first four and one-half months of class were used to learn the Italian language and the last four and one-half months were spent on the Sicilian dialect. We spoke only the learned language in class. We visited

---

*I have disguised his name since I recall he was fearful of Mafia vengeance against his family in Sicily.

wineries where we conversed with native-born Sicilian workers and Italian restaurants where the management or waiters spoke the language. Many years later I would learn from interviews with LCN underboss Jimmy Fratianno that one of the restaurants we visited in Monterey was owned by a "made" member of the San Francisco LCN family. Fortunately, we never disclosed our true identities or background to any of those individuals with whom we spoke. I was amazed that at the conclusion of the course, we could all speak both Italian and Sicilian and could conduct intelligent interviews in these languages.

This was a great time. There were seven of us in the class. We attended classes six hours a day and we studied four hours each night. We had a chance to play tennis and take part in various other activities. In June 1964 my second son, Chris, was born at Monterey by the Sea.

After completion of language school, I was initially assigned to New York City. Fortunately for me, the transfer was changed to Buffalo, New York. I later learned that the Buffalo SAC, Vic Turin, upon hearing he was not going to get an agent from this Sicilian class, became outraged and went right to Hoover and explained that he had the most important microphone in the country in Buffalo, but he had no Sicilian-speaking agents to translate the language. So my official transfer orders were changed to Buffalo.

CHAPTER 3

Smashing the Money Sources

BUFFALO ASSIGNMENT

A fter finding a house in a suburb of Buffalo, which we rented with an option to buy, I began my first assignment as an organized crime agent assigned to the SAC squad.

Upon arriving at the Buffalo office of the FBI and reporting to the organized-crime squad on a freezing Monday morning in early January 1964, I spent the first several weeks reviewing seven years' worth of intelligence files, focusing on Mob activities in western New York State, primarily the Buffalo–Niagara Falls area.

I found that the organized-crime program in Buffalo consisted of one agent, Leon "Andy" Andrews, assisted by three other young, inexperienced agents like myself. One of these, Bill Roselli, became one of my best friends and my partner. Bill had attended the Italian language school and had reported to Buffalo several months ahead of me.

Andy was a phenomenal guy. He was in his late forties or early fifties at the time, and he was one of the most dedicated and hardest working guys I've ever met in the FBI.

Andy was extremely knowledgeable and gave me a complete briefing on the Buffalo family. Buffalo was the headquarters for one of the principal organized-crime families in the United States. Stefano Magaddino, a senior member of the Commission, was the boss of this family. Magaddino was one of the founding bosses of the Commission and one of the most revered bosses within the LCN culture. Later in my career, it would be one of my greatest professional moments to say, "Stefano, we are from the FBI and you are under arrest."

Magaddino's underboss was Frederico G. Randaccio. Andy and the files indicated the capos were believed to be Joe Fino, Peter A. Magaddino, Roy Carlisi, Daniel G. Sansanese, Joseph E. Todaro Sr., Pasquale A. Natarelli, Frank Valenti, and Benjamin Nicoletti Sr. Antonino "Nino" Magaddino was believed to be the consigliere.

As I said, initially there were four of us working with Andy on organized crime. One of the other organized-crime agents resigned from the FBI to enter private law practice and a second was transferred to Rochester, so ultimately, in these early years, it ended up that just Roselli and I worked organized crime in Buffalo. Andy coordinated the organized program and handling all the paperwork for FBI headquarters.

In the years after Apalachin, Andy had identified on his own all of the Mob meeting places and had arranged for hidden microphones to be placed in these locations by FBI surreptitious-entry teams. Buffalo had one of the most important FBI mikes in existence, which was installed in Magaddino's inner sanctum, his office at the Magaddino Memorial Chapel. This was a Niagara Falls funeral home operated as a "front" by Stefano Magaddino and his son Peter A. Magaddino. We also had mikes located in the Camilla Linen Shop, which was the meeting place for LCN members and Magaddino's sons-in-law, Charles A. Montana and James V. LaDuca.

The office at the Magaddino Memorial Chapel was the principal headquarters for Stefano Magaddino and the location where he held court on a daily basis. One of my early assignments in Buffalo was to monitor these conversations with Roselli and prepare the translations for dissemination to other FBI offices throughout the country. In 1964 and 1965, Magaddino's principal concern was with his cousin and fellow LCN Commission member, Joseph Bonanno. Stefano Magaddino spent hours talking about Bonanno with Peter A. Magaddino; his brother, Antonio Magaddino; Fred

Randaccio; and Roy Carlisi. Magaddino had learned Bonanno had expanded his operations into Canada, which, according to the LCN Commission, was supposed to be Magaddino territory. Magaddino was outraged and cursed Bonanno on a daily basis. At Magaddino's insistence, the LCN Commission had ordered Joseph Bonanno to report before the Commission for the purpose of explaining what he was doing in Canada. Bonanno had refused and had sent his son, Bill Bonanno, instead. This further outraged Magaddino. In retrospect, I believe Bonanno's and Magaddino's activities in Canada probably related to the establishment of the Sicilian Mafia heroin-smuggling ring uncovered years later in the FBI's "Pizza Connection" case.

At the time, the FBI had no jurisdiction to conduct narcotics investigations. It would not be until many years later that Congress passed legislation giving the FBI concurrent jurisdiction with the Drug Enforcement Administration (DEA) to conduct narcotics investigations. Investigation by the FBI in the early 1980s determined that a major heroin ring existed throughout the United States. During the 1960s and 1970s, Sicilian "hit men" and drug dealers had infiltrated the United States through Canada. Members of the American LCN called these men "zips." All of the zips were members of the Sicilian Mafia and most were illegal immigrants. They established pizza parlors that were "fronts" for their heroin-smuggling operation. In 1984 this organization was broken up when the FBI and assisting police arrested thirty-one individuals in Sicily and the United States. The records seized from members of this group indicated that between 1979 and 1984 they smuggled $1.65 billion worth of heroin into the United States.

Magaddino would frequently be visited by local public officials, on occasion one well-known major league baseball star who was originally from Niagara Falls, and at least one U.S. congressman came by to pay him homage. They would treat him with great respect, addressing him as "Godfather." It was disgusting, but enlightening to hear.

During the early years in Buffalo we were hamstrung because we had very few federal laws that could be used effectively against the LCN. We had only two federal laws that were useful against the major gambling and bookmaking operations conducted by the LCN, these being the Interstate Transportation in Aid of Racketeering (ITAR) and the Interstate Transportation of Wagering Information (ITWI) statute. These laws carried a penalty of five years, which wasn't enough of a hammer to use against sophisticated mobsters. Each of these statutes required some interstate aspect to the crime. The ITAR law made it a federal offense to travel interstate to commit murder, arson, extortion, or bookmaking. The ITWI statute made it a federal crime to transmit over interstate telephone lines bookmaking information in connection with the operation of an illegal bookmaking operation. Gangland murder was not a federal crime. In fact, most of the LCN criminal activity did not violate any federal statutes: State law, not federal law, covered these offenses.

The Magaddino family was commonly known to street criminals as "the Arm": that is, "You pay the Arm." The Arm controlled all bookmaking in Buffalo, Niagara Falls, and Rochester. They also controlled all illegal craps games and large illegal card games. Burglars and armed robbers were forced to pay leaders of the the Arm a percentage of their illegal gains. This practice was called "paying a street tax."

For the first couple of years, we devised strategies to develop informants within the organization. Aggressive investigations, frequent raids on their illegal gambling operations, and a very active interview program ultimately led to the successful infiltration of the Buffalo family, but it would take several years.

Initially, it appeared that the family was getting most of its illegal profits from: (1) bookmaking; (2) craps games and illegal card games operated by Benny Spano, Benny Nicoletti Sr., and Joseph "Chicago Joe" Scales; (3) illegal skimming from Las Vegas casinos; and (4) major burglary rings being operated by LCN-controlled thieves in Buffalo, such as John C. Sacco, Russ DeCicco, and Gregory Parness, as well as burglary rings operating in Rochester.

As I perused the most recent organized-crime reports beginning that first morning, I couldn't help but reflect on how desperately we needed new laws to be passed by Congress—real tools that would make it a federal offense for members of a criminal group, like the Magaddino Mob, to engage in patterns of criminal acts such as murder, extortion, bookmaking, the infiltration of legitimate businesses, and other insidious criminal activities that were then only state criminal violations. All of these criminal activities against our citizens are coordinated within the LCN family, and because they are conducted by LCN, they affect interstate commerce, so they should be federal violations. We needed a federal statute with some meat on it—substantial penalties. If any of the killers I was now reading about were to face only a year or two in prison, he wasn't apt to "flip" and cooperate with us. We also needed a federal wiretap statute. In addition to turning mobsters into informants, all of us who worked organized crime recognized the need for a new federal law making it illegal to belong to an organization such as LCN.

Skipping ahead in time, congressional counsel G. Robert Blakey wrote and Congress passed such a statute in 1970: the Racketeer Influenced and Corrupt Organizations statute, now commonly referred to as the RICO statute. This statute was signed into law on October 15, 1970, as part of the Organized Crime and Control Act of 1970. RICO's main goal, as conceived by Blakey, was to make it a federal offense for members of an "organization" or "association in fact" to follow a deliberate pattern or sequence of criminal acts that are normally local crimes to further the organization's objectives. The crimes covered were murder, kidnapping, gambling, arson, robbery, bribery, extortion, and dealing in narcotic or dangerous drugs. Even after 1970, this astonishing statute collected dust on the shelves of the nation's best federal prosecutors because they didn't know how to use it. Most simply felt it was "too complicated" to employ against organized crime and we in the FBI didn't fully realize its potential. In fact, the first time Blakey's masterpiece would be unveiled charging La Cosa Nostra as the "association in fact," as I sat there reading, would be twelve years later—and, little could I know then, it would be under my watch in Cleveland.

Meanwhile, the most recent intelligence reports stated that the Magaddino crime family of Buffalo, New York, was one of the oldest and most powerful of twenty-four LCN organized crime families then operating in North America. As I continued skimming the intelligence files that early January morning in 1964, it occurred to me that it had been forty-three years since Stefano Magaddino had fled to Buffalo from possible inter-Mob retaliation for a killing he allegedly committed in August 1921 in

Avon, New Jersey. And from 1921 on, Magaddino, a real-life godfather with a powerful hand and plenty of leadership acumen, vigilance, and cunning, had his tentacles stretching into Ohio, Pennsylvania, and Canada. During the decades that followed, hundreds of millions of dollars poured into the Magaddino crime family's coffers from illegal card and dice games, loan-sharking, bookmaking, major armed robberies, hijackings, burglaries, and narcotics sales. In addition, Stefano controlled the Laborers' International Union Local 210 in Buffalo. Most, if not all, of the officers of Local 210 were members of the Magaddino family. They controlled the laborers' jobs in Buffalo and used the union local to get "no show" jobs for other members. Most of the activity conducted by his soldiers were not federal crimes under our jurisdiction.

In those years, the FBI had no jurisdiction whatsoever in narcotics investigations. If agents of the Buffalo FBI office came up with any information on the importation of drugs from Canada or their sales in Buffalo, federal law wouldn't allow us to do anything other than pass the intelligence on to local police or the Federal Bureau of Narcotics and Dangerous Drugs (FBNDD), now known as the Drug Enforcement Administration (DEA). In fact, in 1964 the FBNDD, traditionally undermanned in field offices across America, had just one agent assigned to the entire Western New York region and the Canadian border abutting our territory. And the man fiercely protected what he considered his individual jurisdiction, as we would do. Whenever we received information concerning illegal narcotics, we simply picked up the phone and called the federal drug agent who occupied a small office off the lobby of the federal courthouse in downtown Buffalo.

THE INFORMANTS

On that first day in Buffalo, after a lunch break with my new colleagues, I returned to the file room in order to review old informant folders. My goal was to identify potential future informants. Needless to say, to successfully investigate the Mob it is absolutely essential to have a few good, solid informants helping you out. You can't really do much without the informants. That's one of the first steps in starting a successful investigation. Without well-placed informants, an investigator is in the dark. You can follow these Mob guys around all day, concluding that they're little more than bums hanging around, with nothing to do and nowhere to go. They just sit around the social clubs talking to each other all day. Occasionally, one will get up, walk out to a public pay phone, and make a call— or meet someone on the street. But if you've groomed an informant among them, he will tell you they are either planning future crimes, engaged in ongoing crimes, or bragging about past crimes.

While reviewing these files during my first week in Buffalo, I was fortunate to identify one potential informant who had been used by an agent before his retirement about two years before. When the agent vacated his office, he simply closed the informant file. I could tell from the file summary that up to the time the informant was closed he was a marvelous source of Mob information.

This particular guy had provided solid information on Magaddino family bookmaking and a number of interstate property violations. In further checking the files, I learned that this former informant was alive and doing well.

The next morning, I drove out to his house. Still an active bookmaker, he was not exactly delighted to see me. But after we talked for a while, he soon realized that if his prior relationship with the FBI was renewed, he could breathe a little easier in his own bookmaking business, even if it meant putting his life on the line for the FBI. At the very least, he knew I wasn't there to make a case against him. I just wanted to reestablish the previous arrangement—he would provide me with information on Magaddino's bookmakers and burglars in exchange for me not targeting him personally for prosecution. If he was square with me, I would not go out of my way to put "heat" on him. Under existing FBI policy, an informant could engage in nonviolent criminal activity if it was in furtherance of an official investigation.

Developing and operating an organized-crime informant is an extremely dangerous but absolutely essential activity. There is a fine line you must walk—you are dealing with a criminal, knowing he is committing crimes that you must overlook for the greater good. An agent must secure the trust of the informant, but he or she has to be extremely careful to not get too close to the informant. Many agents never develop informants because of the fear of getting into trouble, but these are not successful agents and they are not doing their job. Later in my career I would evaluate agents on their informant development, and I have never seen an excellent agent who did not have good informants.

After I secured his trust, this informant provided a great deal of previously unknown information about the Magaddino bookmaking, card games, and gambling activities. He told me that Fred Randaccio, who was then Magaddino's underboss, controlled a number of bookmakers who had to pay "taxes," or a percentage of their income, to Randaccio. He identified four: Nicholas Mauro, Joe Lombardo, Richard Todaro, and Joe Fino. I asked him to get the phone numbers they were using to accept their betting action. When he gave me this information, I opened cases on all four.

To fight the Magaddino crime family effectively, we needed to not only establish a string of informants but cooperate closely with honest local and state officials in order to get the biggest bang for our buck. Many times we would uncover information that did not involve federal violations, but when we were working with people on the local or state level, charges could be filed in those venues against the bad guys.

THE BOOKMAKERS

At about this time, a new commissioner of the New York State Police was appointed by Governor Nelson Rockefeller—Arthur Cornelius, who had just retired as special agent in charge of the Albany FBI Field Division. Arthur immediately set up a special investigative unit within the New York State Police to work on organized crime. Bob Cryan, an FBI agent who had recently retired from the Buffalo office, headed up the unit. Gradually, over a period of time, I became a close friend of Maurice "Mo" Gavin, the local commander of the unit, and his two assistants, George Karulus and

Ed Palaschek. I also made it a point to establish a close relationship with Capt. Hank Williams, commander of the local state police division, called Troop A, headquarted in Batavia, New York.

I also established a great relationship with Capt. Kenneth P. Kennedy, who commanded the Buffalo Police Department's Gambling Squad and who was also highly respected. Ken had a number of outstanding investigators, including Dave Derrico and Joe Dragonette, whom I began working with and grew to admire. Both Hank and Ken were not only graduates of the FBI National Academy, but they were totally dedicated and honorable officers. Each was completely trustworthy. Mo Gavin, Derrico, and Dragonette enjoyed going after the Mob, just as Roselli and I did. They all began working with us like fellow FBI agents.

It didn't take long for me to conclude that the best way we could smash the Arm's money sources was to go after the burglars, bookmakers, and illegal gambling. In most of the illegal gambling and bookmaking operations, which were the source of millions of dollars of yearly profit for the Arm, there was no interstate aspect and they were not federal crimes. When Bill or I developed information concerning these games or bookmaking operations, we would conduct the necessary surveillance to verify the informant information. We would prepare affidavits reflecting our investigation and take these to State Supreme Justice John J. Dwyer, whom we totally trusted, with a request for a state search warrant. We would then take the search warrant to the Buffalo Police Gambling Squad if the location was in the city, or to the New York State Police if the location was elsewhere.

Attacking the bookmakers and their games would disrupt the gambling profits flowing to Stefano Magaddino, Frederico Randaccio, Pasquale Natarelli, Daniel Sansanese, and others. If you hit a book, all betting action is not accepted for that day. And when you hit a book on collection day and grab all the collection records or cause them to be destroyed by the bookmaker, the weekly profit losses can amount to between $100,000 and $500,000 per week. Hitting a game means all the proceeds are negated that day, however large or small. Furthermore, attacking the bookmakers, burglars, fences, and game operators provided us with the opportunity to develop new informants—and, as far as I was concerned, that was more important than the raid.

During my first two years in Buffalo, we conducted an average of three raids per week against Arm bookmakers and illegal games using these state warrants. Much of my time was also devoted to evaluating the intelligence information being picked up on the Magaddino microphones.

Magaddino held court daily in his office and mostly in the Sicilian dialect. Since he was a Commission member, much of his discussion related to other LCN families, so it was necessary to disseminate this information to the other FBI offices. These microphones provided us with tremendous national intelligence information, but unfortunately, we could not use the information in court. However, we were able to prevent several murders by giving well-placed and anonymous warnings. And we were receiving outstanding intelligence information—we now knew more about LCN than they knew themselves. One member might know one bit of information and another would have another piece to the puzzle—we were getting the whole picture. But we could not use the information in court. As I have said, we needed a federal law to make these intercepts admissible in court.

However, on July 12, 1965, the U.S. Department of Justice ordered the FBI to terminate all of our microphones covering the Mob. We were ordered to turn them all off and to retrieve them if possible. I later learned from officials at FBI headquarters that when the attorney general was briefing President Lyndon B. Johnson regarding the FBI corruption investigation of Bobby Baker, the former secretary of the Senate Democrats, Johnson learned that the FBI had a microphone covering an organized-crime associate of Baker. Baker was being investigated for bribery and federal income tax violations. When Johnson learned of these microphones, he allegedly ordered the attorney general to terminate all of the microphones. Incidentally, Baker was convicted in federal court in 1967 on these charges.

Nick "Sonny" Mauro, probably the principal sports bookmaker in Western New York, was selected as our first bookmaker target. A year before, he had characterized himself in testimony before a state organized-crime investigative committee as being a "bookmaker's bookmaker." This meant that he was considered by the underworld as a "layoff bookmaker." To explain "layoff bookmaking" let me use as an example a sports bookmaking operation. Normally, a bettor on a sporting event such as football bets $110 to win $100. There is a 10 percent advantage to the bookmaker, which is called the "vig." Sports bookmakers accept betting action on college and professional football games, professional baseball games, and college and professional basketball games. The ideal situation is to have an equal amount of money bet on each team in a contest, that way he can't lose and he takes the 10 percent vig. Let's say the Buffalo Bills are playing the Denver Broncos. A sports bookmaker in Buffalo will most likely have heavy betting action on the Bills and little on the Broncos. The bookmaker must "balance his books" by "laying off" some of the bets he has accepted on the Bills to other bookmakers. The bookmaker who accepts these layoff bets is a "layoff bookmaker."

So Mauro was very well known. Informants reported that Mauro worked for LCN capo Daniel G. Sansanese Sr. Through my newly developed informants, I was provided the phone numbers of Mauro's current bookmaking location. It turned out he had three phones at his place. Bill Roselli and I set up our surveillance and quickly determined that during the day Mauro and his associate Ralph Velochi would enter the book office around noon every day, leave around 4:00 P.M., and return at about 7:00 P.M. They would then close the book around 9:00 P.M. From our review of his telephone records, it appeared he wasn't involved in any interstate violations. At the conclusion of our investigation, I filed a warrant through the state court, secured the necessary search warrant, and gave the warrant to Captain Kennedy on the morning of September 15, 1964. That afternoon, we raided Mauro's book. His bookmaking office was located in an apartment that was heavily barricaded. After we broke our way into the apartment with battering rams, we arrested Mauro and gathered the evidence he was unable to destroy.

Subsequently, Mauro was convicted and on March 2, 1966, was sentenced to serve one year in the Erie County Jail. The term was highly unusual, but it was based on Mauro's past record. The judge even commented during the sentencing that Mauro proudly described himself as a "bookmaker's bookmaker."

My partner, Bill Roselli, was transferred to his beloved New York City in November 1966, and I soon partnered up with Don Hartnett, a Buffalo native who had just transferred in from the New York FBI office. Don, a former star basketball player at Canisius College, was a twenty-year veteran of the FBI.

After Mauro's release from prison in early 1967, I learned from our informant that he was again operating a sports book. My first step was to check the telephone records. This time, however, I noticed that Mauro was now using interstate phone calls to conduct his operation. He was calling Nello Ronci, a Youngstown, Ohio, bookmaker. The informants told me that Mauro was getting line information from Ronci, who was also handling Mauro's layoff betting. This was a violation of the federal ITWI statute and meant a possible five-year sentence.

We immediately set up a surveillance of this new location. Mauro was observed walking into an office building at 30 Cherry Street with Ralph Velochi and John Barile, who, the informant said, were two of Mauro's telephone answerers and collectors. I contacted the Cleveland FBI office and talked to Marty McCann, one of their organized-crime and gambling experts. He told me that Ronci was well-known to them as a "connected guy" who ran a bookmaking operation in Youngstown. Marty and the Youngstown agents immediately began surveillance of Ronci. We continued this surveillance for several months in order to develop Mauro's pattern of activity and telephone calls made to Ronci.

On February 20, 1967, at 6:30 P.M., Hartnett and I, with the assistance of the Buffalo Police Department Gambling Squad and the New York State Police, raided Mauro's Buffalo operation while the Cleveland FBI office simultaneously raided Ronci's book in Youngstown. We surrounded the Cherry Street building and, because all the doors were heavily barricaded, entered through the second-floor plate glass window using a borrowed Buffalo city "cherry picker." Mauro, Velochi, and Barile were not immediately found.

While searching the second floor, we discovered a secret disguised staircase that led all the way down to the basement. Of course, we went down and within minutes found their phones and all of their records. We walked back to the second floor. It was at that point that one of our agents found the three Magaddino men meekly hiding in another secreted compartment. As Velochi and Barile were being handcuffed, Mauro bolted and jumped out of the second story window. I followed. He landed and, limping slightly, crossed Cherry Street, oblivious to the heavy traffic. I landed safely and chased him across the street, also dodging the traffic. I ended up having to tackle him on the sidewalk. I have to admit, he was a pretty gutsy guy. As I was handcuffing him on the ground, I asked, "What in the hell are you doing running from me? I know where you live." He was out of breath, but he smiled and remained silent.

Our searches resulted in the discovery of extensive documents that tied in with the telephone calls to Ronci in Youngstown. Ronci's records seized in Youngstown corresponded with Mauro's records, so the raids were really quite successful. It turned out they were doing about $100,000 in betting action a day, which was a pretty sizable bookmaking operation for Buffalo. We took the men to the office of the U.S. magistrate, who released them on bond. Mauro, Velochi, Barile, and Ronci were later indicted by the federal grand jury and they appeared before U.S. District Judge John O. Henderson and were released on bond.

The Mauro case was assigned to the newly formed U.S. Department of Justice Strike Force, which operated independently of the U.S. Attorney's Office. This strike force was established by Attorney General Ramsey Clark in 1967. The purpose of the strike force was to concentrate massive forces against organized crime. The lead attorney on the strike force reported directly to the chief of the U.S. Department of Justice Organized Crime Section. The strike force was comprised of representatives from the FBI; the Internal Revenue Service Intelligence Division; the Alcohol, Tobacco, and Firearms Division of the Treasury Department; postal inspectors; investigators from the Department of Labor, and Investigators from selected local, county, and state police departments. All of the representatives were to pool all of their intelligence information for a concerted attack on the key figures of the organized-crime families. This concept was employed by Bobby Kennedy when he focused on Jimmy Hoffa and his sycophants. His efforts were very successful and Hoffa was convicted and imprisoned. Clark initiated the strike forces in response to widespread criticism that he wasn't doing enough about the increasing strength of organized crime. In my opinion, the criticism was certainly justified. SAC Neil Welsh had already assigned me to be the FBI representative on the strike force and this was to be the first case these attorneys handled for the FBI.

Of course, our investigation continued after the original federal indictment since Mauro immediately made bond and, when released, he continued to operate his bookmaking syndicate. Unfortunately, the Mauro case was reassigned from one strike force attorney to another, and each time the case was scheduled for trial, the newly assigned attorney wanted a new indictment containing the most up-to-date information concerning Mauro's ongoing operation. Mauro would be reindicted and it was my job to go out and rearrest him on the additional warrants. I would assemble the force and we would hit his current bookmaking location. I personally raided and arrested Mauro five times based on the original arrest and subsequent indictments. On my final arrest, he commented that I was making him a famous man in Buffalo. Furthermore, he said indignantly, he didn't think it was fair to keep arresting him on the same charge. I laughed and I said, "Your lawyer keeps getting these continuances. Why don't you tell him you want to go to trial." But I actually agreed with him. The fourth assigned prosecutor, Dennis O'Keefe, finally brought the case to trial. After a trial that lasted three weeks, Mauro and his associates, in spite of the truly overwhelming evidence we had gathered on all of these raids, were acquitted. You can imagine my anguish. But years later, long after I left Buffalo, Mauro was arrested repeatedly on new and more serious charges. In 1994 Mauro was tried and convicted in Buffalo's federal court for violation of the RICO statute, a law we did not have in 1967, and sentenced to fourteen years in prison. He is now serving his term at the U.S. Penitentiary in Oregon.

After all the trials and tribulations our office endured in the Mauro case, we then concentrated our efforts on Richard Todaro, Joseph Lombardo, Joseph Vizzi, and other alleged LCN-controlled bookmakers in the Buffalo area. And even in those high-profile cases, the subjects, when convicted, received little or no prison time and insignificant fines. We were finding that the courts did not take the federal interstate gambling laws as seriously as we did.

JOE VIZZI

A good example of the FBI tilting at windmills in the late 1960s and early 1970s was the Joe Vizzi case. My informants reported that Vizzi was a major national horse race layoff bookmaker. We began surveillance of Vizzi in December 1967. His daily practice was to drive randomly around the Buffalo suburbs during bookmaking hours (11:00 A.M. to 4:30 P.M., Monday through Saturday) accompanied by his partner, Richard Raymond. They would stop every ten minutes or so and make their calls from public telephones, receiving layoff bookmaking action. We followed them around from public pay phone to public pay phone for more than four months. Joe began his bookmaking day around 11:00 A.M. With Raymond at the wheel, the two drove through and around Buffalo for about an hour each day, making sure they weren't being followed. We referred to this as "dry cleaning" themselves. When they finally felt secure, they would stop at the numerous corner pay telephones and phones in countless shopping malls, where they would place their interstate gambling calls. The surveillance agents would later identify the pay phone number and I would subpoena the records for the pay phones they were using. I would then have to sit down and review some four to six thousand records each day to determine the specific telephone calls Vizzi had made.

I found that he and Raymond were calling up to sixteen bookmakers every day in Los Angeles, Chicago, Las Vegas, New Orleans, Miami, New York, and Cleveland. We identified all of the bookmakers involved and FBI offices in each of these cities began simultaneous surveillance of the bookmakers in their areas.

Our case resulted in nationwide raids by the FBI on March 1, 1968. Vizzi was the chief coordinator of all the bookmaking action among the various bookmakers, many of whom were LCN connected. The raid received national press coverage and when a person read the newspaper, it would appear that we were really making a dent in the illegal LCN-controlled sports and horse bookmaking. All the bookmakers were convicted in federal court for interstate bookmaking and all received extremely light sentences. Vizzi and Raymond were given fifty-dollar fines. Over time, we were able to develop informants within LCN. But because of the court leniency and the basic weakness of the existing laws, we were as yet unable to have sufficient leverage to "flip" low-ranking mobsters and to make them witnesses against the higher-ups in the Magaddino crime family.

On June 19, 1968, the U.S. Congress passed the Omnibus Crime Control and Safe Streets Act, which in part provided for the use of court-approved electronic surveillance in certain types of cases. This was a major victory for the public against organized crime. We could now use hidden microphones and wiretaps, with the approval of a U.S. District Court judge, and this type of evidence would be admitted in federal and state courts. Unfortunately, Attorney General Ramsey Clark would not allow us to use this statute in organized-crime cases during his tenure.

One of the first cases in which we used court-authorized electronic surveillance (a wiretap) was in the Joseph Lombardo gambling investigation in the fall of 1970. Lombardo and his partner, Frank Stasio, were alleged to be Buffalo sports bookmakers our informants identified as being controlled by the Arm. They were strictly "sports bookmakers," handling bets on professional and college football and basketball, as well as professional baseball. The informants gave me the telephone numbers of their bookmaking office and we set up surveillance of the book location. This investigation was conducted in the 1970 football and basketball seasons, and we believed Lombardo and Stasio were working the book on Saturday and Sunday afternoons and evenings, as well as evenings during the weekdays.

Their bookmaking room was located at an apartment building in Cheektowaga, New York, a suburb of Buffalo. After I secured the telephone records for the two telephones they were using, I determined that they were calling Frank J. Masterana, a well-known gambling figure in Las Vegas.

Our surveillance confirmed the informant's information was correct. The informant placed a number of bets with Lombardo and Stasio by calling the bookmaking office with the bets while I was overhearing the telephone calls. After I secured probable cause, I requested that the Department of Justice approve a request for court authorization to wiretap the two Lombardo bookmaking telephones. It was required that the U.S. attorney general personally approve each application. This procedure was time-consuming and it took me about a month to get the approval. When the authorization was received, Strike Force Attorney Robert Stewart took the electronic surveillance request and affidavits to U.S. District Judge John O. Henderson, who gave us the court authorization. The subsequent electronic coverage confirmed the informants' information and also provided proof that Lombardo and Stasio were getting their betting line from Masterana in Las Vegas, Nevada, thereby making this a federal crime.

On the second Sunday in December 1970, I led a team of FBI agents in a raid on Lombardo's bookmaking location. The Las Vegas FBI simultaneously raided and arrested Masterana. Both of these raids were very successful. We secured records reflecting bookmaking activity, and the records seized in Buffalo and Las Vegas were tied into each other. After Lombardo, Stasio, and Masterana were arrested, they were arraigned before Judge Henderson and released on bond. They were indicted by the federal grand jury on December 30, 1970.

After almost two years of motions, countermotions, and other legal maneuvering by defense counsel, the trial began on January 4, 1972. It took Bob Stewart about three weeks to present our case. He presented the lab examiners who gave expert testimony about the bookmaking records. He presented several of Lombardo's bettors, who had been immunized before the grand jury and testified that they had placed sports bets with Lombardo. FBI agents testified as to the surveillance of Lombardo, Stasio, and Masterana. Bob did his usual great job in the prosecution and we felt we had a winner in this case.

On January 2, after closing arguments, the jury retired to the jury room to deliberate the case. On February 3 they reported to Judge Henderson that they were hopelessly deadlocked. As a result, Judge Henderson had to declare a mistrial and dismissed the jury.

Unfortunately, not too long after, Judge Henderson died and the case was reassigned to another judge. The case languished until long after I left Buffalo. On June 28, 1974, the judge dismissed the case against Lombardo, Stasio, and Masterana because the government had failed to give the defendants a speedy trial.

Another bookmaker reported by informants to be controlled by the Magaddino family was Richard J. Todaro, a former boxer who was unusually slick. I had tried to build a case on him for some time but he always slipped through the cracks. During my first year in Buffalo, my informant reported that Todaro was operating a sports bookmaking office at a specific telephone number and I determined the location where he was allegedly working the sports book. This location was in the middle of Buffalo's West Side, where a sitting surveillance car would attract all kinds of attention. I needed a surveillance post to observe Todaro's comings and goings. Buffalo Boys Town was located nearby and I approached the priest who ran this school to secure a room from which to conduct my surveillance. I told him that I was looking at someone in the area in connection with an official FBI investigation and asked him if I could use a room for several days to conduct the surveillance. The priest was very gracious and he led me to an empty room that faced the street that I needed to observe. Todaro showed up that day around 11:30 A.M. and he was due to work in the book until about 4:00 P.M. About 12:30 P.M., he left in a rush and did not return that night or the next day. I learned from my informant that he had abruptly changed his location to another phone number. I couldn't understand why he would change his location since he had only been at this place for several days. Later I learned that Todaro formerly boxed at Buffalo Boys Town for the priest. You live and learn.

I continued working on the Richard Todaro case off and on and in 1972, after some other cases you will hear about, I located Todaro's new bookmaking location. After several weeks of surveillance, we were successful in securing probable cause for an electronic intercept at his bookmaking location.

Midway through the investigation, I was transferred to FBI headquarters and the case was taken over by Ron Hadinger and Ron Hawley. Their follow-up investigation was very successful. On February 6, 1973, Richard

J. Todaro was indicted by the federal grand jury in Buffalo for violation of the federal gambling business statute and conspiracy. He was also charged with destroying evidence.

There were numerous court appearances, discovery and evidence suppression issues, and even hearings as to whether the U.S. attorney general had actually signed the electronic surveillance request. These hearings and court delays lasted until April 20, 1976, when the trial finally began—three years after the indictment.

The evidence was presented by Strike Force Attorney Bob Stewart and, although I was not there, by all accounts he did a superb job. On April 29 the jury returned a verdict of guilty and sentencing was deferred until June 7. Eventually, on August 17, U.S. District Court Judge John T. Curtin sentenced Todaro to two concurrent prison terms of three years each. Bail was continued pending appeal.

On June 29, 1977, the federal appeals court reversed one of the three-year counts and affirmed the other three-year prison term. Todaro was ordered to surrender to serve his time. On August 2 Todaro's attorney filed a motion for reduction of sentence.

On September 13 Todaro appeared before Judge Curtin for resentencing. Judge Curtin reduced the sentence to six months confinement, with the stipulation that Todaro could be released at the discretion of the Board of Parole after serving one third of his sentence. According to the court docket, Todaro ultimately surrendered to serve his two months on October 4.

Another Todaro who came to my early attention was Joseph E. "Lead-pipe Joe" Todaro Sr., and his son, Joseph Todaro Jr., who reportedly controlled bookmaking operations for the Arm. Our informants reported that Joe Todaro Sr. was a principal figure in the Magaddino LCN family. A review of public-source history reveals that local police attention was focused on the senior Todaro when he was questioned after Charles S. Gerass, age thirty-six, of Tonawanda (a northern suburb of Buffalo), was found trussed, beaten, and shot in the head in September 1965. The press reported that, according to a police report, "Todaro was scheduled to meet with Gerass, a free spending realtor, on the night of Sept. 21, 1965. Gerass left his home to keep the appointment with Todaro, but never arrived at his destination. Gerass' body was found the following night in the trunk of his wife's auto behind a supermarket in the Sheridan Plaza, Town of Tonawanda." This gangland murder was never solved at the time, and this type of murder was not a federal violation. The federal government did not have a federal criminal code covering murder at that time.

In early May 1967 I received a telephone call from my informant who said that Joe Todaro Sr. was sponsoring a "stag party," which was to be held at Panaro's Snowballs Lounge in Buffalo on May 8, 1967. The informant reported that an illegal craps game would be set up in the basement of the lounge. My informant also said that virtually the entire membership of the Magaddino crime family planned to attend this event. After I verified this information with a couple of other informants, I telephoned Ken Kennedy of the Buffalo Police Department Gambling Squad. Ken was ecstatic. He said that he had full authority to conduct a State Liquor Authority (SLA) inspection of Snowballs Lounge, a state liquor-licensed facility. We needed to find out whether all these Buffalo LCN members would show up at one time at the location. If they did, we could tag along under his auspices as he conducted the inspection. He would then have the authority to arrest any of the Magaddino men, and other LCN guests with criminal records, on charges of consorting with each other as known criminals. These charges would probably eventually be thrown out, but it would give us an opportunity to again display to the community evidence that organized crime did in fact exist.

Around 7:00 P.M. on the night of the stag party, we set up our usual surveillance and soon saw that virtually the entire membership of the family was attending this function! Everyone was there except the Magaddinos, who were represented by James V. LaDuca. At exactly 10:00 P.M., Captain Kennedy radioed for the Police Tactical Patrol Unit vans to report to the location. When they arrived, Kennedy motioned for the vehicles to back up to the front and back doors of Snowballs. Along with some fifteen New York State Police officers, Kennedy, Dave Derrico, Joe Dragonette, Don, and I boldly marched into the lounge. Kennedy announced the SLA inspection and that officers would be checking the IDs of everyone on the premises. "Legitimate people," including several local judges and businessmen, were all on the first floor of the restaurant. All the mobsters were in the basement where the illegal games were operating.

Our initial search did not turn up all the LCN figures that we had observed entering the lounge earlier in the evening. The only area that we didn't initially search was the wine cellar, which was locked with multiple outside padlocks. Panaro was ordered to unlock the cellar. After he reluctantly did so, and we brushed past him, we found seven more mobsters sitting on the wine cellar floor, casually sipping wine. We had hit the jackpot! Here were some of Magaddino's key men—Nick Rizzo, Fred Randaccio Jr., Victor Randaccio, Jim LaDuca, Roy Carlisi, Pat Natarelli, and Dan Sansanese. As they walked out of the wine cellar and were handcuffed, Rizzo, who was intoxicated, took a swing at one of the tactical patrol officers, who quickly subdued him.

Some thirty-six organized crime figures were arrested that night by the police department on consorting charges, including the following, who have been identified in U.S. Senate testimony as La Cosa Nostra leaders: Joseph DiCarlo, former LCN leader in Youngstown, Ohio; Frederico Randaccio, Magaddino underboss; Roy Carlisi, Magaddino capo and brother of Chicago LCN boss Sam Carlisi; James V. LaDuca, LCN member and son-in-law of Stefano Magaddino; Joseph Fino, Magaddino capo and future LCN boss in Buffalo; Daniel "Boots" Sansanese Sr., Magaddino capo and future Buffalo underboss; Pasquale Natarelli, Magaddino capo; Sam "The Frenchman" Frangiamore, Magaddino capo; John Cammilleri, Magaddino capo; Joseph "Leadpipe Joe" Todaro Sr., future Buffalo LCN boss; and Victor Randaccio, LCN member and boss of Local 210 of the Laborers' International Union of North America (LIUNA).

Our raid became known as the "Little Apalachin Raid." Panaro's, a notorious Mob hangout, lost its liquor license and went out of business. Todaro Sr. sued us all. Remember that our raid occurred during a time in our history when even the existence of La Cosa Nostra was considered by some to be debatable. In fact, it was at this time that Joe Colombo, one of New York's five LCN bosses, and his league were picketing the FBI field office in New York City.

The main point in Todaro's suit alleged that we were "discriminating against persons of Italian extraction." His suit disregarded the Italian American heritage of our people—Derrico and Dragonette—and my own children, who are half Italian. Several days after the raid, all of the consorting charges were dismissed in local court. Todaro's suit was also later dismissed.

In late 1969 the Buffalo FBI office received information from a complaining witness that he had been fleeced on a gambling junket from Buffalo to Las Vegas, a junket allegedly organized and operated by Joseph Todaro Sr., and his son, Joseph Jr. The Todaros were believed to be partners in the Fortune Travel Service, a "junket" operation based in New York City that was in the business of arranging for inexpensive charter flights from the Western New York area to Las Vegas. Nevada law permits such flights, but in this case the Todaros were allegedly conducting dice games and card games during the chartered flights. During the investigation that followed, we interviewed a number of people who had taken these flights and many of them indicated that they had been "fleeced" even before the plane landed in Las Vegas. The results of the investigation were presented to the federal grand jury.

On Thursday morning, January 8, 1970, we secured arrest and search warrants from U.S. Magistrate Edmund F. Maxwell, executing them by noon that same day. We arrested Joseph E. Todaro Sr., at his home in Tonawanda; his son, Joseph E. Todaro Jr., who lived in Buffalo; and Dominic Chirico, Angelo Vaccaro, and Sam Minkoff, who also were alleged to be part of the operation. Our witnesses said that these men were operating illegal games on the plane during the flight to Las Vegas and making "loan shark" loans to the alleged victims on the plane. The planes flew over areas where gambling is illegal and we believed this constituted a federal violation. It was the opinion of the federal strike force attorneys that conducting illegal card games over areas where gambling was illegal was a violation of the ITAR statute. That was the theory. The witnesses alleged that in addition to losing all their money, they were able to obtain any size loans they wished from loan sharks provided by the Todaros on the flight. Dominic Chirico was a convicted counterfeiter who had been frequently observed chauffeuring Frank Valenti, the LCN capo in Rochester. All those arrested were subsequently indicted for ITAR-gambling and arraigned before U.S. District Judge John O. Henderson. They were immediately released on bond. Extensive pretrial

hearings were conducted, and defense attorneys promptly attacked our affidavits for search warrants. Their principal contention was that this was not a
federal crime. The strike force attorneys did a good job presenting our case,
but the defense attorneys also presented a good defense, claiming that the
activity was not a violation because the gambling activity took place in the
air, not on the ground where gambling was illegal. The judge agreed with
the government, and gave the case to the jury. Unfortunately, the jury saw it
otherwise and acquitted all of the defendants.

Incidentally, some twenty years later, in 1988, according to the U.S.
Senate Permanent Subcommittee on Investigations of the U.S. Senate
Committee on Governmental Affairs, the boss of the Magaddino family
was Joe Todaro Sr., while the underboss was his son, Joseph Todaro Jr.
Neither of the Todaros has ever been convicted of any criminal violation.

One of the principal hangouts of the Magaddino Mob in the 1960s
and 1970s was a gambling club called the Blue Banner Social Club, which
was located on Prospect Avenue in Buffalo, behind the residence of Benny
Spano, a Magaddino man. The club had originally been a large two-story
garage, but the inside now resembled a small but fully equipped Las Vegas
casino. There were various kinds of gambling games and slot machines on
the first floor, while on the second there was a large craps table in a huge
oak-paneled room. Randaccio and his capos would meet there every day
in the late afternoon. This particular location, with its major craps game,
brought in large amounts of money for the Magaddino crime family.

I loved raiding this place. Usually, we would bag half the "made" guys
in Buffalo in these raids, providing us with the opportunity to not only
obtain current mug shots, but also to talk to them while they were under
some stress. We raided this place about every month.

Bill Roselli and I first began our surveillance of the Blue Banner
Social Club in the early 1960s and periodically we would obtain a search
warrant for this location from New York Supreme Court Justice Dwyer.
We would then take the warrant to the Captain Kennedy, and the gambling squad and the FBI Top Hood squad would raid the game that afternoon. We did this on innumerable occasions but nothing would stick in
court. The only way we could get a conviction was if someone testified

that he actually played in the games, and he would have to identify all of the participants. Those games were mostly attended by burglars, small-time thieves, and gamblers who were so fearful of Randaccio and the rest of the Magaddino mobsters that they believed they would end up in a car trunk if they openly cooperated with us. They were probably right. Without their outward help, we continued the raids anyway, to disrupt their activities and to keep these LCN figures off guard. I must say, it was fun and pretty effective at the same time.

In addition, these efforts greatly assisted us in getting informants. On many occasions, Roselli and I would strike up a casual conversation with one of these Mob guys and we would hit it off on a certain level. Some of them were very engaging, with tremendous, outgoing personalities. When I met one that I could talk to as a human being, I would attempt to develop a relationship with him, to win his trust for the purpose of developing him as an informant. I would attempt to meet the prospective informant away from the group. If our friendship developed, I would begin to give the person small tasks. If he agreed to help me, I would eventually give him more dangerous tasks, such as getting detailed information concerning the criminal activities of the LCN higher-ups—information that could be used for Title III microphone and wiretap applications to the U.S. District Court and for search warrants. This worked and a number of informants were developed, several that I used as recently as 1996.

I will give you an example of a typical raid. In early December of 1967, after observing the Blue Banner Social Club for a week or so, I felt I had obtained enough information to get another search warrant from Judge Dwyer. After securing the warrant, I presented it to Captain Kennedy. The last time we had hit the location was the afternoon of October 7, five or six weeks before.

This location, as with all the others that we raided during that period of time, was heavily barricaded. There was a lookout who had a variety of warning bells and buttons at his disposal. All the upstairs windows were boarded up and paneled over.

After we used the battering ram to force our way into the club, the police department arrested twenty individuals, including Magaddino capos

Pasquale Natarelli; Dan Sansanese Sr.; Sam Frangiamore; Albert M. Billi-teri, a Magaddino soldier in charge of the crime family's loan-sharking operations; William S. Sciolino, another Magaddino soldier who was one of the family's principal strong-arm men; and Benny P. Spano, the Magad-dino soldier who actually operated the club. During our continuing search, several of the subjects tried to escape through the roof and scamper down a fire escape, at which point they were, of course, grabbed.

After our search was completed, we were baffled by the absence of Nick Rizzo, who we knew maintained the money, or "bankroll," for the operation. It was obvious that he was hiding somewhere behind the expensively paneled walls. Kennedy and I told the agents and officers to immediately begin chopping down the walls with the axes we always brought on these raids. So we started chopping from one end of the room toward the center. After about ten minutes, when about half of the walls had been destroyed, we heard Rizzo crying out from behind the paneling. "Stop! I'm coming out. I'm coming out." He stumbled out through a secret door, a bankroll of about $70,000 stuffed in his coat pockets.

The noisy activity of the raid caught the attention of all the neigh-bors, who hurried from their homes and apartments to their balconies in order to watch what was going on. You can imagine what this neighbor-hood felt about these hoods, where they and gamblers grabbed all the street parking spaces for blocks around. So as we were leaving with all the Mob guys in handcuffs, the neighbors standing on their balconies and in their front yards began applauding and cheering us on.

The criminal charges we lodged against these men, even if they were to stick, would get each subject a twenty-five-dollar fine in state court. After the arrests, all of the defendants were released on bail. Eventually, the charges were dismissed.

Another location that the Magaddino crime family used as a meeting place, also an illegal craps game, was located on Chicago Street in Buffalo. Kennedy repeatedly raided this location during the mid-1960s with our help. We hit this place an average of twice a month. Each time the raid occurred, we would arrest all participants and give them a lot of publicity. That was not good for their business and was very disruptive.

One of these raids occurred in the first week of December 1967. On December 5, 1967, after receiving new tips from my informants, I set up surveillance at the Chicago Street location, and after verifying our informant's information, I prepared supporting affidavits and presented them to Judge Dwyer, who promptly gave me the search warrant. I turned the warrant over to Kennedy on the morning of December 8, and we executed the raid that night. As we approached the heavily barricaded location at exactly 9:00 P.M., we spotted the lookout. He was parked in an automobile across the street from the club. Within minutes, however, he was taken down by Derrico. We smashed our way into the gambling club with heavy battering rams and found a large dice game going on. We arrested thirty-nine mobsters and citizens that night for frequenting a place of ill repute and "consorting." Among those arrested that night were Magaddino capos Dan Sansanese Sr. and John Cammilleri, soldiers Salvatore Bonito and Rocco Vaccaro, as well as a number of burglars, armed robbers, and bookmakers. As always, we gave them a lot of publicity, with many of their pictures plastered on the front pages of the *Buffalo Evening News* and the *Buffalo Courier-Express*. The charges were eventually dismissed in local court.

THE BURGLARS

Another major source of revenue for Stefano Magaddino and his crime family was burglary. In the late 1960s there was a principal burglary operation underway that was controlled by John C. Sacco, a Magaddino man, who had a front job with the City of Buffalo Streets Department. Sacco had been an old-time burglar and now was a principal fence for the crime family. He had a number of very good burglars working for him, including Russell DeCicco, Gregory Parness, David Nardozzi, Stephen Giordina, Louis Mavrakis, and Frank DeAngelo. The antiracketeering case involving Sacco was assigned to me, and I immediately began to develop intelligence concerning the various burglars in the case. Coincidentally, in early 1968 I received a call from State Police Captain Hank Williams, who said that an individual by the name of Paul Parness had called his office and he was interested in disclosing some things concerning Sacco and his team of bur-glars. Hank asked if I would be interested in working Parness as an infor-mant. Of course, I said that I absolutely would. So Hank introduced me to Paul, who turned out to be the brother of Gregory Parness.

On April 29, 1968, Sacco and Greg Parness burglarized the Joseph Strauss Co. store located in the heart of Buffalo and stole sixty color TV sets, valued at $25,000. The day after the burglary, Paul called me and said that Sacco was planning to ship the stolen TVs to Pennsylvania. Paul said that Sacco had been talking to Russell A. Bufalino, who was the boss of the Pittston, Pennsylvania, LCN family. Paul told me where the TVs were then being stored and I immediately arranged for surveillance of the location. Paul was going to be the truck driver when the stolen TVs moved, so we had some time. I checked Sacco's toll calls and sure enough, there were three calls to Bufalino's apartment in New York City. Bufalino, one of the old LCN bosses, who was one of those arrested at Apalachin—he had a reputation for being very shrewd, so I was very surprised that he would become directly involved with something like this. Over the next several weeks, Paul had a series of meetings with Sacco and Greg Parness con-cerning the plan to ship the TVs to Pennsylvania. The plan eventually fell through and on May 16 we searched the Busti Avenue garage where the TVs were stored and made the recovery. At this time, we did not make any arrests, since we did not want to expose Paul as our informant. However, we had the evidence to eventually charge Bufalino, Sacco, Greg Parness, and several others with conspiracy to violate the federal Interstate Trans-portation of Stolen Property statute.

On August 21, 1968, the residence of T. Edward Hanley, an oil million-aire in Bradford, Pennsylvania, was burglarized of $1.5 million in art trea-sures. Hanley was an oil fortune heir and an avid art collector. Included among the artwork stolen were paintings by Cezanne, Renoir, Goya, and Rodin. Several days after the burglary, Paul telephoned me and told me that Russ DeCicco and Louis Mavrakis had burglarized the Hanley residence. Paul indicated that he and his brother had met with DeCicco at Greg's house in Buffalo the previous evening, and later with DeCicco at his resi-dence. DeCicco needed a fence to handle the paintings. Paul claimed the paintings were still stored someplace in the Bradford area. Don and I decided to set up a sting operation with DeCicco as the focus. Paul was willing to risk introducing an undercover FBI agent to DeCicco as a prospective buyer, with the understanding that he wouldn't have to testify at any trial. We agreed and Gabe Martinez, a very distinguished-looking agent in his early fifties, was selected as the undercover agent. I arranged a meeting between Gabe and Paul so they could develop their respective and coordinated stories. Gabe's story would be that he was an art collector on the shady side out of New York City and that he was very excited about buying the collection. The following evening, Gabe and Paul met with DeCicco, and DeCicco and Gabe negotiated a price for the paintings. DeCicco promised the paintings would be delivered on August 30 in Buffalo.

A few days later I learned from Paul that Greg Parness, Russ DeCicco, and Louis Mavrakis would drive to Bradford on the morning of August 29 to pick up the paintings. Our surveillance squad, now under the control of Don Hartnett, was activated and we observed DeCicco, Mavrakis, and Greg Parness leave the Buffalo area in DeCicco's car on that morning. They did the normal "dry cleaning" procedures, driving through shopping centers and up one-way streets in an effort to determine if they were under surveillance. When they became convinced that we were not following them, they headed for Interstate 90 and entered going west. We followed them up the interstate to the outskirts of Bradford, where we were met by agents from the Pittsburgh office, who assumed control of the surveillance. The Pittsburgh agents followed DeCicco, Parness, and Mavrakis into Bradford, where they approached a gas shack by the highway. They looked around and apparently noticed something about the Pittsburgh surveillance, so they walked past the gas shack. Then the trio turned around, got back in DeCicco's car, and drove back to Buffalo. After they left the area, we contacted the gas company by telephone and secured permission to search the gas shack. We immediately entered the shack and within minutes discovered all the stolen paintings. Although all the paintings were recovered, we still couldn't come up with a case against the subjects without exposing Paul as our informant. However, we did have a conspiracy to transport stolen property back to Buffalo in interstate travel, which could be prosecuted later. Eventually, we would have the testimony of Paul Parness, but at this point we didn't want to reveal his position as an informant.

Sacco was very active as a fence for the Magaddino crime family. He was the principal organized-crime "fence" in Western New York and he had good connections with New York City fences within the Colombo LCN family.

In December 1968, on orders from John Sacco, Greg Parness and Russell DeCicco broke into the Gross Furrier in Buffalo and made off with $150,000 worth of furs. Through Paul, I learned the exact location where these furs were being fenced. Sacco had stashed them at an Auburn Avenue location, a residence in a ghetto area on the East Side of Buffalo. This was, in effect, a "showroom" where prospective buyers of the furs could come and look at the merchandise, trying on the coats if necessary. For two consecutive nights we observed who entered the run-down house to see and purchase the furs. We even observed one defense attorney, who arrived with his wife. By the second night, I had secured a search warrant through the Erie County District Attorney's office. We raided the showroom with officers of the Buffalo Police Department and the New York State Police at about 10:00 P.M. We discovered Sacco had professional showroom-type mirrors and hanging racks for the fur display all over the first floor. We recovered over $125,000 in stolen furs. We also found stolen china and silverware worth about $100,000, stolen a few weeks before from a major burglary of a store on Delaware Avenue. Sacco was not present during our raid so he was not immediately arrested.

About a week later, I learned from Paul that Sacco was fencing about $100,000 in stolen cigarettes from a house located on Amsterdam Street. I secured a search warrant and, with the Buffalo Police and New York State Police, raided this location and recovered the stolen cigarettes.

By January 1969, Paul was ready to testify and we made the decision to "surface" him as our informant and place him into the Federal Witness Security Program. He was one of the first witnesses to use this program. He secretly testified before both the federal and state grand juries, and after we presented evidence that supported his testimony, indictments were returned.

John C. Sacco, Rosario "Russell" Bufalino, Greg Parness, and several others were indicted by the federal grand jury for conspiracy in connection with the stolen TVs. Sacco was indicted by the state grand jury for the theft of furs, TVs, cigarettes, china, and silverware.

On one early morning in January, FBI agents, accompanied by officers of the New York State Police and the Buffalo Police Department, fanned out through the streets of Buffalo. We arrested Greg Parness; Russell DeCicco; his wife, Renée; and Louis Mavrakis for conspiracy to transport the stolen Hanley art treasures across state lines. Sacco and Greg Parness were arrested on both state and federal charges in connection with the conspiracy to transport the stolen TVs to Pennsylvania. Philadelphia agents arrested Rosario Bufalino on the same charges. The remaining Sacco burglars, Stephen Giordina and David Nardozzi, were also arrested.

The first trial turned out to be the federal trial involving the Hanley art treasures—when Paul strode into the court room, you could almost see the shockwaves emanating from the defendants, their attorneys, and their supporters. Paul was the principal witness against his brother and the other three and he did an excellent job. Attending each day of the trial for the following six weeks was Dr. Hanley's wife, Tullah, a former belly dancer from New York. She was some ticket: about seventy years old but very well preserved, she told me during our court break conversations that her political affiliation was "sexually progressive," and that she was a "twelve o'clock woman in a nine o'clock town," referring to her hometown of Bradford, Pennsylvania. To say the least, she was very eccentric. What did surprise us was the fact that she was brash enough to try communicating with Russell DeCicco's wife every chance she got. One day during a break, my fellow case agent Rick Schaller and I asked her what she was doing and she told us that she wanted to get Renée and Russell DeCicco into a "threesome." We told her to stay away from them, but to no avail. Finally, Ed Joyce and John Tarrant, the U.S. Strike Force attorneys who were prosecuting the case, instructed her to stay away from the defendants, at least until after the trial was over. At the conclusion of the trial, Russell DeCicco, Renée DeCicco, Louis Mavrakis, and Greg Parness were convicted on all counts and sentenced to long prison terms.

Unfortunately, several years after the trial, Dr. Hanley passed away. Unknown to Tullah, his will specifically stipulated that many of the recovered paintings be donated to Canisius College in Buffalo. Later Tullah called Rick Schaller and asked if it was possible for the paintings to be returned to her so she could make the Canisius presentation in a special ceremony. "Why not?" he said. Rick took the paintings, under armed guard, back to her Bradford farmhouse.

At the college several weeks later, wine and cheese were served before the presentation ceremony. Everyone was standing around very properly, munching on high-quality cheese, sipping wine, and chatting. A priest was playing the violin. After she was formally introduced by the president of the college in a lengthy welcoming speech, Tullah, with the recovered paintings wrapped with FBI evidence tape lined up behind her, delivered a brief, beautiful, and touching speech in her lilting Hungarian accent. Then she said, with a slight twinkle in her eye, that she would like to share her expertise in the belly dance. Then, without another word, she flipped off her jacket and proceeded to give a sexy belly dance which was completed by a handstand, totally revealing her. Smiling, she got back on her feet and continued the presentation with everyone in the audience frozen-faced and acting as if nothing had happened. Still smiling, she concluded her little speech. Those of us from the FBI roared with laughter all the way back to the office. She had a great spirit. If you'd like more of Tullah, read her book, *Love of Art and Art of Love*. She became a wonderful philanthropist for the arts, giving most of her priceless art collection to the University of Pittsburgh and museums throughout the United States. She passed away on June 2, 1992, at her home in Bradford.

We had a series of other trials, in both federal and county court, where Sacco and all of his burglars were convicted in connection with the Buffalo burglaries. All were sentenced to long prison terms. We lost one defendant, Rosario Bufalino, who was acquitted in his federal trial. But, as you will see, we dealt with him later.

During this period, we had developed several new informants who were providing new and specific information concerning the loan-sharking operation Albert "Babe" Billiteri was running for Stefano Magaddino and his crime family. Loan-sharking is a very lucrative, illegal source of income for the Mob. Cash loans are made on a six-for-five basis, meaning that the borrower must pay the loan shark 20 percent interest on the principal each week. I am not a mathematician, but as I recall this interest rate is over 1000 percent per year. If the borrower does not pay as expected, he is physically threatened and beaten up, if necessary. I recall in one instance, the borrower was a compulsive gambler who owned a drug store. The drug store eventually ended up in the Mob's hands. Based upon this new information, Rick Schaller prepared a detailed affidavit and, after it was approved by FBI headquarters and the U.S. attorney general, he secured federal court approval to install a microphone in Billiteri's home. Billiteri prided himself among his fellow Mob members that his house was never vacant and no one could possibly put a mike in it. He was almost right. We had a hell of a time installing one. His mother lived upstairs, with orders never to leave the house when he and his wife were gone. Furthermore, a huge guard dog lived in the residence. We soon learned from our phone tap that Billiteri and his brood were going to attend a cookout on the afternoon of the Fourth of July. That bit of intelligence was all we needed. Surveillance squad supervisor Don Hartnett quickly devised an innovative strategy for us to make a "black-bag job" entry. We would simply enter in broad daylight.

On the afternoon of July 4, a Buffalo city street repair crew, actually consisting of four FBI agents on the surveillance squad, drove a very official-looking Sanitation Department truck down Ashland Avenue, erecting signs and blocking all traffic in front of Billiteri's house. They entered the manhole in front of Billiteri's home and began working with very loud construction equipment. This was a great diversion. The five of us on the entry team parked our bureau car up an alley and exited. We casually walked to the first-floor side entrance of Billiteri's two-flat residence. Within moments, our lock specialist opened the door and we were in. Don Hartnett came prepared with a pound of raw hamburger meat for the dog. Less than thirty minutes later, two microphones had been installed by our technical guys. No one had noticed us. As we exited the side entrance, Don scooped up the hamburger meat not consumed by Billiteri's nasty Doberman, stuffed the raw meat in his coat pocket, and we returned to the car, very pleased with ourselves. As we chatted and laughed on the drive back to our office, we began to notice a terrible smell in the bureau car.

In his haste, Don hadn't noticed that while scooping up the uneaten hamburger, he had also grabbed a handful of doggy do-do, which was now sweltering in one-hundred-degree heat. So much for that suit.

Billiteri was very free with his talk in the residence, since he felt so secure. He had meetings with his brother, LCN member Matthew "Steamboat" Billiteri, and his loan shark strongmen Albino Principe, Samuel Lagattuta Jr., Pasquale Napoli, and his son, Frank T. Billiteri. His voice would later lead to his downfall. He identified his victims and on many of the conversations we overheard he gave instructions to beat the victims if they did not pay the 20 percent per week interest.

We presented all of our evidence to the federal grand jury. As a result of this very successful Title III electronic coverage and the follow-up investigation, on November 21, 1969, the federal grand jury indicted LCN members Albert M. "Babe" Billiteri, Matthew "Steamboat" Billiteri, and Sam Lagattuta Jr., as well as Albino Principe, Pasquale Napoli, and Frank T. Billiteri, on federal loan-sharking charges.

On Saturday, November 22, FBI agents fanned out in the streets of Buffalo, and within an hour, we had arrested all of the subjects. My new partner, Graham "Des" Desvernine, and I went to Babe Billiteri's residence to get him. He was about 5'7" and 350 pounds; when he walked, he waddled like a fat duck. After we knocked, Babe came to the door still dressed in his silk bathrobe. I told him that he was under arrest for violation of the federal loan-sharking statute and took him to his room, where he changed into his jail clothes. As we were handcuffing Billiteri, the search team arrived and began going though the house. The home was a typical Mob house; it looked pretty shabby outside—so as not to attract the attention of the IRS—but the inside was something else. It was furnished like a palace. The high walls were covered with expensive paintings. He had a treasure of imported furniture in all the rooms, and in his bedroom was a gigantic walk-in closet with hundreds of suits, shirts, and fancy shoes.

Des and I transported Billiteri to the FBI office, where other agents were also bringing defendants. After the processing, the Mob loan-sharks were taken to the county jail.

After Greg Parness and Russ DeCicco were convicted and given long prison terms in the Hanley case, Rick Schaller began talking to Russ and I to Greg. With the assistance of strike force attorney John Tarrant, we cut a deal with DeCicco and Greg Parness. We "flipped" them. They testified against all of the Mob loan sharks, as well as other high-ranking LCN figures in Buffalo and in Pittston, Pennsylvania. Eventually, their prison terms were reduced and they were placed in the Federal Witness Security Program.

Albert Billiteri and all the other loan sharks were convicted for violation of the extortionate credit transactions statute. All of them were given substantial prison terms.

Des and I later "flipped" several other Mob witnesses who helped us convict Frank Valenti, the Magaddino capo in Rochester, and John Cammilleri, a Magaddino capo in Buffalo. This was to become our regular pattern for successfully going after the Mob—convict, sentence, and "flip" key guys, always striving upward toward the boss, Stefano Magaddino.

CHAPTER 4

Magaddino

I f you had asked any law enforcement official in upstate New York during the middle of this century who Stefano Magaddino was, he or she would have promptly answered, "A crime boss who lives in Buffalo." True, but Magaddino was a whole lot more than that. He was the Old World Mafia patriarch who ran La Cosa Nostra in Western New York, Pennsylvania, Ohio, and southern Ontario. Their main criminal activities were murder, narcotics, gambling, loan-sharking, burglary/fencing, fraud, securities thefts, and money laundering through legitimate business.

Who was this legendary aging don? By all accounts, he was considered a traditional "Man of Honor." Was he? My file research turned up some interesting facts.

Known as "The Boss," "The Old Man," "The Undertaker," and "Don Stefano," Magaddino was born on October 10, 1891, in Castellamare del Golfo, Trapani, on the western tip of Sicily. Prior to World War I, the Castellamare region belonged to the infamous Mafioso Diego Plaja, an enormously heavyset man who wore bejeweled rings and necklaces while sweating profusely. According to informants, his bulging belly and cadaver-like yellowish complexion made him appear even more mean than he was. Plaja's daughter married Giuseppe Magaddino Jr., son of Gaspare Magaddino, a mafioso underboss of an adjacent area. Soon after Stefano was born

99

from this marriage, Giuseppe disappeared from Castellamare because he was scheduled for trial on drug-trafficking charges. He later turned up dead in Brooklyn, with a stomach full of bullets.

Meanwhile, back in Castellamare del Golfo, Stefano was related in a distant way to the Bonanno clan that spawned Joe "Joe Bananas" Bonanno, who, soon enough, would rule over his own crime family in America. Bonanno's mother, Catherine Bonventre, a young girl educated by nuns in a Castellamare convent, was Stefano's half-sister. Right after Joe's father, Salvatore Bonanno, married her, he, too, disappeared, winding up in New York's Little Italy. Soon thereafter, Joe was born.

Apparently, Stefano was considered the son of the "black sheep" by most of the Magaddino clan in Castellamare who were not Mafia connected. In fact, many Magaddinos were well placed in both regional and state governments. They never cared for Stefano, even as a young boy. Even as a preteen, he was feared. In addition to being boisterous, demanding, and infantile, Stefano was considered vicious and dangerous. By the age of seventeen, he had already begun his journey into the criminal world. So, with many of the Magaddinos in conflict with him and his mother, he realized there was no future in Sicily. He decided to follow Joe Bonanno to America in 1918.

Stefano became a naturalized United States citizen in 1924. Prior to that time, he had only one serious brush with the law. It seems that in 1921, while living in Brooklyn, the original and largest Castellamarese colony outside of Sicily, the Buccellato brothers, the archenemies of Stefano's father back in Sicily, shot at Stefano and another mafioso, Gaspare Milazzo of Detroit. Although the ambush failed, two innocent people were killed. But, to Magaddino and his "Man of Tradition" values, revenge was a personal responsibility. Within days, the Buccellatos were gunned down on the streets of Brooklyn. Police certainly had their suspicions who the assassins were, but had no proof since all the witnesses "saw nothing." Although he was picked up by the NYPD in New York's Little Italy as a fugitive from this homicide investigation, the police lacked sufficient evidence to charge him, so he was released on the two murders. Soon thereafter, Stefano headed for Buffalo, while Gaspare returned to Detroit.

Meanwhile, in Buffalo, a crime family was already in operation.

Founded by Angelo "Buffalo Bill" Palmeri in 1912 at the onset of Prohibition, the mafiosi combined legitimate wholesale grocery, fruit, and liquor businesses with illegitimate gambling, loan-sharking, and bootlegging. Joseph Peter DiCarlo ruled the crime family between 1912 and 1922, at which time he died of natural causes. Palmeri, who served as underboss and ran the DiCarlo Palmeri Saloon in Buffalo's Italian neighborhood, urged that Stefano take over the family. Hence, Magaddino became the don in late 1922, and in 1931 this Mafia family became one of the founding families in the newly created American La Cosa Nostra. His only real personal tragedy occurred in 1936, when his younger sister was killed when assassins mistakenly bombed her house, which was next door to her brother's.

Magaddino enjoyed a half century without serious interference from law enforcement authorities. He oversaw the expansion of the Buffalo family through northern New York and into areas of Canada. In October 1963 Mafia "songbird" and murderer Joseph Valachi, in testimony during U.S. Senate hearings on organized crime, claimed that Magaddino was the "irrefutable lord paramount" of organized crime in Buffalo, Niagara Falls, and Toronto. At another point, Valachi fondly recalled how at one of the lowest points in his criminal life, Magaddino had loaned him five hundred dollars to tide him over and he was never forced to repay the loan. According to Valachi, Stefano provided the important link in the chain of Mafia influence that stretched from Boston across the Great Lakes area to Minneapolis.

In the late 1930s Magaddino was associated with John C. Montana in the Empire State Brewery. Montana was a trusted lieutenant of Stefano and second in command of the crime family. In fact, the close association with the Magaddino dynasty in the Western New York area was cemented by intermarriage of both families. As I recall, John Montana's son, Charles Montana, married Stefano's daughter.

Montana was a well-known, popular Buffalo businessman who owned the city's largest taxicab company. In addition to serving on Buffalo's city council, he was named the region's "Man of the Year" in 1956. The following year, when he was arrested at the ill-fated Apalachin crime convention, Buffalo went into shock. The resulting exposure and publicity blew his cover as a top man in the Magaddino family. With Stefano's reluctant approval, Montana asked the Commission, the ruling body of the American LCN, if he could return to the rank of a soldier in order not to compromise the Magaddino crime family. Asking for a demotion in order to put the organization ahead of himself was virtually unheard of. The Commission approved, knowing full well that Montana could never be a simple soldier. He died shortly thereafter.

During these years, Stefano built up the Magaddino Memorial Chapel, the Power City Distributing Company of Niagara Falls, and Camellia Linen Supply Company of Buffalo as legitimate front companies.

One of the more laughable incidents during Stefano's stranglehold on organized crime in the Buffalo–Niagara Falls and Toronto areas occurred during the infamous failed crime pow-wow at Apalachin, New York, on November 14, 1957. Not only were some of his clothes and identification papers found on the Joe Barbara premises where the meeting was held, but he escaped the police raid by scampering across nearby muddy fields and woodlands barefoot in his blue suit and shirt and tie.

Interestingly, several months after the Apalachin raid, FBI agents working with the Chicago police listened to a recorded telephone conversation between Stefano Magaddino and Sam "Momo" Giancana, the underboss of the Chicago Mob. "That mess wouldn't have happened in your place," lamented Magaddino. "You bet you're fuckin' right it wouldn't," Giancana said glumly. "I told him Chicago was just right for the big meet. We've got three towns in our territory just outside the city with their police chiefs in our pockets. Our whole area is balled up tight. We should have had that sit-down right here, dammit."

Meanwhile, by 1963, at the age of fifty-eight, cousin Joe Bonanno had lost little of his ambition or hatred of fellow Commission members such as Vito Genovese, Carlo Gambino, Stefano Magaddino, Joe Colombo, Joe Zerilli, Sam Giancana, and Angelo Bruno. Bonanno staked out for himself areas in Canada that he deemed "open" and not governed by other crime families. "Joe Bonanno is trying to plant his flag everywhere," Stefano was overheard moaning on our FBI bugs. According to Mob informant John "Futto" Biello, a captain in the Genovese clan, Bonanno was doing more than that. And he would know. He was a close friend of Bonanno, who had confided that he was about to take over all the New York Mobs by "whacking" his cousin Stefano Magaddino, Thomas "Three-Finger Brown" Lucchese, and Carlo Gambino, as well as Frank DeSimone, head of one of California's crime families. Biello promptly tipped off the Commission. Biello, incidentally, even voted to have his buddy Bonanno killed. Later, informants alleged that Bonanno, who never forgave Biello for his traitorous actions, had him shot in the face four times after being kidnaped off the streets in Miami. Police found his body in the trunk of a car parked in a municipal parking lot. When New York police later asked "Joe Bananas" if he tried to arrange the deaths of the three Mafia leaders, he replied, "Baloney, fantasy, lies."

Meanwhile, the venerable old dons on the Commission hurriedly convened a meeting to deal with the aborted assassinations. They summoned Bonanno to face charges. Of course, Bonanno didn't show up. He hid out in Arizona, using the name "J. Santone." Then, in the next year, he headed for the Toronto area to poach once again on the Magaddino turf. Stefano seethed, then demanded a Commission meeting. On September 18, 1964, the Commission met at the home of LCN underboss Thomas Eboli in Englewood Cliffs, New Jersey. Joe Bonanno failed to appear at this meeting. In the face of such a monumental insult, the Commission took under advisement the advice of Sam Giancana: "Kill him. Just kill him." Ironically, this old-style gangster got what he advocated ten years later. In June 1975 Giancana was shot in the back of the head and killed as he fried a midnight snack of scrambled eggs and sausage in the basement of his suburban Chicago home.

On October 21, 1964, about a month after Bonanno refused to attend the Commission meeting, Bonanno, three of his men, and his lawyer, William Power Maloney, dined in a New York steakhouse. A sixth man joined them around midnight and soon left the table to walk out into a rainstorm to make a phone call from a corner booth. In the early hours of the morning, as Bonanno arrived at his apartment a few miles away, two men stepped out of the bushes and forced him at gunpoint into a car that suddenly drove up. Bonanno was missing for about eighteen months and when he did reappear, he appeared to be in exile at his Arizona home.

Years later, during an interview with Bonanno on *60 Minutes*, Mike Wallace asked in a taped interview from Bonanno's home in Tucson, Arizona, "Who kidnapped you back in 1964?"

"My dear cousin, Stefano Magaddino," Bonanno replied. "Things like that happen. He wanted me out of the way so that he could take over the Bonanno family. He released me after six weeks for many reasons. One was probably he didn't want my blood on his conscience. Also, he feared retaliation from my people in New York who would go up there to Buffalo who weren't afraid of him."

✱✱✱

When Bonanno disappeared, Bill Roselli and I reviewed in detail all the conversations that occurred between Stefano Magaddino, Peter A. Magaddino, and Antonio "Nino" Magaddino on the days just prior to the alleged kidnapping. We discovered a whispered conversation between the three that was barely audible. In this conversation, Stefano told them to get Bonanno and take him to Staten Island and then to the farm. The logs showed that Nino and Peter A. Magaddino then disappeared for several days. Bill and I did the best we could to get a verbatim transcript of the conversation and we immediately advised interested FBI offices and began a search for the "farm." We sent the tape of the conversation to FBI headquarters, where a native Sicilian priest did complete verbatim transcripts. When his report came back a month later, there was no reference to Bonanno or the kidnapping. Bill and I were somewhat embarrassed and we believed we had made a bad mistake in our translation. For years I would joke about this and use it as an illustration of my Sicilian language ability when someone inquired. Years later, we learned different. We were possibly right.

In 1983 Joseph Bonanno wrote his autobiography, arrogantly titled *A Man of Honor*. In this book, he alleges that Nino Magaddino and Peter A. Magaddino were the ones who kidnapped him that night in New York. He states that they drove for hours and eventually came to a farmhouse in the woods, which they entered. He writes that they told him to make himself comfortable. He also writes that Stefano Magaddino showed up the following afternoon. Joe's son, Bill, also wrote a book, *Bound by Honor*. Bill writes that his father did not recognize his kidnappers and that Stefano Magaddino showed up the following day and stayed for a number of days. From our microphones in Magaddino's headquarters, I know that Stefano Magaddino was not missing for any length of time from Niagara Falls during that period. He could have taken a short trip or a series of short trips, which we would not have detected, but if he was missing for more than several hours at a time during the day, we would have known something was up and aggressively attempted to locate him.

Though there has been all sorts of speculation about the kidnapping, including a theory that Bonanno staged the whole thing to avoid an appearance before the federal grand jury in New York. I tend to believe Bonanno when he says he was kidnapped by Nino Magaddino and Peter A. Magaddino of the orders of Stefano Magaddino. Joseph Bonanno claims that Stefano Magaddino visited him frequently. Maybe, but the farmhouse must have been close to Niagara Falls. Joseph Bonanno wrote that he talked Stefano out of killing him by raising the specter of a nation-wide gang war if he was killed. If Stefano would let him go, Bonanno agreed to step down as family boss and retire to Arizona. That may have been the way it happened.

After Bonanno was apparently released, he still was worried that another Mafia boss would try to kill him or attempt to kidnap him. So he headed for South America and Sicily before suddenly reappearing without notice at the U.S. District Courthouse in Brooklyn.

Before the kidnapping in 1964, Stefano Magaddino was obsessed with Joe Bonanno and he continued to rant and rave against him. He began conspiring with an unknown subject, "Gasparino," who was a member of the Bonanno family, to take over the Bonanno family. Magaddino wanted Gasparino to be the boss. Magaddino hated Bonanno and he would talk for hours about how Bonanno dishonored Magaddino and the LCN. He usually referred to Bonanno using the grossest possible profanity.

One day in December of 1964, we learned from the Magaddino microphone that a visitor was coming from New York to see Stefano for a very secret meeting. Stefano did not want any of his capos to be aware of the visitor. The guy was traveling under an assumed name and would be picked up at the Buffalo airport by Peter A. Magaddino. Bill Roselli, Andy Andrews, and I set up surveillance at the airport. There was a blinding snowstorm, but the New York plane landed and we saw Peter at the baggage area. A man approached Peter and they quickly exited the airport and entered Peter's Cadillac, which was parked in a no parking zone outside. We followed the car as it proceeded toward Niagara Falls. When the car came to Grand Island, I put my blue light on and we pulled them over. We walked up to Cadillac and Peter lowered the window. When he saw us, he knew this was no traffic stop. We made them both get out of the car and we patted them down for weapons as they stood in the foot of snow. I then asked the passenger for his identification papers. He reluctantly produced his driver's license. He was Stefano's personal selection as the new boss of the Bonanno family, Gasparino DiGregorio. They were not happy campers. The FBI's discovery of this secret, internal LCN conspiracy was not in their best interests.

Joe Bonanno, interestingly enough, lived until his nineties. His only distinction, of course, was that this real-life former boss survived all the Mob wars of the past century. He spent many of his last years in jail, and he wrote a book detailing the existence of La Cosa Nostra, but he later refused to take the witness stand and was sent to prison for contempt.

In June 1967 Vito Agueci, serving a fifteen-year sentence for involvement in a $150-million-a-year heroin-smuggling ring that operated in France, Italy, Canada, and the United States, testified before a Canadian court that Stefano Magaddino had given the "go ahead" for the creation of the narcotics ring and that, "should any members of the Mafia interfere," he would take care of them.

According to the files, Vito testified that in July of 1960 he was pressured to join the Magaddino crime family by Frederico Randaccio of Buffalo. At the time, Stefano Magaddino had been hospitalized for heart trouble. He had been examined by eight highly regarded heart specialists and all concurred that he indeed had serious heart problems, that his condition was not good, and that with the passing of time he would die. In 1961, as the court waited for a resolution to the matter, Vito's brother

Albert Agueci was found murdered with his arms bound behind his back with wire. He had been strangled with a clothesline. An autopsy report revealed that some thirty pounds of flesh had been sliced from his body while he was still alive. Agueci was found buried on a farm near Rochester. I would later review FBI technical surveillance logs wherein the Magaddino men would discuss the murder in great detail.

With the strength of his brazen empire declining, Magaddino and some of the Commission's other dons decided to breathe life into the LCN and reignite the traditional Old World Mafia spirit into their crime families by smuggling into Canada, then Buffalo and New York, a large number of homegrown Sicilian criminals, known as "zips," who were "made" men in the Sicilian Mafia. These men would operate independent of the LCN families, but they would pay "street taxes" to the LCN bosses in the areas where they operated. These new intruders represented the infancy of the reintroduction of the Sicilian Mafia into the United States and they were the nucleus of the heroin-smuggling ring that would be uncovered by FBI agents years later in the famous "Pizza Connection" case.

More and more, Magaddino considered Canada, especially Toronto and Hamilton, his personal fiefdom. In the mid-1960s we began seeing these zips very frequently showing up on the streets of Buffalo and Niagara Falls.

My first encounter with one of the zips occurred in 1971 when the New York State Police requested my assistance in installing a court-authorized microphone in a Mob restaurant hangout on the West Side of Buffalo. They said that they had to get access to the restaurant to make a secret entry to install the microphone, but it appeared impossible because a Sicilian zip lived over the small restaurant and his job was to guard the restaurant. My friend at the state police gave me the name of the zip and I quickly telephoned the FBI Legal Attaché in Rome. Several hours later he confirmed that this guy was a member of the Sicilian Mafia, a suspected "hit man" who should not have been in the United States.

The state police wanted to go in on a Sunday morning. I agreed to help them. On the next Sunday morning, I went to the zip's apartment at about 9:00 and flashed him a quick badge. I spoke to him in the Sicilian dialect and told him that I was seeking a fugitive from Calabria and he would be attending Sunday mass at a local Catholic church. I asked him if he would assist me in locating this individual by engaging the guy in conversation to verify that the man I suspected was the fugitive, based on his Calabrian accent. The zip was an illegal alien and a Sicilian Mafia member, but he was scared, he did not want to be deported, and he probably thought that I was nuts, but he agreed to accompany me to the church.

We sat in the bureau car outside the church and waited for the imaginary fugitive until I got a coded transmission over the bureau radio from the state police that their mission was accomplished. I told the zip that my information must have been incorrect since the fugitive did not show up and took him back to the restaurant.

The next morning, my friend at the state police called me and said that the hoods had found the microphone. The police had installed what is called a "spike mike" under the zip's bed and when the restaurant opened that morning, the Mob guys noticed sawdust and a small hole in the ceiling. They made a bee line for the zip's apartment. I don't know if he was able to explain himself out of this fix. I do know that after this incident, he was no longer living in that apartment and we didn't see him again in Buffalo.

While Stefano ran his Buffalo family, he was an intimidating man. Although uneducated and illiterate, he was cunning and somewhat charismatic. With a razor-sharp mind, he held court at the Magaddino Memorial Chapel with an iron fist. Furthermore, he was a solid family man, never flashy or extravagant. To the best of my knowledge, he never had a mistress or girlfriend. This was unusual. Most of the Mob guys I have known have had multiple mistresses. It's a "guy thing" with them.

Apparently, Stefano was his most contented self after a huge bowl of pasta with ample portions of meat sauce. With his friends, he relaxed by smoking thick Cuban cigars. He had a special table at the Como Inn, a popular Niagara Falls, New York, restaurant. He had lunch there every day with Peter A. Magaddino, Antonio Magaddino, and any other visiting hood who happened to be in town. Whenever I found myself in Niagara Falls, I would gather several other agents and we would have lunch at Como's, sitting at the table adjacent to Magaddino's. I don't think that helped his digestion. He was easily insulted if peers and underlings didn't shower him with attention, praise, and "respect." Since he was one of the original old-timers, with a crime family long established and currently making big money, Stefano expected to be treated with deference by all LCN types, even by the higher-ranking Commission bosses whose crime families flourished in and around the Big Apple. Although they in turn considered him a major power, he was nonetheless a distant colleague whose throne was hundreds of miles away.

In his later years, during the 1960s, Magaddino began to become very unpopular among his crime family subordinates for his increasing greed with their spoils. He became like New York's boss Joe Profaci and Massachusetts's boss Raymond Patriarca, who were known to have paid their soldiers with counterfeit money. But most of his fellow Commission colleagues considered themselves his allies. In my encounters with him, I found him to be cold and combative, angry and arrogant, which, of course was the role he had to play for his men. Joe Bonanno maintained in his book that Magaddino was essentially a highly depressed, paranoid man with "a shameful sense of inferiority." I would agree with this assessment. Bonanno's education as well as his calm and confidence seemed to threaten Stefano, who figured his suave cousin was always up to some conniving. Their relationship, strained even back in Sicily, slowly deteriorated, even though, as Bonanno claimed, in earlier years he helped solidify Magaddino's place on the Commission and back in Buffalo.

In short, I think that most LCN figures I have known are borderline personalities, riddled with egocentric, narcissistic, and infantile traits. Emotionally, they are stone-cold dead. They are not men of honor. In Magaddino's case, how many did he end up killing, or giving the order to execute?

Who knows?

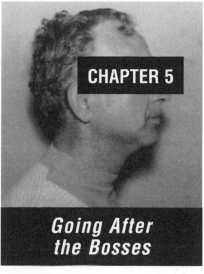

CHAPTER 5

Going After the Bosses

THE BIRTH OF THE WITNESS SECURITY PROGRAM

By early 1968, I had developed three "Top Echelon" Mob informants, two of them "made" members of the Magaddino family of La Cosa Nostra. From these three and others, we were gathering a great deal of detailed intelligence concerning Stefano Magaddino and those associated with him in Buffalo and Niagara Falls. I can't get too specific about how these informants were developed, since one of them is still alive and all of their families would be in jeopardy if I disclosed anything that would identify them. However, I can say that these informants were developed as a result of our aggressive investigations in the early 1960s, the arrests that we made during the 1960s and the resulting pressure we placed on the money-making activities of the Magaddino family. We also capitalized on outstanding intelligence information we received from the microphones and other sources to zero in on the weaknesses within the Magaddino LCN family structure.

Stefano Magaddino became more and more greedy as he got older and this did not escape his close associates. Magaddino was not a popular boss within the family in his last twenty years and there were a number of members who were susceptible to our approach.

111

By 1968 Magaddino was the longest-reigning LCN boss and the most influential member of the Commission. He was the one remaining member of the original Commission. He oversaw the development of the Magaddino family throughout northern New York—actually, in all of New York State outside the city. Frederico G. "The Wolf" Randaccio had replaced John C. Montana as the underboss of the Magaddino family after Montana's death in the late 1950s.

Randaccio was a longtime loyalist to Magaddino who quickly rose through the ranks of the family. He had a reputation as a cold and vicious killer.

Randaccio first came to my attention when I reported to Buffalo and began reviewing the microphone transcripts on the technical coverage of him.

One day in 1961 Andy Andrews, who was coordinating the Randaccio antiracketeering investigation, received a call from our New York office that Alberto Agueci, a heroin dealer associated with the Magaddino family, had jumped bail in New York and was on the lam and believed to possibly be headed to Buffalo. The following day, Andy monitored a conversation from a hidden microphone installed in Mogavero's gas station, a daily hangout of Randaccio's, that indicated Alberto Agueci was there and was trying to meet with Stefano Magaddino. Andy told me he rushed out of the office to Mogavero's, which was just east of the Peace Bridge to Canada. Agueci was not there, nor was Randaccio or Daniel Sansanese. He checked Magaddino's residence, the Magaddino funeral home, and all of Randaccio's and Sansanese's normal hangouts, but he could not locate them or Agueci. On the next day, Sansanese and some of the others showed up at the gas station and Andy heard them discussing Agueci and talking about how Agueci was trying to get something out of Magaddino in lieu of Agueci not testifying about Magaddino's involvement in the narcotics ring. The log indicated they laughed and said that they had tied up Agueci with his hands behind his back and used a rope as a garrote to strangle him. They said they strung a rope around his neck, running the rope around his legs behind his back, and let him strangle himself when his legs began to pull against the rope. Before Agueci died, they used a knife to cut off his penis, which they said they stuffed in his mouth—

because he was threatening to talk. The file indicated Agueci's body was found several months later, buried on a farm near Rochester. Sansanese and these others were bad people who needed to be taken off the street, but the tape was not admissible—we could not use it in court.

One morning in the winter of 1967, the Buffalo City Treasurer's Office was robbed by a lone white gunman in a daring stickup that netted the robber many thousands of dollars. He got away clean. When the FBI office was notified several minutes after the robbery, calls went out over the FBI radio and we all responded to the scene. City Hall employees were stunned, since this was the first time the office had been robbed. We conducted the normal investigation, linking up with the Buffalo Police Robbery Squad, interviewing all the witnesses, conducting investigations at neighborhood offices in an effort to get a description of the bandit, and conducting an outside investigation in an effort to get a description of the getaway car and the getaway route. Later on in the afternoon, a Buffalo bank was also robbed by a lone white gunman, resulting in a major loss to the bank. As was customary, calls again went out over the radio to us and we responded to this robbery, which was unrelated to the City Hall job. We did our normal investigation at this location as well, hooking up with detectives on the robbery squad, conducting interviews of the witnesses, conducting investigations in the neighborhood in an effort to get a description of the getaway cars, and so on. No information of significance was developed on the day of these two robberies.

In the early evening hours, two teletypes were sent to FBI headquarters detailing the two robberies and indicating the plans we had for the investigation to solve the cases. At FBI headquarters, a supervisor received these two teletypes. He reviewed them and, as was normal procedure, he prepared summaries of the teletypes for review by Director Hoover. However, to save time, he put the teletypes together and combined the summaries into one summary. When the teletypes got to Hoover, he reviewed them and came to the erroneous conclusion that the two robberies were the work of one very active armed robber. He wrote on the summary "Exert all efforts to identify this robber!! Keep me advised of developments." Bingo! This became a "Bureau Special." The FBI assistant director called SAC Neil J. Welch and instructed Welch to assign significant man-power to this "case" to get it solved quickly. Welch protested that these were two unrelated robberies and we were working both of them actively. The assistant director didn't want to hear this. No one back in Washington had the guts to tell Hoover that these were two independent robberies. The only thing out of the ordinary was the City Hall job. One of the Buffalo FBI office's senior agents, Gordon Eddy, was assigned to head the "Special," and Frank Conners, Bill Badgley, Bill Roselli, and I were assigned as case agents to do the "grunt" work on the case. We worked very closely with the Buffalo Police Robbery Squad, and soon one of our informants reported that the robbery had been committed by a young street tough, Pasquale "Paddy" Calabrese.

We were aware of Calabrese. He was an up-and-coming LCN associate who was slated to be inducted into the Buffalo family. We had previously observed Calabrese meeting with Frederico Randaccio during our frequent physical surveillance of Randaccio. The investigation immediately focused on Calabrese and soon we had witness identifications and sufficient information to charge him locally for the City Hall robbery. We turned over our information to the Buffalo Police Department and Calabrese was arrested for the City Hall robbery, arraigned before a local judge, and sent to the Erie County Jail in lieu of high bond. Calabrese sat in jail for a few days; on the third day, he called the FBI office. Bill Badgley and I responded, traveling to the county jail to interview Calabrese. Paddy knew both of us from our investigations of Randaccio and Sansanese. He wanted to get out of jail and he was angry that he had not been provided with an attorney. It was only later in the interview that I realized he expected that an attorney would be provided by the Mob. Calabrese was anxious to determine if a deal could be made to get him out of this scrape. He said that he was involved with people we were interested in putting in jail. I asked him who he was referring to, and he said, "Freddie Randaccio and Pat Natarelli." What a break! Frederico Randaccio was the underboss and Pasquale "Pat" Natarelli was one of the leading capos in the family. We told him that we would be in a position to make a deal after we debriefed him. We needed to know the details of his involvement with

Randaccio and Natarelli. Bill Badgley and I talked to him for the next three days and he described a number of robberies and burglaries he had conducted or was planning under the direction of and in conjunction with Frederico Randaccio and Pasquale Natarelli. He also detailed a hotel guest robbery in California that he had conducted under Randaccio's direction with LCN members Steve Cino and Charles Caci, aka Bobby Milano. We immediately went to see Bob Peloquin and Tom Kinnally, who had just come to Buffalo as leaders of the U.S. Justice Department Strike Force against organized crime. To make a long story short, we had Calabrese released to our custody and, after he was fully debriefed, he testified before the federal grand jury.

This was the first instance in my personal experience proving my belief that their Omerta, or vow of silence, was a myth. On June 29, 1967, as a result of Paddy's testimony and our follow-up investigation, Frederico Randaccio, Pasquale A. Natarelli, Stephen A. Cino, Charles Caci, and Louis Sorgi were indicted by the federal grand jury for violation of the Hobbs Act, a rarely used statute that was originally passed by Congress to be utilized in relation to labor racketeering. Simply stated, the statute makes any robbery or violence that affects interstate commerce a federal crime. The City Hall job, as much as the California hotel guest robbery, were violations of that statute. Arrest warrants were issued for all five of these mobsters.

The strike force decided to use deputy U.S. Marshals and several local police officers to make the arrests of this crew, rather than the FBI agents who actually put the case together. This really angered us. We had made the case and deserved to have the opportunity to make these arrests. In the arrest situation, there is always the possibility of picking up additional evidence or getting the cooperation of one of the subjects. This was my first look at how some of these strike forces would operate and I did not like it for a minute.

Calabrese was an outstanding witness. He was highly intelligent and very articulate. Randaccio, Natarelli, Cino, Sorgi, and Caci were all convicted. Judge John O. Henderson ordered that all of the defendants be remanded to jail, pending sentencing.

On December 11, 1967, the defendants appeared before Judge Henderson. Bill Badgley, Bill Roselli, Frank Conners, and I were in the front bench of the spectator gallery. Randaccio was sentenced to twenty years in prison. Natarelli and Cino also received twenty years in prison. Charles Caci and Louis Sorgi were given ten years in prison.

We then relocated Calabrese and his family. Calabrese was the first federal witness ever relocated by the U.S. government. We gave him and his wife new identification papers, Social Security cards, and, through personal friends in the business community, we made a business history for him that would stand scrutiny. This was the beginning of the Federal Witness Security Program (commonly referred to as the "witness protection program"). Congress later passed legislation in 1970 making the Witness Security Program official. Since his relocation, Calabrese has helped us on some other very sensitive investigations. He has led a very full and happy life with his family and he has been very successful in business where he is living. I have not heard from him for several years, but I am proud that I had a part in his relocation. He turned out to be a fine person.

Randaccio was released from prison in the late 1990s and it is my understanding he is "retired" in Buffalo. Steve "The Whale" Cino was also released about the same time. I have heard that he transferred to the Los Angeles LCN family shortly after he left prison. He was indicted for extortion in U.S. District Court, Las Vegas, for his role in the extortion of long-time local hoodlum Herbie Blitzstein. He was convicted and on August 31, 1999, Cino was sentenced to fifteen years imprisonment. At sixty-one, with a host of medical maladies sure to keep prison doctors hustling, not even Cino would book the odds he'll ever leave prison alive.

On January 8, 2001, Charles Caci and his brother, Vincent Caci, each pleaded guilty in U.S. District Court, Las Vegas, to one count of conspiracy to participate in an enterprise engaged in racketeering activity. Their guilty pleas stemmed from a plan to sell counterfeit traveler's checks for fraudulent use. The indictment, which was returned in 1998, identified Vincent Caci as a capo in the Los Angeles LCN family. On July 27, Charles Caci, who is a professional singer under the name Bobby Milano, was sentenced to four months confinement in his Palm Springs, California, home. Vincent Caci was sentenced earlier to six months confinement.

MAGADDINO IN THE CROSSHAIRS

Getting back to Steve Magaddino, back in 1968 Ray Kruger, an experienced agent in the Niagara Falls Resident Agency, was assigned the Magaddino case. Meanwhile, I was attached to the FBI office in Buffalo with responsibility for tracking organized-crime figures living in Buffalo. The only case that existed on Steve Magaddino was what was then referred to as an antiracketeering (AR) or intelligence-type case. The investigation had used wiretaps to gather intelligence information on him, but they had nothing that would hold up in court.

Magaddino was not under investigation for any specific federal crime. As a matter of routine, the AR cases were kept open on all LCN figures, since they are always committing some crime, as repositories of information and as a way to follow their daily activities. This is done to develop information about specific crimes they commit. When information about a specific crime is received, a "substantive" investigative case is opened and worked just as any other reactive crime case, such as a bank robbery.

As for Magaddino himself, he had not been arrested or charged for any offense since 1921, when he was arrested for those two murders in New York. When the only witness disappeared, the case against Magaddino was dismissed. Although Magaddino was present at Apalachin, he was one of several who managed to get away. Now he was seventy-seven years old and he appeared to be totally insulated from prosecution.

During the latter part of his criminal career, Magaddino was a notoriously greedy and cheap LCN family leader who treated those closest to him with contempt. He had loyal capos, such as Danny G. Sansanese Sr., Sam Pieri, Joe Fino, Sam Frangiamore, and Roy Carlisi, backing him up. With their help, he ruled through sheer fear and intimidation. Sansanese was made from the same mold as Magaddino: short, ugly, and vicious. Although I will deal with him later in this book, I will say that Sansanese was one of the most vicious and sadistic men that I encountered in La Cosa Nostra. His contract killings always consisted of mutilating the victims in the grossest and most terrible ways before they were killed. Later, I would learn that he was also a personal coward, as many of these LCN figures are.

As for Magaddino, he was a small man, about five feet tall, skinny with a beer belly, and bald. I figured from my courses in undergraduate psychology at Georgetown University, as well as from observing his actions, interviewing him, and listening to his ranting and ravings on the FBI microphones, that he had a major "little man" (or inferiority) complex. His wife was perpetually dressed in black, the typical Sicilian mourning dress, and either praying or chanting the rosary. She was doing the right thing: Magaddino needed her prayers.

One day in August 1968, SAC Neil J. Welch called me into his office and closed the door. He said that he was very concerned that we didn't have anything going on Magaddino, one of the most powerful racketeers in the United States. Welch asked if I thought I could put together a case against Magaddino. I responded that I was certain we could make a case against the old guy. Welch said he had been led to believe that Magaddino was so insulated that we could never touch him. I told Welch that was "a lot of baloney," and I said I hoped that he would give me a shot at Magaddino. He smiled and said, "You got it. You hook up with Ray Kruger and see what you guys can come up with." I immediately called Ray and arranged to meet him that same afternoon.

Kruger and his sidekick, Alan "Smoky" Burgess, were terrific agents and they welcomed any assistance. Recently assigned to Niagara Falls by Welch, they had been trying to figure out how to go after Magaddino. The Mob boss had been thumbing his nose at us since the FBI started investigating him in 1957, certain he was somehow immune. Each time we had served him with one of many subpoenas over the past five years, he checked himself into a hospital. One of his highly paid heart specialists would simply provide an affidavit or testimony that due to heart problems, Magaddino was practically on his deathbed and would certainly meet his maker if called before a tribunal.

Meanwhile, during the previous six months, I had learned from the two informants in his crime family that Stefano Magaddino had a personal sports book operated by capo Benny J. Nicoletti Sr. At this time, after the incarceration of Frederico Randaccio, Peter A. Magaddino, Stefano's oldest son, had taken over as underboss of the family. According to my two informants, who had learned the details of the sports book operation from Benny Nicoletti Sr. and Peter A. Magaddino, Benjamin "Sonny" Nicoletti Jr., an aspiring hood and the capo's son, was actually the operator of the book. He answered the telephones, took the bets, made the collections, paid off the bettors, and met other collectors. Sonny would settle up with Nicoletti Sr. every Tuesday evening. Nicoletti Sr. would then meet Peter later that night and hand over the week's receipts. Peter would then bring the proceeds to Stefano. From my third informant I learned the phone numbers and the locations where Sonny was operating the bookmaking office. Sonny changed the location of his "office" every three weeks in order to avoid detection. But when the location changed, my informant would get the new number and pass it on to me. Sonny's "office" was usually in a dilapidated apartment building in a low-rent area of Niagara Falls or North Tonawanda, New York.

Our task was to establish an interstate connection to the case and corroborate the information being received from the three informants. This was done by contacts with other informants, police intelligence sources, the examination of telephone records, and, most important of all, surveillance of the principals involved.

The surveillance part was extremely difficult. Niagara Falls was a small community that was literally owned by the Magaddinos. Any unusual activity on Ray's part in Niagara Falls was immediately noticed by so-called legitimate people and called in to Stefano Magaddino. For example, on one occasion, Ray was spotted walking into a clothing store by one of the Magaddinos. The next time Kruger went into that store, he was told by the owner to stay out, that Peter A. Magaddino had come in and demanded to know what Kruger was doing there. The owner apologized, but said he didn't want to have any trouble with the Magaddinos.

So the Mob was closely scrutinizing all our activities. Our surveillance had to be done so discreetly it could not be observed.

Upon reporting to Buffalo as SAC in the mid-1960s, Welch was briefed on how hard it was to conduct surveillance of these hoodlums with our bureau-looking vehicles. We got feedback from informants that the mobsters routinely watched our office and that they knew our license numbers and descriptions of all our cars, and were capable of monitoring our radio transmissions. The office of one of the their attorneys was located directly across the street from the FBI office.

Unknown to the Magaddinos and their attorneys, Welch had ordered Don Hartnett and me to find an off-premise location where we could establish a highly specialized surveillance squad. That meant a location where no one would know who we were or what we were doing. We discovered a perfect location in Williamsville, an eastern suburb that is convenient to both Buffalo and Niagara Falls. Don established the squad and was made its supervisor. The squad, which was staffed by some twenty experienced surveillance agents, several of whom were formerly assigned to conduct sensitive surveillance over a long period of time in New York.

Pete Sofia was one of the agents transferred to Buffalo from New York. He had learned the trade following around some of the most sophisticated spies in the world. Without question, he was the finest surveillance agent I have ever known. Pete had a unique talent for making himself invisible to the surveillance subject. This was before the FBI had female agents, but soon thereafter we began to routinely use wives, girlfriends, and female FBI support employees to provide "cover" and assist in the surveillance. Furthermore, the surveillance agents were allowed to grow beards and wear scruffy clothing.

Don Hartnett and his newly assembled team worked out of a location that to all observers appeared to be little more than a private company. No one knew who we were or what we were really doing. Certainly no one would have believed we were FBI agents. All of our surveillance operations originated and were supervised from this location. Don even went so far as to purchase and rent specialized vehicles, such as sports cars, convertibles, foreign-made autos, and specialized trucks disguised as bread trucks or delivery vans.

Congress had passed the Omnibus Crime Control and Safe Streets Act, which had become law on June 19, 1968, and which permitted us to use court-authorized electronic surveillance. But the liberal Ramsey Clark/Warren Christopher Justice Department would not allow us to use this technique, even against the most powerful mobster in the United States.

From telephone company records, I learned that the bookmaking location being manned by Sonny Nicoletti Sr. was located in North

Tonawanda, New York, just south of Niagara Falls. Our investigation began in the early part of the 1968 baseball season, so the book was operating daily during the afternoon and in the evening. It wasn't long before our surveillance began corroborating the steady stream of information from the informants. For example, we verified that Sonny Nicoletti entered the book around noon every day, leaving after 4:00 P.M., returning again about 6:00 P.M. where he remained until nearly 9:00 P.M. Our surveillance further revealed that each Monday, Sonny met with Pasquale "Patsy" Passero, Gino Monaco, Sam Puglese, Michael A. Farella, and Louis C. Tavano. My third informant told me that all these guys were collectors for Sonny who also worked the craps game operated by Nicoletti Sr. in North Tonawanda for Steve Magaddino. During the previous four years we had joined the New York State Police in raiding this game on numerous occasions. But the Magaddino Mob kept reopening it.

During our surveillance, I had one of my informants telephone the book and make bets on the various baseball games with Sonny. I listened in on our extension phone so I could later testify that bets had been made by informants on certain dates and at certain times. Our surveillance also verified that every Tuesday, Sonny would again meet with his collectors, who handed paper bags over to him. Then he was driven over to the Round-the-Clock Restaurant in Niagara Falls, New York, to meet with Ben Nicoletti Sr. On each occasion he would pass one large paper bag to Nicoletti Sr., who in turn drove directly to Peter A. Magaddino, usually waiting at a table in the Your Host Restaurant in Niagara Falls. The surveillance showed that Peter always took the paper bag from Nicoletti and drove directly to the Magaddino Memorial Chapel. Peter usually entered the funeral home at around 4:00 P.M. He and Stefano Magaddino would usually then leave the funeral home, Peter driving Stefano to his home in Lewiston, New York.

During our three months of continued physical surveillance the crime family's pattern of activity never varied except for the locations of some of the restaurant meetings. The book location changed about four times during that period of the investigation, although I continued to observe the bets going into the book from one of the informants.

Toward the end of our investigation, another of my informants revealed that Dan Sansanese, Sam Pieri, and Joe Fino, three of Magaddino's capos, were extremely upset with Stefano Magaddino. Apparently, he cut their percentage of profits from the bookmaking, gambling, and loan-sharking activities. Usually, each Magaddino capo received a large year-end bonus, normally in the range of $50,000. That year, Magaddino announced they were not going to get a bonus for 1968. I thought this was rather interesting since Magaddino's personal sports book was the largest in northern New York and he had to be making at least $20,000 a week.

After subpoenaing the telephone records and long-distance telephone calls from the telephone bookmaking location and for all of the home locations of the principals, I realized that Sonny was making long-distance calls to telephone numbers in Niagara Falls, Ontario, from the bookmaking location, indicating that he was making these calls to lay off betting action. This is a common practice for large bookmakers.

Ray Kruger learned from his investigation that these telephone numbers were known bookmakers in Ontario. Through close liaison with the Royal Canadian Mounted Police and the Ontario Provincial Police, Ray determined that Sonny was using these Ontario bookmaking operations to lay off his betting action. As I explained earlier, for a bookmaker to be successful, it is necessary to balance his books; that is, to have equal amounts of money bet on each side of a baseball or football game. He makes his money in the 10 percent spread that each bettor is charged. In order to balance the books, Sonny was compelled to have a "layoff" bookmaker where he could place his balancing bets. These telephone calls gave us our federal violation.

In early November 1968 we began putting the case together on paper and preparing affidavits for search and arrest warrants. An examination of these affidavits made it very clear that the Magaddinos were in classic violation of the ITAR-gambling statute. This meant that a conspiracy existed from the lowest Mob collector all the way up to Peter A. Magaddino and his father, Stefano, to operate an illegal bookmaking operation through the use of interstate or international telephone calls. We verified all of the informants' information through the three-month surveillance. And through his Canadian law enforcement sources, Ray was able to further verify the facts in our investigation.

After Ray and I prepared the Complaint for Search Warrants, the Complaint for Arrest Warrants, and our supporting affidavits, we took them to the newly appointed U.S. attorney, Andy Phalen. I had informed Andy several weeks ago that we were working on this case, so he was not surprised. After reviewing our material, Andy concurred that we had probable cause for the arrests and search warrants of all the residences of each of the subjects, with the exception of Stefano Magaddino. Andy disagreed that we had probable cause to search Stefano Magaddino's residence since none of our informants had actually seen any bookmaking activity in Magaddino's residence. I strongly disagreed, pointing out that Stefano's residence was the most important location that needed searching. More than one of our informants had hearsay information that gambling records and Stefano's proceeds from the gambling activity would be found in his residence. Our informants believed Stefano Magaddino had a major stash of cash hidden at home. He was so relaxed because he had not been arrested or searched since 1921. Stefano Magaddino believed his home to be the most secure place on earth.

Andy could not be swayed. Furthermore, he told us that because of Magaddino's serious heart history he would not give us the authority to actually arrest him. Ray and I were furious. We believed we had established probable cause for Stefano's house search and his arrest. But Andy would not change his mind and we had no recourse. I suspect that Andy was fearful that Magaddino might have a heart attack and die on us or that we would come up "dry" on the search, causing embarrassment. I didn't buy that, but Andy was the U.S. attorney and it was his job to make these kinds of decisions, so I had to respect that. Andy approved all the search and arrest warrants except for the Stefano Magaddino home search and his physical arrest.

Our plan was to execute the warrants on the following Tuesday, November 26, 1968, after surveillance determined a pass had been made of the brown paper bag containing the week's bookmaking receipts. On Monday, November 25, Ray and I took the complaints and affidavits to U.S. Commissioner Ed Maxwell, who promptly approved them and issued us search warrants.

On the following day, our surveillance determined the exact same pattern occurred as it did during the past three months. Don Hartnett informed me that Sonny met with Benjamin Nicoletti Sr. and turned over the paper bag containing the records and Stefano's split of the weekly bookmaking proceeds to him. An hour later Nicoletti met Peter Magaddino at the Your Host Restaurant in Niagara Falls and Peter then drove to the funeral home to meet with Stefano Magaddino.

Earlier in the day on November 26, a "closed in briefing conference" was held in our office with approximately 150 FBI agents, local police officers, and officers of the New York State Police. A "closed in briefing conference" is one in which no conferee can make a telephone call after the conference begins until after the arrests are made. The search teams were briefed by Welch, Ray, and me. Each participant was provided a packet of search warrant locations, which included the bookmaking location apartment, the residences of the collectors and book operators, and the residences of Benjamin Nicoletti Jr., Benjamin Nicoletti Sr., Peter A. Magaddino, and the Magaddino Memorial Chapel. In addition, we had search warrants for all of them personally, as well as their arrest warrants. Immediately after the briefing, teams of ten fanned out in what would be the most important attack ever undertaken against the Magaddino empire. We timed the raids to take place when the Nicoletti bookmaking operation was in full swing. I was assigned to arrest Peter A. Magaddino and to head up the search at his residence. At about 6:05 P.M., Ray, fellow agent Tom Shaughnessy, and I drove to the Magaddino Memorial Chapel, where we encountered Peter A. Magaddino as he was leaving the Magaddino headquarters. I told him that he was under arrest and handcuffed him and placed him in the back seat of Shaughnessy's bureau car.

Peter appeared to be very shocked and asked, "What for?" When I told him that it was for interstate bookmaking, he appeared somewhat relieved. Tom advised him of his rights and he refused to make any statement. I told him that I was leaving to go search his house. This appeared to upset him and he said that we could not do that. I laughed and said, "Watch us." Tom Shaughnessy and another agent that I do not recall drove Peter to the FBI office in Buffalo where he was processed.

I immediately drove to Peter's home in Niagara Falls, where the search was already happening. When I arrived, the other agents were in the process of going through the master bedroom. Behind the bed, a hidden door was discovered that led to a secret compartment about five feet wide and five feet deep. Within this compartment were three dark brown suitcases. We pulled the cases out of the hidden closet, placed them on Peter's bed and opened them, discovering that each was stuffed with money, a total of $473,134. Upon discovery of this cash, I called Peter's wife into the room and asked if she could explain the huge amount of cash in the suitcases. She appeared stunned as she looked down at the cash. Then she began cursing. "That son of a bitch! I wanted to take a trip to Sicily this summer and he said we couldn't afford it." She added that the money must be her husband's, since she did not know it was there. None of us could know at that moment that the discovery of the these three bulging suitcases of cash would soon lead to Stefano Magaddino's downfall in La Cosa Nostra.

Meanwhile, back at the funeral home, the searchers discovered the records Peter had delivered to Stefano that day, as well as Stefano's share of the week's bookmaking proceeds, $38,000 in twenty-dollar bills. Tom Shaughnessy discovered identical records on the person of Peter A. Magaddino himself when he was arrested. Other bookmaking receipts tying into these records were discovered on Benjamin Nicoletti Sr. as well as on each of the collectors. Sonny Nicoletti was due to show up at the bookmaking office at 7:00 P.M., but he didn't appear, undoubtedly because he somehow learned about the other arrests. He was, therefore, a fugitive, although he surrendered several days later accompanied by his attorney.

After the raids, I telephoned my two member informants to tell them of the cash we found in Peter's house. They both reminded me that Magaddino had told the Buffalo capos that they were not going to get their normal cash bonuses that year since he was so cash light. The informants predicted that when the capos learned about the hidden cash there was going to be plenty of trouble. And there was.

The searches were so successful that Andy Phalen gave us an arrest warrant for Stefano Magaddino and search warrants for what was called "Mafia Row," the homes owned by Stefano Magaddino, James V. LaDuca,

Vincent Scro, and Charles A. Montana, on Dana Drive in Lewiston, New York. LaDuca, Scro, and Montana were "made" guys who were also Magaddino's sons-in-law. The warrants were executed simultaneously on the evening of Friday, November 29. Welch, Don Hartnett, Agent Terry Kelly, the search crews, and I proceeded to the Magaddino residence in Lewiston to execute the search warrant.

As Welch, Hartnett, Kelly, and I walked up to the front door of Stefano's house, James V. "Jimmy" LaDuca hurried over from his house next door and asked me what we were doing. I actually liked LaDuca. He was a very friendly, humorous, and engaging guy. One time he told me that he was in line for the first *Godfather* movie and when he got to the ticket counter, the girl told him the theater was filled. He said he told the ticket seller, "You've got to let me in. This is about my family."

After I informed LaDuca that we were there to arrest the old man and to search his house, as well as LaDuca's house, he opened the front door of the Stefano Magaddino residence and stepped aside. The living room looked like a chancery. There was a papal blessing from Pope Pius XII hanging on the wall near the front door. Paintings of saints and Jesus hung on most of the walls, and in the first-floor master bedroom, there was a statue of the Sacred Heart dressed in very rich linen garments on top of a large television.

Meanwhile, Stefano's wife, Carmella, was seated in the living room in her mourning attire. She wept, prayed, and chanted the rosary. Welch and I walked into the first-floor master bedroom and discovered Stefano Magaddino lying in bed with an oxygen mask over his face. I walked over to the bed and told him, "Stefano, we're with the FBI and you're under arrest." He immediately began chanting "You're trying to kill me! You're trying to kill me!" in his thick Sicilian accent. Magaddino continued chanting, "You're trying to kill me," as Terry Kelly and I began the search of his room. When I opened the nightstand drawer, I found a loaded .38 Colt revolver. Magaddino didn't miss a beat. He leaned forward and, with his eyes still tightly closed, said, "I have a permit for that." As Terry and I began searching under the mattress, Welch walked in. We were pulling the mattress up pretty high to search for additional weapons or contraband and

Magaddino began to bounce around on the bed rather violently. He continued to chant, "You're trying to kill me." Welch walked over and checked his pulse, adding, "I believe this old man is having a heart attack." I laughed. We had a cardiologist on standby waiting outside in a bureau car for just such an emergency. I walked out and asked the doctor to come in. After a quick examination of Magaddino, he announced that Stefano was not having a heart attack. In the meantime, Carmella had passed out. So the physician was asked to evaluate her condition and, after a brief examination of her, he said she was okay, too.

Interestingly, in the richly furnished finished basement, there was a long board of directors table with twelve stuffed leather chairs around it. The chair at the head of the table was much higher than the rest and obviously was the one usually occupied by Old Man Magaddino. I made up my mind that this would be the area where we would place microphones, if the Justice Department ever allowed us to use them.

But, just as I figured, Stefano's Magaddino's home and walk-in safe were empty. The searches of the Scro, LaDuca, and Montana homes were also futile. We were too late. They knew or suspected that we were coming and they had stripped their homes of all monies and any incriminating evidence. They didn't even have an address book.

Subsequent to the completion of the searches, U.S. Commissioner Ed Maxwell was brought to the house for Magaddino's arraignment. Stefano was released on $50,000 bond.

We would return to the Magaddino home one more time. As I expected, immediately after the search and arrests, affidavits were filed by Magaddino's doctors stating that Magaddino could not attend court because of his heart condition. If he were forced to attend, they argued, he would undoubtedly die. Several weeks later we returned with U.S. District Judge John M. Henderson to arraign the LCN boss after he was indicted by the federal grand jury. Welch and I took Judge Henderson on a quick tour of the house and pointed out to him the basement table and the chairs. I asked him what this looked like and Judge Henderson exclaimed, "It's a fucking courtroom!!"

For the next two years, countless hearings occurred in federal court over Magaddino's health and other challenges to our search warrants. Not too long after our raid, Andy Phalen left the U.S. Attorney's Office and took a job in New York City. U.S. Attorney Ken Schroeder replaced Phalen and assumed responsibility for the prosecution of the case. Almost immediately after the indictment and arraignment of the Magaddino subjects, the strike force began an internal battle with Schroeder to take over control of the prosecution of the Magaddino case. Eventually, the bureaucrats in Washington backed the strike force and the case was reassigned to them. They got the case, but they didn't do anything with it and it languished. Ken Schroeder was an outstanding U.S. attorney who was totally dedicated to his job. Richard J. Arcara, who was also in his office, was a great attorney. I wish they could have kept the Magaddino case.

In the meantime, my informants reported that after learning about all the cash that was recovered at Peter's house, LCN family members were so outraged they wanted to kill Stefano Magaddino. The only thing stopping them was their fear of the Commission in New York. LCN rules absolutely prohibit killing a family boss without the Commission's approval. Within a month of our raids, the Magaddino family members met and voted Stefano Magaddino out as boss and Peter out as underboss. Salvatore J. "Sam" Pieri became boss and Joseph M. "Joe" Fino was named his underboss. My informants reported that Sam Pieri and Joe Fino then flew to New York to appear before the Commission in order to present the new structure of the Buffalo crime family. At that initial meeting, Magaddino still had the backing of the Commission, but soon thereafter he was formally kicked off of the Commission. He had helped establish the Commission back in the 1930s, was one of the original members, and now he was gone, in disgrace. This information was corroborated by investigation and informant information from New York.

Our case never came to trial. Magaddino's defense attorneys established through the testimony of a string of heart specialists that he could never stand trial because of his heart condition and his prosecution was placed in "limbo." Judge Henderson ruled that he could not be brought to trial and that he could not be tried in absentia. The defense also attempted to establish in these endless court hearings that I received the information concerning the bookmaking operation from the microphones that had been installed in Stefano's office between 1961 and July 12, 1965. Of course, this was ridiculous. Sonny Nicoletti was not even working the personal Magaddino bookmaking operation in 1965. When I was ordered to identify my informants in court, I refused. Their lives would have been over if I gave up their names. One of the most concrete philosophies in the FBI is that you protect your informants' identities at all costs. Besides, we couldn't try the big guy.

At the conclusion of the hearings, which occurred over the following twenty-four months, Judge John O. Henderson ruled our warrants were indeed lawful and that I did not have to disclose the identity of my informants. But the bottom line was that Stefano Magaddino would never have to stand trial. Magaddino and his fellow defendants continued with their appeals and eventually, in 1973, the U.S. Court of Appeals ruled that our warrants were "tainted" because of the microphone coverage in the early 1960s.

Magaddino was virtually a prisoner in his own house and, in 1974, he finally died in disgrace from that much-anticipated heart attack.

Pieri Succeeds Magaddino

When Sam Pieri became boss, I immediately launched an intensive investigation of his activities. I had already been assigned his antiracketeering case and had accumulated a great deal of intelligence information. He had been released from prison several years before after doing time for a major heroin conviction. After his release from prison, Pieri transferred to the Cleveland LCN family and moved to Youngstown, Ohio, with Joseph J. DiCarlo. Their initial presence in Youngstown caused friction between the Cleveland LCN family and Pittsburgh LCN family and a number of bombings and gangland killings followed. In the early 1960s Pieri and DiCarlo were run out of town by the Pittsburgh LCN families. Pieri and DiCarlo returned to Buffalo and rejoined the Magaddino family. When Pieri returned to Buffalo, he primarily hung around Santasiero's, a well-known West Side restaurant. He conducted his stolen-property-fencing operation over the various pay telephones located in the area. I located a "fixed plant," an apartment in the area, and began periodic surveillance of him. The U.S. attorney general would still not allow us to use court-authorized technical surveillance, so when I saw him use the pay phone, I would note the time and get the phone record under subpoena from the telephone company. I learned that Pieri was in close touch with Anthony J. "Lib" Liberatore, a notorious Cleveland racketeer, and Curly Montana, another Cleveland hoodlum. Pieri was also in close touch with Carmen "Junior" Persico and Donny "Donny Shacks" Montemorano, two members of the Colombo family. I also identified through these surveillances Pieri associates who were being used by Pieri in various capacities. Ultimately I began talking to some of these individuals, and before long, I had two new informants.

As a result of the new informants, I was now able to more closely follow Pieri's activities. On occasion, we would learn of Pieri's travel plans and when Pieri was going out of town, we would follow him to identify his criminal associates and try to figure out what they were doing. My friend Sean M. McWeeney was now in New York working on the Joe Colombo squad, so he covered Pieri while Pieri was in the Big Apple. I was also in close contact with the Cleveland FBI office and there I developed a close friendship with Martin P. "Marty" McCann, who would cover Pieri on the many trips he made to Cleveland. Through this surveillance, we learned who Pieri's contacts were. They were all LCN members who were involved in property crimes or narcotics. Developing the intelligence information was nice, but we had to have some specific knowledge of what Pieri was doing to effectively take him out.

In January 1970 I received information from one of my informants that Sam Pieri was in Jacksonville, Florida. Pieri had called back to the source and indicated he was returning with some hot jewelry he wanted to fence in either Buffalo or Cleveland. According to the source, Pieri would be returning on January 16, 1970. I immediately checked with the appropriate airlines and could locate no flight reservation. Pieri was undoubtedly traveling under an alias. Fortunately, the informant was later able to furnish me with Pieri's exact flight plans.

Des Desvernine and I established surveillance at the Buffalo airport and sure enough, Sam Pieri and two unidentified men disembarked the midafternoon flight from Jacksonville. Pieri was carrying a briefcase, which appeared to be rather heavy. They picked up their other luggage and took a taxicab to the Continental Inn, located just across from the Buffalo airport. Each of them, including Pieri, checked into the hotel with what were later determined to be phony names.

After putting their luggage in their rooms, they proceeded to the hotel bar where Pieri remained in close guard of his briefcase. Later in the day, about 6:30 P.M., they were joined at the restaurant by Victor Randaccio, an LCN member who was the brother of former LCN underboss Fred Randaccio. Victor was also the business agent of Local 210, the LCN-controlled Buffalo LIUNA local. The four spent most of the evening in the hotel bar, and around 11:00 P.M., Randaccio left and Pieri and his two associates, who were referred to as "Tony" and "Paul," returned to their rooms.

Des and I continued the surveillance through the night. I called Don and he activated the surveillance squad the next morning, a Sunday, at 6:00. Beginning at 8:00 A.M., we had a continuous stream of disguised FBI agents, accompanied by their wives or girlfriends, in and out of the restaurant and the Continental lobby. About 9:00 A.M., Pieri, Tony, and Paul entered the restaurant and were soon joined by Victor Randaccio. The surveillance teams were all around them and were in a position to overhear some of their conversation. I soon learned that Pieri and the others had been talking about taking the "stuff" to Cleveland.

Victor indicated to Pieri that "Lib" was expecting them. As I have indicated, I knew that Anthony J. Liberatore, was an LCN associate of both Pieri and Randaccio. Liberatore was an official of LIUNA in Cleveland who had been released several years before from the Ohio State Penitentiary after serving about thirty years of a life sentence for murder. While in prison, Lib had been close to Pieri's brother, LCN capo John "Johnny Ray" Pieri.

At 10:30 A.M., after finishing their breakfast, the four entered Randaccio's car and drove out of the hotel parking lot. They drove to Interstate 90, where they proceeded west toward Cleveland. I called Welch on the radio and related what was happening. Welch quickly telephoned U.S.

Attorney Ken Schroeder, who authorized us to stop the vehicle and arrest the subjects for conspiracy to commit interstate transportation of stolen property. He passed on this information to us and we stopped the car, arresting all subjects. The other previously unidentified subjects were determined to be Tony Romano, a LCN figure from Florida, and Ralph W. Jacobs, who also lived in Florida. We recovered the briefcase, which contained stolen diamonds and jewelry. We later determined its value at $300,000. For the next several months, Agent Cecil Miller and I traveled all over the United States with this jewelry, attempting to identify its owners. Ultimately, we determined that most of the jewelry was from a 1969 Pittsburgh, Pennsylvania, jewelry store robbery and from a home burglary that occurred at Saratoga, New York, in August, 1969.

At the preliminary hearing before the U.S. magistrate, Pieri's attorney moved for the identity of my informant; in order to protect the identity, we decided to present the case to the federal grand jury and have the charges temporarily dismissed by the magistrate. The case was subsequently presented to the federal grand jury, which returned a six-count indictment charging Pieri, Randaccio, Romano, and Jacobs with interstate transportation of stolen property. We arrested all of them again and they were released on $25,000 bond.

Their trial began in early June 1970. The government's case was tried by U.S. Attorney Kenneth W. Schroeder. Des and I were not allowed to be in the courtroom because we were witnesses, but we talked to Ken every evening and he indicated the case was going in well. Our surveillance agents had testified in an outstanding fashion and the victim witnesses were just completing their testimony.

On the morning of June 17, I received a shocking telephone call from an informant. The source said that Pieri had, several minutes earlier, given juror #6 a $100 bill and that he was planning to meet with the juror to give her some more money on the following morning. I alerted Welch, and Des and I went to the courtroom, where we waited for the next break. We grabbed Ken and told him about the developments. At the first opportunity, Ken briefed Judge Henderson, who instructed that we continue our investigation of the alleged bribery.

On the morning of June 18, we had an extensive surveillance operation in the lobby of the courthouse. The blind man at the candy stand was even an FBI agent. About 9:40 A.M., juror Marilyn Smith (not her real name) came into the lobby and walked up to the candy stand. After making a purchase, she hesitated and waited by the elevators, passing up about three cars. Several minutes later, Pieri entered the lobby and, after looking all around the lobby, he approached Smith. He spoke several words to her and gave her a piece of paper. They smiled at each other and she entered the elevator. He waited for the next elevator and also entered. The results of this surveillance was immediately given to Ken Schroeder, who advised the judge. The judge requested that we provide affidavits concerning our observations of the June 18 contact between Pieri and the juror. We immediately prepared the affidavits and Ken provided them to Judge Henderson.

Des and I were later called to the courtroom by Judge Henderson. When we arrived, he dismissed juror Smith and instructed her to accompany us out of the courtroom. We told her that we had some matters to discuss with her concerning her actions as a juror at this trial. We took her to the FBI office located several floors below the courthouse level and, after advising her of her rights, began the interrogation. She initially denied ever seeing Pieri out of the courtroom or ever having talked to him. Even when confronted with the surveillance that morning, she denied seeing or talking to Pieri. Only when confronted with surveillance photos of the meeting did she admit to seeing and having a short conversation with Pieri. She denied anything improper. After about three hours of conversation and interrogation, she finally admitted accepting the $100 bribe from Pieri on June 17. She said that when Pieri gave her the money he said, "There's more where this comes from." He told her to meet him on the following morning (June 18). Smith told us that she showed the $100 bill to two fellow jurors who were traveling back and forth to court with her and told them that Pieri gave her the money. Upon seeing the $100 bill and hearing the story, one of these jurors, Mildred H. Dally (not her real name), told her, "If you get more money, I'll be a lookout and watch for the police." The second juror who learned about the $100 Pieri bribe, Michael E. Robbins (not his real name), asked Smith for five dollars to get his pants out of the cleaners and they made plans to go to play bingo together with the remaining money. After we obtained a signed statement from Smith, the interview was reduced to an affidavit which was filed with Judge Henderson. He immediately dismissed jurors Dally and Robbins and instructed them to accompany us out of the courtroom.

Dally and Robbins both admitted to the events that had occurred on June 17 and June 18. They both furnished signed statements admitting that they and Smith had agreed to find Pieri and the other defendants not guilty on all charges because of the $100 and the fact they thought Pieri was a "good dresser" and a "nice guy." They said that they hoped he would provide more money before the end of the trial.

I could not believe it. Three jurors bought in a multimillion-dollar LCN case for $100. This sure jarred my confidence in the jury system, at least temporarily. We were now left with only twelve jurors and no other alternates. On the evening of June 18, we learned from one of our informants that Pieri had sent "killers" to try to find Smith and kill her. By that time, we already had her in protective custody. Pieri was also attempting to get to another juror who had a brother who was a member of Local 210. Pieri was successful in getting to this juror, and after I learned of this and passed the information on to Judge Henderson, he was dismissed from the jury on June 23, 1970. At this point, Judge Henderson called Des and I into the courtroom and ordered us from the bench to arrest Pieri for jury tampering and bribery. We gladly cuffed Pieri and took him out of court. We gave him a pretty hard time verbally during this interview, although he didn't tell us anything. He was released on $100,000 bond. He later told my informant that this was the worst anyone had ever talked to him in his life. Since we had only eleven jurors remaining, the trial was declared a mistrial and the remaining jurors were dismissed.

Ultimately, Pieri was indicted by the federal grand jury and subsequently tried before U.S. District Judge John T. Curtin. He was convicted on all charges. At the time of sentencing, Judge Curtin strongly lectured Pieri on the severity of his crime and how jury tampering and bribery attacks the very foundation of our judicial system. He sentenced Pieri to five years imprisonment, although Pieri was facing a possible twenty years on the charge.

We never retried the ITSP conspiracy case. Des and I "flipped" one of the other defendants and he became one of our most valuable organized-crime informants in the property and labor area until his death years later.

Pieri did his time, was released after a little more than four years, and almost immediately he connected with a "diamond burglar" who was actually undercover FBI Agent Dick Genova. Dick was recruited by Pieri to be his driver, thereby making the agent a witness to all of his activities. Pieri violated his parole, was returned to prison, and died from testicular cancer. A fitting end.

JOE FINO BECOMES BOSS

According to our informants, Pieri was succeeded as boss by Joseph M. Fino, and Daniel G. "Boots" Sansanese Sr. replaced Fino as underboss. Sansanese earned this nickname because several years earlier he was caught shoplifting a pair of boots from a local department store.

In 1971 Nicholas R. Fino was operating a horse bookmaking operation for his brother, Joseph Fino. In view of his LCN position, we quickly moved to make a case against Joe. This case was assigned to Ron Hadinger. Ron took the case to Bob Stewart, an outstanding and recently assigned strike force attorney. Bob ultimately became the one who handled all future FBI organized-crime cases in Buffalo. He was (and is) a brilliant attorney who has the work ethic of a great FBI agent—which from me is a high compliment. Our surveillance soon identified Joe Fino's book operators as Joseph M. Giallella and Nicholas Alberti and his collectors as Tom Cherico, Gaegano Agro, Joseph Randazzo, and Anthony Tripi. Giallella had long been a "telephone" answerer for the Arm bookmaking operations. In fact, about four years before, Bill Roselli and I had attempted to develop him as an informant in a rather unorthodox fashion. We determined that Giallella was working Randaccio's book at a specific address and we went over to this spot before Giallella arrived at the book. The bookmaking location was located in a run-down area of town. The house was vacant, abandoned, and unlocked, so we went inside and hid in a closet. About twenty minutes later,

Giallella showed up and, after installing the door barricade bars, he sat down at the two telephones to begin taking the betting action.

We let him do his business for about forty-five minutes before we made our presence known. We burst out of the closets and he almost had a heart attack. We talked to him for a while on that day, but he was afraid; he would not cooperate and he declined to talk to us again.

Getting back to the Joe Fino book, we conducted surveillance of the book locations and obtained court authorized wiretaps on the location under Title III. The tap quickly determined that Joe Fino, Nick Fino, Joe Giallella, Nicholas Alberti, Thomas J. Cherico, Gaegano C. Agro, Joseph Randazzo, and Anthony J. Tripi were operating the bookmaking operation in violation of the illegal gambling business statute, which carries a five-year prison term. We secured fifty search warrants for the bookmaking office locations, all of their homes, their automobiles, and several bank deposit boxes we had identified through the investigation. These raids were conducted by teams of about forty FBI agents, officers of the Buffalo Gambling Squad, and New York State Police detectives. The raids took most of the day and they were very fruitful. We found guns and extensive bookmaking records.

After the searches, the evidence was presented to the federal grand jury and on September 15, 1971, Joseph M. Fino, Nicholas R. Fino, Joseph M. Giallella, Nicholas Alberti, Thomas J. Cherico, Gaegano C. Agro, Joseph Randazzo, and Anthony J. Tripi were indicted by the grand jury for two counts of violation of the illegal gambling statute and conspiracy. We arrested them all and they were released on bond, awaiting trial.

DAN SANSANESE GOES DOWN

The trial began in April 1972. During the third week of the trial, I got a call from one of my informants that LCN underboss Daniel G. Sansanese was working on fixing the Fino case. I went to see the informant immediately. The source said that Sansanese had contacted Sam Levitch, a local furniture dealer. Sansanese told the source that Levitch had an employee whose daughter was a juror on the Fino case. Des and I went to see Levitch and he confirmed that Sansanese and his girlfriend, Vivian, had come to his furniture store. Levitch said that he had known Joe Fino and Daniel G. Sansanese for about forty years. Sansanese inquired about this employee, whose last name was Rizzo, and he told Levitch that Rizzo's daughter was on the jury. Levitch then told us that Sansanese had asked him if "anything could be done." Levitch said that Sansanese told him he would be back in about ten days, indicating to Levitch that Sansanese expected him to talk to Rizzo. Levitch was extremely scared of Sansanese, and rightly so. We put a protective surveillance on Levitch starting that day. Des and I went to see Sansanese with a federal grand jury subpoena. He was his usual obnoxious self and refused to be interviewed and I gave him the subpoena. During this contact with Sansanese, I noticed he had "dead eyes"—when you looked into them, there was nothing there. In later years, I would see this trait in other killers. He appeared before the federal grand jury and lied his ass off. He denied the conversation details and came up with a cover story that we thought we could break. He said that he and his girlfriend were looking for furniture for her apartment. Immediately after we left Sansanese, Des and I went to see the girlfriend. She was a secretary for one of Sansanese's attorneys. She said that they were looking for furniture for Sansanese's house. The devil is in the details!

In the meantime, the Fino jury heard the case and convicted all of the subjects except for Joe Fino, who was acquitted. Des, Ron Hadinger, and I investigated the statements made by Sansanese to the federal grand jury and we were successful in gathering evidence that would prove he lied in his testimony.

Several days later, intelligence officers from the state police came to our office with an audiotape, which they played for Welch, Don, Des, and me. The tape contained a conversation between Danny Sansanese and his closest LCN underling, Billy "Billy the Kid" Sciolino. Sciolino was reporting to Sansanese that he had been watching my neighborhood and making passes by my residence on Evergreen Drive in Tonawanda. He was aware of my general schedule leaving in the morning and getting home. Sansanese and Sciolino then discussed the feasibility of throwing a hand grenade through the large plate glass window of my small ranch house. Sansanese said that he didn't care who was home as long as I was one of them. I had a wife and four children. It appeared that they were still trying to make up their minds as to whether this was a smart thing to do. FBI agents have traditionally been "off limits" for LCN physical retribution for practical reasons. The LCN guys know from several isolated instances that we will retaliate. As the old saying goes, "You guys might have two hundred professional killers, but we have ten thousand."

I was, to say the least, very concerned, but I had a warrant for Sansanese in my pocket. He had just been indicted by the federal grand jury for perjury. We asked the officers to stay close to their source and to let us know if anything else was heard.

The following morning, Ron Hadinger and I went to the Sansanese residence on Nancycrest Drive in West Seneca, south of Buffalo, to arrest him. It was about 10:30 A.M. Sansanese answered the door in a fancy blue silk robe and slippers. We told him that he was under arrest for bribery and jury tampering and I instructed him to get changed so that we could go downtown. I followed him into his bedroom and noticed that his bedroom phone was wrapped in pillows and buried in the closet. It looked like he was a little paranoid. He and I had a very serious conversation. After I finished talking to him, Sansanese said "Mr. Griffin, I don't know what you are talking about. I have never said anything bad about you," over and over again. He repeated his denials all the way downtown and over to his arraignment. He made bond and left the courthouse. Later in the week, we heard from the state police. They said that Sansanese had contacted Sciolino right after he was released on bond. Sansanese told Sciolino that they should forget about the whole thing and that he should never go near my home again. Sansanese told Sciolino that he had no idea how I knew, but that I did. Sansanese said that I was crazy and that I would kill both of them if I heard anything else.

Danny Sansanese went to trial before Judge John Henderson for perjury and our case was presented by Strike Force Attorney Bob Stewart. It was pretty much a cut-and-dried case. Sam Levitch testified. We presented follow-up witnesses verifying that Sansanese was in the store talking to

Levitch and Des and I testified about our interview with Levitch. After about an hour of deliberation, the jury returned and found Sansanese guilty of perjury. Sansanese was sentenced to five years in prison and he was immediately taken into custody. He later died in prison. Billy Sciolino was killed several years later in a daylight Mob hit at a Buffalo construction site. By that time I was no longer in Buffalo, but I heard the LCN put out the word that he was an FBI informant. To the best of my knowledge, he was not. But paranoia can kill you.

LCN Capo Frank J. Valenti

In April 1972 I learned from an informant that Frank J. Valenti of Rochester, New York, and Joseph Zito Sr. of Batavia, New York, were "shaking down" Depew, New York, contractor Joseph Laraiso. Valenti was an LCN capo and he ran Rochester for the family. Zito was a "made" guy who usually was involved in bookmaking activities around the Batavia racetrack. I sent the lead to our Rochester Resident Agency and one of the organized-crime guys interviewed Laraiso, who denied that he was being victimized. The informant continued to report that the extortion was continuing and that Zito and Valenti were going to take over his business. When I got the report back on the Laraiso interview, I talked to Des and we decided to take another run at Laraiso, a highly respected contractor who owned the Twin Village Construction Corporation in Depew, New York.

That evening, we went out to see Joe Laraiso at his residence south of Buffalo in Lancaster, New York. Laraiso appeared very nervous, but he invited us in and took us to a small office off the dining room. The three of us sat down and I began the conversation by telling him basically what we knew. I told him that we knew he had been shaken down by Valenti and Zito for at least the last two years and that we knew he had submitted fraudulent bids on a Buffalo paving project at the instruction of Valenti.

Des interjected that we knew he was the victim and that these hoods would not stop until they owned his business. We talked in general about what would happen to him if he came out with the truth and Des told him the only answer was to cooperate, since, no matter what, he was going to lose his business. We said the Witness Security Program was always an option. It is always best to stand up to these people. We knew Laraiso was an honest person, but he was in a bad fix. The Mob had targeted him and they would not let up until they owned him. If he had come to us two years before, maybe we could have prevented the initial shakedown, but unfortunately he did not.

After thinking quietly about this matter for several long minutes, Laraiso said that Zito had been shaking him down for about $1,000 a week since 1970. He said that in January of that year, City of Batavia officials had begun refusing his bid paving requests on Batavia public construction projects. They told him that his bid would not be considered.

Shortly thereafter, Joe Zito came to his office in Depew and said he wanted to talk to Laraiso. Zito went on to tell Laraiso that he understood Laraiso was having a problem getting his bids accepted, and he offered a solution to the problem. He said that the bids would be accepted if Laraiso paid the three city officials $300 each. Laraiso gave Zito a $900 check for fictitious services and the next week, the bids were accepted. When Laraiso accepted these terms, he was now owned by Zito. Several days later, Zito came back to see him and Zito demanded more money, $1,000 a week to ensure that future bids would be accepted.

Laraiso subsequently made several weekly payments of $1,000, but he later balked because he was not making enough money to make any more payments. When he refused, Zito pulled a revolver out of his belt and said Laraiso had to go with him to see the number one man.

Zito took Laraiso at gunpoint to Zito's car and they drove to a farm near Rochester, New York. Zito took him into the house and they were ushered into the living room by the home's occupant, who Laraiso recognized as Frank Valenti. Valenti told Laraiso that he ran the labor unions that Laraiso's workers belonged to and that if he did not continue making the payments to Zito, he would cause serious labor problems for Twin Village Construction.

Laraiso knew that all of his workers belonged to LIUNA, which was a Mob union. Laraiso was scared to death and he told Valenti that he would continue making the payments. While taking Laraiso back to Depew, Zito commented that if Laraiso did not continue to cooperate, "We will knock on your door in the middle of the night and we will kill you and your family." Laraiso continued making the weekly payments to Zito, who began giving him instructions on what bids to submit. Zito gave him an obviously phony rigged bid and ordered him to submit it to the Batavia city officials. He refused and he was again taken before Valenti .

Valenti was very angry and he told him to follow Zito's instructions. Valenti told him that if he ever talked and disclosed Valenti's name, Laraiso would end up in a cement mixer. Valenti told him that he owned his company in name only and that the company was now Valenti's. Laraiso said that he felt helpless, so he continued making the payments to Zito, but now Zito demanded an additional $1,000 for Valenti.

As Joe Laraiso told this story, he seemed to relax. He had wanted to get this off his chest for a long time. I told Joe that if we could have stopped this before it reached the Valenti level, we might have had a chance. Valenti was a vicious killer and he would not hesitate to come after Joe and his family if he felt the least bit threatened. We told Joe that his best bet would be to enter the Witness Security Program and testify against these men.

We asked Joe if he would provide a signed statement and he agreed. He was now determined to take control of his life and go after these people. Joe was a very courageous guy. He then called in his wife and explained what we had been discussing. She began crying, but quickly regained her composure. She then became angry and told Joe that he had her total support no matter what he decided to do. She was also very courageous.

We told them to sit tight and we would be back to see them the next day. They had two young children and this would mean Joe would have to sell his business and the home that he built for his family. But he had no choice. Valenti would never let him rest.

On the following morning, Des and I went to the U.S. attorney's office and talked to Ken Schroeder. We told him the story and he was as outraged as we were at "these dirty bastards." But he also knew that we had Valenti. I told Ken that we could verify most of Joe's story from records.

All of the payoffs had been made by check, even the payoffs to Valenti. These guys were vicious, but stupid. We made a few calls and got the approval to get the Laraiso family into the Witness Security Program.

Des and I rounded out the investigation. Joe provided us with all of the pertinent documents, and all the evidence was presented to the Federal Grand Jury by Ken Schroeder and Strike Force Attorney Robert C. Stewart. As soon as Joe completed his grand jury testimony, the family entered the Witness Security Program. They moved out of their residence that day and Joe put his business up for sale. Des and Rochester agent Hugh Higgins later assisted Joe in the sale of all of his New York assets.

On May 19, 1972, the Buffalo federal grand jury returned an indictment charging Joseph Zito Sr. and Frank Valenti with federal extortion and violation of the extortion provisions of the Hobbs Act. Later that morning, we went to Valenti's home in Henrietta, New York, near Rochester. Valenti answered the door and, when he saw us, he tried to slam the door shut. I stuck my foot through the door and pushed my way in. Hugh Higgins and Des followed and we grabbed Valenti, who began to struggle. Hugh told Valenti that he was under arrest and cuffed him. He was very upset. When he heard the charges, he knew that he was gone.

I heard from my informant that, after making bond, Valenti had sent one of his henchmen, whose name I do not now recall, out to locate Joe Laraiso. When the henchman discovered Joe and his family were gone, he reported this news to Valenti and Valenti told the guy that he had delayed too long in trying to find Joe. My informant reported that Valenti had this guy shotgunned to death. His body was later found in a Rochester-area field with his middle torso cut almost in half by the blast.

Joseph Zito was not at his residence when the raiding party arrived to arrest him and he became a federal fugitive. Zito was located several weeks later by Rochester agents and taken into custody. He also made bond.

Zito and Valenti were tried before U.S. District Judge John O. Henderson. Ken Schroeder presented the government's case in his usual outstanding, professional manner. Joe was a brilliant witness and after spending very little time in deliberation, the jury found Valenti guilty on all counts.

Judge Henderson immediately sentenced Valenti to eighty years in federal prison. Zito received a 111-year sentence. They were both immediately sent to federal prison. Valenti died several years later in jail, a broken man.

Des, Hugh Higgins, and I were in the courtroom that day and we hoisted a few brews later that night to Joe Laraiso and his family. They were honorable people: just what the Witness Security Program was designed for.

Several years later, Des decided to see if Zito would consider cooperating. We knew he had contact with Russell Bufalino, the boss of the Pittston, Pennsylvania, LCN family, and he could provide testimony against the remaining LCN "crew" in Rochester. Des made contact with Zito when he was imprisoned at the U.S. Penitentiary in Atlanta, Georgia. Zito agreed to meet with Des and then agreed to cooperate. Des called me in Washington and we arranged to move Zito to a secure witness section in the Metropolitan Correctional Center in San Diego, California. During one of his telephone discussions, Zito told Des that he would have to check with his attorney and put down the phone. When Zito came back on the phone, Des asked him who his attorney was. Zito replied, "John Dean."

Zito later entered the Witness Security Program while continuing to serve his prison term, and testified against the remaining Valenti associates in Rochester and against Pittston LCN family boss Russell Bufalino at Bufalino's first trial for extortion. All were convicted and sentenced to long federal prison terms. Zito also testified against the corrupt public officials in the Batavia city government and a number of individuals who were fixing races at Western New York racetracks. As can be seen, after Magaddino, his successors, Sam Pieri, Joe Fino, Daniel Sansanese Sr., and Frank Valenti, were immediately targeted when they assumed the top positions in the Buffalo family. By the end of 1972, Pieri and Sansanese were in jail. Valenti was in jail. Joe Fino had so far eluded us. But by that time we were talking to his son, Ron, who was the business manager of Local 210. Until I left Buffalo, I frequently interviewed Joe and he was always a gentleman and respectful of what we were doing. From conversations I had with Joe, I suspected that he may have known that Ron was cooperating with us, but he loved his son and he may have wanted Ron to get out of the rackets. Ron would become one of our best sources against LCN and a good friend; you will hear much about Ron later. Don Hartnett, Ron

Hadinger, and Des Desvernine were still working on making a case against Joe Fino when it was time for me to leave Buffalo.

In June 1972 I was transferred to the Organized Crime Section at FBI headquarters as a supervisor. The tour in Buffalo had been a great experience, both professionally and personally. Two of my sons, Kevin and Shawn, were born during the Buffalo years.

The Magaddino case was still pending when I left. As I have said, Magaddino lived in disgrace until his death in 1974. Carmella's prayers didn't do him any good. To her dismay, the church refused to give him the full Roman Catholic funeral rites.

CHAPTER 6

Another Washington Assignment—
This Time We Investigate Ourselves

On July 6, 1972, my last day in the Buffalo office, which was also the day of my going-away dinner, I heard an urgent call over the FBI radio while en route to the office. It was around 7:00 A.M. and an airplane hijacking was underway at the American Airlines tarmac at the Greater Buffalo International Airport. I was instructed to report to the scene.

Upon arrival, I learned from the newly assigned SAC, Dick Ash, that one Charles Smith had stabbed his wife and her boyfriend at their home. Both had been rushed to Deaconess Hospital, where they were reported to be in critical condition. After the attempted murders, Smith drove from their residence directly to the airport. He dashed down the American Airlines ramp toward an aircraft that was being prepared for the 6:25 A.M. flight to Rochester. One of the ground crew spotted Smith and immediately alerted other airline personnel, who telephoned the FBI and the Cheektowaga Police Department.

Smith's first demand was a shouted order to airline employees that he be flown out of the country. After Ash had the plane surrounded, we could see Smith seated at the door of the aircraft. He was holding his three-year-old daughter aloft, screaming that he would kill her if he was not provided a pilot. Clutching her in his left arm, he pointed a four-inch switchblade knife at her chest. The little girl's screams could be heard above all the noise of the planes taking off and landing. Even above the airline's auxiliary power unit buzz the screams could be heard.

Using a bullhorn, Dick Ash attempted to negotiate with Smith. He first asked Smith for permission to board the aircraft. Smith shouted back, "No! If you do, you'll both be dead." He added, "I'm not gonna wait much longer." Again, Dick attempted to negotiate with him. But Smith shouted, "Shut up and get me a pilot. If I don't get one, the little girl's gonna die." Dick again asked Smith if he could come aboard and whether he would let the little girl go. Slowly, Ash established a rapport with Smith. A few minutes later, Dick pulled me aside and asked if I had spotted a way to get aboard the aircraft surreptitiously. I had been talking to one of the mechanics who told me there was a gangplank that began in the tire wheel well and ended at a trap door under the pilot's seat in the cockpit. I told Dick about this and he told me to try to get aboard the aircraft. We had snipers from both the FBI and the Cheektowaga Police Department already in place around the aircraft should it become necessary to take Smith out.

I put on an airline mechanic's uniform, climbed into the wheel well, and began crawling up through the aircraft. It took about ten minutes and eventually I saw the grate that had been described to me. I was able to reach up through the grate and push the pilot's seat back. After I removed the grate and climbed into the closed cockpit, I could see Smith through the peephole in the cockpit door. He did not know I was there. He was standing about three and a half feet from the cockpit door and near the door to the aircraft. Periodically, he would raise his daughter up and place the knife at her throat or her chest. Because he was lifting her by the back of her clothing behind her neck, he would be distracted and look away. Meanwhile, he continued to talk to Dick, who was shouting to him on the megaphone.

Ash was able to persuade Smith's mother, Lily Smith, to come down to the ramp and talk to him through the megaphone. He wouldn't respond. She collapsed after he refused to talk to her and had to be taken from the scene by ambulance. Dick then tried to get someone else to intercede with Smith. His parish priest, Rev. Frederick Henton, drove to the scene in order to talk Smith into vacating the aircraft with his daughter. But he did not respond.

I was waiting for just the right moment to jump out of the cockpit and disarm Smith. I finally had an opportunity when he lowered the knife from his daughter's throat and held it at his side. At that point, I shoved the door open and put my .38 to his back. I shouted, "Drop the knife! Drop the knife!" Stunned, he dropped it out of the aircraft. Calmly, I said, "Let's go down the ramp and end this whole thing." Dazed, he looked at me for a moment, then nodded. With my .38 still at his back, we slowly walked down the ramp. Although the little girl had only what appeared to be a slight cut on her nose, there were bloodstains all over her little nightgown. She was rushed to St. Joseph's Hospital and later released to the custody of Smith's mother. Apparently, the blood on Smith's clothing and on his daughter's nightgown came from her mother and her mother's boyfriend.

So the incident was concluded without further injury to anyone, and I got back into the bureau car and drove on into Buffalo to pick up my stuff. Of course, the news media had been present during the attempted hijacking, taking a lot of pictures. One appeared on the cover of the July 9, 1972, edition of the New York *Daily News*, which was required reading at FBI headquarters. When I reported to Washington, D.C., on Monday morning, July 9, and walked into the Organized Crime Section office, everyone had copies of the front page of the *Daily News* taped to the walls of their cubicles. They were essentially saying, "Okay, hotshot. You're back here in the funny farm now, so you better get in line." We all had a good laugh.

THE FBI ORGANIZED CRIME SECTION

The assignment to FBI headquarters was not something that I was looking forward to. It was strictly a desk job, basically shuffling paper. I was assigned as "supervisor of the Midwest offices" in connection with various organized-crime violations. My responsibilities included reviewing all the reports that came in, providing "guidance" to the field (what a joke) and processing requests from the field for Title III wiretaps and microphones. I found processing the Title III requests especially interesting and felt I was really accomplishing something for the good of the country and the field when I got one of these handled quickly. But virtually all of this new assignment was routine and dull. Already I was weighing my options for getting back into the field. I felt like I was a field agent infiltrating FBI headquarters. Being assigned to FBI headquarters as a bureau supervisor or executive is similar to the mandatory assignments of military officers at various points in their careers to the Pentagon. This headquarters assignment was the first step for an FBI agent who wanted to eventually get his own office. But it wasn't a good assignment if you liked action.

FIRST INSPECTION ASSIGNMENT

After two years at headquarters, I was handed another assignment, which was also a step in the process of getting my own office. I was assigned to the Inspection Division as an inspector's aide, and for a year I traveled throughout the world conducting audits and internal inspections of FBI offices. Not only was this assignment interesting, it was also informative, since I was provided the opportunity to see how other FBI offices were managed. During that year, which I spent mostly on the road, I routinely went out on inspections for three weeks, returned to Washington for a week, went out for another three weeks, returned for a week, repeating the process throughout the year. During this time my fifth child, dear Jennifer, was born.

While at headquarters and on the inspection tour, I would meet and become friends with Floyd Clarke, Tom Kelly, Jim Greenleaf, Tom Sheer, Jim McKenzie, Dana Caro, Glen Young, John Glover, John McCurnan, John McGinley, Jim Ahearn, Tony Daniels, Gordy McNeill, and others who would eventually be fellow leaders in the FBI and lifelong friends.

Our group of inspector aides was the first wave of younger supervisors brought into FBI headquarters after the death of J. Edgar Hoover. Prior to Hoover's death, the inspection staff consisted of agents in their late forties and fifties. But our group was of a younger generation; most of us were in our mid-thirties. This was the era of the leisure suit, if you will remember. My first inspection trip was San Juan, Puerto Rico. As were most of my colleagues on the plane trip to this lovely island, I was wearing a leisure suit. I was particularly proud of this leisure suite—it was an exquisitely tailored pale yellow number. When we deplaned at the San Juan airport, the welcoming party of FBI agents, including the SAC and ASAC, did not recognize us as inspectors because we were not wearing business suits and, since we did not know them personally, we walked right past them. They finally paged us and caught up with us at the baggage area. I was disappointed one day during the inspection, when I returned to my hotel room and discovered that someone had stolen my yellow leisure suit. The thief didn't take anything else from the room.

INTERNAL INQUIRY OF TOP FBI OFFICIALS

This inspection tour was hard work, but also a lot of fun. During the Miami inspection, a friend of mine in the Miami office loaned me his membership to the Jockey Club, so most of us hung around there when we were not working or sleeping. I remember one evening, we were at the bar and our chief inspector was sitting across the bar from me. He was sitting next to this gorgeous blonde and I mouthed to him, "Bob, why don't you ask her to dance?" and he mouthed back to me, "She's too old!" She asked the bartender for another drink and when we heard her voice, we all recognized her—she was the lovely, ageless Zsa Zsa Gabor. But Bob still didn't ask her for the dance.

On the New York inspection, Floyd Clarke, Jim McKenzie, and I wanted to find a place to work out, so I contacted the hotel switchboard and they gave me the name of a health club nearby. We went to the place that night, and after our intense workouts, we all entered the sauna. As we were sitting there, sweating in our gym shorts, we began listening to the others in the sauna— and for the first time we really began paying closer attention to the surroundings. We immediately realized that these guys were all gay. Floyd, Jim, and I looked at each other and we quickly left the sauna, got dressed, and got the hell out of there. Jim asked us to take an oath that we would not tell anyone that we had mistakenly gone to an at least partially gay gym. I laughingly told him that I would never tell this story unless I decided to write a book.

Upon completion of this assignment in early February 1976, I returned to the Organized Crime Section at headquarters, where I was promoted to unit chief of the Intelligence Unit. This internal unit within the Organized Crime Section oversaw the operation of all confidential informants in the Organized Crime Program. Although short in duration, this assignment became one of the most fascinating of my career. I learned the depth of our informant coverage in the organized-crime field. You can tell how well an office is doing by just examining its informant program. An office that doesn't have quality informants cannot do the job for the American people. As I previously indicated, I would later use this criteria to judge how well an agent under my command was doing. If an FBI agent doesn't have quality informants, the agent is not doing his or her job. It is difficult and dangerous to properly operate informants, but it is essential to the job.

Shortly after I reported back to the Organized Crime Section in 1975, I received a call from Assistant Director Dick Ash. As you will recall, Dick had been the SAC in Buffalo during my last months there. He had recently been brought into headquarters to head up the Identification Division. Dick requested that I immediately report to his office for a briefing. I took the elevator up to his executive office and upon entering I was surprised to see two current special agents in charge, two deputy assistant directors I knew, Tom Sheer, and eight other special agent supervisors like myself. "Wow! What's up?" I wondered. After we had all assembled, Dick announced that he had been charged by Director Clarence M. Kelley to conduct a major internal inquiry. He said that he had personally selected all of us in the room to conduct the investigation. Dick further explained that the investigation would concern all current FBI officials, up to and including the director, and that the assignment could potentially have a very negative effect on our careers. Dick told us that in the course of this investigation, we would be taking a good look at the all-powerful Administrative Division. This is the FBI division that handles the money, makes promotions and demotions, and selects the officials of the FBI.

Therefore, he wanted it understood that we could withdraw from the investigation right then and there. Of course, none of us did. Dick also told us that the investigation would include a thorough inquiry into the nefarious allegations that had been made against J. Edgar Hoover and other FBI officials since Hoover's death in 1972.

The major allegation was that the FBI had paid kickbacks to the U.S. Recording Company, a company that manufactured recording devices that were purchased by the FBI. Associated with the FBI for many years, this company had been the bureau's exclusive source of recording devices. There were also allegations that the FBI Exhibits Section and the FBI Electronics Section had performed special services that were considered unethical and improper for Hoover and other FBI officials over the years. There were allegations that some of the bureau funds were handled in an improper manner. In addition, there was an allegation that a former FBI official and several current Bureau officials held monthly poker parties at the Blue Ridge Club, a private social club near Harper's Ferry, West Virginia. Allegedly, this club was the location where Hoover's personal files had been taken and destroyed in a fire. Dick explained he had a directive from Director Kelley to conduct the inquiry based upon conversations that Kelley had with Attorney General Edward Levi. Dick concluded by saying this investigation was basically our last chance to clean up the FBI's reputation in regard to these charges. If we couldn't do the job, the Department of Justice would take over the Inspection Division, which it had been trying to do ever since Hoover died.

These allegations had previously been looked into by an inspection team but Attorney General Levi told Director Kelley that he was not satisfied with the results of the Inspection Division's inquiry. I saw the inspection report and I would agree with Levi. Dick said that we would report directly to John M. Dowd, a special attorney in the Criminal Division of the Department of Justice, who would be coordinating the Justice Department aspects of this case. He, in turn, would report to Michael E. Shaheen, a counsel for the Office of Professional Responsibility in the Department of Justice.

During the first week of the investigation, we established our investigative plan, organizing it structurally as we would any major criminal investigation in the field. We interviewed all current and most former FBI headquarters officials. Because of the complex nature of the investigation, and since the matters under investigation were varied and often unrelated, we devised a system for easy retrieval of the information. Very sophisticated indices and filing systems were created so that the names of all persons interviewed could be indexed and all items of interest cross-referenced. Pertinent records from the Department of Justice and the FBI's Inspection Division were also appropriately filed and indexed.

Since the major allegation involved the relationship of the FBI with the recording company, we decided to give this aspect of the investigation first priority. Since the second allegation involved the activities of the Radio Engineering Section of the FBI Laboratory, the Exhibits Section, and the Property Management Section of the Administrative Division, we determined these matters would be investigated immediately after the recording company issue was resolved.

During the first several months of the investigation, we conducted extensive reviews of numerous U.S. Recording Company (USRC) and FBI records relating to bureau purchases from the USRC. Two additional special agent accountants were added to our staff and the four accountants continued the audit.

We conducted an extensive accounting investigation of USRC sales to the FBI to determine the description and quantity of the equipment sold to the bureau. We also determined the cost basis of this equipment in order to determine the markup on the equipment sold by USRC. USRC books were reviewed to not only determine the annual sales volume of the company but also the portion that could be attributed to sales to the FBI. On a random basis, certain equipment was selected to be physically inventoried and accounted for. This was a monumental effort considering that USRC sales records covering the years from 1968 to 1975 had to be reviewed and analyzed.

At the conclusion of our intensive and thorough USRC investigation, we were happy to report that there was no evidence of kickbacks or payoffs to any FBI officials. In addition, there was no evidence that the president of USRC or any other company official had received any fee or payment from the FBI for acting as a source of equipment purchases. Absolutely no evidence was found indicating any improper or illegal activity on the part of this company, its officials, or FBI officials. Furthermore, there was a consensus among those interviewed that USRC had indeed provided the FBI with good service in both supplying and repairing electronic equipment. This company also functioned as a "cutout," that is, appropriately concealing the identity of the ultimate consumer, the FBI. Many of those interviewed believed that this cutout arrangement worked well, protecting the bureau. This presumably kept foreign intelligence agencies and organized crime groups from determining the type and amount of electronic equipment that we were purchasing.

We then began interviewing employees in the Radio Engineering Section and the accountants began the audit of the various FBI funds, which were the subjects of these allegations. These included the FBI Recreation Association Fund, the Special Agents Mutual Benefit Association (SAMBA) Fund (health insurance), and the Confidential Fund.

At the conclusion of the Radio Engineering Section aspect of the investigation, we began extensive interviews of former and current employees of the Exhibits Section and the Property Management Section. Toward the end of the overall investigation, we focused on the allegations concerning the Blue Ridge Club near Harper's Ferry, as well as other matters that surfaced during the entire investigation.

With regard to the allegations concerning the Radio Engineering Section of the FBI Laboratory, we interviewed all its current and former employees and determined that they indeed had been asked over a period of years to perform a number of unusual tasks. Much of their work dealt with the repair and maintenance of equipment at the residence of the late J. Edgar Hoover. Almost all their efforts were justified on the grounds of national security, that is, the need to prevent anyone's gaining access to the director's residence—the fear of enemies gaining access to his residence to install electronic surveillance devices. The Radio Engineering Section either simply handled the installation or repair of electronic equipment at the residence or had one of their men supervise a commercial firm doing the job. Most of this work was totally justified. But some of this work would have been initiated after a casual remark by Hoover to his executive assistant, Helen Gandy, and some of it was questionable. It was believed that because the director occupied such a highly responsible national position everything possible should be done to relieve his mind of "petty" considerations. Examples of services performed by the Radio Engineering Section for Hoover included the repair of his television sets, installation of an outdoor light, installation of lights submerged in a fish pond, servicing the furnace, repairing the garbage disposal unit, and the like. An automatic window opener with a remote control device was also designed, built, and installed in the director's bedroom. This electronic window was designed, built, and patented by the Electronics Section under Associate Director Clyde Tolson's direction, with three of the windows actually constructed and two installed. One was installed in Hoover's bedroom at his residence and another installed in Lyndon B. Johnson's bedroom at the White House when he was president of the United States. The third window was built for Johnson's Texas ranch, but was never installed. We recovered this window from the ranch during the investigation.

These windows were built by FBI Laboratory personnel during working hours and using material purchased by the United States government. This was wrong. We felt that most of the activities were initiated by the Electronics Section either as a gesture to curry favor with Hoover or to anticipate potential problem areas at his residence.

One hilarious example of one of the services performed: we were told that the director once remarked to Helen Gandy that he was having a dinner party for Hedy Lamarr at his residence and he hoped the "moon" would be out for the occasion. Gandy called the assistant director of the FBI Laboratory and informed him of the comment. The assistant director immediately dispatched an electronics crew to Hoover's residence. To assure that the "moon" was in fact going to be out, the crew installed a globe high in the oak trees behind the Hoover residence, which, when turned on at night, appeared to be a full moon. This globe was installed with an on-off switch located on a discreet wall in one of Hoover's hallways. So if the sky was overcast and the moon wasn't out, Hoover could switch the moon on. This globe remained at the residence for years, until the wires holding the electrical equipment started to kill the tree. At that point, a crew from the FBI Laboratory removed it.

With regard to the allegations concerning the Exhibits Section, we interviewed all its current employees and many of the retired employees. In the early 1950s, in response to increased demands from the field divisions for exhibits to be used in trials, an FBI Exhibits Section was established and staffed with a variety of craftsmen skilled in carpentry, woodworking, model building, and painting. We learned from our interviews that the employees of that section were used for repairs and maintenance at the Hoover residence. As was the case with the misuse of the Radio Engineering Section, personnel from the Exhibits Section were dispatched to Hoover's house many times based on casual remarks made by the director to Helen Gandy. All these jobs were performed under the mantle of national security. Wallpaper was touched up, furniture was repaired, sod was installed in the lawn, a portico was designed and built over the front door, and rooms were painted and wallpapered when Hoover went on vacation.

Pieces of furniture were manufactured in the Exhibits Section for Hoover, which he presented to some of his subordinates as Christmas gifts, anniversary presents, and so on. These items included tables, a bar, jewelry boxes, and a stereo console, all constructed from FBI stock material with no labor costs billed to Hoover.

During the course of our investigation, an Exhibits Section employee produced a diary and hundreds of photographs documenting abuses of the section between 1962 and 1971. This diary contained the nature of the projects, the dates the services were performed, for whom they were performed, and who worked on the projects. Color photographs of the furniture and other items built in the Exhibits Section for the personal use of FBI officials were produced.

On July 7, 1976, based upon the diary and the photographs, Jim Greenleaf and I interviewed Associate Director Nick Callahan, the number two man in the FBI. After casually examining the photographs, he commented, "We shouldn't have let them have a camera down there." He then candidly admitted having the Exhibits Section construct fences at his home and getaway cottage, as well as other personal projects for him. When we reported the facts about this to Director Kelley, he promptly fired Callahan, a forty-year veteran of the FBI.

The inquiry also revealed that John P. Mohr, the former number three man in the FBI, now retired, had a number of items built for him by the Exhibits Section, including a wine rack valued at approximately one thousand dollars and a gun cabinet designed and built supposedly as a trophy case for his New York office.

Dowd and other attorneys in the U.S. Department of Justice Public Integrity Section determined that the statute of limitations had run out and no action should be taken against either Callahan or Mohr. One inspector, an ultimate Washington sycophant who was responsible for many special services provided to the officials, was fired and prosecuted for theft of government property.

At the conclusion of the Exhibits Section investigation, we focused upon the allegations involving the Blue Ridge Club. Sandy Smith, a reporter for *Time* magazine, had previously written that Hoover's personal files were believed to have been burned at the Blue Ridge Club shortly after the director's death. The suspicion was reinforced when a congressional investigator en route to the club to check out the allegations heard over the radio that the Blue Ridge Club had just burned to the ground.

Based on the stories in the national news media in late 1975 concerning the fire that occurred at the Blue Ridge Club on November 23, a more formal investigation was undertaken to determine the cause of the fire. This provided us with the opportunity to identify all those who had played poker at the club. All were interviewed under oath.

The Blue Ridge Club, originally known as the Blue Ridge Rod and Gun Club, was organized in 1880 by a group of hunting and fishing enthusiasts. Approximately seventy-seven acres of land were purchased along a remote stretch of the Potomac River in Loudoun County, Virginia, near Harper's Ferry, West Virginia. The clubhouse was constructed around 1894. When the original clubhouse burned in 1921, a second was constructed, opening in 1923. The club's membership remained at around thirty-five throughout its entire history, but in recent years, escalating costs had dictated that the club expand its membership. In 1975 the club was sold for $100,000 to one of its members who owned a large construction firm in Washington, D.C. John P. Mohr was then the assistant director of the Administrative Division and one of his friends had a membership in the club. Based on his friend's membership, Mohr held sporadic poker parties there, with fifteen to twenty FBI officials. They would begin playing on Friday evenings, with the games concluding on Saturday afternoons. Meals and lodging were paid for by each individual who attended, at a cost of approximately twenty-five dollars per occasion. No information concerning any improprieties surfaced during our inquiry into the poker parties.

As mentioned, a staff investigator for the House Select Committee on Intelligence was en route to the club when he heard over the radio that it had been destroyed by fire the previous evening. This gave rise to a great deal of speculation concerning arson, because of his impending visit. No evidence of arson was detected and no involvement by any present or past FBI official was found.

In addition, during the course of our investigation and interviews with persons associated with the club, no evidence was ever uncovered suggesting that any FBI files had ever been stored or taken there for destruction.

During the investigation, Tom Sheer and I were dispatched by Ash to Harper's Ferry. We drove to the Blue Ridge Club and saw that it had, in fact, been totally destroyed. We previously learned from interviews of former FBI officials that the "in-crowd" at FBI headquarters—those within the all-powerful Administrative Division—had casual, infrequent poker parties at the former club. We were unable to discover any information about Hoover's files having been taken to the club and destroyed. In fact, to our knowledge, Hoover never attended any of the legal gambling parties.

During the first day of our investigation at Harper's Ferry, Tom and I determined that the fire had been accidentally ignited by the caretaker's seven-year-old son. The boy explained that he was on the second floor of the club playing with safety matches, flipping them up against the white curtains in his room. He said that when one of the curtains caught fire and the fire ran up the wall, he became scared and ran downstairs, where he joined his dad, who was watching a televised football game. He didn't tell his father what had occurred upstairs, waiting to see what would happen. He said that about twenty minutes later, heavy smoke started pouring through the walls and the two could see that the club was totally ablaze. He said that he and his father then escaped the building prior to its total destruction. We interviewed the boy in his parents' house trailer and obtained a signed statement from him. Since neither he nor his mother was literate, the two X'd their signed statements. This investigation could easily have been resolved by Sandy Smith, who would have arrived at the same conclusion we did.

Based upon our charter from Attorney General Levi, we were instructed to determine not only what was done personally for FBI officials but also what was done for other United States government officials. This was included in the charter because of the allegations concerning the window that had been fashioned for former President Johnson. During our interviews of the people in the Exhibits and Electronics Sections, we were not only asking them about the services they performed for former FBI officials, but also about services performed for other government officials, including the attorney general himself. To our surprise, we learned that the sections had both performed services for attorneys general, including installing locks, installing alarm systems, and shaving doors for the installation of new carpeting.

During our investigation, we reported periodically to Dowd's office, both in person and via written reports. After significant details had been developed concerning the abuses of the Exhibits Section and the FBI Laboratory and reported to Dowd's office, much of our confidential information began to appear in the local and national press. It was difficult to assess the impact these leaks had on our investigation. Many of those we interviewed did express dismay about the publicity and expressed reservations about being totally candid. Of course, we complained to Dowd about the leaks and, for a while, the leaks stopped. He appeared as concerned as we did about the leaks, but after a time, the leaks resumed.

All was quiet until information concerning personal services for Director Kelley surfaced. We were shocked to discover that subsequent to his appointment as director of the FBI, Director Kelley had allowed the Exhibits Section install drapery cornices in his home. This installation was made at the specific direction of the associate director, who justified the work on national security grounds. The valance issue became a major thrust of Shaheen's and Dowd's interest. We had developed this information and waited approximately a month before it was reported to Dowd's office. The next day, the valance story was in the *Los Angeles Times*. And by this time, we had concluded our entire investigation and submitted our closing report, but no one would close us down. I felt that we were being kept alive so that we could be directed to go after Kelley.

We also looked into the activities of the attorney general's special guard detail. This detail was formed in 1969 based upon threats to the life of Attorney General John Mitchell and his family. The detail has always been staffed by FBI agents assigned to either FBI headquarters or the Washington field office. We learned that special agents performed numerous errands for a previous Attorney General, as well as baby-sitting his daughter. FBI cars were routinely used to take attorneys general and their families on vacation. We also established that locks and security devices had been installed at the residences of various former attorneys general and the current attorney general, Ed Levi. These examples are not all-inclusive but only represent a sample of the types of services performed by FBI agents for the attorneys general. In addition, we found that there had been a pattern of gift-giving between the attorneys general and the special agents assigned to protect them. The Department of Justice was leaking information that Director Kelley had exchanged Christmas gifts with his assistant directors and the national press was making Kelley look like a felon. There was a double standard working here and everything that we turned up relating to Kelley was leaked to the press, but the information concerning the attorneys general was not leaked.

It became apparent to me that someone in the Justice Department was intentionally leaking information concerning our investigation in an effort to damage Director Kelley and the FBI. I concluded that no effort had been made by the department to stop the leaks and they continued. The FBI didn't want to make the residence of the FBI director or the attorneys general accessible to someone who could be a Soviet agent or a criminal. The valances, door shaving, and gift giving among personal friends should have been no big deal. But in Director Kelley's case, they were making it a big deal.

At the conclusion of our investigation, we were able to prove that there was no corruption involved in the FBI's relationship with the U.S. Recording Company. There were certainly numerous abuses of power on the part of Hoover and other FBI officials involving their use of the Exhibits and Electronics Sections for personal use. But we determined there was no embezzlement involving any of the funds we looked at, with the exception of the inspector who was fired and prosecuted. It was now time for us to move on; our work had been completed and now we were just sitting on our hands, watching the news leaks, mostly critical of Kelley.

One morning, the nine of us who were the original special agent supervisors assigned to the case discussed the matter and decided to conduct further inquiry regarding the current attorney general in order to once and for all nail down the allegations we had received about the attorneys general. In actuality, we believed that when Levi learned we were asking questions about him, he would close down our investigation.

I called my friend Floyd Clarke, who then headed up the attorney general's protection detail. I told Floyd that we needed to interview all of the special agents assigned to the detail that day. Floyd wanted to know why we wanted to interview his guys and I said that it related to the U.S. Recording Company investigation and at that point I couldn't provide any more details. We worked out an arrangement whereby we would interview individually all of the agents during the late morning and afternoon of that day.

We assigned one or two interviews to each team of agents. When the agents on the guard detail reported to our office for their interviews, we informed them that we were conducting an official investigation at the request of the attorney general and needed to ask them about services that had been provided for the attorney general by the Exhibits Section, the Electronics Section, and the guard detail. We also asked about any gifts that had been exchanged between themselves and the attorneys general. It was determined that locks and security devices had been installed in the residences of most of the recent attorneys general, including Attorney General Levi. Some of the attorneys general, including Attorney General Levi, had other work done at their residences by the Exhibits Section, including shaving doors for the installation of new carpeting. We also determined that there was a pattern of Christmas gift giving between the attorneys general, which included Attorney General Levi, and the special agents assigned to protect them. The agents assigned to the detail were extremely

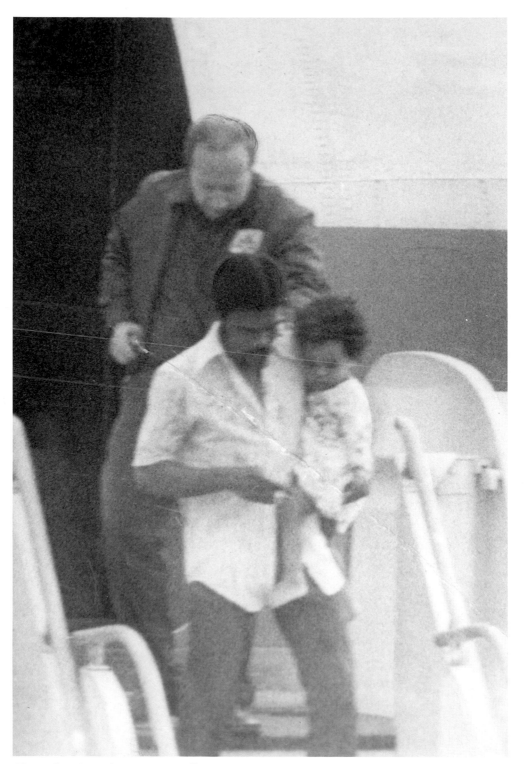

The author, Special Agent Joe Griffin, arresting attempted air-hijacking suspect Charles Smith on July 6, 1972, at the Greater Buffalo International Airport. (Buffalo Courier-Express *Collection, Butler Library, Buffalo State College*)

BUFFALO FAMILY THEN

Frederico "The Wolf" Randaccio

Stefano Magaddino

Peter A. Magaddino

Benjamin Nicoletti Sr.

Salvatore J. Pieri

Albert Randaccio

Anthony Romano

Joseph Fino

Nicholas Fino

John Sacco

Daniel G. Sansanese Sr.

(FBI File photos)

Joseph Todaro Sr.
BOSS

Joseph A. Todaro Jr.
UNDERBOSS

Gaetano A. Miceli

Leonard F. Falzone

John A. Pieri

Joseph R. Pieri

Daniel G. Sansanese Jr.

Victor J. Sansanese

Benjamin L. "Sonny" Nicoletti Jr.

Donald C. "Turtle" Panepinto

Frank J. "Butchie" Bifulco

Robert J. Panaro

Joseph P. Rosato

John R. Catanzaro

Bart T. Mazara

Vincent S. "Jimmy" Sicurella

All of the above, with the exception of Joseph Todaro Sr., Gaetano A. Miceli, and Benjamin L. Nicoletti Jr., were banned from Local 210 because of their connection to organized crime activities. Todaro Sr., Miceli, and Nicoletti Jr. were not members of Local 210. *(FBI File photos)*

The residence Buffalo Mob boss of Stefano Magaddino, which was raided by the FBI in 1968. *(FBI file photo)*

The suitcases and more than $500,000 in cash seized by the FBI from the residence of Buffalo underboss Peter A. Magaddino on November 26, 1968. This raid ultimately led to the ouster of longtime LCN boss Stefano Magaddino. *(FBI file photo)*

Buffalo FBI support employees, including Barbara Bartus, and Special Agent Tom Shaughnessy with the author in December 1968. The support employees are modeling stolen fur coats recovered from LCN fence John C. Sacco. *(FBI file photo)*

Former FBI Director Clarence Kelley with the staff that investigated allegations against former Director J. Edgar Hoover and other high-level FBI and Department of Justice officials in 1975. This was the birth of the FBI Office of Professional Responsibility. *(FBI file photo)*

Angelo Lonardo

Milton "Maishe" Rockman

Anthony Liberatore

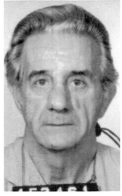
James T. "Jimmy the Weasel" Fratianno

John Scalish

James T. Licavoli, aka "Jack White"

Anthony D. Liberatore

Ken Ciarcia

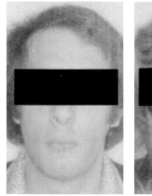
Jeffrey Rabinowitz

Geraldine Rabinowitz.

Hartmut "Hans" Graewe

Billy Bostic

Some of the principal figures involved in the gang war that ultimately led to the downfall of the Cleveland LCN family. *(FBI file photos)*

LCN boss James T. "Jack White" Licavoli meeting with underboss Leo Moceri in the sumer of 1977. Moceri would later be killed by the West Side faction of the Cleveland organized-crime family. *(FBI file photo)*

The author with special agents Bob Kroner and Larry Lynch, and other FBI agents and police officers during a 1978 raid on one of Licavoli's casino operations in Youngstown, Ohio. *(FBI file photo)*

The author with special agents Bob Kroner and Marty McCann celebrating after a narcotics raid in Youngstown, Ohio in December 1976. *(FBI file photo)*

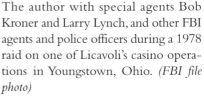

Anthony J. "Tony Lib" Liberatore (inset) and members of the Ferritto Gang after their arrest for the murder of Cleveland police officers Virgil Bayne and Gerald Bode on December 18, 1938. *(FBI file photo)*

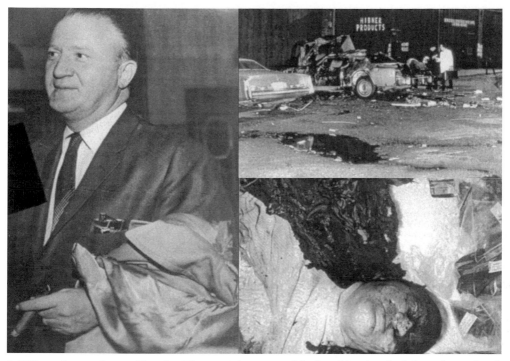

LCN numbers racketeer Shondor Birns and the scene of the bombing in which he was murdered on March 29, 1976, by West Side mobster Keith Ritson. *(Cleveland, Ohio, Police Department)*

LCN figure John Nardi and the scene of the bombing outside Cleveland Teamsters Union headquarters, where he was murdered on May 17, 1977. *(Cleveland, Ohio, Police Department)*

West Side gang leader Danny Greene and the scene of his bombing murder on October 6, 1977, at Brainard Place in suburban Lyndhurst, Ohio. *(Lyndhurst, Ohio, Police Department)*

LCN member Alfred "Allie" Calabrese and the scene of a car bombing outside his residence. The bomb planted in his automobile was intended for him, but his neighbor was killed in the explosion while attempting to move the car. *(Cleveland, Ohio, Police Department)*

Outside Carmen Zagaria's tropical fish store, where several mobsters met violent ends at the hands of Hans Graewe. *(FBI file photo)*

LCN narcotics dealer Joey Giamo meeting with West Side gang leader Carmen Zagaria at Zagaria's tropical fish store. Giamo would later be killed in the fish store and temporarily buried within its walls, shown in the inset. *(FBI file photos)*

FBI surveillance photograph of LCN capo Tommy Sinito meeting with Cleveland boss Angelo Lonardo. *(FBI file photo)*

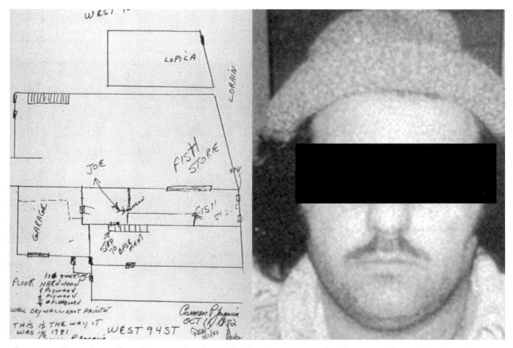

Carmen Zagaria and a diagram he furnished FBI agents after he was "flipped." The diagram shows where drug dealer Joey Giamo was initially buried in the basement of the fish store. *(FBI file photos)*

U.S. Navy divers, FBI divers, and divers from the Lorain County Sheriff's Department recovering the body of murder victim Keith Ritson in October 1982. *(FBI file photos)*

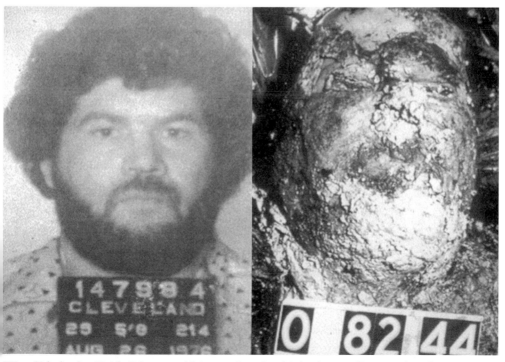

West Side leader Keith Ritson and his remains after his body was discovered at the LaGrange quarry in October 1982. *(FBI file photos)*

U.S. Navy divers, FBI divers, and divers from the Lorain County Sheriff's Department recovering the body of murder victim Joey Giamo at the Jacquway quarry on October 29, 1982. *(FBI file photos)*

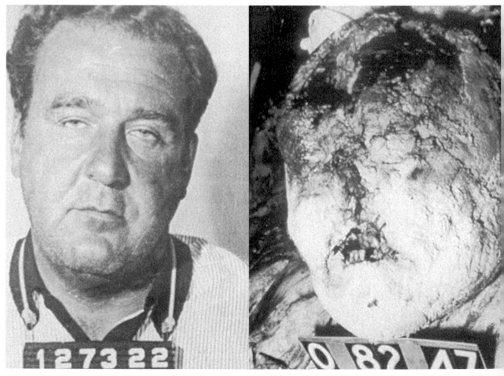

Drug dealer Joey Giamo before and after his deadly encounter with Hans Graewe. *(FBI file photos)*

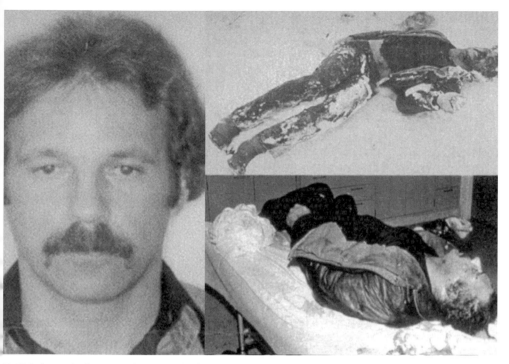

LCN drug dealer David Perrier before and after his deadly encounter with Hans Graewe. *(FBI file photos)*

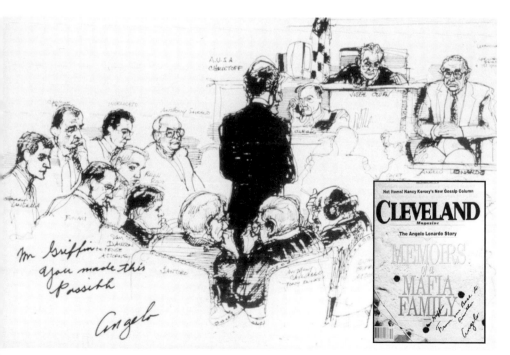

Drawing of Angelo Lonardo during his testimony in the Commission case in New York, in October 1986. Inset: A cover of *Cleveland* magazine, with comments by Angelo Lonardo. *(Cleveland magazine)*

The residence of Cleveland mobster James T. Licavoli, which was bugged by FBI agents in 1977. *(FBI file photo)*

FBI surveillance photograph of James T. Licavoli meeting with Martin "Mutt" DeFabio in front of Cleveland LCN headquarters—the Card Shop—in 1977. *(FBI file photo)*

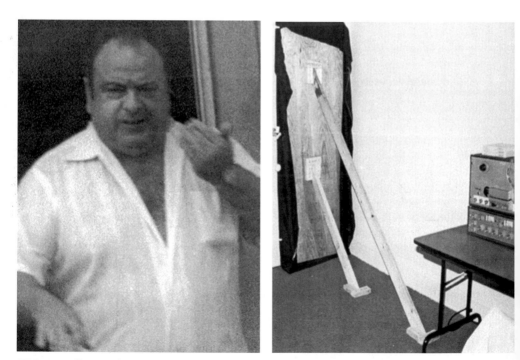

FBI surveillance photograph of reputed Los Angeles LCN underboss Carmen Milano leaving the Card Shop in 1977. *(FBI file photo)*

Photographs of the FBI monitoring post for microphones planted in the Licavoli residence in 1977. *(FBI file photo)*

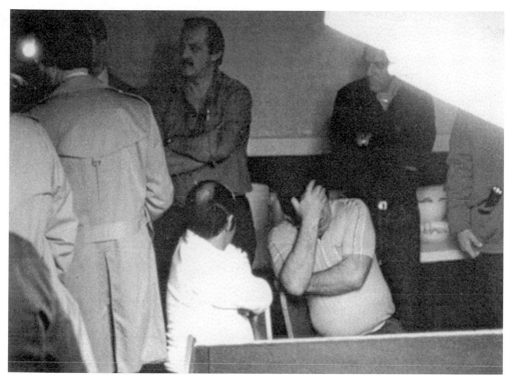

Scene of the FBI raid of the Card Shop on January 8, 1988. *(FBI file photo)*

Special Agent Dave Drab interviewing Marin DeFabio during the Card Shop raid on January 8, 1988. *(FBI file photos)*

The author during a press briefing at the Card Shop, shortly after the FBI raid of the Cleveland LCN headquarters. Special Agent Dave Drab is placing a notice in the window indicating that the building has been seized under the RICO statute and is now U.S. government property. *(FBI file photo)*

Quest Consultants International: (l to r) Jack O'Rourke, Leoni Flosi, Bob Seigalski, and Joe Griffin.

reluctant to cooperate with us. They liked and respected Levi and they were very loyal to him. However, they were told in the strongest language possible that it was absolutely essential they cooperate with the investigation in order to protect their jobs.

On the following day, Special Attorney John Dowd called Assistant Director Dick Ash and informed him that based upon a review of our final report and consultation with other Department of Justice officials, he concluded the investigation was complete and we should shut down the investigation. This is exactly what we hoped would happen. We should have been shut down at least a month before. The bottom line was that neither Director Kelley nor Attorney General Levi had done anything wrong.

Many years later, when I was SAC in Cleveland, former Director Kelley called me and said he would be coming through town in connection with his Kansas City consulting business and asked if I could meet him for dinner. I really liked Kelley. He was a "man's man" and a great FBI director. During this pleasant meeting, I casually asked him if he had ever heard how our investigation had been closed. He laughed and said he was afraid to ask Attorney General Levi, but he had heard something about a "rampaging elephant." I then told him the story and we both got a good laugh.

Upon completion of this U.S. Recording Company inquiry investigation, I reported back to the Organized Crime Section as chief of the Intelligence Unit, where I remained for several months. In late spring of 1976 I received a telephone call from Ed Hegarty, who was then assistant special agent in charge of the Cleveland FBI office. Ed told me that he had just been transferred to the Inspection Division as an inspector and wanted to know if I would be interested in replacing him in Cleveland. He said that the special agent in charge, Roy McKinnon, had asked him for a recommendation. After Ed brought me up to date on the Cleveland division, I told him I would be very happy to be assigned to the Cleveland office.

Within several weeks, I received my orders to report to the Cleveland FBI office as assistant special agent in charge. It didn't take me long to get on a plane and go back to the field, which I loved. My family remained in Fairfax, Virginia, for about a year until our house was sold.

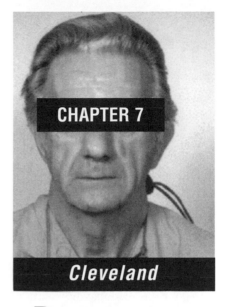

CHAPTER 7

Cleveland

CLEVELAND FBI OFFICE REORGANIZATION

I reported to Cleveland in April 1976 as the new assistant special agent in charge and first met Roy McKinnon, the special agent in charge. I knew him only by reputation. McKinnon was a highly respected SAC and was becoming a legend in the FBI. He was considered an "agent's SAC," which meant he looked at things from the point of view of a street agent. That was also my view. McKinnon liked to become very familiar with all the key investigations underway in his division and made it a point to be involved at crucial times in these investigations, without getting in the way. I liked McKinnon immediately. Marty McCann, supervisor of the Organized Crime Squad, had previously briefed me about McKinnon and I came to agree with his high opinion of the man. He was going to be a great SAC to work for and to learn from. The Cleveland office had an excellent reputation in the FBI. I was familiar with its work, since I had "supervised" Cleveland's organized-crime investigations at FBI headquarters.

McKinnon gave me a detailed briefing on the Cleveland Division. During that first meeting, he told me that Jackie Presser, an international vice president of the Teamsters International Union, was a top echelon informant of the Cleveland Division. Jackie had been developed by Marty McCann years before. McKinnon said that Presser was furnishing extensive, valuable information concerning the La Cosa Nostra situation nationally and in Cleveland, as well as the LCN's successful efforts to infiltrate the gaming industry in Las Vegas. I was surprised to hear about Presser since I was most recently the chief of the Intelligence Unit at FBI headquarters, which supervised all FBI informants in the organized-crime program. I was familiar with the names of all of the top echelon informants and Presser was not among those that I knew. McKinnon told me that Presser was handled on a different level by the assistant director of the Criminal Investigative Division, not by the SAC of the Cleveland Division. Because of the sensitive nature of his position, his informant reports were sent directly from McCann to the chief of the FBI Organized Crime Section, who coordinated the information received for the assistant director. Presser's status as an informant was highly guarded and protected, since he was furnishing information on the most high-level activities of La Cosa Nostra, activities of the Commission, and the LCN infiltration of Las Vegas. The informant reports were disseminated to the field as if the informant was a "bureau source," with no indication the information was coming from someone who lived in Cleveland. This was an effort to protect his identity.

On the first day, I was introduced to McCann's principal relief supervisor, Pat Foran, whom I also liked immediately. Foran knew I didn't have a place to stay and that the government did not at that time provide much in the way of temporary housing funds. He said he had a big house and asked if I would be interested in staying there. I gladly took him up on this offer and stayed at his residence for several months until he and his fiancée, Cassie, were married. We became good friends and I developed a high regard for him as a supervisor and as a person. I later moved to a one-room efficiency (bed folds out of the wall) at the Westlake Hotel. The place was run-down and dilapidated. I would end up staying there for about a year, since the housing market in Washington was slow and we couldn't sell our house. My little daughter, Jennie, called this the "messy hotel." The hotel was later converted into condos and it is now quite beautiful.

During my first six months in Cleveland, McKinnon and I evaluated the division's manpower and we decided to reorganize the office along "target squad" lines. He gave me the responsibility of coordinating all of these target squads, which I greatly anticipated. It would be exciting to get back into organized-crime street work.

Up to that point in the FBI, offices reacted to criminal violations and assigned their manpower accordingly. Each case was treated equally. The most important organized-crime investigation or $20-million white-collar crime was treated the same as a five-hundred-dollar unarmed bank robbery. The cases were assigned when received and each agent had to have a similar number of cases, no matter the complexity. An agent usually had fifty or sixty cases at one time.

In the target squad concept (we called it "proactive"), the most important cases on a particular squad are determined and massive manpower resources are dedicated to these few cases. You might have the whole squad working on just one case. This concept was developed by Neil Welch in Buffalo.

FBI Director Clarence M. Kelley had already established the overall priorities for the FBI to be organized crime, white-collar crime, foreign counterintelligence, terrorism, and public corruption, so our Cleveland plan was consistent with Kelley's overall bureau plan. We set up target squads in each of these overall priorities. We also established a specialized surveillance squad, which, I was surprised to learn, Cleveland did not previously have. This was the ninth largest FBI office in the country, so a specialized surveillance squad was certainly needed. At the time, the only offices that had these specialized squads were New York; Washington, D.C.; Philadelphia; Detroit; and Buffalo. We sent questionnaires to all the agents inquiring about their interest in being assigned to specific squads and we attempted to accommodate them as best we could, based on their investigative expertise and desires.

We gave the new surveillance squad to Terry Sheehan, who until that time was a mainstay on the bank robbery squad. Sheehan was a dedicated agent, very intelligent, an excellent organizer, and a leader. He quickly found an undercover location from which the surveillance squad could operate. Initially, we assigned eight agents to the surveillance squad, which he called the SAM Squad; however, circumstances would dictate that this squad would ultimately become one of the largest squads in the division, and more than twenty agents would be assigned to it.

During the first several months of my Cleveland days, I had a lot of time on my hands, so I set out to conduct detailed research concerning the organized-crime situation in Cleveland. The Cleveland organized-crime family began in about 1913 with some young toughs, members of a street gang called the Mayfield Road Gang. The file indicated that they had been recruited by a local newspaper to break up a rash of beatings, shootings, and truck highjackings relating to an unidentified newspaper circulation war in the Cleveland area. The street gang consisted of young hoodlums from a small Italian American district called Murray Hill.

With the coming of Prohibition, the Mayfield Road Gang became active in bookmaking and liquor, taking advantage of Cleveland's harbor and frontage on Lake Erie to bring illegal liquor across the lake from Canada and servicing other harbor cities. To maximize their profits, they soon built a small bootleg empire by infiltrating the sugar industry, servicing hundreds of small operators of illegal stills, and then buying back the finished product for resale.

By the early 1920s the Mayfield Road Gang had been taken over by the Cleveland Mafia family and the boss was Joseph "Big Joe" Lonardo. During Prohibition, Lonardo became wealthy as a dealer in corn sugar, which was used by the bootleggers to make corn liquor. Many of Lonardo's gang members had previous killing experience in the newspaper circulation wars.

As huge profits began to flow, the money was "laundered" by investing it in gambling casinos in Las Vegas and resort hotels in Florida. Around 1926 one of Lonardo's top henchmen, Joe Porrello, left Lonardo's sugar wholesaling company and, with his six brothers, set up his own corn sugar business on Woodland Avenue in east Cleveland. During the summer of 1926 Joe Lonardo returned to Sicily to visit his mother and family. He left his brother and business partner, John Lonardo, in control of the corn sugar business. During Joe's six-month absence, John lost much of the business to the Porrellos, who took advantage of John Lonardo's lack of business savvy, with assistance from some of Lonardo's disgruntled employees. Upon his return, Joe Lonardo tried peaceably to get his business back from the Porrellos. These talks led to no resolution.

On October 13, 1927, Joe and John Lonardo went to meet with the Porrellos at the Porrello barber shop. As the Lonardos entered the rear room of the shop, two gunmen opened fire and Angelo Porrello ducked under a table. Both Joe and John Lonardo were killed. The Porrello brothers were arrested and Angelo Porrello was charged with the murders. All charges were later dropped for lack of evidence. Joe Porrello succeeded Joe Lonardo as boss of the Cleveland Mafia family.

On December 5, 1928, Joe Porrello and his underboss, Sam Todaro, hosted the first known national Mafia meeting, which was held at the Statler Hotel in Cleveland. Many major Mob leaders from the United States attended. The meeting was raided by the Cleveland Police before it actually began. Joe Profaci, leader of the Brooklyn, New York, family, was the most well-known of the gangsters arrested. He was the founder of what is today known as the Colombo family. Vincent Mangano, the founder of what is today the Gambino family, also attended and was arrested.

Later, Angelo Lonardo, the eighteen-year-old son of Joseph Lonardo, drove with his mother to the Porrello stronghold on the corner of East 110th Street and Woodland in Cleveland. Angelo sent word to the Porrellos that his mother wished to speak to Salvatore "Black Sam" Todaro. Todaro was then a Porrello lieutenant, and Angelo believed he was responsible for his father's murder. As Todaro approached to speak with Mrs. Lonardo, Angelo pulled out a gun and emptied it into Todaro's body. Todaro crumpled to the sidewalk and died.

Eventually, Angelo was arrested and charged with Todaro's murder. He was convicted and sentenced to life but he was released approximately one year later after winning a new trial; the charges never resurfaced.

Another individual, Frank Milano, was moving up in the Mayfield Road Gang. Moe Dalitz, of Las Vegas fame, was also associated with the Mayfield Road Gang. In the 1920s Dalitz opened two illegal casinos, the Beverly Hills Club and the Lookout House, for the Cleveland Mob in Covington, Kentucky. He also opened two other illegal casinos for the Cleveland Mob, the Mound Club and the Pettibone Club, on the outskirts of Cincinnati, Ohio, on the Ohio River. Dalitz was known as the "Santa Claus of the river" because he paid everyone involved in the enforcement of gambling laws, including politicians, police, and judges. He was one quoted as saying, "How do I know that this is illegal, with all of the judges and politicians coming to my joints every night?" In the 1940s Dalitz moved to Las Vegas where he owned and operated the Desert Inn Casino and Hotel. He died in 1989 as a respected retired Las Vegas businessman.

In 1931 the Cleveland family of La Cosa Nostra emerged, and Frank Milano was selected as the boss. After numerous attempts on their lives, on February 25, 1932, while Raymond Porrello, his brother Rosario, and Dominic Gulino, who functioned as their bodyguard, were playing cards at East 110th Street and Woodland Avenue in Cleveland, the front door burst open during the early morning hours and a hail of bullets from sub-machine guns ended the lives of the three men. This shooting was Cleveland's most deadly Mob hit ever and ended the attempts by the Porrello family to take over the La Cosa Nostra family.

On January 30, 1935, Frank Milano, boss of the Cleveland family, entered Mexico, where he was granted a permanent immigration visa on April 13, 1942. He attempted to run the family from Mexico, but in 1942 he resigned as boss and named Alfred "Big Al" Polizzi as his successor.

On October 19, 1944, Al Polizzi, boss of the Cleveland family, pleaded guilty to charges of failing to pay federal liquor taxes and was sentenced to prison. After his release in 1945, he moved to Coral Gables, Florida. He was succeeded as boss by John Scalish, and Anthony Milano was named as underboss.

Scalish ruled the family until his death in 1976. During the period when Scalish was boss, the Cleveland family received skim money from the Las Vegas casinos in which they had a hidden interest. "Skim money" is casino gambling winnings that are secretly taken out of the casino before the daily count is made; therefore, this money will not show up on the casino's books and no taxes will be paid on it. Skimming is accomplished by a crooked inside employee who must be fairly high up in the management of the hotel, usually in the counting room. This skim income was so lucrative that Scalish pretty much allowed the traditional organized-crime activities, such as gambling and loan-sharking, to be independent in Cleveland. Scalish was rich and he didn't want to attract any attention, or "heat," to himself. Alex "Shondor" Birns, a Jewish racketeer closely associated with Scalish, took over the black-numbers operation in Cleveland during this period. The numbers racket is a very important racket for the Mob and, since the wager is not large (usually a quarter to a dollar), the victims are usually in the poorer communities. The bettor bets that a series of three numbers will show up on some predescribed series of numbers, such as the payoff prices at a specific racetrack. These bets add up: A lucrative numbers operation can take in over $1.5 million a day. Birns paid a percentage of this business to Scalish. As a teenager, John Scalish was a stickup man and a burglar. In 1933 he was convicted of robbery, receiving a sentence of ten to twenty-five years in prison. Interestingly enough, two years later he was pardoned by the governor and emerged from prison to rejoin his former associates in the Mayfield Road Gang. Scalish maintained his control over the Cleveland La Cosa Nostra family for thirty-one years and maintained a low profile during most of this period. He made few new family members during his reign and the family membership became old.

Agent Pat Foran's informants reported that Scalish was receiving monthly payments of more than $50,000 in skim money from Las Vegas casinos. According to these informants, the skim was being delivered by Milton "Maishe" Rockman, Scalish's brother-in-law and his business partner in a vending machine business called Buckeye Vending. Rockman made monthly trips to Las Vegas when he picked up the skim money. The informants reported that Rockman usually drove one of his own automobiles on these trips. We soon began outlining Rockman's daily activities in the hope of eventually getting microphones in his office and automobiles.

In May 1976, however, John T. Scalish died during heart surgery. Scalish had a long history of heart disease and opted to undergo this surgery knowing that he basically had a fifty-fifty chance of survival. At his deathbed was his brother-in-law, Milton Rockman. Rockman reportedly claimed that just prior to dying, Scalish had whispered to him that James T. Licavoli, who was known on the street as Jack White, should take over as boss of the family.

LICAVOLI BECOMES BOSS

Licavoli was an unlikely candidate for boss. He previously had operated and coordinated the loan-sharking and gambling operations run by the Cleveland family. He was not articulate and was rather unimpressive in appearance. Licavoli could usually be seen in the summer months sitting in front of the "Card Shop" or one of the other Mob hangouts on Murray Hill, dressed in slacks and a stained undershirt.

Licavoli reluctantly took over as boss and named his cousin and best friend, Leo "The Lips" Moceri, as underboss. Moceri was a vicious killer who was the primary hit man for the Cleveland family.

Licavoli named Anthony "The Dope" Delsanter as consigliere and Angelo Lonardo as a capodecina.

Scalish's failure to "make" any new members in the Cleveland family left a wide gap in its leadership. There was no "middle management" to assume control.

THE GREENE/NARDI WAR BEGINS

After Scalish's death, Anthony Milano, the former underboss, teamed with his nephew, John Nardi, and began scheming to take over control of the family from Licavoli. Nardi was a "made" guy, and was secretary-treasurer of Teamster Vending Machine Local 410. He soon joined forces with Daniel Greene, an Irish racketeer and former longshoreman. Greene was an arrogant and allegedly fearless killer who would aid Nardi as his principal muscle man in the gang war that followed.

After Scalish died and Licavoli became boss, Nardi and Greene went after Leo Moceri. On August 22, 1976, Nardi and Moceri met in Little Italy at the Feast of the Assumption celebration and were seen having a serious argument. Moceri was last seen driving away from the feast. His blood-soaked car was later found in a parking lot at an Akron, Ohio, motel. Much later, we learned that he was killed by two of Greene's henchmen, Keith Ritson and Hans Graewe. When Moceri disappeared, Licavoli knew that he had been killed by Greene and Nardi and he was outraged. Moceri was not only Licavoli's underboss, but he was also his best friend. He sent out orders that both Greene and Nardi be killed. Angelo Lonardo was named underboss, replacing Moceri.

Upon the disappearance of Moceri, it became apparent to us that a bloody gang war would soon be underway. McKinnon and I began moving additional manpower to the surveillance squad and to the organized-crime squad since this squad would have the responsibility of investigating any gangland murders that occurred.

FBI headquarters charts the assignment of agents within an FBI field office through a mandatory monthly reporting system. We soon began to get complaints from the divisions at FBI headquarters that were not involved in organized crime investigations, claiming we were not giving enough attention to reactive crime such as bank robbery, but we decided to take the heat. Our bank robbery success was higher than most FBI offices, so we knew we were on the right track. About that time, the Cleveland Division received our annual inspection from headquarters and we were mildly criticized for using too much manpower on organized crime, but that was only the beginning. Things were beginning to happen in Cleveland.

Licavoli assigned the overall responsibility for the Nardi and Greene "hits" to Tony Delsanter, who initially put out the word that both Nardi and Greene should be killed in an "open contract," which meant that any member or prospective member who got the opportunity should kill either or both of them. Joseph Gallo, Albert "Allie" Calabrese, and Pasquale "Butchie" Cisternino, all of whom were young thugs who would later become members of the LCN family, began their efforts to murder Nardi and Greene.

In September 1976 they attempted to kill Nardi as he was leaving the Italian-American Brotherhood Club on Mayfield Road in Little Italy, on the East Side of Cleveland. As he was walking to his car, they opened fire with semiautomatic pistols. They missed.

Several weeks later, Greene's people retaliated by placing a bomb in Albert Calabrese's 1975 Lincoln Continental. Calabrese had parked his car in a neighbor's driveway. When the neighbor attempted to move the automobile for him, he was blown to pieces by the bomb that had been placed under the driver's seat.

In March 1977 another attempt was made to kill Nardi and Greene, this time at the Cleveland Hopkins Airport. They had gone to New York City to meet with Paul Castellano, boss of the Gambino family, concerning a beef deal that Greene had been working on in Texas. Cisternino and Calabrese put a bomb under Nardi's car, which was parked in the airport lot, and activated the bomb. They then awaited Nardi's and Green's arrival to detonate the bomb by remote control. They had rented a room at the airport hotel and were looking through the motel window at the parking lot. When Nardi and Greene returned to Cleveland, they walked to the car and entered the vehicle. The remote control device failed to detonate the bomb. Cisternino and Calabrese ran frantically through the hotel lobby, pushing the button to activate the device, but to no avail.

After this, Angelo Lonardo went to New York and met with Paul Castellano to discuss Nardi and Greene. It was agreed that Castellano would have Nardi and Green killed the next time they came to New York on the meat business. However, the opportunity never arose and they did not travel to New York again.

John Nardi's normal practice was to park his vehicle in a gas station on Carnegie Avenue near his Teamsters headquarters. However, on May 17, 1977, he parked in the Teamsters parking lot. While he was inside, an automobile loaded with explosives was driven into the parking lot and parked next to Nardi's Cadillac. When Nardi left the Teamsters hall later that day, he got into his automobile and the bomb was detonated electronically with a remote control device. Nardi was killed instantly.

When Nardi was killed, we opened a RICO-murder investigation on James Licavoli, code-named "GANGMURS." Pat Foran assigned this case to Tom Kimmel and Bob Friedrick, two of his top agents who had been classmates at the U.S. Naval Academy. We also opened up potential top echelon informants files on most of the associates of Licavoli and Angelo Lonardo, with the view of gathering information concerning these associates in an effort to compromise them and turn them into informants. This was a fortunate decision, as you will later see.

At least six attempts were made to kill Greene during the 1970s. On one occasion, bombs were detonated on the front and back porches of his residence; Greene, who was in bed with his girlfriend, fell from the second floor to the basement, but neither of them was injured. The house was totally destroyed, but Greene landed on top of a refrigerator with not a mark on him. On another occasion, LCN associate Mike Frato attempted to shoot Greene while he was jogging in a downtown Cleveland park. Greene pulled out a .38 revolver from his jogging shorts and shot Frato to death. Greene called the police and reported the shooting. Greene was defending himself and he claimed self-defense. He was not charged.

In February 1977 Marty McCann retired. I was really disappointed. One of the reasons I had wanted to serve in Cleveland was to work with Marty. Marty took a job as director of corporate security with LTV Steel Company, whose office was also located in downtown Cleveland, so McKinnon and I stayed in close touch with him. McKinnon named Marty's primary relief supervisor, Pat Foran, as the new supervisor of the 9 Squad. Pat was an outstanding agent. He is extremely intelligent and totally dedicated to his work. He began his career as I had. He was a night clerk in the New York office while attending college full-time.

McKinnon and I continued to beef up the manpower in the organized-crime program. We gave Pat the opportunity to select any agent in the division, so he had the cream of the crop. Bob Friedrick, Tom Kimmel, and Ken Andrews were a few agents who would be keys to our success. They were classmates at the U.S. Naval Academy and had entered the FBI at about the same time. They were all decorated veterans of Vietnam and, although in their first office of assignment in the bureau, they were outstanding agents. Tony Riggio was an outstanding informant agent and a great interviewer. Dave Drab would also turn out to be one of the best. He was a very hard-working and intelligent agent who was also well liked. Dean Winslow was later added to the squad. He was an experienced agent who was a tireless worker. He and I were usually the last to leave the office at night, and sometimes he would still be there when I left. He would also be a key to the future successes in Cleveland. Rich Hoke and Neal Berkowitz also later came to the squad and they were superb agents. I am leaving some out because of my failed memory, but these agents were representative of the outstanding agents assembled on the 9 Squad.

MOB MOLE IN CLEVELAND

In July 1977 Roy McKinnon was transferred to San Francisco as special agent in charge, and I remained as acting special agent in charge, waiting for McKinnon's successor, Stan Czarnecki, who had been ordered to Cleveland. On August 12, 1977, I received an urgent telephone call from McKinnon. He requested that I go to a public pay phone and call him back at his private phone in the San Francisco FBI office. I left the office and drove to the first public telephone booth I could find. I called McKinnon back at his office.

His voice sounded as if he was shaken and he told me he had just received an urgent telephone call from Larry Lawrence, a retired San Francisco agent. Larry said that many years ago, he had developed James T. "Jimmy the Weasel" Fratianno as a top-echelon criminal informant and had handled him for several years until Fratianno stopped cooperating. Larry said that he had just received a call from Jimmy, who was now the acting boss of the Los Angeles LCN family. Jimmy told Larry that he had just been in Cleveland visiting with James T. Licavoli, the boss of the Cleveland family.

During this meeting, Licavoli told him that he had someone in the FBI who "was giving us information." Licavoli showed Fratianno a list of approximately twenty informants, a copy of an FBI document designated "SD" with a number that concerned an informant, and a copy of a report marked "Anti-Racketeering" concerning Licavoli. Fratianno recalled some of the names on the informant list and when Roy related these to me, I recognized some of those as being the potential criminal informants we had opened earlier in the investigation. I recognized the designation on the "SD" document as that of a former high-level informant of the San Diego Division, and, of course, I also recognized the "Anti-Racketeering" report.

This was terrible news and could not have come at a worse time. We were at the height of the RICO-murder investigation involving John Nardi and were attempting to prevent the planned murder of Danny Greene. I immediately called Pat Foran, Mike Kahoe, and Don Pierce. Foran, of course, was the supervisor of the organized-crime squad, and Kahoe and Pierce were two of the top investigators in the division, whom I totally trusted.

I briefed all three concerning my conversation with McKinnon. Pat and I made plans to travel to San Francisco on the following day. I assigned the leak investigation to Kahoe and Pierce, with instructions that no one else in the office was to know of the existence of this investigation. At this point, we had no idea where the leak was coming from, although there was no question that there was a major leak. Someone with access to the information leaked had to be a longtime, experienced employee, and it could be an agent or a support employee.

The next day Pat and I flew to San Francisco, where we arranged to meet with Fratianno. Fratianno repeated the information he had given to his former contacting agent. Fratianno added that Licavoli had told him that he received the documents from Anthony Liberatore. Liberatore was a made member of the Licavoli family who was functioning as a capo-decina. He was also then a high-ranking official of the Laborers' International Union of North America (LIUNA). Fratianno was extremely fearful that Licavoli would learn of his prior status as in informant.

Jim Ahearn, one of McKinnon's ASACs and a close friend of mine, was assigned the job of staying in touch with Fratianno and attempting to extract more information from him. At this point, Fratianno agreed to make one more trip to Cleveland in an effort to get more details from Licavoli.

I learned during my conversations with McKinnon that FBI headquarters had previously ordered that no contact be made with Fratianno because of a pending investigation of him in Los Angeles. We decided to temporarily ignore these instructions. We needed his help as an informant and I was already making plans to force him to surface and testify. I called Ed Sharpe, the chief of the FBI Organized Crime Section, and briefed him on the leak. He also agreed that we should follow up with Fratianno.

Based on Fratianno's information, we launched an even more intensive investigation. Mike Kahoe, who was the office general counsel, and Don Pierce were instructed to conduct a very discreet investigation, which would not be known to anyone else in the office with the exception of incoming SAC Stan Czarnecki, McKinnon, Foran, and me. I instructed Kahoe and Pierce to begin preparing dummy documents concerning Licavoli and to place these in our files, where we could watch them. At that time, we also began preparing dummy informant files, which is where the potential informant files we had opened earlier came in handy. The individuals in these potential informant files were not really informants, but you couldn't tell that from the file or the master list. Whoever received that list must have been really confused, because *everyone* was on the list—talk about paranoia.

Foran accelerated search warrants in connection with the GANG-MURS investigation. We installed hidden, closed-circuit television cameras in key locations at the FBI office where there is no expectation of privacy, such as the informant room, over the copy machine, and over the file cabinet area where the organized-crime files were located.

Ed Sharpe at FBI headquarters located a very young-looking FBI agent in the Washington field office and he was assigned as an undercover agent who began working in the Cleveland office as a clerk. We pulled out all of the stops. We were in a major LCN gang war and we didn't know who we could trust in our own FBI office. This was going to be a struggle, but I was convinced that we would ultimately come out on top.

Several weeks later, Stan Czarnecki reported in as special agent in charge and I immediately took him out to lunch and briefed him concerning the major GANGMURS investigation and the leak. Not surprisingly, Stan was stunned by this news. This was not something he wanted to hear about his new office, but he was a cool customer. After I explained what we were doing to solve the leak case, he smiled and told me, "Joe, you run with it. It sounds good to me." We then began serious efforts to secure microphone coverage on Licavoli.

Based on the Nardi murder and the information we were receiving that Licavoli was attempting to kill Greene, we were starting to develop probable cause that Licavoli was violating the RICO-murder statute. The entire 9 Squad and the surveillance squad were now being used exclusively on this case.

Licavoli's residence was right in the middle of Murray Hill, near Mayfield Road. It was impossible to conduct surveillance of this area without being detected. Licavoli had a crew of young wannabe punks who routinely patrolled the area at night and would challenge any car or vehicle that was not familiar to them.

We decided that we had to infiltrate Licavoli's neighborhood. Lucy Vonderhar, an attractive blonde agent on the surveillance squad, and two male agents posed as young medical students attending Case Western University, made inquiry at several locations on Murray Hill, and were able to rent a two-room apartment across the alley from Licavoli's house, which we could use as a "lookout." They took up surveillance of Licavoli from this residence.

I continued to be personally involved in this investigation. I met every morning with the 9 Squad and got several briefings each day from Pat Foran.

Ahearn continued his efforts in San Francisco to get more cooperation from Jimmy Fratianno. On August 24, 1977, he and Jimmy flew to Cleveland with Jimmy's promise to meet with Licavoli. He met with Licavoli, but Licavoli did not disclose any more information about the leak.

During that last week in August, FBI Organized Crime Section Chief Ed Sharpe called me and requested that I give a briefing to Associate FBI Director Jim Adams concerning the GANGMURS case and the leak investigation. Ahearn, Foran, and I went to Washington to meet with Adams and we gave him a full briefing on our progress concerning these two cases. This briefing was extremely important to us since we needed Adams's approval to continue dealing with Fratianno. At the conclusion of this meeting, Adams gave us his blessing and he continued to give us his total support throughout the investigative ordeal.

By the end of August 1977, Tom Kimmel and Bob Frederick had successfully developed sufficient information to secure a court-authorized electronic surveillance on Licavoli's residence. They and Mike Kahoe prepared affidavits requesting this authority under the RICO statute. This was exactly the type of case the RICO statute was designed for. In these affidavits we alleged that the Cleveland family of La Cosa Nostra was the "association in fact" under the RICO statute and that murder was being committed by LCN family members to further this enterprise. To the best of my knowledge, this was the first time the FBI used the RICO statute wherein La Cosa Nostra, as an organization, was charged as the "association in fact."

We secured the court authorization from U.S. District Court Judge Frank Battisti several days later and we waited for an opportunity to make entry into Licavoli's residence to plant the microphones. Licavoli had a housemate, Paul Cirricullo, aka Paul Lish, who handled all of Licavoli's investments and served as his bodyguard. He was always present at Licavoli's residence when Licavoli was not present.

On September 1 Licavoli took a trip to Florida. When Licavoli left town, we went on alert and prepared to make entry into the Licavoli residence to plant the microphones at the first opportunity. Cirricullo remained at the house twenty-four hours a day. Our time was running out. Each night the entry team—consisting of our technical agents, Ken Andrews and Mike Philips, as well as Bob Friedrick, Tom Kimmel, and me—sat in a van parked near Murray Hill and waited for our opportunity. We had only thirty days to install the microphones. If the thirty-day period passed, we would have to get new authority from the federal court, which would take invaluable time. But we got a break. On the night of September 8, for the first time, Cirricullo walked out of the house and went to the Roman Gardens, a restaurant located approximately four blocks away. He sat down at the bar and began drinking with some of his Mob associates. Andrews quickly picked the side entrance lock and we made entry into the Licavoli residence at approximately 10:30 P.M. Outside surveillance agents reported that Cirricullo continued drinking at the Roman Gardens bar.

Licavoli's residence was sparsely furnished and hardly what you would expect of a La Cosa Nostra boss. Several of the walls were covered with photos of nude females, which reminded me of a fraternity house. Over the back door hung cloves of garlic in clusters. The living room was furnished with threadbare furniture, two color television sets, and stereo equipment; and expensive golf clubs were stored in a closet. Two upstairs closets contained dozens of expensive suits. A brick addition contained a paneled recreation area with a well-stocked bar and a sauna.

We put microphones in the recreation area and over a table in the living room, which appeared to be where Licavoli would sit and have conversations. It took the technical agents about four hours to install the microphones and string the lines to our surveillance post across the street.

At approximately 2:00 A.M., the agents at the bar called on the radio that Cirricullo was getting ready to leave the Roman Gardens and he appeared intoxicated. I told everyone to speed up; we had to get the hell out of the house. The outside agents reported that Cirricullo had left the bar and was now staggering toward the residence. Mike was on the roof making a final connection to the telephone line. As Cirricullo approached the house, I told the surveillance agents to stop him on a pretext, since we were still inside. Two of the outside agents walked up to him, identified themselves, and inquired of Licavoli's whereabouts. Cirricullo was completely drunk and his responses were incoherent. Several minutes later I gave the word that we were out and Mike was off the roof, and they cut Cirricullo loose. Cirricullo was so drunk that the next day he did not remember what had transpired the night before, so we were home free.

The microphones were operational for several months, until Carmen Marconi, the alleged Mob wiretapper who was routinely used by Licavoli and his associates, did a sweep of the Licavoli residence and discovered them. When they found the mikes, I initially suspected that Licavoli had been tipped by his "mole" in the FBI. However, this was not the case. No one in the main office, other than the key people on the 9 Squad, knew of the mikes. We purposely had them monitored out of the main FBI office. However, I would later learn that the existence of the microphone coverage was widely talked about at the weekly strike force briefings. Every agency representative on the strike force was kept abreast of what we were receiving on the microphones. This was not right; there would have been time later to share this information, not while it was ongoing. This was the first time that I began to seriously distrust the judgment of the leadership of the Cleveland Strike Force. Up to that point, I had not disclosed to them that we had a leak in the office that was the subject of a major investigation. I now knew that I had done the right thing. If they had been made aware, the leak investigation would have been the topic of much conversation among the seven or so strike force representatives and at their agencies, thus compromsing our investigation.

Later, our investigation determined that Cirrciullo was dating a secretary to one of the federal judges, but further investigation, including an interview of the woman and the judge, indicated she was not the problem. The investigation indicated that Licavoli routinely had Marconi "sweep" his residence every several months.

Prior to the microphone discovery, we had to make one additional entry to repair the microphone equipment. This entry was made without any problem. The microphone coverage was very productive and we overheard Licavoli discussing the planned murder of Danny Greene.

Pat Foran interviewed Greene on a number of occasions and told him that he was the target of an open contract and that the Licavoli group was actively trying to kill him. Greene was aware of this and told Pat that they "know where to find me." During the same period, Greene did a number of interviews on local television and openly taunted Licavoli and the La Cosa Nostra family, calling them "maggots and pigs." Greene, dressed in his Irish green suit and wearing a Celtic cross, continued baiting Licavoli and his henchmen, laughingly telling them to "come and get me." Greene thought he was invincible.

On October 6, 1977, Danny Greene had an appointment at Brainard Place in Lyndhurst, an eastern suburb of Cleveland. At approximately 2:00 P.M., he parked his green Lincoln Continental in the Brainard Place parking lot. Unbeknownst to Greene, there were two hit teams also parked in the lot. After Greene entered the dentist's building, LCN member Ron Carabbia and Raymond W. Ferritto parked a bomb-laden car next to Danny's green Lincoln and began the wait. A backup hit team, consisting of LCN associates Ron Guiles and Louis Aratari, was stationed in the parking lot with high-powered rifles. They were prepared to shoot Greene if the bomb did not detonate. At approximately 3:15 P.M., Greene left his dentist's office and walked to his car. As he got into his Lincoln, Ron Carabbia pushed the remote control device, blowing up the 1970 Chevrolet that Carabbia and Ferritto had parked next to Greene's automobile. Greene was blown to bits. His right arm was thrown about thirty feet from the car and his legs were blown off. Ferritto drove the getaway car and Ron Carabbia was crouched in the back seat.

You will remember that luck is an important link in any successful investigation. Our luck held in this instance. As Ferritto and Carabbia were driving out of the parking lot in their 1973 Plymouth getaway car, two honest, observant citizens, a man and his wife, were driving by the Brainard Place parking lot. They saw Ferritto and Carabbia pull out onto the highway. Their attention was attracted because of Carabbia's crouching in the back seat of the car and the gigantic explosion that had just occurred in the parking lot. The wife, who was the daughter of a Berea, Ohio, police officer, wrote down the license plate number of Ferritto's vehicle and she asked her husband to drive abreast of the car so they could get a good look at the mens' faces. The woman then sketched a drawing of Ferritto. Upon arrival at their residence, the wife called her father.

On the day of the bombing, I had taken off early in the afternoon to attend my son's football game. At approximately 3:30 P.M., I was paged by Pat Foran. Pat told me that Greene had just been killed and he gave me directions to Brainard Place. I rushed to the scene. By this time, Lyndhurst police officers had established a crime scene investigation, which was under the command of Chief Roger Symthe and Det. Joe Wegas. Greene was lying beneath the car. His arms were blown away and his legs were detached from the torso. Shortly thereafter, Joe Wegas received a call from his office. The Berea police officer had contacted the Lyndhurst Police Department with the information from his daughter and her husband. This was a tremendous break in our investigation. We quickly initiated an investigation into the license plate provided by the officer.

On the following day, Wegas picked up the sketch, and investigation of the license plate number quickly led to suspect Raymond W. Ferritto, a known hit man who lived in Erie, Pennsylvania. He was known to be associated with both the Cleveland La Cosa Nostra family and the Los Angeles family, with its transplanted former Cleveland members, Carmen and Peter Milano.

We put together a task force to work this RICO-murder case, as well as the Nardi murder. Those assigned to the group included the Lyndhurst Police Department; the Cuyahoga County Sheriff's Department; the

Cleveland Police Department Intelligence Unit; the Alcohol, Tobacco, and Firearms Division of the Treasury Department; and the FBI. This unit worked together for the next two years under the direction of Pat Foran, putting together this major RICO investigation.

As the investigation became centered on Raymond Ferritto, a federal search warrant was obtained by Tom Kimmel and Bob Frederick for the Ferritto residence in Erie. The warrant was immediately executed and during the search we recovered registration documents for Ferritto's 1973 Plymouth getaway car and copies of *Cleveland* magazine with photographs of Danny Greene circled. An examination of the registration certificate for the getaway car determined that it had been registered at the same time and place as the 1970 Nova that served as the bomb car. This evidence tied Ferritto directly to the bombing.

Based on this information and the information from the two eyewitnesses, Ferritto was indicted by the federal grand jury in Cleveland and immediately arrested by Pittsburgh FBI agents for RICO-murder and on state murder charges in Ohio, which carry the death sentence. This was the first LCN hit solved in Cleveland, but it was not to be the last. Ferritto was incarcerated in Erie, Pennsylvania, and two weeks later he was moved to the Cuyahoga County Jail in Cleveland.

THE HIT MAN FLIPS

During this time, no attorney was hired for Ferritto by Licavoli and his associates. Licavoli was so cheap he didn't want to spend the money for Ferritto's defense. Ferritto realized that he was on his own and he would not stand for it. On the twenty-second day of his incarceration, Ferritto decided to call the FBI. He placed a telephone call to the Pittsburgh FBI office and asked to speak to one of the Pittsburgh agents who had arrested him. He told the agent that he did not want to call the Cleveland FBI office because he was aware that there was a major leak there. Ferritto said that he wanted to talk and he wanted a deal. The Pittsburgh agents called me, and I told them that we were aware of the leak and were pursuing the matter with a very discreet and closely held investigation. I called Foran and told him about the call, and we agreed that Kimmel and Frederick would meet the Pittsburgh agents and arrange to interview Ferritto. After Foran briefed Strike Force Chief Doug Roller and I talked to County Prosecutor John T. Corrigan so that we were all on the same page, Kimmel and Frederick went to see Ferritto. Ferritto was extremely angry at Licavoli and said that he was willing to cooperate in connection with the Greene murder if he could cut a deal. Ferritto told the agents that he had knowledge implicating James Licavoli, Angelo Lonardo, Ron Carabbia, Tony Delsanter, Tom Sinito, John Calandra, Pasquale Cisternino, and Alfred Calabrese Jr.—virtually the entire Cleveland LCN family—in the murder of Greene. Ferritto was willing to plead guilty to the Greene murder, to provide the details of the plan, and to testify against all of the other conspirators in return for consideration on his own prison sentence. He was told that we would consider his offer and get back to him. Foran and I briefed Roller, his assistant, Steve Olah, and County Prosecutor Corrigan. All of the attorneys were elated at the turn of events and approved our cutting a deal with Ferritto. We quickly got the deal approved by FBI headquarters and the Department of Justice in Washington. Our first step was to secure a non-Mob attorney for Ferritto, which we quickly did.

The following day, FBI agents took custody of Ferritto and moved him to a "safe house." Friedrick and Kimmel began the long, detailed debriefing of Ferritto. Ferritto told them that he had been working on the Greene killing for about a year. He said that he had met with Delsanter, Licavoli, Lonardo, Cisternino, Carabbia, Calandra, and Sinito in connection with the murder. He said that on the morning of October 6, he and Pasquale Cisternino carefully worked on assembling the bomb on a kitchen table in a rented apartment where he was staying with Cisternino. Ferritto could not remember the name of the building, but we identified it through investigation as the Winchester Hills apartment building on Chardon Road in Willoughby Hills, Ohio, east of Cleveland. Ferritto subsequently identified photographs of this location as being where they had rented the apartment. Ferritto said that Cisternino brought in the parts for the three dynamite-stick bombs early that morning in a brown paper shopping bag. He said there was a nine-volt battery, some blasting caps, some metal clips, brown wax paper, and black electrical tape, which had been purchased the day before at a local department store. He also said there was a remote control device, an eight-inch-square black box with an antenna, and a police radio scanner used to monitor police calls. Ferritto said that Ron Carabbia was also in the room with them when they were working on the bomb.

Ferritto said that he, Cisternino, and Carabbia then went to the apartment building parking lot, where he saw a maroon Chevrolet Nova. Cisternino told him that this was the car they were going to use to carry the bomb. Ferritto said he noticed a heavy metal box had been welded to the inside of one of the doors on the passenger side of the car. Carabbia told him the bomb would be placed in the box, which also contained a lot of bolts and nails. Then he drove the blue Plymouth, which had also been left in the apartment building parking lot, and took the bomb with him. Carabbia drove the Nova and said that a "backup hit team" should already be there. The two arrived at the Brainard Place building in Lyndhurst at about 2:00 P.M. Ferritto said that he followed Carabbia to a car in the parking lot occupied by a guy Carabbia referred to as Tony, and another man. Carabbia said, "These guys are here to help us." They talked about where they could get a good view of the door. They were going to try to use a rifle to kill Greene and wanted a clear view of the door. The rifle attempt was to be made first because they didn't know if a parking space would be available next to Greene's car. Ferritto said he walked back to his car, where he was joined by Carabbia.

A short time later, a green Lincoln came into the parking lot, and Greene got out of the car and entered the building. The backup hit team did not fire. Tony and his partner pulled over and said they saw somebody watching them in another car. They were both scared and Carabbia told them to leave. Ferritto said a few minutes later the car that was parked next to Greene's car pulled out.

Ferritto took the bomb and placed it in the iron box attached to the door and activated the bomb. He threw a green blanket over it and went back to the Plymouth. Ferritto drove the bomb car into the vacant spot next to Greene's car. Ferritto said he rejoined Carabbia and then drove the Plymouth from the parking lot to a nearby phone booth. Carabbia went into the phone booth, where he had a good view of the parking lot, and waited for ten or fifteen minutes. When Greene came out of the dentist's office, Carabbia got into the back seat of the Plymouth and Ferritto made a right turn toward the freeway. Carabbia was in the back seat as Ferritto drove away. As Greene approached his car, the bomb was detonated. Ferritto added that he saw pieces of the car flying through the air. Ferritto said that he and Carabbia returned to the apartment, where Cisternino was waiting. There was little conversation before they both left and Ferritto headed home to Erie. Once he got home, he said, he got ready to go to a party. Ferritto noted that Carabbia called him two days later and said he had heard that witnesses saw a blue car leaving the bombing scene.

According to Ferritto, he had attended a meeting several days before the bombing on a boat at Mosquito Lake near Warren, Ohio. Warren is located east of Cleveland, near Youngstown, Ohio. At the meeting were Pasquale Cisternino, Ron Carabbia, Angelo Lonardo, James Licavoli, and John Calandra. Ferritto said that the conversation on the boat dealt with plans to kill Greene. Someone had a tape recorder and played a tape in which he heard Greene's girlfriend make a dental appointment for him at 2:30 P.M. on October 6. That's when they decided to give it a try, Ferritto told us. He said he had been recruited in late 1976 by John Calandra and Tony Delsanter to kill Greene.

He said that he first became involved in the death plot during a phone conversation with an old friend, James T. "Jimmy the Weasel" Fratianno, in May 1976. Fratianno, a West Coast mobster, told Ferritto he was in Warren and wanted to meet him. The next day, Ferritto and Fratianno met at the Town and Country Motel and Cocktail Lounge in Warren, where Fratianno told him about Licavoli's efforts to kill Danny Greene. Fratianno asked Ferritto if he would be interested in doing the hit. Fratianno told him that "they're having some problems in Cleveland." Fratianno said that if Ferritto was interested he should talk to Tony Delsanter and "maybe you could make some money on it." Fratianno said that Greene was trying to muscle in on gambling operations in Cleveland and that something had to be done about him. Ferritto told Fratianno that if they wanted somebody taken care of—killed—he was interested.

Ferritto went on to say that toward the end of May Fratianno again called him from Warren and requested a meeting the next day at Cherry's Restaurant, near Warren. He met Fratianno, who was accompanied by Tony Delsanter, a man that Ferritto had known since 1956. Delsanter told Ferritto that the hits were on Teamster boss John Nardi and Danny Greene. Fratianno said that they were attempting to muscle in on Licavoli's rackets and they had to be taken care of. Ferritto said he asked Delsanter, "What's in it for me?" Delsanter said, "I'll have to ask Jack White. He's the boss."

Ferritto said that his next meeting in connection with the murder contract was in August 1976, when Ron Carabbia met with him at Cherry's Restaurant. On this occasion, Carabbia was accompanied by Pasquale Cisternino. Initially, Ferritto told us that he was with Pasquale Cisternino when they detonated the bomb, but he eventually changed his story to the honest version and admitted that he was with Ron Carabbia, who actually pushed the trigger on the remote control device. Ferritto said that Cisternino was the one who gave him the Nova bomb car and the Plymouth getaway car, which were registered sequentially at the same time. He said this was one of the most stupid things he had ever seen and was what caused him to be linked directly to Greene's death. He said he had been trying to get even with Cisternino.

Ferritto said that after a year of stalking Greene, he had almost given up the job as being impossible until he got the phone call from Ron Carabbia on October 3 at his Erie residence. The following day he met with Carabbia in Warren, Ohio, and Carabbia took him to the Mosquito Lake Yacht Club.

This information concerning James Fratianno was very interesting to us all. Up to this time, Jimmy had played hardball, refusing to cooperate further and he said he would never testify. He was now in the middle of a capital murder case and facing possible execution. He had introduced Ferritto into the murder conspiracy and he therefore became a principal coconspirator. We had him. He now had to cooperate or he was a dead man, one way or the other.

The massive leak investigation continued. And there were some unbelievable administrative screw-ups. We had six out-of-town agents assigned to do the monitoring of the closed-circuit TV coverage. These agents were selected because they did not know any FBI employees in Cleveland. They worked from a separate floor in the federal building in which the FBI office was located. One day, the clerical office manager came into my office and said that FBI headquarters was listing more agents on our staff than we actually had. I looked at the list and discovered that headquarters had added the TV surveillance agents and the undercover agent to our official list of agents. I took the list and told her that there was some mistake and I would get it clarified at headquarters. I called headquarters and raised hell. They said that they would try to do better in the future.

Prior to Stan Czarnecki's arrival and subsequent to Ray Ferritto's call to the Pittsburgh agents, the Pittsburgh SAC called me after learning from his agents that there was a leak in the Cleveland FBI office. He told me that because of the leak, he believed Pittsburgh should control of the Cleveland GANGMURS case and he said he was requesting FBI headquarters reassign the case to Pittsburgh as the office of origin—the controlling office. I told him that we were working on the leak and that it didn't make any sense to assign the GANGMURS case to Pittsburgh since the murders and all related activity had occurred in Cleveland. He would not listen to me and he insisted that Pittsburgh should take over the case. Although I was acting SAC, in actuality I was only an ASAC and he was trying to intimidate me— he was trying to steal our case. I finally told him off, using some strong profanity, unaware that he was sitting in his office in the presence of his entire supervisory staff talking to me on a speaker phone. This was very embarrassing to him, being told off by a young upstart ASAC—and he was pissed. He called FBI Assistant Director Don Moore in Washington and told him that I had refused to allow him to take over this case, that I had told him off, and that he believed Pittsburgh should take over the investigation. As a result, several weeks later my new boss, Stan Czarnecki, and I were ordered to report to Washington to meet with the Pittsburgh SAC at Moore's office.

Stan and I flew to Washington and met with Moore, who was a close friend of Stan, the Pittsburgh SAC, and me. Stan and I were in the process of explaining our situation to Moore, giving our side of the story, when Don's secretary rushed into the room and told me that she had an urgent call for me. I quickly walked out of the office and went to her phone.

The call was from Tom Bader, one of our supervisors in Cleveland. Tom was unaware of the leak investigation. Tom said that something was funny in that the office manager had just come into his office and told him that one of the clerical employees had just received an agent's paycheck. This, of course, was our undercover agent. I couldn't believe it. I told Tom this must be a mistake. I told him to retrieve the check and give it to my secretary, and that I would handle it when I returned to Cleveland. I told him there were probably two FBI employees with the same name. I walked back into Don's office fuming. I proceeded to tell Moore how screwed up I thought FBI headquarters was—they couldn't even properly coordinate the administrative aspects of an undercover operation inside the FBI—and he agreed. After listening to the Pittsburgh arguments, Don ruled that Cleveland would keep the GANGMURS RICO-murder investigation and control it. He sent the Pittsburgh SAC packing, not to my surprise.

Jim Ahearn continued his efforts to secure Fratianno's cooperation, but he would not budge. After we finished interviewing Ray Ferritto, I called Ahearn and told him that Fratianno was involved in the Greene hit. Fratianno had introduced Ray Ferritto into the murder conspiracy and he was involved in the planning of the Greene murder. Ahearn contacted Fratianno and he denied knowledge of the Greene hit. Jimmy Fratianno continued to refuse to furnish additional information or to testify. For this reason, we needed a hammer, and now we had it. I told Ahearn that we were going to charge Fratianno with capital murder and then we would see what he really knew.

"JIMMY THE WEASEL" FLIPS

The strike force presented our investigation to the federal grand jury and on December 5, 1977, James T. Licavoli, Angelo Lonardo, Pasquale "Butchie" Cisternino, John Calandra, Thomas J. Sinito, James T. "Jimmy the Weasel" Fratianno, Ray Ferritto, and Alfred "Allie" Calabrese were indicted for RICO-murder in connection with the deaths of John Nardi and Danny Greene. They were also indicted on the same day by the Cuyahoga County grand jury for aggravated murder with specifications, which carried the death penalty; aggravated arson; conspiracy to commit murder; conspiracy to commit arson; and engaging in organized crime.

On December 5, at about 3:00 P.M., Foran, Kimmel, Frederick, Lindhurst Chief Roger Symthe, Det. Joe Wegas, and Det. Rocco Polutro of the Cleveland Police Department Intelligence Division, and I met at my office to plan our arrest strategy. Other officers and agents assembled and at 4:20 P.M., seven teams of agents and detectives fanned out and began making the arrests. Ferritto was, of course, in our protective custody. Within an hour, all of the Cleveland hoods had been taken into custody. Ahearn and McKinnon arrested Fratianno, who soon changed his tune.

Everyone except Ferritto and Fratianno appeared in federal court and were released on bond, at which time they were rearrested by officers of the Cleveland Police Department Intelligence Squad on the state charges. All of the subjects eventually made bond and the investigation continued.

Ray Ferritto pleaded guilty to the federal and county charges. He agreed to testify against all of the defendants in both the federal and county charges before he was sentenced. We agreed to recommend a reduced sentence if he testified to the truth. If he did not tell the whole truth, all deals were off.

Jimmy Fratianno also entered guilty pleas to all charges and he was taken into protective custody by Cleveland FBI agents. His surfacing as an FBI informant and witness caused a national firestorm within La Cosa Nostra. He was the acting boss of the Los Angeles LCN family and at the time the highest-ranking LCN figure to enter the Federal Witness Security Program.

The investigation and searches in connection with the Greene and Nardi murders continued. The apartment identified as being used by Cisternino, Carabbia, and Ferritto to make the Greene bomb was located and subsequently searched. These guys were sloppy. We found a large quantity of ammunition, a pistol, a police radio scanner, a switchblade knife, a rifle arm rest, a note with the description and license plate number of Greene's car, a list of thirteen Cleveland police radio frequencies, alligator clips, electrical wires to battery terminals, and a roll of electrician's tape containing Ferritto's fingerprints. Ferritto said he had spent the last night before the Greene hit at this apartment with Cisternino. This search was very instrumental in corroborating Ferritto's future testimony.

LCN associate Kenneth Ciarcia was identified through the investigation as one of those who had secured the rifles that were to be used by the backup hit team. Ciarcia was arrested on both state and federal charges in March 1978 for the Greene murder. Ciarcia formerly worked as a salesman at Crossroads Lincoln-Mercury in the Cleveland suburbs. In the search for evidence against Ciarcia, we had searched his area of the dealership in early 1978.

THE MOB MOLE IS UNCOVERED

On the evening of March 8, 1978, Harry Lum, the owner of Crossroads Lincoln-Mercury, called George Grotz at home. Grotz was the FBI agent who had been in charge of the earlier search at Crossroads. Lum told Grotz that he had found some FBI documents in an area at Crossroads that had not been searched by Grotz earlier. Grotz immediately went to meet Lum at the Lakeside Holiday Inn, which was located near the FBI office. Lum told Grotz that he was planning to fire Ken Ciarcia and he was searching for Ciarcia's personal effects at the dealership, which he planned to take to the Justice Center, where Ciarcia was being held on the Greene murder charges. Lum said he found a black box encircled with cloth tape in his conference room, which was not part of the prior search warrant. Inside the black box was a Fruit Loops cereal box. He said he opened the box and found some photocopies of FBI documents inside. The heading on the documents was "Federal Bureau of Investigation." Lum said he did not tell Ciarcia about finding the documents. Grotz immediately called me and Stan Czarnecki, and we rushed to the office to meet with him. I telephoned Pat Foran, Mike Kahoe, and Don Pierce, who all came to the downtown FBI office.

We arrived at approximately 12:15 A.M. and met with George Grotz. He showed us the cereal box that contained copies of FBI documents and a handwritten list of names and numbers—the purported informant list. Also enclosed was the document marked "SD," and an antiracketeering report concerning James T. Licavoli.

Kahoe and Pierce had previously worked on the bank robbery squad.

Upon seeing the handwritten list, Kahoe said, "Look at the little O's over the I's, instead of dots over the I's. That's Geraldine Rabinowitz's handwriting." Rabinowitz was a longtime FBI employee and probably one of the most trusted clerks in the office. We were totally shocked. Rabinowitz had submitted her resignation several weeks before and this was to be her last day at work.

Stan and I returned home with instructions that Rabinowitz and her husband be placed under surveillance until she reported to the FBI office at 8:00 A.M. Upon her arrival at the Cleveland office, Stan called for her to report to his office. She probably thought he was calling her to tell her how upset we were that she was leaving. When she sat down by Stan's desk, I advised her of her Miranda rights and gave her the rights form to sign. She signed the form and tentatively asked us what this was all about. Stan handed her the plastic-enclosed list of purported informants that we had recovered. She looked at the list and broke down in tears. She confirmed that this was her handwriting and she began her confession.

She said that in December 1975 she went to a Christmas party at Pesano's Restaurant in Valley View, Ohio. At this party, her fiancée, Jeff Rabinowitz, introduced her to Kenneth Ciarcia, who was his boss at the Crossroads Lincoln-Mercury auto dealership. She and Jeff began socializing with Ciarcia. Sometime during 1976 she saw Ciarcia at a party and during a conversation with him, she told him about a civil court case she had initiated to evict a renter and recover funds from him. He told her that he had some connections and he might be able to help her with this case.

In January of 1977 Ciarcia quit working at Crossroads. Ciarcia started dating a girl named Noreen around that time. Sometime in the early spring of 1977, Ciarcia and Noreen asked Geraldine and Jeff to their residence for dinner. This was the first time Ciarcia and asked her about her employment. He took her into the living room, where no one else could overhear their conversation. He started a rambling conversation about how he was fed up with everything and used to have contacts but now because of his lack of contacts he was unable to get his son-in-law a job. Ciarcia then asked her if she knew what was going on in the Cleveland FBI office. He specifically asked her about James Licavoli and Tony Liberatore. He asked her if she could check and see what she could find out about these two individuals and she said that she would. She said that at this point, she began planning to get money from Ciarcia.

About two weeks after this dinner party, Ciarcia called her and asked her again to find out about Licavoli and Liberatore. She then told him that there were volumes on these two. He asked her if she could find out what was going on presently with regard to them. She said she would do what she could. A week or two later, she searched the FBI case index and found the report on James Licavoli, dated February 2, 1977. She got this report from the organized-crime file section. After photocopying the report, she called Ciarcia and told him that she had something that may help him. She made arrangements to meet him at his house on Richmond Road that evening. Geraldine and Jeff Rabinowitz, who was now her husband, drove to Ciarcia's residence, where she gave him the report. Ciarcia asked her if he could keep the report and she said no, she wanted the report back. But he kept it anyway.

A week or two after she furnished this initial report, Ciarcia called Geraldine again and asked her about numbers that were on one of the front pages of the report. She told him that these numbers referred to informants. He asked her if she could find out who the informants were and she asked him why he wanted to know. Ciarcia said they wanted to find out who was talking about them to the FBI. He said no one would be harmed; they just wanted to know who not to talk to. Geraldine explained to Ciarcia that the FBI used numbers instead of informants' names so that they could not be identified. Ciarcia asked her if she could identify any of the informants. He asked her a number of questions about informants during several conversations. He also told her he was going to have her civil court case taken care of.

In late spring or early summer of 1977, Ciarcia again called Geraldine and engaged her in conversation about the identities of informants. She told him she didn't know what else she could do for him. He asked her to find out, if she could, about Tony Liberatore, James Licavoli, and himself. He also mentioned a man by the name of Tommy Lanci. She recognized Lanci's name. He worked at Diamond's clothing store in downtown Cleveland, where she shopped. She said that Ciarcia told her Tommy Lanci was his nephew. She checked FBI indices for Ciarcia and advised him there was nothing on himself or on Lanci and nothing current on Liberatore. He asked if there was anything on Licavoli and she said that she would find out.

In the summer of 1977 she went to the closed files and pulled a copy of the most recent report concerning James Licavoli, which was dated May 4, 1977. She took his antiracketeering report to the copy room and made one copy.

About a week later, she went to Ciarcia's house and gave him this report. He again started asking her questions about the symbol numbers and informants' identities. He asked her again if she could try to get them. She said she would try.

In late July 1977 she went into the informant room at the Cleveland FBI office and, when she saw that no one was there, she looked at a list of approximately ten names of informants. This list had names and symbol numbers, which she copied by hand. She said she thought the informants were all top-echelon informants.

As it turns out, this was after Pat and I had opened all the potential top echelon informant files on most of Licavoli's associates.

At the end of the week, Ciarcia called and told Geraldine that her court case had been "fixed" and asked her if she had anything for him. She told him that she had a couple of names for him. He asked her to bring the information to the Crossroads dealership, where he was waiting with Tony Liberatore. She said she drove to the Crossroads dealership, where she met with Liberatore and Ciarcia. Liberatore spoke up and assured her that no one was going to get hurt if she helped them. Ciarcia asked to see the list and she turned it over to him. At this time, Liberatore also told her that he was trying to handle her civil case and said that he knew a lot of people. She didn't realize that her case had not actually been taken care of, as Ciarcia said. She refused to turn over the list to Liberatore and Lanci and told them that she was not able to get rid of her old house and she needed a down payment for her new house. Liberatore said, "We'll take care of that." Liberatore started to ask her about the IRS and wanted to know if the FBI was tied in with them. She said they were not, that the FBI and IRS were separate agencies.

Liberatore left the office for a few moments and came back with $1,000 in wrapped money, which he gave to Geraldine. He then asked to see the list. She asked him why he wanted it. She gave him the list of informants. He took the list and copied it on another sheet of paper. She left the office as Liberatore and Ciarcia were examining the list. Ciarcia called her the following weekend and said that a review of the Licavoli report indicated a lot of other informants that were not on the list that she had given them. He asked if she could get more names of informants. She told him that she would see what she could do.

On one Monday in August 1977, Geraldine said she went into the informant room again and, after observing that no one was there, she took three-by-five inch cards from a file cabinet and copied down in longhand the symbol numbers and identities of all the informants contained on them. She called Ciarcia and told him that she had it. He said that they needed it right away. Ciarcia told her that Liberatore had to leave town because the heat was on. She went to Ciarcia's residence that night and she gave him the list. He said he did not recognize any of the names on the list. She told him that was good. She then asked Ciarcia what she was going to get out of this and she said that she wasn't going to furnish any more information.

In September 1977 she received another call from Ciarcia at the Cleveland FBI office. This time, he said he needed a current report on James Licavoli. She went to the organized-crime file cabinet, which is called a "rotor," and pulled the most recent report, dated August 24, 1977. She photocopied the report and about two weeks later she met with Ciarcia and turned the report over to him.

In September or early October 1977 she went to court with her civil case and appeared before a county judge. He ruled against her and she lost the suit, after having been promised by Ciarcia and Liberatore that the suit was being taken care of.

Shortly thereafter, Ciarcia and Noreen were married. Geraldine and Jeff attended their wedding reception. Ciarcia told Jeff to keep her away from the people who sat at a reserved table in the front of the room. The only person Geraldine recognized at the table was Tony Liberatore. While going through the food line at the reception, she got in line directly behind Liberatore. He made casual conversation but later, while she was seated at her table, Liberatore came over and sat down. The band was playing very loudly so she was unable to hear him well, but she recalls him asking her if she knew anything about FBI cases in California. She said she explained that California is covered by three other FBI offices and she did not have access to West Coast information.

After Danny Greene was killed, Ciarcia called her and asked her what the FBI reaction was to Greene's death. She said that nobody had gotten too excited over it and he asked her to see if she could find out about it.

In August 1977 Ciarcia told her that he would have a man install carpeting at the new house that she and Jeff had started to build. Some time later, a man from Carpet Concepts in Painesville, Ohio, called and gave her an estimate on the carpeting, which was about $5,000. She called Ciarcia and told him that this was more than she could afford and he told her not to worry, that the carpeting was a wedding gift.

In October 1977 after Geraldine had lost the court case, she told Ciarcia that she needed $15,000 to put down on the new house. She said that she had counted on this amount from her court case, which he and Liberatore had told her would be fixed. She and Jeff went to Ciarcia's house that night and met with Tommy Lanci, Kenny Ciarcia, and Tony Liberatore. Liberatore told her, "You've been nice to us and we want to help you out." He asked how much money she needed and she told him that she needed $15,000. Liberatore told her that he couldn't possibly give her that much money and they began an argument. Liberatore then told her that he would lend her and Jeff $15,000 with no strings attached. He said he would not be knocking on her door and asking for any more favors. She told him she did not know when she could pay him back and he said, "You can pay me back when your old house gets sold."

The following day, she and Jeff went to Ciarcia's house and met again with Tony Liberatore. He gave her a paper bag containing $15,000 in cash. She left the money with Noreen, who took the cash to a Shaker Heights savings and loan association where Tom Lanci's wife worked. Noreen got a cashier's check for $14,900 and Kenny kept $100 for himself. Jeff deposited the cashier's check in a savings account at the Third Federal Savings and Loan in the western suburb Parma, Ohio.

Geraldine and Jeff were married on November 4, 1977. In December 1977 she and Jeff took the money from the savings account and put it in escrow on the new house. After Ray Ferritto was arrested, Ciarcia started calling her, wanting to know when the money would be paid back. He implied that if she could get additional information from the FBI office regarding the current whereabouts of Ray Ferritto there wouldn't be such a rush to get the money back. She told him that she didn't know where Ferritto was being kept and Ciarcia became very hostile toward her.

In the middle of December Ciarcia called her again. He was very angry with her because she had not told him beforehand about the arrest of James Licavoli and the others charged with him in connection with the Nardi and Green murders. Ciarcia again asked her if she could determine where the FBI was keeping Ferritto. She said she didn't know where he was and that she would not try to find out.

In January 1978 she and Jeff paid $4,000 to Ciarcia, a partial payment on the $15,000 loan. In that same month, Jeff called Ciarcia and asked when they would be getting the carpet that Ciarcia had promised as their wedding present. Ciarcia told Jeff that they were not going to get the carpet.

In late February 1978 Geraldine said she heard that there was a possible leak in the FBI. When she heard this rumor she was very upset and scared. Jeff called Tony Liberatore and arranged for her to meet with him at the L & K Restaurant on Route 303 in Brunswick, Ohio. She met Liberatore at the restaurant and he told her that, in the fall of 1977, he had given Ciarcia $3,000 for her and he wanted to know if she had gotten it. She told him no, that Ciarcia had not given her any money. She told him that the FBI was aware of the fact that there was a leak in the Cleveland office and that she was scared. She was going to resign from the FBI in order to get away from it all.

Liberatore told her that she was being foolish, that she shouldn't give up her job with the FBI, and that she was not the only leak. He did everything he could to talk her out of quitting. He told her that she should not be worried, that she never gave them any information on the Greene killing anyway.

Fortunately for us, the informant list had been "salted" shortly after the Nardi murder, when we had expanded our efforts to develop additional organized-crime informants by opening an extensive number of additional potential top-echelon informants. These individuals are not actually informants, although they do have an informant file, symbol number, and file number. The files were basically investigative files that we used to collect intelligence information on criminals close to James Licavoli and Angelo Lonardo.

The list that Geraldine had copied contained some legitimate informants, but basically it was a list of Licavoli-Lonardo associates. In addition, we learned later that Liberatore had added the names of some of his enemies to the list before he gave it to Licavoli.

There was one disappointment. The closed-circuit TV coverage conducted by the out-of-town agents didn't work. The agents monitoring that coverage should have seen Geraldine in the informant room copying down the list, but they failed. She also lifted Licavoli's file from the organized-crime squad rotor and copied several of his reports, and they missed that, too.

We had, however, found the leak. We were elated. After more than six months of investigation, not knowing who could be trusted in the office, we had our LCN "mole." Geraldine said that she would plead guilty to all charges and she would take her medicine. She also told us that she was sorry for what she had done and she would testify fully against all involved. We could now institute new, tighter security procedures in the informant room without alerting the spy in our midst.

After she completed her confession to us, Stan and I arrested Geraldine and turned her over to Mike Kahoe and Don Pierce, who took a detailed, signed statement.

On March 9, 1978, Jeffrey Rabinowitz was interviewed by agents Thomas H. Kirk and Anthony T. Riggio. He furnished a signed statement admitting his part in the bribery scheme with Liberatore and Ken Ciarcia. The Rabinowitzes were later indicted by the federal grand jury for federal bribery. These charges carried a sentence of fifteen years and/or a $15,000 fine. They both pleaded guilty to these charges and agreed to testify against Liberatore and Licavoli. After their testimony, they were each sentenced to five years in prison.

When the employees at our office learned of the betrayal of Geraldine and Jeff Rabinowitz, the morale of the office dropped to an all-time low.

No one could understand how an employee with Geraldine's record and accomplishment could become a source for the Mob. Her supervisor told me that it was as if he had lost his daughter. I walked around the office and saw only shame on the faces of her many friends—we all felt so violated. She had risked the lives of our informants and so many of the agents working on the case. I knew I had to do something to lift spirits in the office—the successful prosecution of these people would do that, but the cases were proceeding too slowly.

An outstanding undercover operation had just surfaced in New York. An old friend of mine, Joe Pistone, had just completed a very successful effort to infiltrate the Colombo LCN family. I was aware of the operation because of my prior assignment to the FBI Organized Crime Section in Washington. He had worked undercover for eight years as Donnie Brasco, an apparent small-time hood and burglar. His heroic effort was so successful that he had gained the complete trust of the leadership of this family and he was proposed for LCN membership. After he had amassed a mountain of evidence against members and leaders of this family, and before he was inducted into the family, FBI headquarters pulled him out against his wishes. He wanted to stay in the role, but FBI leadership believed it was entirely too dangerous for him to continue. I sympathized with Joe, but I knew the bureau was right. A shooting war was imminent within the family and Joe would have been right in the middle of it.

Joe's story was really inspiring. He had lived apart from his family—his wonderful wife, Peggy, and their beautiful daughters—for eight years. He and his family had endured this suffering for the American people—so he could do his job as an FBI agent. I called Joe and explained what had just happened in Cleveland. He knew the whole story; everyone had heard about our traitor. I told him I needed someone with an inspirational message who could restore the morale of our support employees. He said he would be glad to come to Cleveland to speak with our employees.

Joe came to Cleveland the next day and met first with the supervisory staff and then with all the employees. After his talk, I saw the renewed pride in the faces of all our employees. I will always be grateful to Joe for making that trip to Cleveland—and, of course, for the heroic work he did.

THE FIRST LICAVOLI TRIAL

Since we had both federal and county charges filed against Licavoli and the others, a decision had to be made as to which charges to try first. Foran, Kimmel, Friedrick, and I attended numerous meetings between the strike force and the county prosecutors and we all ultimately agreed that it would be best to try the local murder case first, since it carried the possibility of a death sentence.

The first trial began in Cuyahoga County Court in February 1978. The trial judge was James J. Carroll, one of the most respected judges on the county court. Jury selection took thirty-one days and the whole trial became a marathon. County prosecutors Carmen Marino and Eddy Walsh presented 125 of our witnesses, including star witness Ray Ferritto. He was on the stand for three days. The strike forces in Los Angeles and San Francisco needed Fratianno's testimony against LCN leaders in their jurisdictions, and Fratianno balked at giving testimony in this trial. Fratianno said he did not want to testify in Cleveland because he still had relatives living there. Foran and I urged Strike Force Chief Doug Roller to take a strong stand and insist on using Fratianno, but he folded and an agreement was made with Fratianno's attorney, Dennis McDonald, and the West Coast strike forces that we would not use Fratianno in the first county murder prosecution. I believed this to be a mistake; Fratianno reacted only to pressure and the death penalty is a lot of pressure. This was to be the first of many battles I would have with the Cleveland Strike Force leadership. As time would tell, we needed Fratianno at this first trial.

As I previously indicated, I didn't tell Strike Force Chief Doug Roller about our leak investigation until after we had arrested the Rabinowitzes. Roller and Steve Olah, his chief assistant, were very angry with me for not advising them earlier about the leak. They didn't understand that this leak case was strictly on a "need to know" basis, and they did not need to know. I had been the first FBI strike force representative on the first Department of Justice strike force in Buffalo, and I knew how they handled information. When one agency is working a major investigation, it is the subject of conversation and gossip among all of the agency representatives— everyone wants to know what's going on, even if they aren't involved and have no need to know. At this time, I told Doug and Steve that I knew they had made all of the agencies aware of our microphones in Licavoli's house while they were in operation, and that I didn't like it one bit.

I attended many of the key court sessions, including the days when some of the key witnesses, including Ray Ferritto, were testifying. Marino and Walsh did a great job with this long prosecution.

On May 25, 1978, Foran called me from the courthouse and said we had a verdict. Foran, the entire 9 Squad, and I rushed over to Judge Carroll's courtroom and we took our seats just as the jury was entering the courtroom. We listened with anticipation as the jury delivered its verdict to the judge. I knew we had a problem when Judge Carroll read the first verdict, finding Tom Sinito not guilty on all charges. If they weren't going to convict Sinito, I knew we had also lost Licavoli, Lonardo, and Calandra. They acquitted Licavoli, Lonardo, Sinito, and Calandra. The jury convicted Ronald Carabbia and Pasquale Cisternino of aggravated murder and aggravated arson. We got the soldiers but missed the bosses. Judge Carroll sentenced Carabbia and Cisternino to two consecutive life terms and the bosses walked out of court, still facing the federal RICO charges. We were all devastated. All that work for the past two years and we got only the workers. The only consolation was the pending federal RICO-murder indictment against all the bosses and soldiers, including those convicted in the state case. And I was convinced we had a good case.

Anthony J. Liberatore

Tony Liberatore involved himself in the Greene murder by hiring and equipping the backup hit team of Louis Aratari and Ron Guiles. His ultimate goal was to take over the Cleveland LCN family.

Liberatore was a vicious killer, but he was able to con some in the religious, business, and political communities of Cleveland. At the time of the Greene murder, he was on the Regional Sewer Board Authority and he routinely socialized with the cream of Cleveland society—mayors, bishops, city councilors, and business leaders.

In 1938, at the age of sixteen, Liberatore already had a long juvenile record for armed robbery dating back to when he was nine years old. On December 18, 1938, shortly after 11:00 P.M., Liberatore, Carl Ferrito (no relation to Ray Ferritto), Mario "Tony" Gallina, and three other punks from the Murray Hill area of Cleveland had just robbed Mullen's Oil Company, a gas station on Buckeye Road. As they were driving away in Liberatore's black Lasalle, two Cleveland plainclothes officers, Virgil Bayne and Gerald Bode, spotted them and gave chase. Liberatore and his pals were in the midst of a two-week rampage of armed robberies of gas stations and small restaurants. When the Lasalle finally pulled over to the side of the road, Officer Bode approached the driver's window and ordered the punks out of the car. Officer Bayne was on the passenger side of the car frisking one of the subjects when gunfire suddenly erupted from the Lasalle. Officer Bayne was killed instantly when a bullet struck over his right ear and passed through his brain. Officer Bode went down when a bullet tore a large chunk out of his heart. The killers dashed to the Lasalle and fled. Although mortally wounded, Officer Bode managed to get to his feet, retrieve his revolver, and fire six shots at the Lasalle, leaving bullet holes in the sedan's license plate. He died shortly thereafter at St. Luke's Hospital.

An army of police officers responded to the murder scene and mounted a manhunt for the assailants. Liberatore and the others were arrested about four hours later, after a high-speed chase during which they exchanged gunfire with the arresting officers. Four guns were recovered from the car.

All six denied involvement in the murders and armed robbery. Liberatore explained the powder burns on his hand by claiming that his gun, a .25 caliber revolver, discharged accidentally after the officers were already dead. At his trial, Liberatore took the stand and testified, "My gun accidentally went off when I stumbled as I was picking it up from the ground where I had tossed it." He was learning to be a con man even at that age. The autopsy determined that the fatal shots to the officers were from a .38 caliber weapon, which was seized from Ferrito, who was given the electric chair. Liberatore was tried for these murders and given life without the possibility of parole.

While in the Ohio State Penitentiary in Columbus, Liberatore became associated with Yonny Licavoli, a cousin of James Licavoli, and other Mob figures such as John "Johnny Ray" Pieri, brother of former Buffalo LCN boss Sam Pieri. These "made" men had tremendous influence at the prison and through them, Liberatore was able to get plush prison assignments, such as assistant to the prison chaplain. In 1946 Liberatore was transferred to the prison camp at London, Ohio, near Columbus, where he continued to receive favorable treatment. There he served as chauffeur and tutor to the superintendent's children. From London, Liberatore began his quest to get out of prison. He sent his first request for executive clemency in 1948, which was denied by Ohio governor Thomas J. Herbert. Governor Frank J. Lausche denied his second request in 1950.

In early 1957 Cleveland FBI informants began reporting that funds were being collected by Murray Hills LCN hoods and East Side numbers operators for the "Tony Liberatore Fund." In December 1957, following Governor Lausche's election to the U.S. Senate, Lt. Governor John W. Brown assumed the governorship for an eleven-day period between Lausche's resignation and the new governor's swearing in. Without any consultation with Cleveland police officials, Brown commuted the sentences of five convicted murderers, including Liberatore.

According to press reports at the time, public outrage was overwhelming in Cleveland. Famed Cleveland mayor Anthony J. Celebrezze called the commutations an "inexcusable error." Celebrezze roared, "The governor by his action is condoning and encouraging the killing of policeman by young hoodlums." The sentencing judge at the original trial in 1939, Judge Lee E. Skeel, said, "No one ever asked me about it and if they had I would have objected strenuously. I have tried a lot of murder cases and hardly any was worse than this one." Cleveland Police Chief Frank Story proclaimed it was "one of the most shameful things I ever heard."

Brown blamed it all on Governor Lausche, claiming he was merely honoring a commitment made by Lausche, an allegation that Lausche strongly denied. Lausche angrily responded, "If I had been governor, not a single one of those commutations would have been granted. My only conversation with Governor Brown was to warn him on granting commutations. In 1946 I turned down requests on behalf of Gallina and

Anthony Liberatore, who killed two policemen." Brown then claimed, "As I raised my pen over those commutation papers on my desk, I said: 'Dear God, guide me. If what I am about to do is right, let the ink flow.'"

Whatever the reason, ink flow or money flow, Liberatore's life sentence without the possibility of parole had been reduced to second degree murder, making him eligible for parole after serving twenty years in prison. Liberatore was released from London Prison in 1958. He quickly joined Local 860 of the Mob-dominated LIUNA and immediately became a business agent. I could locate no record that Liberatore ever worked on a single job site. Physical labor was not his game. He was an "enforcer" and provided the muscle when the local became involved in disputes with employers. This belief is enforced by an incident that occurred in Warren, Ohio, on August 7, 1960. Liberatore and suspected bomber Cecil W. Angelberger were driving in a rented black Ford that was stopped by the Ohio State Police, who suspected the car was stolen. After a chase that ended in a cornfield, Liberatore and Angelberger were arrested at gunpoint. They both claimed they were out of town on union business. Since this arrest was outside Cuyahoga County, Liberatore was in violation of his parole but, unfortunately, no action was taken by Ohio authorities. On the day following the arrest, police returned to the arrest scene and found a gym bag containing a pistol and a dynamite bomb rigged to be placed in an automobile.

Police could not link Liberatore to the gym bag and filed no charges. Liberatore was convicted of reckless driving and resisting arrest, receiving ten days in jail and a $200 fine. Angelberger was also known as a "union enforcer." Angelberger later was killed when a dynamite explosion blew his head off in the "bomb workshop" at his Hinckley, Ohio, farm.

By 1965, Liberatore had been elected business manager of LIUNA Local 860 and he was working his way into the legitimate society of Cleveland. On July 28, 1972, Governor John J. Gilligan granted Liberatore a full pardon for the 1938 police murders, notwithstanding the Ohio Adult Parole Authority recommendation that included allegations of involvement with organized crime and living beyond his means. Gilligan said in a statement reported by the Cleveland *Plain Dealer* that Liberatore "was found to be free of any known criminal involvement and enjoys an excellent reputation in the business and labor field." Gilligan also said that he believed Liberatore would in all probability live up to the standards of good citizenship.

During this period, Cleveland FBI informants were reporting that Liberatore was becoming actively involved with Danny Greene. Liberatore's star continued to rise. In 1975 Cleveland mayor Ralph Perk appointed Liberatore to the board of the newly created Northeast Ohio Regional Sewer District. This placed Liberatore in direct supervision of more than $500 million in public money scheduled to fund construction contracts over ten years.

In 1976, when I first reported to Cleveland as assistant special agent in charge, I made a courtesy call on Mayor Perk. At the time Perk was on a campaign to rid the city of "filth" and he had ordered that all *Playboy* magazines be taken out of the Cleveland airport newsstands. He had stacks of the *Playboy*s on and around his desk. After he proudly told me of his efforts at the airport to get rid of the *Playboy*s, I told him that this was nice, but that he had a more serious problem on his hands. I told him that Tony Liberatore was a mobster and cop killer and that he should remove Liberatore from the Regional Sewer Board. Perk told me that Liberatore was innocent of the police killing since Governor Gilligan had given him a pardon. I assured him that Liberatore was not innocent; he was a cop killer and a very bad guy. Perk said he would look into the matter, but he took no action. Liberatore continued his pretense of being an upstanding Cleveland labor leader.

We later learned that after the death of John Scalish, Liberatore believed that his chance to become the major power in the Chicago LCN family was near. Liberatore met with James Licavoli, Angelo Lonardo, and John Calandra and offered his services to kill Greene. He also told them about his source in the FBI and passed the stolen FBI documents to Licavoli in an effort to curry favor.

We learned that Liberatore was the one who hired Louis J. Aratari and Ronald A. Guiles to kill Greene. Liberatore was to pay each of them $5,000 for the killing. Tom Lanci was able to secure the weapons from his uncle, Kenneth Ciarcia, who worked as sales manager at Crossroads Lincoln-Mercury.

After the Greene killing, Liberatore instructed Aratari to kill Greene's close associates, Kevin McTaggart, Keith Ritson, and Brian O'Donnell. He said he would pay $5,000 for each hit. Liberatore told them, "Get those three Irish kids and we got the whole town."

Aratari and Guiles decided to first go after O'Donnell. On the evening March 1, 1978, Aratari was in a stolen car parked near O'Donnell's Islander Inn on Pearl Road in Middleburg Heights, awaiting O'Donnell's arrival. He had three "hit guns," including two sawed-off shotguns and a .357 magnum revolver. Unfortunately for him, he did not escape the attention of the Middleburg Heights Police, who approached his car and ordered him out at gunpoint. The police seized the guns and made the arrest, charging him with stealing the car and possession of illegal firearms.

This was a major break for us. With this latest arrest, Aratari knew that we would now be able to possibly link him to the Greene murder conspiracy and that he would be facing the death penalty. Shortly after entering his cell, he told the officers that he wanted his first call to go to the FBI. He had decided that he did not want to go to the electric chair or spend the rest of life in prison. Foran dispatched two of his top guys, Tony Riggio and Tom Kirk, to the Middleburg Heights police station to talk with Aratari. After several hours of questioning, Aratari gave a complete confession concerning his involvement in the Greene murder. He implicated Liberatore, Tom Lanci, and Ken Ciarcia in the murder conspiracy and told how they had obtained the bomb car and Ferritto's getaway car from Crossroads Lincoln-Mercury. He said that Lanci had instructed them to go to an Arthur Murray dance studio, where a woman provided the weapons they would use in the Greene hit. They went to the studio and picked up a .30-06 rifle. He said that later in September they met Liberatore at a restaurant, at which point Liberatore told them that "two professional hit men" had been hired and that Aratari and Guiles were to back them up.

Aratari said that on October 6, 1977, he and Guiles met Ferritto and Ronald Carabbia in the parking lot at Brainard Place in Lyndhurst. They asked Ferritto and Carabbia "What do you guys want to do, shoot him or blow him up?" It was decided that they would make the attempt to blow up the car first and if that failed, the backup team would shoot Greene. We know how that turned out.

Based on this new witness, agents George Grotz and Doug Domine located Ron Guiles that morning and confronted him with Aratari's confession. After some great interviewing, Guiles broke down and admitted his involvement in the Greene murder. He furnished a long, detailed, signed statement implicating himself, Liberatore, Lanci, Ciarcia, and Aratari. He corroborated the information furnished by Aratari. We now had two new witnesses to use in the current trial and any future trials.

The evidence gathered was immediately presented to the Cleveland federal grand jury and on March 3, 1978, the grand jury returned a sealed indictment charging Liberatore, Tom Lanci, Ken Ciarcia, Louis Aratari, and Ronald Guiles with RICO-murder and arson. Liberatore, Ciarcia, and Lanci were also charged with the bribery of Geraldine Rabinowitz. Federal warrants were issued for their arrest.

We had three teams of FBI agents, Cleveland police, and Lyndhurst police fan out to make the arrests of Liberatore, Lanci, and Ciarcia. Lanci and Ciarcia were immediately located and arrested. They refused to make any statements and were taken to jail. Liberatore was not located and it was determined that he had left his residence about twenty minutes before the agents arrived.

We were unable to locate Liberatore and on May 27, 1978, he was added to the FBI Ten Most Wanted Fugitives list.

Interestingly enough, while on the FBI Ten Most Wanted Fugitives list, Liberatore remained a member of the Cleveland Regional Sewer Board and the business manager for Local 860 of LIUNA. For months after he fled on the RICO murder charges, Liberatore continued to receive salaries from both positions. It wasn't until July 1979 that the sewer board stopped mailing his checks to his residence; they placed the checks into an escrow account until the criminal case against him was heard. He remained as business manager for Local 860 of LIUNA and was paid for the entire period. Local 860 later named its headquarters the Anthony J. Liberatore Building in his honor.

During Liberatore's flight, Kenneth Ciarcia and Thomas J. Lanci were tried on state charges in connection with Greene murder and, based on the testimony of Aratari and Guiles, they were convicted. They were given life sentences.

Over the next year, international searches were made for Liberatore and raids were conducted in New York City, Los Angeles, New Orleans, and Miami—to no avail. During the last week of March 1979 Mike Kahoe, one of the case agents on the leak investigation and the one who had been most active in the Liberatore hunt, advised me that one of his informants believed that Liberatore might be back in town. The informant said he had heard that Liberatore, disguised in a wig and beard, had attended a prize fight at the Cleveland Coliseum several days before. We canvassed all of our informants again and soon learned that Liberatore was probably back in town for the last time and he was preparing to flee to Sicily.

On Sunday, April 1, 1979, Mike Kahoe called me at about 10:00 P.M. and told me that his informant had just learned where Liberatore was staying. He was holed up at a dump home located on Reeves Road, in Eastlake, which is a small suburb east of Cleveland. This house was owned by a contractor whom we knew to be an associate of Liberatore. I immediately alerted Pat Foran and called Stan Czarnecki, and we drove to the office to meet Foran, Kahoe, and the 9 Squad agents. Lyndhurst Police Chief Roger Smythe, Det. Joe Wegas, and Det. Rocco Palutro, all of whom were still very much involved in the investigation, were also there. We quickly made our arrest plans and departed the office in ten minutes, en route to Eastlake in five FBI squad cars. At 12:44 A.M. our raiding team of fifteen agents and officers, led by Stan, surrounded the Reeves Road residence. Stan got on the megaphone and called for Liberatore to surrender. When he got no response, he ordered us to kick the door in. Foran and Kahoe pushed through the door and we rushed into the home. We found Liberatore alone, asleep in one of the small bedrooms of this sparsely furnished, modest residence. Liberatore was bearded and we found a wig and sunglasses by his bed. In the nightstand was a loaded .32 automatic. In a suitcase we also found $2,500 in cash and a current passport in a phony name, which he was undoubtedly planning to use. Additionally, we found two more wigs and several fake goatees in the suitcase. Liberatore, appearing dazed, refused to make any statement, so he was taken to the FBI office, photographed, printed, and taken to the Cuyahoga County jail lockup to be charged with RICO–murder and federal bribery.

During trial preparation, the first two strike force attorneys assigned to this case asked to review the stolen informant file list when they were going over the evidence. The case agents came to me questioning why the list had to be further disseminated. I appealed to Doug Roller that I did not believe a further review of the list was necessary. I also told him I had heard that these two attorneys were considering leaving the department and going into criminal defense work. Doug refused my request, stating that these two attorneys had to try the case and if they felt they needed to review the list, they reviewed the list. I took the list to them for their review. They reviewed the list, long and hard, in my presence. Several weeks later, both resigned the strike force and went into private defense practice.

When the two attorneys left the strike force, the Liberatore case was assigned to John Sopko, and a second departmental attorney, Abraham "Abe" Poretz, was brought in from Washington, D.C., to assist John. Both of these attorneys declined to review the informant list, saying it was unnecessary. John was a great attorney who is, at this writing, an official of the Department of Commerce in Washington, D.C. Abe was also a brilliant attorney who started out his prosecutorial career on the staff of famed New York district attorney and governor Thomas E. Dewey. Abe was like a history book and extremely sharp.

Abe and John presented the evidence gathered by the 9 Squad to the federal grand jury and the grand jury returned a superceding indictment (follow-up indictment after the first indictment) charging James Licavoli, Anthony Liberatore, Pasquale Cisternino, Tom Lanci, Kenneth Ciarcia, and John Calandra with federal bribery in connection with the bribery of Geraldine Rabinowitz.

In June 1979 I was promoted and transferred back to Washington as an inspector. This transfer was a normal progression in the process of ultimately becoming a special agent in charge. I was looking forward to this assignment because, if I did a good job, it meant I would be getting my own office in the near future.

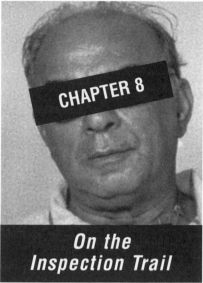

CHAPTER 8

On the
Inspection Trail

My old friend Dana Caro was now the assistant director of the Inspection Division and he teamed me up with another good friend, Norm Zigrossi, whose last assignment had been assistant special agent in charge in Minneapolis. Norm and I had worked together when I was a street agent in Buffalo and he was working organized crime in New Orleans. While in Minneapolis, Norm had been on an extended detail directing the investigation of the cold-blooded murders of FBI agents Ron Williams and Jack Coler, which had occurred on the South Dakota Pine Ridge Indian reservation in 1975.

Norm and I partnered on several inspection trips together at FBI offices in Phoenix; San Juan, Puerto Rico; Miami; and New Orleans. Our sixth trip was to Mobile. When we arrived in Mobile from New Orleans, Hurricane Frederick was lurking in the Gulf of Mexico. We were joined by Brian Hyland, a good friend and another FBI inspector who was just reporting in from the inspection of another office.

That Mobile trip was some experience. The office had some minor problems and we were initially critical of several of their administrative operations. The SAC was not happy with us, to say the least. The office loaned us several bureau cars to get back and forth to the office from our hotel, and on the fourth day of the inspection, Hurricane Frederick hit Mobile with all its force. Our inspection crew was staying at a Holiday Inn downtown and Norm, Brian, and I had stopped at a bar near the hotel after work. In our macho way, we decided to wait until the storm hit before we returned to the hotel. When the lights went out in this dingy bar, we walked out carrying a six pack of beer to enjoy while watching the storm back at the hotel.

When we got to the street, we were shocked, never having experienced a hurricane. The wind was so strong, it was almost impossible to walk. We barely made it to our car and I drove the two blocks to the hotel in the blinding storm. We were the only ones stupid enough to be on the road. When we entered the hotel, most of the guests were lying on mattresses in the hallways outside their rooms. We decided to watch the hurricane from my room, which had one glass wall overlooking the pool. The palm trees were completely bowed over by the tremendous force of the wind. This lasted for about a half hour until the roof and glass wall of the room blew out and we were soaked. We spent the rest of the night in the hall. We discovered the next morning that one of the bureau cars had been totaled when portions of hotel roof had been blown onto it.

The next week I received orders to report to Louisville, Kentucky, as special agent in charge of the Kentucky Division of the FBI.

When I returned to Washington before reporting to Louisville, Director Bill Webster summoned me to his office, where he gave me a thorough briefing on a case that was called the "State case," an investigation of allegations of corruption in the Kentucky state government. I realized that I had not been scheduled to go out as an SAC so early, but he explained that he had selected me to go to Kentucky because he needed someone in Louisville with experience in running major special investigations. He explained how important this investigation was and I assured him that I would do my best.

I reported to Louisville in November 1979. This was a great assignment. Louisville had good FBI work and was a great place to live and raise a family. However, I realized this was only for a time. I knew that I would be moved on after several years. My family remained in Cleveland for the first year because the housing market was not good and we could not sell our Cleveland residence.

Upon my arrival in Kentucky, I discovered that the State case was assigned to an outstanding agent by the name of Jim Huggins. The facts about this case and the resulting widespread corruption that we uncovered in state and local government is an other story, which I will not go into here. Jim was on the right track and the case couldn't have been in better hands.

In Kentucky, the problem was corruption in state and local government, not organized crime, but we could use the same approach that we used in Buffalo and Cleveland—the target squad concept—to attack the corruption.

So during my first several months in Kentucky, we reorganized the investigative squads under the proactive target squad concept, with emphasis on the widespread corruption that existed in the state. Being an SAC is very similar to being a coach. The key to having a successful FBI office, as in sports, is having the best people in the key spots. In Louisville, I had Jim Blasingame, an old friend and great guy, as ASAC. Mike Griffin (no relation), Tom Kneir, Ed Armento, and Jim Huggins were the key supervisors. They were the best. With these guys running their investigations and squads, I could have put the place on automatic pilot, but that was not my game. We had a lot of fun in Louisville.

Meanwhile, back in Cleveland, the first bribery trial began on June 5, 1980. I went back to testify and spent several weeks there during the trial. Midway through the trial, Ray Ferritto refused to testify. He was the only one who could link Cisternino and Carabbia to the bribery plot, so charges against these two were dismissed. This was not a severe blow to us, since both were already serving life sentences without the possibility of parole for their parts in the Greene hit.

We pulled out all the stops, and for the first time in Cleveland, we used James T. Fratianno as a witness at this trial. He had already entered a guilty plea to the federal RICO-murder charges and had been given time served while he was testifying against other LCN leaders throughout the country. Fratianno was still reluctant, but I believed he was essential to our case and everyone agreed. We convinced him that he was the most important witness in this bribery case, which originally brought him to us in the first place, to save his skin. Fratianno was an engaging guy and an outstanding witness. He testified about the meetings with Licavoli, during which the latter revealed he had a woman in the FBI who was providing inside information. Fratianno said that he asked Licavoli if the woman could find out anything about the West Coast and he was told she could not. Geraldine and Jeffery Rabinowitz also testified truthfully and were very effective. At the conclusion of the case Abe was very confident, as were we all. But, as they say, you can't predict a jury. They returned guilty verdicts on Liberatore, Ciarcia, and Lanci, but acquitted Licavoli, Cisternino, and Calandra. The boss and LCN capo had beaten us a second time. Liberatore was sentenced to twelve years in prison for his bribery of Rabinowitz. Ciarcia was given nine years and Lanci, who was also serving a life term on the Greene murder, was given eight years imprisonment.

During my second year there, my family joined me, and several months later, I was transferred. Director Bill Webster called me and told me that there was still work to be done in Cleveland. He was sending me back as special agent in charge. I couldn't have been happier.

CHAPTER 9

My Return to Cleveland

I returned to Cleveland as special agent in charge in the summer of 1981. By this time, my old job as ASAC had been split into two, so I now had two ASACs, Dick Schwein and Phil Urick. Bill Esposito, Joe Martinolich, and Larry Collins would later become ASACs in Cleveland during my years there. Director Clarence Kelley and his successor, Judge William Webster, had established a policy that, when an ASAC slot was open, the office SAC could personally interview each of the candidates and make a recommendation for the position selection. Fortunately, the FBI headquarters career board went with my recommendation in each of these appointments. These guys were the best of the best. Bill would later become associate director of the FBI. Joe later served as SAC in Detroit and Larry retired as SAC in Chicago.

I couldn't believe that the Licavoli federal RICO-murder case was still sitting on the strike force shelf, gathering dust. Doug Roller was now the strike force chief in Chicago and his former assistant, Steve Olah, was now the new Cleveland Strike Force chief.

The Licavoli case was the most important organized-crime investigation in the office and nothing was being done with it. Supervisor Bob Friedrick and the case agent, John B. Sommer, were just as frustrated as I was and they told me that Cleveland Strike Force Attorney Steve Olah would not move the case forward to trial.

I set up a meeting with him the second day I was back. Before the meeting, I paid a courtesy call on the new U.S. Attorney Bill Petro and apprised him of my concerns. He said that he would take the case if Olah did not move on it. This was very reassuring, since many U.S. attorneys would be inclined to defer to the strike force. I walked over to Olah's office, which was located several blocks away. After exchanging pleasantries, I got right to the point. When I asked him why the case was not scheduled for trial, he said that he was working on other things. This was outrageous. I told him that this was the most important case in his office and I would not hesitate to take the case to the U.S. attorney's office if he didn't get off his ass. There was strong friction immediately with him, since he resented me telling him what to do, but I had no choice. We had to get this case moving. Greene and Nardi were murdered in 1977 and the indictments were handed down on December 5, 1977, over four years before. This was my first skirmish with the new leadership of the Cleveland Strike Force, but it wouldn't be my last. Bad blood between us would continue for the rest of Olah's time with the Cleveland Strike Force. The case was finally scheduled for trial in May 1982.

THE SECOND RICO-MURDER AND BRIBERY TRIAL

On June 18, 1982, a jury was selected for the trial of James T. Licavoli, John T. Calandra, Anthony D. Liberatore, Pasquale Cisternino, and Kenneth Ciarcia, all charged with RICO-murder in connection with the bombing murders of Danny Greene and John Nardi, and wirh bribery—five years after they were indicted. Liberatore, Cisternino, and Ciarcia were returned to Cleveland from where they were incarcerated to stand trial.

Abe Poretz returned to Cleveland from Washinton and he and John Sopko did a magnificent job of presenting our case. After opening statements, I was the lead witness. John and Abe used me to introduce evidence concerning the overall investigation and specifically details about the bribery of Geraldine Rabinowitz and the theft of the FBI documents.

Ray Ferritto, who had dropped out of the Witness Security Program, refused to testify, which was initially a real blow to our case. He was subpoenaed, took the stand, and declined to testify, invoking his Fifth Amendment rights. Judge William K. Thomas ordered him to testify and granted him immunity, but Ferritto continued his refusal, so the judge locked him up for contempt. I believed that Ferritto had cut some type of deal with Licavoli, since Ferritto was now back in Erie, Pennsylvania, and living out in the open. He had appeared on television and he did not seem to fear for his life. However, this problem with Ferritto was quickly resolved with a brilliant move on the part of the prosecutors. John and Abe convinced Judge Thomas to allow the government to read to the jury Ferritto's prior testimony regarding these murders. This was permissible in federal court since the defendants and attorneys were the same in both trials. When Ferritto's testimony was read to the jury, it was probably better than him actually testifying from the stand. He gave very strong testimony in the first county trail about the Greene murder and he personally implicated each of the defendants in the conspiracy. As I recall, Strike Force Attorney Steve Jigger read the testimony and he did a masterful job.

We were able to play for the jury portions of forty days of tapes recorded on the microphone we placed in Licavoli's residence. This evidence was very damning. Licavoli frequently discussed the planned Greene hit and, since the microphone was in place on the very day of Greene's murder, the jury could hear Licavoli's elation when he learned that Greene had been blown to smithereens.

John and Abe presented six witnesses who were in the Witness Security Program and I'm told that this is the largest number of relocated witnesses ever used in one prosecution. This was our last shot at the bosses and we had to make it stick.

Jimmy "The Weasel" Fratianno made a reappearance and was an excellent witness. He was extremely important. In this RICO case, we were specifically alleging that the Cleveland family of La Cosa Nostra was the organization that was benefitting from the killing of Nardi and Greene. Jimmy was present when John Calandra and Anthony Liberatore were "made" members of the LCN family, so his testimony concerning the existence of the LCN family and the initiation ceremony was admissible. Jimmy said that he walked into the Roman Garden Restaurant, where Calandra and Liberatore were being "made" in the basement. No new LCN members had been inducted for many years in Cleveland and Jimmy had to give the oath to them because Licavoli and Lonardo had forgotten the words. Jimmy was a very engaging guy and the jury loved him. He also testified at length about the bribery scheme.

Tom Lanci made his first appearance as a witness. Mike Kahoe had "flipped" him and Lanci had agreed to testify. Lanci was serving a life sentence after being found guilty of the Greene murder in county court. In return for his truthful testimony in this case, he was allowed to plead guilty to involuntary manslaughter in county court and the original life sentence was thrown out. He was given a five-year prison term.

Lanci's testimony was also devastating, particularity to Liberatore. When being questioned by Abe, Lanci testified that he was brought into the murder conspiracy by Liberatore. Lanci gave Louis J. Aratari the high-powered rifle he used as one of the backup hit team. Lanci testified that Tony Liberatore told him and Aratari that if they could kill Greene, they would be in good with Licavoli, since Licavoli believed it was taking too much time to kill Greene.

After the Greene murder, Liberatore told Tom Lanci, Ron Guiles, and Aratari that Licavoli wanted to kill Kevin McTaggart, Keith Ritson, and Billy Bostic, who were Greene's closest associates. Lanci obtained pictures of McTaggart and Bostic and personally delivered them to Licavoli. He also testified that he helped Tony Liberatore make copies of the FBI documents given to them by Geraldine Rabinowitz. During the previous county trial, an FBI surveillance agent had testified to a damaging conversation overheard between Licavoli and John Calandra that was picked up by the hidden microphone in Licavoli's living room. When Calandra left the Lacavoli residence after this conversation, the agent identified him from his surveillance post and said that Calandra had a "little white dog" with him. The defense strongly attacked this testimony and the credibility of the surveillance agent. After this testimony and while awaiting for county court to resume, Calandra had commented to Licavoli and Lanci that he should "never [have] had the little white dog with him." Lanci was permitted to testify to this conversation.

Louis Aratari and Ron Guiles, the back-up hit team who were present when Greene was blown up, both testified for the first time and their testimony nailed Liberatore, Licavoli, Calandra, Carabbia, and Cisternino. Geraldine and Jeff Rabinowitz also repeated their testimony concerning the bribery on the part of Liberatore and Licavoli.

Because of the unusually large number of relocated witnesses, Abe told the jury in his summation that this was a case where the soldiers had turned against the generals. That it was.

On July 4, Abe Poretz and John Sopko completed our case. In final arguments, to defend the use of the relocated witnesses, Abe told the jury, "If you are sick, you go to the best doctor. If you are in legal trouble, you go to the best lawyer. So in this case, we went to the experts who happened to be low-level mobsters and we have used them as witnesses." The government rested, after ten weeks of testimony. The defense put on no case and, in closing arguments, attempted to attack the credibility of our relocated witnesses.

On the following Monday, Judge Thomas read to the jury fifty pages of instructions on how to apply the complex Racketeer Influenced and Corrupt Organizations (RICO) Act to this case. The jury was ordered to be sequestered and began its deliberation. I was very happy with the flow and essence of the trial. John and Abe did a great job and John Sommer made an outstanding effort in organizing the evidence. Agents from the 9 Squad participated in the preparation for trial and in presenting the evidence. I was so proud of all of them. Now we waited to see what would happen.

At 3:30 P.M. on July 8, 1982, John Sommer called me and said we had a verdict. I joined the 9 Squad agents and we rushed to Judge Thomas's court. Shortly thereafter, the jury was brought to their jury box and was asked for its verdict. The verdict sheets were given to Judge Thomas and he began reading the verdicts.

James T. Licavoli was found guilty of two counts of RICO-murder. John Calandra was found guilty of two counts of RICO-murder. Anthony Liberatore was found guilty of two counts of RICO-murder and RICO-bribery. Ronald Carabbia was found guilty of two counts of RICO-murder. Pasquale Cisternino was found guilty of two counts of RICO-murder. Kenneth Ciarcia was found guilty of two counts of RICO-murder and RICO-bribery.

Judge Thomas set the sentencing date as July 30, 1982. The convicted defendants remained free on bail, except for Liberatore, Ciarcia, and Cisternino, who were already in prison.

About four hours before the Licavoli verdict, the Cleveland federal grand jury returned a very significant seventy-two-count RICO-murder and RICO-narcotics indictment against some other subjects. More about this later in this chapter.

Upon leaving court that day, Licavoli and Calandra lost their cool and physically attacked local news channel 5 cameraman Rich Geyser and *Plain Dealer* reporter Diana McNees. They first went after McNees, grabbing her camera and her camera bag and swearing at her. Calandra grabbed Geyser's camera, throwing it to the ground, and Licavoli struck Geyser repeatedly with his cane.

On July 30, 1982, the Greene murder defendants all appeared in Judge Thomas's courtroom for sentencing. The first to be sentenced was James Licavoli, who was seventy-seven years old. Licavoli was given seventeen years and Judge Thomas immediately revoked his $400,000 bail and remanded him to prison. Thomas lectured Licavoli and told him there was no doubt that he was the boss of this conspiracy. John T. Calandra, sixty-seven years of age, was given fourteen years. Calandra, who cried the entire time, had his bail doubled to $400,000 and he was released pending appeal. He later surrendered and was sent to prison. Anthony D. Liberatore, who was sixty years old, was given a fourteen-year prison term to run concurrently with the twelve years he was already serving for the bribery. Pasquale Cisternino, who was forty-three years old, was given a twelve-year sentence to run concurrently with two life terms he was serving in state prison for the local murder charges. Kenneth Ciarcia, who was serving a life term for state murder, was given a twelve-year prison sentence to serve concurrently with the ten years he was given for bribery.

Toward the end of August, John Sommer and other 9 Squad agents began reporting to me that Licavoli, Liberatore, Cisternino, Lonardo, Sinito, Gallo, and the imprisoned Mob defendants in the other case, who had just been indicted and were lodged in Cuyahoga County Jail, had the run of the jail and were being allowed to order special food from Murray Hill. The informants reported that Licavoli had actually taken over the Catholic chaplain's office and he was using this as his headquarters. Licavoli was attempting to run the Mob from jail. I passed this information on to the press and to my distant cousin, Bishop Jim Griffin, who promptly straightened out the chaplain. I also made a formal complaint to Sheriff Gerald T. McFaul, who was unaware of what the jailer was doing. The Cleveland *Plain Dealer* newspaper conducted its own investigation and determined that 367 of 455 special visiting passes granted in that August were for visits to the eleven organized-crime figures who were held in the jail. Sheriff McFaul immediately corrected the problem and fired the chief jailer responsible.

Eventually all the appeals were declined and all the Greene and Nardi murder defendants were sent to prison, where those still alive remain serving their terms.

AN LCN BOSS CONVICTED

During the extensive debriefing of James "Jimmy the Weasel" Fratianno, he told us that during a visit to New York City in September 1976, he met Pittston LCN boss Rosario "Russell" Bufalino at a restaurant in Manhattan. During this meeting, Bufalino asked Fratianno to kill Jack Napoli, who was in the Federal Witness Security Program. Napoli was scheduled to testify against Bufalino at a federal extortion trial coming up in New York City. Fratianno agreed to perform this murder and Bufalino gave him what he said was Napoli's address. Fratianno said that he made an unsuccessful effort to locate Napoli. Bufalino was subsequently tried in federal court on the extortion charges and Napoli testified against him. One of the other witnesses against Bufalino was Joe Zito, who we earlier "flipped" in Buffalo. In 1977 Bufalino was convicted and he was sentenced to four years imprisonment.

Cleveland agents took Fratianno to New York City, where he testified before the federal grand jury concerning Bufalino. In May 1981 Bufalino was indicted by the grand jury on federal charges relating to this witness murder conspiracy. On May 8, 1981, FBI agents in New York arrested Bufalino on these murder conspiracy charges, several hours after he was released from prison on the prior extortion charges.

Bufalino's trial began in October 1981, with Jimmy Fratianno as the star witness. On October 23, 1981, Bufalino was found guilty and on November 17, 1981, U.S. District Judge Kevin Thomas Duffy sentenced him to ten years imprisonment. After serving seven and a half years, Bufalino was released in 1989, when he was sent to a Kingston, Pennsylvania, nursing home. Bufalino died in February 1994, still living at the nursing home.

Fratianno also testified extensively and was responsible for the convictions of most of the leadership of the Los Angeles LCN family.

BUSMARK INVESTIGATION

During our earlier investigation of the Nardi and Greene murders, we conducted extensive surveillance of Angelo A. Lonardo, sixty-six years old; Tommy Sinito, thirty-nine years old; and Joseph Gallo, forty-four years old. We noted that the three were frequently meeting with Carmen Pasquale Zagaria, age thirty-eight, and Hartmut "Hans" Graewe, age thirty-seven, who was also known as "the Surgeon." Our informants reported that Zagaria and Graewe were major Cleveland drug dealers. Because of this information, in 1978, during my previoius assignment as ASAC, we opened a RICO-narcotics case on Lonardo and the case was assigned to Dean Winslow, a hard-working, experienced, and dedicated agent on the 9 Squad.

Prior to the Greene murder, there were two organized-crime factions in Cleveland—the West Side Gang, headed by newcomers John Nardi and Danny Greene, and the East Side Gang, the traditional, recognized Cleveland LCN family, headed by James Licavoli and underboss Angelo Lonardo.

After Danny Greene was murdered, his principal henchmen, Keith

Ritson, Kevin McTaggart, and James Coppola, contacted Licavoli in hopes of making peace. As a result, in July 1978, the weakened Greene gang was not only allowed to take over the independent gambling operations throughout Cleveland's West Side, but also continue to run their multimillion-dollar drug ring. The profits of these activities were to be split equally between the West Side Gang and the Cleveland LCN. Our informants reported that the peace agreement was negotiated principally by LCN associate James Coppola. The Cleveland LCN family thereby became partners in Greene's narcotics operation, now operated by Carmen Zagaria.

This marijuana-cocaine-heroin ring was suspected of being the largest in northern Ohio, handling over $20 million in drugs a year. Zagaria's principal henchmen were Kevin McTaggart and Hans and Fritz Graewe. The Graewe brothers were first-generation Americans whose father, a former Nazi SS officer, taught them to kill when they were children. Informants reported that Hans was a serial killer who was frequently used by the Cleveland LCN family for contract hits.

Our investigation of Zagaria's drug ring was code-named "BUS-MARK," and officially began in March 1978. Informants reported that Sinito and Gallo, who handled the actual day-to-day activities of the Cleveland family for Licavoli and Lonardo, were personally involved in the Zagaria drug ring.

We opened our case with the long-range goals of not only determining what the association was between the above-mentioned mobsters, but also getting a court authorized wiretap on Carmen Zagaria. Dean Winslow put together a task force consisting of agents from the 9 Squad, officers of the Cleveland Police Department Intelligence Squad, and the Cuyahoga County Sheriff's Department Narcotics Squad. At various times throughout the investigation, other local, state, and federal agencies—such as the Bureau of Alcohol, Tobacco, and Firearms and the Lorain County Sheriff's Department—assisted our investigation.

The basic duties of the involved law enforcement agencies were split almost from the beginning. For example, the Cleveland Police Department and the Cuyahoga County Sheriff's Department assisted the FBI's surveillance squad and conducted their own surveillance, while the FBI used its resources to develop confidential informants and cooperative witnesses and to review and correlate records, such as long-distance toll calls, rental car and motel costs, and other pertinent documents. One of the investigative tools we used in this type of an investigation was the "pen register," a court-authorized device that provided us with the telephone number being called from a suspect's telephone as the call was being placed. We obtained pen registers on Sinito, Gallo, Zagaria, and other subjects as they were identified and correlated the information gathered.

The case remained a covert investigation until May 1981. During that phase, we used numerous investigative techniques, such as the pen registers, hidden microphones (or other electronic surveillance), physical surveillance, grand jury subpoenas, and confidential informants. All these investigative techniques were productive. The investigation established the connection between Angelo Lonardo, Joseph Gallo, Thomas Sinito, and Carmen Zagaria. It was determined that this group had, in fact, a narcotics and gambling relationship; that Zagaria basically ran the narcotics aspect of the association; and that the low-level soldiers who reported directly to Sinito and Gallo assisted Zagaria. The investigation documented numerous trips to Florida for the purpose of picking up narcotics during 1979, 1980, and 1981. The investigators hoped to get a wiretap on Zagaria and use that tap to get evidence on Sinito and Gallo. However, an unusual twist developed. They came up with sufficient information to obtain court authorization to install hidden microphones in Joe Gallo's office. As a result, in early 1980, Cleveland FBI agents secured court approval to install hidden microphones and wiretaps in Gallo's office at Orange Place in Beachwood, Ohio. This was another historic moment: the first court-authorized electronic coverage order obtained by the FBI based solely upon narcotics violations.

Numerous coded conversations between Sinito, Gallo, Zagaria, and others, were overheard and subsequently decoded. Two especially important conversations were picked up and decoded. One occurred on December 16, 1980, between Joseph Gallo and another organized-crime member. In that conversation, Gallo talked about the Cleveland LCN family: how it was organized and what problems there were with the family. Gallo admitted working for Angelo Lonardo, who he described as the "underboss" of the

Cleveland LCN family. Gallo said that Lonardo was one of the most respected underbosses in the country. The second conversation took place on December 26, 1980, when Joe Gallo and an associate had a detailed forty-five minute talk about the marijuana business in Florida.

Besides these two conversations and the various coded exchanges that dealt with Zagaria's narcotics dealings, there were also discussions related to arson, gambling, loan-sharking, corruption, stolen property, murder, and perjury.

By April 1981 the investigators determined it was necessary that the investigation become overt so that search warrants could be obtained in order to gather physical evidence, including drugs and drug paraphernalia. Additionally, they felt that witnesses were necessary to corroborate the other evidence they had developed. During the summer of 1981, they conducted approximately ten searches from which physical evidence was discovered that substantiated all of our previous investigations. In addition, a number of the low-ranking drug dealers were charged with violations in state court, while an interview campaign was initiated by 9 Squad agents.

Our first real break came when Don Newman, a drug "mule" for Zagaria, contacted Dean Winslow and requested a meeting. Dean met him later that day and Newman told him that he wanted to cooperate. Newman told Dean that the Zagaria drug gang had already committed a number of murders and he was fearful he would be the next to go. We immediately placed Newman in the Witness Security Program and the debriefing began. Dean began an interview campaign in an effort to turn other Zagaria criminal associates. Dean learned from Newman that Greg Hoven, one of Zagaria's three top associates, was the most likely individual to "flip." He was totally knowledgeable about all of the activities of the Zagaria drug ring, but he had not personally participated in any of the murders. So Dean concentrated on Hoven and during an interview in December 1981, Hoven agreed to cooperate. He also entered the Witness Security Program and 9 Squad agents began his debriefing. From Newman and Hoven, we first learned the details of a series of murders committed by the Zagaria ring. Based on this information, we immediately launched a RICO-murder investigation of Zagaria and his associates.

A third protected witness, Linda Potter, stepped forward, providing additional narcotics information and details concerning the deaths. For the first time, we had concrete evidence that the West Side Gang was responsible for the deaths of Keith Ritson, Edward "Ted" Waite, William "Billy" Bostic, and Curtis Conley, all of whom were criminal associates of Zagaria.

On July 24, 1981, I led a search team to the Graewe farm, which was located about one hundred miles south of Cleveland. Although we searched relentlessly for two days, we came up dry. But our efforts were making headway. We conducted searches of the homes of all of the subjects and recovered rings and watches belonging to Ritson and Bostic.

During the winter of 1981–82 we received information from our confidential sources that the Zagaria drug ring was attempting to locate Newman and Hoven so that they could be executed. We also learned that they were discussing the assassination of Dean Winslow. We immediately moved the Winslow family out of the area for their safety, but Dean insisted on remaining to continue the investigation. We considered the intelligence to be reliable and we became even more convinced when another of Zagaria's drug ring associates, James Coppola, telephoned the Cleveland FBI office and asked to speak with Bob Friedrick. Coppola said he was involved with Zagaria and he wanted to cooperate. He said that he didn't want to go to jail and he was fearful for his life. When he was interviewed, he revealed additional details about the Zagaria narcotics operation and the deaths of Ritson, Conley, Waite, and Bostic. More important, he confirmed that Zagaria and Hans Graewe had discussed "hitting" Agent Dean Winslow. "That gang is nuts and crazy Hans Graewe is totally out of control," he claimed. Coppola remained on the street for a number of months, acting as an informant, gathering information from the Zagaria ring while wearing a hidden body recorder. He was successful in recording statements by Hans Graewe concerning the murders of Keith Ritson and Billy Bostic.

On July 8, 1982, an indictment was returned against Angelo Lonardo, Tom "The Chinaman" Sinito, Joseph Gallo, Carmen "Mr. C" Zagaria, Hans "The Surgeon" Graewe, Frederick "Fritz" Graewe, and Kevin McTaggart. The RICO-murder and RICO-narcotics indictment consisted of seventy-two counts, including the Continuing Criminal Enterprise statute, the RICO statute, several IRS counts, and more than sixty drug violations. The seventy-two counts accused these individuals of a multimillion-dollar nar-cotics-smuggling operation and the murders of Orville Keith, Keith Ritson, Ted Waite, William Bostic, Curtis Conley, David Perrier, and Joseph Giamo.

This indictment was returned several hours before LCN boss James Licavoli and his subordinates, John Calandra, Tony Liberatore, Ron Carabbia, Butchie Cisternino, and Ken Ciarcia, were convicted for the Greene and Nardi murders under the RICO statute. Liberatore and Ciarcia were also convicted for bribing former FBI clerk Geraldine Rabinowitz. As I have said, this was one great day for the good guys!

We met early in the morning on July 8 and the arrest teams spread out to arrest all the suspects. Lonardo, Sinito, Gallo, McTaggart, and the Graewe brothers were arrested without incident. We couldn't locate Zagaria and he became a federal fugitive. A month later, he was added to the FBI's Ten Most Wanted List.

During the second week of September 1982, Agent Dean Winslow spent virtually all of his time negotiating with Paul Zagaria, brother of Carmen, for the surrender of Carmen Zagaria, who by this time was one of the most wanted fugitives in the world. Finally, on September 22, Paul told Dean that Carmen would surrender at his mother's grave at a West Side Cleveland cemetery. Carmen wanted to "say goodbye to her," since he had dared not attend her funeral earlier that month because he knew we would be watching.

At 7:00 the following morning, we drove three bureau cars to the cemetery and waited. The day was dreary and there was a heavy fog. It was like a scene from an Alfred Hitchcock movie. At around 8:30, we saw a new black Cadillac Seville enter the front gates of the cemetery and drive toward us. It was Paul's car and two men were in the front seat. Top Ten Fugitive Carmen Zagaria and his brother got out of the car and approached the grave. Both knelt on the ground and said a quiet prayer. Then Carmen rose and walked toward us with his hands held high. He was officially placed under arrest by special agents Dean Winslow and Carmelo LoParo.

CARMEN ZAGARIA FLIPS

We transported Zagaria to our downtown FBI office. After being photographed and fingerprinted, Carmen was escorted to an interview room where Winslow began his questioning. Dean explained that at this time we didn't care about talking to him for information about himself since we had him "cold." We were only interested in getting his cooperation. He asked if we would allow his wife, Diane, to come to the FBI office and we agreed. Carmen was allowed to call his wife and she agreed to drive to our office. He was also allowed to call his father, Patsy, in order to alert him that he had been arrested.

After visiting with his wife, Carmen said that he wanted to think about the matter before making any decision. He was then escorted to the U.S. District Court, where he appeared before Judge John Manos, who ordered that he be held without bail. Since we hoped to put a little pressure on him to testify, we did not take him to the normal place of incarceration but to the Portage County Jail in Akron, Ohio. On September 27, at around 12:30 P.M., Carmen called Agent Winslow from the jail and requested that he come over for a visit. Dean immediately briefed me and took off for Akron with Bob Fiatal, one of his fellow 9 Squad agents.

After Dean and Bob arrived at the Portage County Jail and were taken to Carmen Zagaria, who was in a waiting room, Carmen began by saying that he feared for his family. Then he launched into the disadvantages of cooperating with the FBI. No questions regarding Zagaria's guilt or innocence were asked. He was told that because of this he was not going to be advised of his rights by Dean Winslow. No admissions of guilt or innocence were made by Zagaria. The interview was concluded at 5:05 P.M. A few days later, Winslow and Fiatal paid another visit to Carmen at the Portage County Jail. Carmen said that he had been in touch with his attorney, Michael Drain, and would give the FBI his final answer about cooperating with us some time during the next week.

On October 5 Carmen called Winslow and said that he would plead guilty to all charges in the RICO-murder and RICO-narcotics indictment and testify against all the subjects in return for leniency at his sentencing before Judge Manos. After being briefed by Dean, I telephoned Donna Congeni, who was handling the federal prosecution. She was as elated as I was. With Carmen's testimony, we now had a good shot at Lonardo, Sinito, and Gallo. In short order, Donna called me back and said that she had talked to the county prosecutor and he had agreed to the deal. We now had a star witness who could put what was left of the LCN family in jail for the rest of their lives.

We transferred Carmen to a newly established safe house, where our questioning of him began. Carmen said that he was first introduced to Keith Ritson by his partner, Jim Coppola, after the death of Danny Greene. At that time, probably in January 1978, Coppola arranged a $3,000 loan from Carmen Zagaria to Keith Ritson.

JOHN CONTI MURDER

Ritson explained to Carmen that he needed the money to pay off a homicide detective to cover up one of his killings. Carmen said that the same detective also covered up Ritson's murder of John Conti, a criminal associate of Ritson. Ritson told Zagaria he killed Conti with an ice pick, which he always kept over the visor in his car. Danny Greene wanted to go into the jukebox business and he didn't want to start from scratch, so he decided to take over John Conti's thriving jukebox business. Conti owed Greene a lot of money over a gambling debt. Conti had agreed to sign the business over to Greene in exchange for the debt, but later backed out of the deal. This infuriated Greene, who ordered the hit on Conti.

Ritson told Carmen that he had picked up Conti on a ruse and drove him to Akron, where he stabbed the unfortunate guy eight to ten times with his ice pick. Ritson searched the corpse, removing a diamond ring from Conti's hand. He said he left the body at an Akron construction site so that it would be found. Ritson gave the ring to Jim Coppola, who had the diamonds removed for him. This information was extremely important since it corroborated everything Coppola told us.

SHONDOR BIRNS MURDER

During the 1960s and 1970s, Shondor Birns controlled all of the illegal numbers rackets on the East Side of Cleveland and he probably paid a "street tax" to the Chicago LCN. On March 29, 1976, Birns got into his 1976 Continental and was blown to pieces. The killer used C-4, a gray, puttylike explosive that is utilized primarily by the military. A handful of this explosive can split a car in half. The C-4, loaded with a blasting cap, was attached to wires beneath the seat of Shondor's vehicle. The wires were part of a seat belt warning buzzer. Danny Greene was picked up by the police department and questioned, but no charges were filed.

Ritson told Carmen that he (Ritson) was responsible for the murder of numbers kingpin Shondor Birns. Carmen said that Danny Greene had borrowed $75,000 from a friend of Birns. When Greene didn't repay the loan, the friend went to Birns, who paid the loan off for Greene. Birns then went to Greene for repayment. Greene wouldn't see him and sent Ritson to see Birns. Ritson told him that Greene wasn't going to pay. Birns contacted a black-numbers racketeer for assistance. This individual threatened both Greene and Ritson in an attempt to get the money back for Birns. In a rage, Greene decided to have Birns killed and ordered Ritson to do it. Ritson had a special bomb made, three times more powerful than necessary, to ensure that Birns would die. Ritson was well aware of Birns's normal schedule and placed the bomb under his car while it was parked behind Christy's Lounge on West Twenty-fifth Street in Cleveland. Ritson knew the approximate time Birns would return to his car, so he set up his alibi by going to Jim Coppola's bar in order to be present when the bomb was expected to go off. Ritson told Carmen that while talking with Coppola at the bar, he glanced at his watch and laughed, "Shondor should be gone by now."

Again, this information confirmed what Jimmy Coppola had already told us when he was debriefed. By now, fortunately or unfortunately, both Greene and Ritson were dead and there would be no prosecution.

Enis Cernic Murder

Carmen said that in 1978 Ritson had told him he set off a bomb under LCN associate John Delzappo's car on April 5, 1977, which killed Hell's Angel's member Enis Cernic. Ritson told Carmen that Cernic had been used by Greene on prior occasions to plant and detonate bombs. Because Cernic "knew too much" about Greene's and Ritson's activities, Greene decided to eliminate Cernic in a setup. Ritson wired Delzappo's car with a live battery placed in the trunk in such a way as to create a flow of current throughout the car. Later that day, Greene and Ritson drove Cernic over to Delzappo's car, where they dropped him off. Cernic got out of Greene's green Cadillac with a bomb package. When he attempted to wire the bomb package to the undercarriage of Delzappo's car, the current flowing from the hidden battery detonated the bomb in Cernic's face. At the time of the explosion, Greene and Ritson were already driving away from the scene. Ritson explained to Carmen that Greene decided to use this particular method of detonating the bomb because it allowed Greene and Ritson to be free of any telltale hardware, such as a remote control device, if they were stopped in the immediate vicinity by the police.

Carmen said that at the end of 1979, subsequent to his entry into a marijuana venture with Sinito and Gallo, he met with the two at the Holiday Inn on Wilson Mills Road. At that meeting, Sinito suggested that Carmen consider becoming a member of the Cleveland LCN family. Gallo added that John Scalish had been too easy and had maintained a freeze on new membership for over fifteen years. Thus, there was a gap between the old members, such as Licavoli and Lonardo, and the younger members, such as Sinito and Gallo. In addition, Sinito described James Licavoli and Angelo Lonardo as being too easy. Gallo stated that when the leadership structure changed, he and Sinito would not only be in charge but also would rule with "iron fists." Carmen asked if Joseph Iacobacci Jr., also known as "Joe Loose," was a member. Neither Sinito nor Gallo commented. Carmen recalled that when Gallo originally introduced him to Joe Loose, Gallo had said that Loose could be trusted completely. This was the only person ever introduced to Carmen by Gallo about whom such a statement was made.

Another meeting occurred in a coffee shop located in the office building where Gallo had his business on the East Side of Cleveland. Carmen said that Kevin McTaggart also accompanied him to this meeting. Gallo pulled Carmen off to the side and said he knew that Carmen had established control over the West Side, which is what he (Gallo) wanted. Gallo again indicated his wish that Carmen would become a member of La Cosa Nostra, although it might take a while to convince Licavoli and Lonardo because of Carmen's involvement with narcotics. Gallo said he had been given a free pass to distribute narcotics because he was one of the few people making money for the organization.

Gallo went on to explain to Carmen some of the rules of the organization, which included not fooling with another member's wife or killing a member for money, although it was permissible if a member went against the organization. Carmen said that both Kevin McTaggart and Hans Graewe, who were sitting over to the side, overheard portions of this conversation. After the meeting, Hans Graewe told Carmen that he felt it was to all their benefit if Carmen joined LCN. Hans said that if Carmen were a "made"guy, he believed this would get them not only "out-of-town" contracts, but also money from Las Vegas. Graewe even suggested they "blast everybody" and take over the entire Cleveland operation. Graewe said that if Carmen gave the word, he would kill the "two cousins," Sinito and Gallo.

Leo "Lips" Moceri Murder

With regard to the murder of Leo "Lips" Moceri, Carmen revealed that during the 1978 Assumption Day fiesta in Murray Hill, Keith Ritson and Hans Graewe grabbed Moceri when he was driving from the celebration. As Lips was leaving Murray Hill area that night, Ritson bumped his car. When Moceri climbed out of the car to investigate, Ritson pulled a gun on him, tied him up, and forcibly shoved him into his own car trunk; then he fatally stabbed Moceri with his icepick while he was lying in the trunk. Ritson told Carmen that Hans cut up the body and buried it at an unknown location. Ritson then drove Moceri's car to Youngstown, a Mob town in eastern Ohio, so it would appear that the Youngstown people had killed Moceri. Ritson claimed that John Nardi contracted the killing, with Ritson receiving $25,000. Ritson used the money to purchase a house.

Carmen said that around this time, Nardi gave an additional contract to Keith Ritson, who in turn passed the contract on to Hans and Fritz Graewe. This contract called for the killing of a man who lived across the street from Tony Liberatore. Fritz and Hans had a scope rifle and had the man's home staked out. When he walked out into the driveway, Hans and Fritz were eating sandwiches and missed their opportunity. The Graewe brothers, however, were also angry with Ritson since he had failed to provide them with full information concerning the contract. This contract was later withdrawn by Liberatore.

ORVILLE KEITH MURDER

After Carmen's introduction to Hans Graewe in 1978, Graewe confided how he had obtained $14,000 he had initially invested in Zagaria's narcotics operation. Graewe explained to Zagaria that he had received the money in a deal with Orville Keith. Keith, who had owned a house on Archwood Avenue in Cleveland, sold the home and received a large sum of cash. Graewe explained to Keith that he could make up to four times his investment. All he had to do to get $100,000 back as his share of the profits in a heroin deal was to give Graewe $25,000. Keith was delighted and gave Graewe the $25,000. Graewe told Carmen that he used a portion of the $25,000 to buy a Chevrolet Suburban and invested the remainder, approximately $14,000, in Carmen's narcotics operation. When Orville Keith did not receive his share of the profits from Graewe, Keith began pressuring Graewe for his money. At one point, Keith was so upset that he threatened to go to the cops concerning the $25,000 rip-off, even though this would expose him as a drug dealer.

Meanwhile, Graewe became increasingly agitated toward Keith because Keith constantly pressured him for the $25,000. As a result,

Graewe began discussing ways of murdering Orville Keith. Graewe considered wringing Keith's neck and throwing his body down a sewer, where it would be eaten by rats. He even talked about asking Keith to change a flat tire on his car so that he could drop the car on him. Graewe thought about running Keith down with his car after asking him to pick something up in an alley.

Graewe also told Zagaria that at about this time he tried to kill Keith in what would appear to police as a hunting accident. While at his farm Graewe asked Keith to place some targets on tree limbs so that Graewe could practice his shooting skills. According to the plan, Graewe would shoot at the tree limbs and branches as Keith hung the targets until a bullet ricocheted and killed him. Graewe believed that any homicide investigator would determine that the bullets had actually ricocheted and Graewe would be exonerated. Graewe said that he fired at least twenty or thirty bullets at Keith in this manner but none were on target. Later, when Carmen asked Keith about it, Keith laughed that Hans had kept shooting in his vicinity when Keith was setting up the targets. Keith described Graewe as a "real corker."

Then Graewe got serious about his planned murder of Orville Keith. Graewe asked Carmen if he could borrow a friend's boat that was docked at the Edgewater Yacht Club. He then told Zagaria about his plan to murder Orville Keith. Graewe said he would meet Carmen at the yacht club at around 11:00 the night of the murder. At that time, Graewe would arrive with a fifty-gallon drum containing the body of Orville Keith. Hans Graewe would have blasted Keith, then cut him up, and placed him in the fifty-gallon drum. Carmen said he agreed to assist Graewe only if he did not have to be present when Keith was killed. On the day of the murder, Graewe provided Carmen Zagaria with a box containing a chain and welding rods that Carmen was to take to the boat before Graewe arrived with the fifty-gallon drum and Orville Keith's body. Carmen noticed that inside the box was also a five-shot .38 caliber revolver. With this in mind, and since Carmen felt he could not trust Graewe, Carmen also carried a .38 caliber revolver in his boot, ripping his pants so that he would have easy access to the .38 in case Graewe should try something.

On the night of the planned murder, Zagaria took the box to the boat and went on board. He tried to contact Graewe through his pager, with no success. Carmen was finally able to get in touch with Graewe by calling him from a phone at the yacht club. Meanwhile, Graewe was at a bar located on West Twenty-fifth Street near Clark, drinking with Keith. Graewe said that everything was ready except for Orville Keith, meaning that Keith was not yet dead. A few hours later, Zagaria called again. This time Graewe was extremely angry. He shouted he was unable to get Keith to a location where he could kill him. Graewe would have to bring Keith on board to complete the job. Graewe asked Carmen if he had anything in his car that could be used to hit Keith. Graewe told Zagaria he could lure Keith to the boat by telling Keith that he was about to meet a heroin dealer on a boat, since the source would be coming down from Canada.

When Graewe and Orville Keith eventually arrived at the boat, Keith was introduced to Carmen Zagaria. It was still daylight when the two arrived in Fritz Graewe's blue Chevrolet Malibu. They boarded the wooden boat. Carmen remembered that Orville was wearing white shoes and that it took quite a while for the two to reach the boat because Graewe gave Keith a tour of the marina.

As it grew dark, Keith suddenly sensed something was up and grew nervous. Zagaria tried to appease him. According to plan, he told Keith that they were going out on the lake to make a major dope deal and that once the deal was completed, they would ride over to Captain Frank's Restaurant and have a good fish dinner. Graewe added that Carmen was well connected with the Canadians coming over from the other side of the lake. Carmen told Keith that he didn't have to come along if he didn't want to and, after a pause, Keith agreed to go with them. Carmen said he made the suggestion because he hoped he might still be able to get out of the killing. While cruising out into open water, Carmen walked out to the front of the boat with Orville Keith. But Keith was still somewhat agitated and retreated to the back of the boat. At this point, Graewe walked up to the front of the boat and asked Carmen to get something to hit Keith over the head with while Hans talked to him. Carmen agreed to hit Keith with a cue stick that was on the boat. But when Carmen picked up the stick, he just couldn't go through with it. After the boat had cruised about five miles from the Cleveland shore the boat's only engine stopped running. Carmen attempted to restart the engine but the battery was dead. At this time Keith, still suspicious, was sitting in the rear of the boat with Hans. Carmen thought Hans would stop the murder after Zagaria told them they would be unable to consummate the dope deal now that the boat had broken down.

Graewe didn't believe Zagaria, thinking his comment was merely a diversion. Hans said that he had a pistol, which he called his "Roscoe," in his box and wanted to know where the box was. Graewe casually removed the five-shot .38 caliber revolver from the box and walked back to his seat next to Keith. Keith asked how they were going to get back. It was approximately 11:00 P.M. They had been cruising for a little less than an hour.

Graewe turned to Keith and said, "Orv, look at the ducks." Keith turned his head to the starboard side of the boat to look in the direction at which Graewe had pointed. Then, from approximately three feet away, Hans fired one shot into Keith's left temple. Instantly, Keith collapsed back in his chair, blood spurting from his head. Graewe was laughing. "Look at that stream. It's just like a hose." Graewe bent over and shot Keith in the left side of the head, the bullet passing entirely through Keith's head and into the wall. With this, Graewe laughed again. "My buddy Orv sure knows how to relax." His eyes wide open, Keith's tongue hung out of the side of his mouth. Keith's body was slouched back in the chair, dead.

Graewe grabbed Keith's bloody chin and said that Keith made him sick. He then shot Keith through the right eye, then the left eye, and then right between the eyes. Laughing, he said that he shot Keith in this manner so he couldn't look up or down or be able to see where he was going. He said that Keith's head would be just like the miniature castle Carmen had in the aquarium in his fish store for the fish to swim through. Graewe had completely emptied the .38 pistol into Keith. In a way, Carmen was relieved because he knew Graewe had no more ammunition. Carmen would not have to protect himself. Carmen told Graewe to pick up the cartridges and throw them and the pistol overboard, which Graewe did. At this time, the boat was approximately a quarter of a mile from a water-intake structure that navigators call "the crib" and slowly drifting in.

Graewe began wrapping Keith's body in canvas and chains. The chains were tied together with welding rods. Graewe then got the extra anchor from below and secured it to the chains. Graewe took the anchor and began beating Keith's face with it, repeating over and over, "You make me sick. You make me sick." Graewe smashed Keith's face extremely hard some five to ten times.

Hans turned to Carmen and asked for a knife so he could cut Keith's belly open. Staring at the blood covering Graewe, Carmen said he didn't have one.

Carmen and Graewe then took Keith's body, which was wrapped in chains, welding rods, and the anchor, and threw it into the water. Carmen told Graewe that since the motor had conked out they would be unable to return to shore. Graewe was surprised since he thought that the story of the boat's breaking down was faked. Hans said that since he had done his job, it was up to Zagaria to clean up. Graewe walked down to the boat's cabin compartment and promptly went to sleep.

Carmen discovered that Keith's blood had seeped through the floorboards into the engine compartment. He had to thoroughly wash this area, as well as the boat deck. He worked until five or six o'clock in the morning and by that time the boat had drifted out about ten or twelve miles.

While Carmen cleaned the boat, Graewe slept like a baby in the cabin. When he finally awoke, he jumped overboard in order to wash himself and his clothes. He stayed in the water for over an hour since he was concerned about somehow being examined by the authorities. He also relieved himself, laughing, "Orville needed a last meal."

Carmen discovered that not only were the boat's flares wet, but he had no distress flag. Although several small boats passed, no one heeded their distress signals. Later that night, they were able to signal a passing sailboat with a flashlight and the Coast Guard was notified. Before the Coast Guard arrived, Carmen told Graewe to stay below deck, which he did. The Coast Guard threw Carmen a rope, which he tied to the boat, and instructed that they cut the anchor. The Coast Guard towed the boat all the way to the break wall before receiving another emergency call and had to leave. The Coast Guard cut their rope and told Carmen they would be back in an hour or two. Although the boat began to drift out again, the Coast Guard did return and towed them back to the Edgewater Yacht Club. Carmen told the Coast Guard that he was the only person on board and gave them a phony name.

Upon arriving at the Edgewater Yacht Club, Carmen saw his brother, Paul, and Jim Coppola standing on the dock. Paul was extremely upset and was carrying a gun because he thought something had happened to Carmen. Paul left the marina when he saw that Carmen was okay. Coppola said that Carmen's wife, Diane, was extremely upset and Carmen immediately called her. The Coast Guard never saw Hans Graewe.

Several months after this murder, Keith's body washed ashore and it remained unidentified in the Cuyahoga County Coroner's office until Carmen began talking to us. After this debriefing, Agent John Summer, knowing that Keith lived in the area of West Twenty-fifth Street, went to nearby Deaconess Hospital to see if Keith had ever been treated there. He located several X rays which he took to the coroner. With these X rays, the coroner was able to make a positive identification of the body as that of Orville Keith. Keith's family was later given $10,000 from the Ohio crime victims fund.

Carmen said that Hans Graewe told him about Graewe's second wife, Debbie, who had to get the death certificate of his first wife changed to "natural causes" before Debbie could apply for welfare in Guernsey County. Hans had murdered his first wife in a fight in a Cleveland biker bar, where he not only punched and threw her to the floor, but then climbed on the bar and jumped onto her chest, killing her instantly. Carmen told us that Hans derived extra pleasure and satisfaction from running over dogs and cats with his vehicle whenever he could. On some occasions, Graewe would repeatedly drive around a block in order to hit a certain dog. Graewe would also drive up on curbs and over sidewalks in order to hit animals. On one particular occasion, Graewe ran over a dog and repeatedly drove around the block in an attempt to hit the stricken dog's owner. Graewe was also known for his propensity for stopping his vehicle when he saw a dog or cat either on the sidewalk or in the windows of houses. He would then shoot the dog or cat and immediately leave the area, laughing. Graewe also on many occasions went to the stockyards on West Sixty-fifth Street and shot steers.

JOE BONARRIGO MURDER

Zagaria said that in February 1980, Licavoli had put out a contract on LCN associate Joe Bonarrigo. LCN member Joseph Gallo told Zagaria that he had given the contract to kill Bonarrigo to someone else but he was willing to pay $25,000 if Zagaria killed Bonarrigo. Zagaria said that Gallo had specified, on James Licavoli's instructions, that Bonarrigo was to be "put in a bag," and his body disposed of so that it would not be found.

When Bonarrigo was murdered and his body found, Kevin McTaggart told Carmen he had given the contract to unidentified members of the Cleveland Hell's Angels. Carmen said that the Angels were able to carry out the contract. But Zagaria said that one of the Angels was injured in the fire that started after the murder of Bonarrigo; McTaggart said that Hells Angels members received $5,000 for this contract.

KEITH RITSON MURDER

Keith Ritson was arrested by the Cleveland Police Department on narcotics charges and he was released on bond. When Ritson was arrested, Gallo and Sinito became concerned that Ritson would "flip" to save his skin. Discussions began between the West Side members—Sinito, Gallo, Zagaria, Graewe, and Coppola—regarding taking Ritson out. Hans Graewe entered into the conversations for several reasons, mainly because he wanted Ritson's portion of the gang's gambling profits. Graewe was also concerned that Ritson might become a law enforcement informant in order to get out of the narcotics charge. Ritson was aware of Graewe's involvement in the Orville Keith murder, so he was a threat.

Early in the investigation, we had tried to "turn" Ritson on several occasions—at that time we desperately needed an inside source to solve these murders—but Ritson would not talk.

The fact is, Ritson never dreamed of turning. Of course, the Cleveland Mob didn't know the truth, so the decision was made to hit Ritson. Carmen said that Coppola telephoned Ritson and asked him to come over to Carmen's tropical fish store for a meeting. Unaware that he could possibly be a target since, to his knowledge, he hadn't incurred anyone's wrath, Ritson appeared as requested. Carmen, Graewe, and Ritson conversed as normal in the rear of the fish store for quite some time.

Ritson sat with one leg folded over the other and Carmen later discovered he had been concealing a gun. While Carmen was on the telephone, Graewe casually got up, walked into the hallway situated in back of Ritson's chair, and headed toward the men's room.

As Carmen finished his telephone conversation, he looked up and spotted a gun sticking out from the bathroom area. As he hung up the telephone, Graewe shot Ritson once in the head. Carmen told us that all he could see prior to the gunshot was the gun barrel, and not Graewe.

As Ritson slumped in the chair, one of his legs shifted and a .22 automatic dropped to the floor from under his pant leg. Graewe exited the bathroom hallway and laughed about how the blood was spurting out of Ritson's head. Graewe grabbed a red plastic kitty litter tray and put it next to Ritson's head, trying to catch as much of the spurting blood as possible. The blood, however, was also dripping down the back of Ritson's head and onto the floor behind and underneath Ritson's body. Graewe picked up a piece of insulation and placed it on Ritson's head to stop the stream of blood.

When he put the insulation on Ritson's head, Hans commented, "Here's your scarf." Ritson was wearing a gold Omega wristwatch worth approximately $800, a boxing ring with two gold gloves with diamonds in the palm, and a gold necklace. By this time, we had already recovered the watch, ring, and necklace at various search locations in connection with this investigation.

Ritson had been carrying about sixty dollars in cash, a beeper, and his gun and holster. Also present on the body was $175, which Zagaria had given him earlier in the day for a cocaine transaction. Graewe rifled the body and returned Zagaria's $175, keeping all the other valuables for himself. Zagaria put the gun and holster in his pocket; he would give both away that night.

As Ritson's blood flow started to subside, even before the insulation was placed over the wound, Graewe kept commenting, "A little lower. A little lower. A little lower"—meaning that the blood was pumping more and more slowly. According to Zagaria, Graewe talked about taking a hatchet to the body. But Carmen argued with Graewe about chopping up the body in the fish store.

Hans's murder weapon, a .38 revolver, had been hidden in the store all the time and was one of several guns Carmen kept at different locations throughout the building. Several minutes later, after Ritson had almost completely bled out, the corpse shifted. Hans immediately walked out, retrieved the .38 revolver, which had been placed back in its original spot above a refrigerator in the fish store, returned to within ten feet of Ritson, and shot him again in the head. Hans laughed again, "That'll make you relax."

At this point Carmen walked over to a cabinet, took out a sheet of heavy plastic, and placed it on the floor of the back room. With Ritson's body still slumped over in the chair, Zagaria turned the chair over so that Ritson fell onto the plastic sheet. As he did so, the chair collapsed into several pieces. Cursing, Carmen wrapped Ritson's body, tying it with electrical wire around the plastic in the areas of Ritson's feet and shoulders. As Carmen finished up, Graewe cleaned the blood off the gun, beeper, and the sixty dollars he had taken off Ritson. He then took the pan of blood and dumped it into a bathtub, picking out the clots of blood that were forming and throwing them in the toilet. He laughed, "You cleaned up after me on Orville's murder while I slept. Let me clean this up while you sleep." His cleanup effort was not fully successful.

After we talked to Carmen, Agent John Summer, who is also a forensic scientist, went to Carmen's tropical fish store and recovered blood that had seeped into the flooring. This blood was positively identified by the FBI Laboratory through DNA as belonging to Keith Ritson. Incidently, the work of John Summer in this investigation was extremely important. He was able to discover blood evidence of each of the victims killed in the fish store. The DNA identification of each of the victims in the fish store was great corroborative evidence supporting Carmen's eventual testimony in this case.

After the cleanup effort, Carmen paged Jim Coppola, who returned the call. Carmen told Coppola that they needed his assistance immediately at the fish store and that he had to come down and help them. Carmen and Graewe then moved the body into a room, referred to as the "blue room," next to the back door, and nailed that door shut. Graewe and Carmen were sitting in the back room near the cash register when James Coppola arrived an hour later. As Coppola entered the unlocked fish store, Graewe walked toward him, smiling and waving the watch he had taken from Keith Ritson. Coppola asked where Ritson was and Hans laughed, "He's in there," pointing toward the "blue room" area. Coppola remarked, "I can smell it. Just like the other guy I smelled at my bar." Coppola meant the smell of death and was referring to the murder of a customer in his bar, The Stubborn Mule, a few months before. Carmen and Hans wanted Coppola to help them remove the body since they didn't trust Graewe's vehicle for transporting the corpse. Coppola was driving his Mercury but said he didn't want to be involved since his girlfriend was in the car waiting for him. Graewe and Zagaria asked him to take her home and return to assist them in removing the body.

When Coppola left the fish store, Carmen remembered waiting a minute or two, then looking out the window. He watched Coppola drive off in the opposite direction he should have taken to his girlfriend's home. Neither Graewe nor Carmen thought he would be back. Approximately thirty minutes later, Coppola called. When Carmen answered, he asked for Graewe, refusing to talk to Carmen. Coppola told Hans that he wouldn't be assisting in the disposal of the body. Of course, Carmen was extremely upset and blamed Graewe because of the way he flaunted Ritson's jewelry and teased Coppola when he was there. Carmen did not have a vehicle at the fish store and Graewe had only his Chevrolet Suburban, with which he was having problems.

Hans went out and was successful in starting up the truck. Since he got the vehicle started and they no longer expected Coppola, they decided to move Ritson's green Lincoln, which was still parked on Lorain Avenue. Carmen put on a hooded sweatshirt so no one would recognize him. He wore the same gloves he used to clean up Ritson's blood.

With Hans driving behind him, Carmen drove Ritson's vehicle south on Ninety-fourth Street to the end of Almira, east on Benison Avenue to Seventy-third, and then into the Zayre Bowling Alley parking lot, where he left Ritson's vehicle in a remote area. Carmen thoroughly wiped the car clean with his gloves and then climbed into Graewe's truck. The two returned to the fish store. Hans decided that he should drive his Suburban with the corpse in it to his brother Fritz's residence and get things together in order to dispose of the body. At this point, Zagaria argued with Graewe about being unprepared to dispose of the body.

Unconcerned, Hans left the fish store and was gone for about an hour and a half. When he returned at around 8:00 P.M., he had Fritz's red pickup truck with a camper shell. It was empty except for a moving dolly and heavy chain.

They loaded Ritson's body on the five-foot dolly and wrapped it with the chain spiraling around the body. The chain was affixed together with a 12-2 Romex wire. Then they wrapped additional electrical cord around the body and dolly.

Hans suggested taking the body to Jacquay quarry, but Carmen argued against it since neither of them knew the location that well. They pulled Fritz Graewe's pickup truck to the rear of the fish store and placed the dolly with Ritson's body in the back. The two then placed strips of insulation and plywood over the body, securing the dolly with two-by-fours. The box with the insulation, the broken chair, and Ritson's shoes was stored temporarily at the store.

The next morning, Carmen burned the box, chair, insulation and shoes behind his residence. Graewe poured paint thinner on the floor where the blood stains were still visible. Hans said he knew of an old well near Columbia Station, west of Cleveland where they could drop the body. Hans then decided to take the corpse to his old swimming hole, another quarry near LaGrange, Ohio, a western Cleveland suburb.

Carmen remembered driving through the town of LaGrange because of the old town square and the Kitchen Cabinet Store located at one of the corners of the square. When they arrived at Hans's swimming hole it was approximately 10:00 P.M. They noticed that lights were still on in a building near the quarry. They decided to wait, and about a half hour later they watched as a man left the building and drove his truck down the driveway. After the vehicle was out of the area, they drove onto the property and backed the truck to the edge of the quarry. The two then pulled the dolly out of the camper and dropped it over the edge.

As they pulled out, the man who had recently left the building returned. Hans said he would kill him if he spotted them. They waited about fifteen minutes and the fellow left again. They immediately pulled out and left the scene. Carmen and Graewe then pulled up to the Normandy Bar and had several drinks.

Carmen later spotted Fritz Graewe showing off Ritson's boxing ring to Kevin McTaggart. Zagaria, Hans, and Fritz argued over this and Hans finally took the ring away from his brother. Later that day, Hans gave the ring to Carmen and asked him to hold it until he could have it remade or melted down. Carmen placed the ring in his pocket and carried it around with him for several days. When Hans didn't ask for it back, Carmen put the ring into his safe deposit box at the bank.

TED WAITE MURDER

Carmen told us he had knowledge of another murder, that of Ted Waite, who was a fire adjuster. He said that in 1966, he had teamed up with Waite to perform construction jobs on residences and businesses that had fire damage. Carmen referred to this business as the "fire-chasing" business. In 1968 Waite refused to pay Carmen his share of a large construction job. Carmen made several attempts to collect, but to no avail. Then Waite disappeared and Carmen did not see him again until 1978. In late 1978 Carmen saw Waite with Kevin McTaggart at Jim Coppola's bar.

Carmen said he later learned from McTaggart that McTaggart was now in the fire-chasing business with Waite. Carmen told us that McTaggart later actually moved into Waite's house on the West Side of Cleveland. Carmen said that McTaggart developed a sexual relationship with Waite's daughter and his wife. As a result, Waite and McTaggart discontinued their business relationship and McTaggart moved out. Carmen said that in late 1978, he was with McTaggart, Hans Graewe, and several others drinking at the Golden Anchor Lounge on the West Side of Cleveland when Waite walked into the lounge. When McTaggart saw Waite, he whispered to Carmen and the others that Waite was an FBI informant. Waite drank by himself for about a half hour and then returned to his car, returning almost immediately and announcing that the tires on his car had been slashed and the car battery was stolen.

Carmen said that several weeks later, he heard a rumor that Waite had disappeared. When he asked McTaggart and Hans Graewe if they had killed Waite, they didn't respond and they both laughed.

JOE KOVACH MURDER

During our interviews with Carmen, he said that Keith Ritson told him that "they" had to get rid of drug dealer Billy Bostic because Bostic knew about a murder Ritson had committed several years before. This murder victim was Joe Kovach, who owned a fire-chasing business. Ritson wanted to take over the business and he decided the best way to accomplish this was to kill Kovach. Ritson told Carmen that he and Kevin McTaggart watched Kovach's house one morning until Kovach came out to go to his car. Ritson said he walked up to Kovach and shot him in the head at point-blank range with his .45 caliber semiautomatic pistol. Then he and McTaggart drove away without anyone noticing them.

BILLY BOSTIC MURDER

During the second week of June 1980, Bostic appeared at the fish store while Hans was talking with Carmen Zagaria. Almost immediately Graewe and Bostic got into a heated argument because Graewe didn't trust Bostic to keep his mouth shut. Bostic left, reappearing about a week later at around 10:30 A.M. He found Zagaria sitting with McTaggart and Graewe. While Bostic walked around the various rooms of the store, Hans pulled Kevin aside to whisper something. Zagaria became alarmed over what McTaggart and Graewe were talking about and ordered them not to "mess around" with Bostic. McTaggart replied, "Me and Papa are going to take care of him." Concerned about the presence of a number of men doing construction and repair work to the building, Zagaria answered, "If you're going to do it, do it another day and in another place." McTaggart and Graewe both indicated that they wouldn't do anything that day.

An hour or so later, around noon, Zagaria had to leave the fish store for a meeting with his accountant and, later, his lawyer at the Blue Fox Restaurant on the West Side of Cleveland. After nearly four hours of meetings, Zagaria returned to the fish store.

When Zagaria got out of his car to enter the front door of the fish store, he noticed that Bostic's car was no longer parked nearby and that the workers were still present. After Zagaria walked into the fish store, he saw McTaggart and asked where Bostic was. McTaggart replied, "I don't know. Ask Papa." At that point, Hans Graewe appeared through a curtain near the steps to the basement. "Nothing happened, did it?" Zagaria asked, Graewe laughed, "Kevin's a corker. They can get him for murder, but they can only get me for malpractice. Go downstairs, someone's taking a shower."

Zagaria immediately descended the stairs into the basement and saw the body of William Bostic lying face down, his head in a hole on the floor near a broken water pipe which had been spewing water into the basement for almost a year. Bostic was lying with his hands out to the side and his palms turned upward. As soon as Zagaria saw the body from the steps, he turned around and saw that one of the carpenters had followed him into the fish store and was following him down the stairs to the basement.

Zagaria quickly turned and stopped the guy from walking any further and seeing the corpse. Carmen walked him back up to the first floor of the fish store. When McTaggart noticed the carpenter coming up the stairs, he demanded, "What are you doing down there?" The man did not respond and Zagaria accompanied him out through the front door of the store and onto the sidewalk, where Carmen told him not to come back in. McTaggart asked Zagaria, "Did he see anything?" Zagaria replied, "No." McTaggart added, "If he did, he would've been next."

Shortly after this, Hans also asked Zagaria if the worker had seen anything. Replying that he had not, Zagaria became very upset with both Graewe and McTaggart. He said he thought they were not going to do anything to Bostic. He said adamantly that this one was theirs and he was not going to do anything about it. Graewe replied, "He had to go. He made me sick from years back."

Around this time, Zagaria noticed that Fritz Graewe had entered and was in fact making trips up and down the basement stairs to get water from the broken pipe for the construction workers. Zagaria immediately began getting rid of all the workers in and around the building, insisting they quit work early and walk across the street to have a drink on him. He took out his wallet and gave the workers a twenty-dollar bill to buy drinks for all those working on the building.

After Zagaria got all of the workers out of the building, he locked it up and continued arguing with McTaggart and Graewe over their lack of discretion in killing Bostic with so many people present in the building. Graewe and McTaggart explained how the murder occurred. Hans said that he, McTaggart, and Bostic began discussing how to break out portions of Zagaria's basement wall in order to allow access from one portion of the basement to another. The passageways would be part of the plan to open up the dice game in Zagaria's building. Bostic said he would decide where the holes would be made in the walls. He took a piece of chalk and walked down the basement steps.

Through a predetermined plan, Hans had passed the .38 caliber revolver to McTaggart, who would shoot Bostic when the signal was given. Hans, with a flashlight, went first down the stairs, Bostic second, and Kevin third. As Hans turned around the corner into the basement room in which Bostic was to be killed, he said, "Duck your head." This was the signal for McTaggart to shoot Bostic.

As Hans turned the corner, McTaggart shot Bostic twice in the back of the head with the .38, the same gun that had been used to kill Keith Ritson. Carmen knew that this weapon was kept in Fritz Graewe's garage and a file had been used to change the lands-and-grooves configuration inside the gun barrel after the Ritson shooting so that an identification could not be made.

When the shots were fired, Bostic slumped down on one knee. Hans grabbed one arm, while McTaggart took hold of the other. They dragged Bostic's body over to the broken water pipe and placed him on the floor, allowing water to run over his body and drain away the blood. McTaggart said that the two bullets did not exit Bostic's skull and were "still in the helmet."

According to Graewe and McTaggart, Bostic was carrying a .45 caliber pistol at the time he was shot, although Zagaria never saw the weapon. Hans said he drove Bostic's car, with Kevin following in another, to the parking lot at the rear of the Sears store located on Lorain near West 110th Street. Zagaria asked them who watched the body while they were gone, with so many of the workers still around. Graewe and McTaggart replied that they left Fritz Graewe there to make sure none of the workers walked down the stairs to the basement.

Zagaria was still irate about the recklessness McTaggart and Graewe had shown when they killed Bostic. He noticed that Kevin was beginning to get very nervous about what he had done. Carmen again said to Graewe and McTaggart that he would not assist them in disposing of the body and that he was leaving. At this point, Hans turned to his brother, "Fritz, go get the ambulance. We've got an emergency." He handed him the keys. Zagaria explained to us that Hans referred to his Volkswagen bus as "the ambulance."

Fritz took the keys and within a few minutes he pulled the Volkswagen near the rear door of the fish store. Hans then said to Fritz, "Give me my surgical tools." Before he left, Zagaria saw Fritz give Hans a bag from the vehicle. Hans chuckled, "I've got to serve my apprenticeship. No, I mean my internship," as he walked down the stairs to the basement. Within a few minutes, Zagaria heard chopping noises coming from the vicinity of where he had last seen Bostic's body, near the rear door. He asked Fritz, "What's that noise?" Fritz laughed, "He's a real corker."

McTaggart smiled. "Papa's down there on his internship." Carmen walked down the basement stairs until he was in a position to see Hans holding a fifteen-inch long meat cleaver in his right hand raised over Bostic's left hand. At that instant, Carmen said, he turned away and began walking back up the stairs when he heard the apparent strike of the cleaver.

Reaching the top of the stairs, he asked McTaggart, "Do you know what he's doing?" Kevin laughed, "Yep. Papa's serving his internship in the basement of a tropical fish store." Carmen turned away and said he was going home. But McTaggart asked if he would wait until Bostic's body was loaded into the bus. Visibly upset, Zagaria said softly, "You guys are nuts. Hans doesn't have any respect for me or you anymore and we're all going to end up in prison."

Ascending the stairs, Hans said to Zagaria, "I didn't mean anything but the guy made me sick." He added, "Carmen, I didn't kill him. Kevin did and Kevin's in a lot of trouble. I can only get it for malpractice. Operating without a license."

At about 6:00 P.M., McTaggart and Fritz and Hans Graewe returned to the basement to begin the job of bringing Bostic's body up the stairs. They shouted to Carmen, who remained on the first floor, for assistance. Again, he refused to help. Then Fritz noticed an old mattress in a corner of the basement and pulled it over to Bostic's body. The three placed the corpse on it and carried it upstairs. Carmen refused to look at the bloody torso as it was brought up. Hans laughed, "Go ahead and look at him. He looks like a turkey." The mattress bearing Bostic's dismembered body was then placed in Hans's Volkswagen bus and covered with insulation and a piece of plywood from the construction area of the building. While Carmen stood some distance away, Hans approached him from behind, grabbed Zagaria's hand, and shoved it into the bucket containing Bostic's hand and blood. Hans laughed, "Your buddy wants to shake your hand goodbye." Stunned, Carmen instinctively withdrew his hand, now covered with blood, and he realized what Hans had done to him. Hans and Fritz roared with laughter.

Hans handed the bucket to Fritz and told him to put it next to the body inside the Volkswagen bus. When Fritz placed the bucket toward the rear of the bus, Hans said, "No. I think I want him to ride up front with me." At that, Fritz retrieved the bucket and placed it on the floor of the bus in front of the passenger seat.

Prior to this, Hans Graewe chuckled to the others that he had "a helluva time" cutting through the back of Bostic's head. In order to decapitate the body, he rolled Bostic over onto his back and slit his throat with the knife so it would "open up like a hinge." Hans explained he used the cleaver to decapitate Bostic from the front of his neck. "Now I know how to do it," he told the others seriously. He then sent Fritz down to the basement to retrieve his "surgical tools." The tools, including the .38 murder weapon, were brought up and placed in the bus. Zagaria watched in disbelief as Hans drove away alone in his bus. Fritz and Kevin followed in another vehicle.

Shortly after they left, Carmen suddenly realized he was all alone in the fish store with Bostic's blood still spattered all over the basement floor and walls. Carmen locked the place up and returned home until nine or ten o'clock that evening. After a shower, he drove to the Country Kitchen, located on 150th Street. At about 10:30 P.M. he was paged by Kevin McTaggart. Zagaria immediately returned the call and McTaggart said casually, "Everything went okay. We got rid of that thing. We'd have called sooner but it would have been long distance." The next morning, at approximately ten o'clock, Zagaria went back to the fish store and found Fritz Graewe washing the basement floor and walls and picking up bone chips and pieces of flesh. Fritz smiled after showing him the bone pieces, "I should take these home to my dog." Carmen didn't respond. He walked over to the broken pipe and diverted the water that was still spewing out to wash down the area of all traces of Bostic's remains. The water then washed out through a drain hole.

Several days later, Carmen met with McTaggart and Hans Graewe at the Golden Anchor Bar, at which time they explained how they disposed of Bostic's body. Hans said they drove east and parked near a swamp where he handed Bostic's head to Fritz to throw into the murky waters. Apparently, Fritz didn't toss the head far enough because Hans made him wade out to where the head had landed in order to throw it further into the swamp. Hans laughed as he told Zagaria, "We gave the gloves (hands) to Fritz's dog to eat."

Carmen wasn't certain, however, if this had really been done. Hans added that they dumped Bostic's torso about twenty feet from the road in an area where there were a lot of trees and greenery. "I don't give a damn if the body is found because then everyone will know I'm serious."

Special Agent John Summer later went to the fish store, where he was successful in locating dried blood belonging to Billy Bostic.

About a year after Bostic was murdered, Carmen saw Fritz Graewe at the Golden Anchor celebrating his anniversary with his wife. At that time, Fritz was wearing Bostic's diamond ring with the initials "W.B."

CURTIS CONLEY MURDER

One time, while attending a meeting at the Golden Anchor, Carmen Zagaria and Kevin McTaggart learned that a competing drug dealer named Curtis Conley had offered a contract to kill Kevin McTaggart. The payment for the hit on McTaggart was to be an unspecified amount of cash and some cocaine. Neither Carmen nor Kevin had any idea why Conley would want McTaggart dead. Their guess was that Conley may have thought McTaggart was part of a previous cocaine rip-off that in fact had been conducted by Jimmy Coppola. A short time later, Carmen received a telephone call from Cleveland hoodlum Tony Occhionero requesting a meeting with Zagaria at the Howard Johnson hotel in the University Circle area of Cleveland. At the meeting, Occhionero informed Zagaria that Conley had offered him $20,000 or a pound of cocaine to kill McTaggart, and an additional $25,000 or the remainder of the kilo to kill Carmen Zagaria. Zagaria asked Occhionero if he would talk with Conley to explain that Zagaria was not responsible for the drug rip-off.

As a consequence, a meeting was set up with Curtis Conley, Kevin McTaggart, Tony Occhionero, and others at the L and K Restaurant in Berea, a suburb south of Cleveland. Zagaria said that he explained to Conley that he had nothing to do with the drug rip-off. Zagaria believed he was under FBI surveillance so he cut the meeting short. Nonetheless, all the participants felt that the hits on McTaggart and Zagaria had been rescinded and would no longer be sought.

About a month later, in June 1980, however, Joe Gallo called Zagaria and asked him to bring McTaggart over to his (Gallo's) office in Orange Village, on Cleveland's East Side. After arriving, Zagaria was pulled aside by Gallo, who told him that Conley had approached a friend of his to kill McTaggart for $20,000. Zagaria asked Gallo to tell McTaggart the same story and Gallo did so.

Two or three days later, Occhionero again met with Carmen at a Denny's Restaurant located on West 150th Street and informed him that Conley had again approached him to kill McTaggart for a pound of cocaine. Occhionero said that if he killed McTaggart, Conley would double the payment to hit Carmen. Conley even provided Occhionero with a floor plan of the Golden Anchor Lounge showing how easily he could set up McTaggart and Zagaria for the kill.

Occhionero offered to have Conley sit down with Zagaria in an effort to calm Conley down. He said that he had to leave to meet with Curtis at the Dutch Pantry, located down the street.

Zagaria called Kevin and asked him to come over immediately. Shortly thereafter, they drove over to the Dutch Pantry and saw Tony Occhionero meeting with Curtis Conley. They then saw Conley and Occhionero climb into Conley's black Chevrolet and drive north on West 150th Street to Lorain and from there to West 130th Street, in the vicinity of McTaggart's home. It was obvious that Curtis was showing Tony where Kevin lived, as well as other areas frequented by McTaggart, to assist in the hit he believed Occhionero was going to do for him. After watching Conley point out various locations frequented by McTaggart, Carmen and Kevin then saw them drive to the vicinity of Zagaria's residence and saw Conley point it out to Occhionero.

In early July Occhionero again met with Carmen and showed him diagrams provided by Conley for the hits on Zagaria and McTaggart, which Conley wanted done at the Golden Anchor Bar. Occhionero said he would be glad to set up Conley at a meeting in Occhionero's warehouse on 123rd Street. His plan was simple.

Occhionero would tell Conley that he would be willing to take the contract if Conley provided him with the pound of cocaine prior to the actual murder of McTaggart. After Occhionero took the cocaine from Conley, Zagaria and McTaggart could take care of Conley any way they wanted.

Two days before Conley's murder, Zagaria had a conversation with Joe

Gallo on the East Side of Cleveland near Gallo's office. During their talk, Joe suggested that Carmen "go along with Tony Occhionero and take care of business." Gallo continued, "Tony has the setup. Don't take anyone along with you. If you need someone, I'll go with you." Tony would entice Conley into leaving the cocaine with him, explaining that it would be given to James Licavoli. Carmen said he thought this would give Conley the impression that Licavoli was in on the deal and approved the killing of McTaggart and that he might also be willing to engage in future cocaine deals with him.

In early July 1980 Zagaria picked up McTaggart at his house on West 130th Street. Kevin armed himself with .38 caliber and .32 caliber pistols. Then the two drove over to Occhionero's warehouse on East 123rd Street. Tony, who was awaiting their arrival, suggested that Zagaria and McTaggart "blast" Conley inside the warehouse; Carmen felt that a severe beating and a rip-off of Conley's cocaine would be sufficient to stop him taking out contracts on others, the three nonetheless decided to kill him there. By prior agreement, Occhionero would get the pound of cocaine brought by Conley. McTaggart, armed with the .32 revolver, handed Zagaria the .38. He commented that this was the same weapon used to murder Ritson and Bostic. It was also agreed that if Conley somehow survived, Tony would keep the pound of cocaine. As they conversed, Zagaria discovered there were only three .38 rounds in the revolver.

Occhionero offered him two .38 caliber wadcutter rounds, explaining that they were in fact "dum-dum" rounds. ("Wadcutter" bullets are rounds produced for target practice. The projectile is flat on the end so that the bullet makes a clean hole in the target.) As the three men waited for Conley to arrive, Tony suddenly became very agitated and started shooting his .22 caliber automatic into the walls and ceiling of his warehouse. Zagaria was concerned about the noise since there was a towing service next door. In order to get rid of the two mechanics who strolled out of their building to find out what the racket was all about, Carmen telephoned the towing service and claimed his car had broken down in a remote area of Cleveland and needed immediate assistance. He said he'd pay anything to have them come and get his car started. The two mechanics left immediately.

After this call, Tony telephoned Conley's house and learned that Curtis was on his way. Occhionero, Zagaria, and McTaggart decided that Tony would initially greet Conley inside the warehouse and send him into the back office. Meanwhile, Zagaria and McTaggart would hide in the office's patio area immediately to the right of the warehouse overhead doors. They would then "do whatever they had to do," and Tony would leave with the cocaine.

About half an hour later, Conley pulled up to the warehouse and knocked on the door. Tony suggested he drive his black Chevrolet into the warehouse and park it there. After Conley climbed out of his car, the two discussed the drug deal for about ten minutes before Tony asked him to come into the office with him.

As Conley entered the office, he saw Zagaria crouched down in the patio area and became very frightened. Zagaria claimed that he rotated the cylinder of his revolver so that the first two shots into Conley's chest were of the wadcutter rounds. After he fired, Conley instantly turned and raced through the warehouse to his car and a parked truck near the door. While he was running, Zagaria fired the remainder of his rounds at Conley as the petrified man attempted to hide under the truck. Zagaria walked over and pulled Conley out from underneath the truck and began to beat him up. After hitting him in the head and face several times with his fists, Zagaria called Kevin and said, "I think you've got a bone to pick with this guy." Zagaria again struck Conley, who had fallen to the floor in a daze. Upon seeing McTaggart approaching, he said in a low voice, "Kevin, take the stuff and leave me alone. I didn't mean nothing."

With his gun raised, Kevin shouted, "Move, Carmen," and shot Conley in the side, slightly to the rear of his right arm. Conley continued to struggle as if the shot had no effect on him and he again attempted to crawl under the truck. Zagaria again pulled him back, at which point McTaggart grabbed Conley by the forehead and shot him in the back of his head near the neck with his .32 caliber revolver. Zagaria did not believe that McTaggart's .32 round exited Conley's head. Conley died instantly as Kevin fired the second shot into him. Shortly after the second shot, McTaggart became very nervous and, according to Zagaria, appeared on the verge of crying. Carmen asked, "Why did you shoot him the second time, Kevin?" McTaggart answered, "He was running out of gas, so I just finished him." Kevin must have believed that Zagaria had already fired several shots into Conley and that he was simply finishing him off.

Now McTaggart wanted to leave the warehouse. Carmen said, "No. Are you nuts? We have to do something with the body." The two then carried the corpse back to Conley's vehicle and placed it near the trunk. At that point, Occhionero returned and asked, "Is everything over?" When they searched Conley's body for the keys to the trunk they could not find them. About a half hour later the keys were located on the warehouse floor near the office. They then opened the trunk and threw Conley's body in.

McTaggart took Conley's wristwatch off and Occhionero removed the ring Conley was wearing. Conley's hairpiece had fallen off during the struggle and McTaggart found it under the truck where Curtis had attempted to hide. Zagaria agreed to drive Conley's car—containing his corpse—to wherever Occhionero wanted to take it.

From the warehouse, Zagaria drove to the Sheraton Hotel in the vicinity of Euclid and Interstate 271 on Cleveland's East Side. He parked the vehicle in the hotel's parking lot near the side entrance, locked it, and waited for Kevin to arrive. McTaggart was supposed to have been following Zagaria with Occhionero but it wasn't until several minutes later that he arrived alone. While he was waiting for Kevin to arrive, and because he noticed that a puddle of blood was forming under the trunk of Conley's car, Carmen decided to move the vehicle again. From the parking lot, Zagaria drove south on Interstate 271 and got off at the Bishop Road exit. He parked the car in the Poppin' Fresh Pie store parking lot between Bishop and Chardon Roads. The car was parked in a space where the trunk extended over a grass strip. McTaggart, who had followed him, picked up Zagaria and drove him back to the warehouse so they could give the keys to Conley's car to Occhionero for disposal, but upon arriving they discovered that Tony wasn't there. Unable to reach him by telephone at the Howard Johnson Restaurant near East 105th Street, the two returned to their respective homes.

Later that night, Occhionero called Zagaria and asked him to come to the Dutch Pantry on West 150th Street right away. Zagaria drove over and handed over Conley's car keys. The two agreed to meet the following day, July

6, 1980, at around noon. Late the next morning, Zagaria and McTaggart drove to the Soho gas station located on Vrooman Road near the exit of Interstate 90, where they met Occhionero. During their brief meeting, Tony told them that he had buried Conley in a shallow grave nearby. He claimed that he had to break Curtis's legs in order to get them to fit into the grave.

Carmen asked if anyone had helped him, and Occhionero replied that he had done it alone. Zagaria said nothing but felt that Occhionero could not have accomplished the job alone. He believed that Joe "Joe Loose" Iacobacci had helped Occhionero bury Conley. Occhionero also claimed that he had moved Conley's car and washed it of all the blood and traces from Conley's body.

Zagaria said that Occhionero then turned to McTaggart and said, "You ought to give me Conley's watch." McTaggart retorted, "You got the ring." Kevin turned to Carmen and offered to sell the watch to him for $1,000. Zagaria, however, said the watch was probably worth much more and offered to give him $1,250. McTaggart gladly accepted the offer.

At this point, Occhionero told Zagaria that he would sell him the pound of cocaine that he took from Conley for $20,000. The three then got into Carmen's car and drove a short distance away down a private road, where Zagaria tested the cocaine's quality. Even though Zagaria determined that the cocaine was of poor quality, the next day he agreed to pay Tony $20,000 for it. About a month later, Zagaria paid Tony the $20,000 for the coke. Kevin later met Carmen at the Golden Anchor Lounge and sold him Conley's wristwatch for the agreed-upon price of $1,250. Later, the watch would be appraised at $5,800 by Seivert's Jewelers.

DAVID PERRIER MURDER

Carmen had met David Perrier in the fall of 1980 at the Dutch Pantry, where LCN capo Tom Sinito introduced him to Zagaria and Tim Van Newhouse. Zagaria had arranged to have ten pounds of marijuana delivered to Perrier, who was dealing drugs for Sinito. In mid-December 1980 Zagaria was sitting with Sinito and Gallo at the Country Kitchen on West

150th when Perrier, who had been sitting at a side bar, started making insulting remarks about "the old man," James Licavoli. When Perrier complained out loud that Licavoli had not buried anybody in a long time, Sinito was forced to settle everybody down at the bar and take Perrier aside and talk to him. Sinito returned to the bar and said that the police were surveilling him.

About three or four days later, Zagaria met with Sinito at Cleveland's Pesano's Restaurant. Sinito said that Perrier had apologized to James Licavoli, kissing Licavoli's feet and hands. Sinito added that Perrier was basically a reliable guy who had collected on loans for Sinito. Furthermore, he had been Sinito's bodyguard in the past. But now he was "going backward, just like Keith Ritson."

Toward the end of December, Zagaria again met with Sinito in order to make another payment of marijuana and gambling profits. Again, Sinito brought up Perrier, who he said was tough and a "good guy to have on your side. . . . But the son of a bitch is getting out of line again. He's bad mouthing everybody, beating up his ex-wife, and spitting in the face of Paul Lish, an old-timer who lives with Licavoli." Sinito explained that several weeks before, Perrier had gotten into an argument with Paul Ciraculla, also known as Paul Lish, at the Italian-American Brotherhood Club and ended up spitting in his face. Sinito feared that the FBI would learn of this incident and begin putting pressure on Perrier to talk. If this happened, Sinito believed Perrier would turn on him. Sinito added that if things didn't work out they may have to put Perrier "where Ritson is." He then asked, "Is there room where Ritson is?"

In the last week of December Sinito called Zagaria at his house and said that things had not worked out the way they hoped and that he would meet Perrier one last time to straighten things out. About a day later, Zagaria met Sinito and Gallo. Sinito said he had driven Perrier to Angelo Lonardo's home in an attempt to have Perrier apologize to Lonardo personally for his prior acts. Instead, Perrier argued with Lonardo. Lonardo was so incensed that he wanted to kill Perrier right there in his own garage. Sinito was able to pacify Lonardo despite the fact that Perrier had not cooled down and was shouting that he had buried a lot of people and had never been adequately compensated. Sinito said that he would probably have to kill Perrier and asked Zagaria if he knew of any deep holes or water where he could dump Perrier.

Carmen told Sinito to bring Perrier's corpse to the fish store and he would help dispose of it. Sinito again asked Zagaria for help and Carmen said that if Sinito could not find anybody else he would assist him. Sinito then suggested that he lure Perrier to Zagaria's building on West Ninety-fourth and that either he or Carmen could shoot him. Sinito added, however, that he had some things to do for the holidays and would have to postpone the killing until after New Year's.

On or about the morning of January 2, 1981, Sinito called Zagaria at home and said he would "bring the guy down to the building to put the kitchen in," meaning that he would bring Perrier to Zagaria's building. Carmen asked Sinito to call him back at the Golden Anchor Bar at around noon. Sinito called later to say that "the guy couldn't make it," postponing matters until the next day. The following day, Sinito called Zagaria and arranged to meet him at 2:00 P.M. at the Golden Anchor.

To Linda Potter, who was the barmaid, Sinito appeared very pale and nervous. Sinito told Carmen that James Licavoli and Angelo Lonardo wanted Perrier killed. He asked if he could take a look at Zagaria's building, which meant that Zagaria had to stop by his house and get the keys. Arriving at the building, they went inside. Sinito suggested that when he brought Perrier to the site either he would shoot Perrier or Zagaria would be waiting there and would shoot Perrier. Sinito said that Angelo Lonardo had told him to take Zagaria along on the murder since Zagaria would know what to do and could be trusted. Sinito and Zagaria left the building, devising a scheme that consisted of putting Perrier's body into his own car and then parking Perrier's car somewhere where it would be found. Sinito told Carmen that "both Jack and Ang" would appreciate Zagaria's assistance and that Zagaria could name his price for the assistance. Zagaria could take either Fritz or Hans Graewe along and, if he did, pay them whatever they wanted. Sinito then dropped Carmen off at the Golden Anchor.

The following day, Sinito again called Zagaria at his home and said that the guy who would "fix the kitchen" would accompany Sinito to Zagaria's building at around 1:00 P.M. They arranged for Sinito to enter through the back door.

Carmen arrived at the building at about 12:45 P.M. and found the back door lock frozen shut. Zagaria walked over to Ohio Freight, next door, and purchased a flashlight and batteries. He then entered his building through the front door and, using the flashlight, made his way through the basement of the building and opened the rear door through which Sinito was to bring Perrier. When Zagaria opened the door, Sinito was standing there.

He explained that he and Perrier were on their way to Zagaria's building in Perrier's car when the car broke down at the Soho gas station on West Boulevard and Lorain. Sinito walked over to Zagaria's building from there. Sinito showed Carmen the small .22 caliber revolver he was carrying.

Sinito expressed concern about using Perrier's car to dispose of his body. Sinito asked if Carmen knew of a spot where they could dump Perrier. Zagaria said that because of the extreme cold, any water would be frozen over. Sinito suggested that Carmen call Fritz Graewe and that Graewe's truck be used.

Zagaria suggested they put the matter off until the next day and that he would then be able to get Hans to assist. Sinito, however, was anxious and replied that he was still under tremendous pressure from "the old guys" to kill Perrier. Zagaria and Sinito then drove over to the Soho station in Zagaria's car and picked up Perrier, who had arranged to have his vehicle towed over to the East Side.

Zagaria learned from Perrier that Sinito had promised to provide him with a hundred pounds of marijuana, fifty thousand amphetamine pills, and a couple of kilos of cocaine that was stored in Carmen's basement. Perrier was concerned over how he was going to transport so much dope. The three men then drove over to the Country Kitchen Restaurant on West 150th. At the Country Kitchen, Zagaria agreed to find another vehicle. He tried calling Fritz, but could not reach him and feigned calling others. Perrier then called a cousin who agreed to allow him the use of his car. He was to bring the car to the Country Kitchen. Since Zagaria did not want this cousin to see him, Carmen told Perrier that he and Sinito would meet him at the Soho station.

Sinito and Zagaria proceeded to the Soho station and Perrier later pulled into the parking lot of the Olliger Drugstore, which was across the street. Perrier got into Zagaria's vehicle and the two drove to the nearby Snow White Donut Shop. Perrier said he had a location on West Sixty-fifth Street where he could stash the narcotics. Sinito pulled Zagaria to one side and asked if they could kill Perrier in the garage of Zagaria's building, leaving Hans to dispose of the body the following day.

Zagaria told Sinito that if they did, one of Zagaria's workers was likely to discover the corpse, although he knew there were few people working in the building at that time. While Sinito was making three or four phone calls, Perrier told Zagaria, "Nobody, including Jack and Ang, appreciate what I've done, except for Sinito. I've buried ten or twelve people, driven bomb cars in the bombing of Nardi and Greene. In fact, it was Sinito who picked me up after the Greene bombing."

After Sinito finished making his calls, Perrier said he needed to make a call. As he did, Sinito told Carmen that he had just talked to "the other guys" and they said he had no choice but to kill Perrier. Sinito offered Zagaria Perrier's ring for his immediate help.

Sinito suggested that Carmen call Hans or Fritz Graewe to set things up. Zagaria called Fritz and asked if Hans was at home and if Fritz would assist Zagaria in a "job" the following day. After that call, Zagaria told Sinito that the next day he would have a vehicle, plus Fritz and Hans Graewe, and the three would handle the matter. Zagaria dropped Sinito and Perrier off where Perrier's cousin's car was parked. Off to the side, Zagaria whispered to Sinito that he would have Hans and Fritz in place to take care of the matter. Sinito would not have to do anything.

The following morning, Zagaria received a telephone call from Sinito, who said that "the other guy decided to take off last night" and that he would meet Zagaria at the Poppin' Fresh Restaurant on Northfield Road at noon. Later that morning, Hans arrived at Zagaria's and said that Fritz had called him to say that Carmen had a "job" for him.

Graewe and Zagaria then drove to the Poppin' Fresh Restaurant to meet with Sinito and Joe Gallo. Sinito was pale and shaking visibly. Graewe sat by himself while Zagaria talked to Gallo and Sinito. Sinito explained that he had killed "that punk" Perrier. Apparently, Sinito emptied his .22 into Perrier but he did not die, so he had to shoot Perrier with his .38. He said he drove Perrier outside of Cleveland where he threw Perrier's body into a ditch. He drove around for several hours, then returned to ensure that Perrier was in fact dead. Sinito said that at one point Perrier had put his hands up to his face and asked him not to shoot him anymore. "Just let me die in peace," he begged.

Gallo said he was surprised that Sinito had it in him to kill. He suggested that Sinito get drunk, which is what Gallo did after he killed someone.

A few days later, Carmen was at the Golden Anchor when Perrier's girlfriend, Linda Potter, came in, looked around, and walked straight up to Zagaria and McTaggart. She said she knew all about what had happened, and not from what she had read about Perrier in the newspapers. Carmen told Potter that he didn't know Perrier. Carmen turned away, commenting that he didn't know anything about Perrier or his disappearance.

JOE GIAMO MURDER

Meanwhile, in the late summer of 1980, Joe Giamo, who lived outside of Miami and was a major narcotics source for Tom Sinito, was introduced to Zagaria and soon became one of his major drug sources. During one of the drug transactions, Giamo suggested to Zagaria that he should deal directly with him, thereby cutting out Sinito and Gallo. Fearing this was a "test," he immediately went to Gallo and told him what Giamo had suggested.

Sinito was outraged and demanded they not only rip off a large quantity of narcotics from Giamo, but also torture and kill him.

In September 1980 Sinito tried to convince Gallo and Zagaria to go along with the plan. However, Zagaria didn't like the idea. He argued that even though he had numerous problems with Giamo on various narcotics deals, and numerous arguments over payments and the quality of the narcotics, Zagaria still felt that Giamo was an "all right guy."

Sinito piped up that Zagaria owed the "old men," James Licavoli and

Angelo Lonardo, a lot of money and this proposed rip-off murder was the way that he could make things even. Zagaria explained that they were splitting the narcotics profits evenly, one-third each, and as a result he would be getting nothing for doing all the work and taking all the hassles for killing Giamo.

Sinito answered that if Zagaria would take care of Giamo, he and Gallo would give him an additional $30,000. Zagaria admitted he was currently $11,000 behind on interest payments to the "old men." Finally, Sinito told Zagaria that if he helped sponsor the rip-off murder plan, they would be even. Zagaria agreed to do the deed.

Carmen confirmed that Hans would be with him at his residence when he contacted Giamo to set up a meeting at the fish store at 8:00 that night. Later, Hans and Carmen left Zagaria's residence and drove over to the Golden Anchor in order to not only establish an alibi but also to provide Zagaria with an excuse to show up late for the 8:00 P.M. meeting. Zagaria and Graewe then drove from the Golden Anchor to the fish store and arrived there shortly after 9:00 P.M., parking next to the new garage in the rear of the fish store. Carmen and Hans entered the store and went to a room located between the garage and the store.

There, Zagaria started his "torpedo" heater to warm up the room. After a few minutes inside the office of the fish store, Carmen excused himself to use the telephone located in another area of the store. He had to walk through the garage in order to get to the phone.

While he was doing this, Giamo walked up to him and began a discussion, which quickly became an argument because Zagaria had been over an hour late for their eight o'clock meeting. Knowing that Hans Graewe was in the store ready to kill Giamo, Zagaria tried to irritate Giamo to the point that he would leave.

But Giamo asked if they could go into the fish store since it was so cold. Zagaria refused. Giamo then accused Zagaria of trying to cheat him by hiding things in the garage. Giamo persisted to the point where Zagaria walked into the garage area and continued the argument. At this point, Giamo could hear the torpedo heater in the office and insisted that something was going on inside the building.

Whatever it was, Giamo wanted to see it. So Giamo and Zagaria entered the room between the garage and the fish store that contained the heater. The argument continued, along with another one about wet marijuana. It seems that Zagaria didn't have a place to heat and dry out the marijuana with the exception of the small room that they were standing in. Zagaria stepped back, remaining on the side of the room closest to the exit door. The heater was located close to Giamo, who was standing near the door leading into the store. The argument grew in intensity.

Suddenly, Giamo pulled out a .38 automatic and began shaking the gun at Zagaria, shouting about how tough he was. Giamo said that it had taken him twenty years to get rid of his reputation and that Zagaria and Sinito were not as bad. Giamo ranted on and on about how the two were screwing him.

At that point, Hans shot Giamo in the back of the head with a .22 rifle from the other side of the room. Giamo fell backward toward Graewe, and his gun, which had been pointing in the air, went off. Zagaria remembered hearing glass breaking in the other room and assumed that one of the two front windows had been shot out by Giamo's bullet.

Giamo fell so that his bloodied head lay in the doorway between the back room and the fish store area. His gun fell to the floor and slid away. Zagaria saw that Graewe had taken a position at the end of a partition in the fish store and had fired the .22 rifle from there.

Hans walked a short distance away and climbed up on a stack of lumber in the fish store area. From this new spot, he aimed the rifle and shot Giamo in the head three more times. Zagaria asked Graewe what he was doing and Hans replied, "I'm dotting the eyes." Climbing down from the stack of lumber and slowly approaching Giamo, Hans placed the muzzle of the rifle to Giamo's chest near the heart and fired two additional rounds into the corpse. Graewe noticed a slight vapor emanating from the blood oozing out of Giamo's body and commented, "You're really smoking, Joe." Hans then went through Giamo's pockets and removed his jewelry, which consisted of a watch, a ring with what appeared to be a diamond, and a crucifix. Hans placed a piece of insulation under the dead man's head and made several comments about Giamo's having had a weapon with him.

As Zagaria looked away from the body, Hans picked up a piece of clotting blood and placed it on Zagaria's arm. Zagaria was infuriated and complained about Giamo's having killed there in the fish store. He also said they hadn't prepared for hiding the body or cleaning up the mess.

Zagaria retrieved a water heater carton from the basement, placed several pieces of insulation in it, and placed Giamo's body into the carton. They carried it to a corner near the back door; they would worry about it later.

Carmen and Hans wiped up as much of the blood as they could, pouring twelve to fifteen bottles of drain cleaner on the blood-stained floor. Graewe picked up the six empty shell casings near the stack of lumber in the front part of the store. The rifle and Giamo's body remained in the store overnight.

Shortly after the killing, while Graewe was doing most of the cleanup work, Zagaria walked out and started Giamo's car, driving it to Ninety-fifth Street near Denison, where he parked it. Zagaria then walked back to assist Graewe. Carmen estimated that it required some forty-five minutes to move the car, clean up the fish store, and hide the body.

Later, Zagaria drove Giamo's late-model black car to the airport and placed it in the short-term parking area. Hans followed Carmen in Zagaria's vehicle. After picking Zagaria up, Hans drove to the Golden Anchor to reestablish their alibis for the evening. Carmen estimated they arrived at the Golden Anchor about 11:30 P.M. While at the Golden Anchor, he telephoned Joe Gallo and told him that "the package had been mailed." After Zagaria allowed himself to be seen in the Golden Anchor, he returned home and went to bed.

The following morning, a Sunday, Zagaria picked up Hans and they proceeded to the fish store. It was about 9:00 A.M. Fritz Graewe arrived a short time later in his red pickup truck to help dispose of the body. The three discussed whether Giamo's body should be disposed of in the same manner as Ritson's body was, that is, dumping him in a Cleveland area quarry. It was agreed that the quarries would probably be frozen at that time of the year. Fritz suggested they just dump the body and let the authorities find it. But Zagaria was completely against that idea. He wanted the body hidden. Carmen decided that he would conceal it in the basement area of his building at Ninety-fourth and Lorain. He would place the body against a wall and build a room around him. Fritz was given a hundred dollars and sent to the K-Mart on West Sixty-fifth to purchase sand with which to cover the body.

Once Fritz returned with the bags of sand, a sand bed about four inches thick was poured and the box with Giamo inside was placed on the sand base. The top of the box was cut open and additional sand was placed inside with the body. Sand was also placed above the box to a height of approximately five feet. A framework of two-by-twos and plywood was then placed on the outer edge so the sand would not slip over. On top of the five feet of sand which contained the box with Giamo's body, debris such as broken equipment and machines, including old juke boxes, as well as other garbage was placed on top until it reached the ceiling level. All of this was again braced with two-by-twos and plywood. After completing Giamo's creative grave, that is, roughing it in with the two-by-twos and plywood, the Graewe brothers and Zagaria broke off for the day.

The following morning, they returned and constructed a brick wall around Giamo's body. Suddenly, Zagaria's main concern was the grave's location. Since he had been getting a lot of heat from the FBI lately, it eventually dawned on him that the body could easily be found in a raid or if he went to jail and had to sell or remodel the building.

So, in early December 1981, Hans and Carmen removed Giamo's body from the wall in order to dump it in the Jacquay quarry. They were both amazed that the body was still in good condition. They tied the remains up with wire and put them into the trunk of a borrowed Cadillac. When they were within about a quarter of a mile from the quarry, they ran out of gas. Since Hans and Carmen were concerned about leaving the vehicle alone with the body in it, they decided to push the vehicle to the quarry. There, they maneuvered the vehicle off to the side of the road, took Giamo's remains out of the trunk, and began to drag them to the quarry. Because of the muddy conditions, they encountered difficulty in carrying the body, so Graewe returned to the Cadillac, opened the trunk, and pulled out a sledgehammer and a double-edged ax. When he returned, he placed both on top of the remains and the two dragged the collection an additional thirty yards. Then, exhausted, they stopped.

Graewe asked Zagaria to check on the car. Carmen did so and when he returned he found Graewe whacking Giamo's head off with the sledgehammer. Hans smashed Giamo's head two or three times in this manner. Angrily, Zagaria grabbed both the sledgehammer and the double-edged ax and tossed them into the water in the quarry.

Hans explained that he was knocking the head off so that the bullets in Giamo's brain would fall out. He said this was necessary since the gun which he had used to kill Giamo was at Fritz's house. Graewe and Zagaria then threw Giamo's remains into the water. The unweighted body floated in the water. Hans and Carmen returned to the car where they discussed what to do with the car.

They walked about two miles to a bar. There, Hans called Fritz to come and pick them up. When Fritz arrived, the three drove back to the quarry with a full can of gas and attempted to start the car. While this was taking place, a police car pulled up, undoubtedly because the officer wanted to see what the trouble was. When Zagaria spotted the patrol car, he panicked and ran into the trees to hide.

As the police car came to a halt behind the black Cadillac, Hans started it, waved at the cop, and drove off, leaving Zagaria in the woods. Zagaria stayed hidden in the woods near the quarry for the remainder of the night until Hans returned at about five o'clock the next morning.

During the night, Zagaria was scared because of activity in and around the quarry. Carmen said that a police car drove by periodically. On one occasion, the police officer parked his vehicle near the quarry, rolled down his window, and spoke to a young woman who was also parked near the quarry. Zagaria believed that no one noticed Giamo's body floating in the quarry, or there would have been a huge commotion.

By the time Hans picked him up, Carmen was almost frozen because of his all-night vigil. The two decided to drive to Lawson's Hardware, located near the Blue Dolphin, in order to purchase some rope so they could retrieve Giamo's body.

There was no rope available at Lawson's, but as they climbed back in the car, a Cleveland *Plain Dealer* newspaper truck pulled in and Zagaria was able to obtain four feet of twine from the driver. They returned to the quarry and tied the twine together to form a rope.

They tied a tire iron to the end of the rope, and they were able to throw it out and latch on to Giamo's body. They dragged the body to a corner of the quarry and there they piled rocks on it to hide it from view.

Several weeks later they returned to the quarry with three stolen manhole covers and more wire. Hans said he wanted to chop off Giamo's jaw so he could hang it in his barn. Zagaria said, "Sure," but asked Hans if he could borrow his hatchet for a moment. When Graewe handed him the hatchet, Carmen heaved it into the quarry. While they were attempting to tie the manhole covers to the body, there was a snowmobile accident in a field next to the quarry and the two had to hide behind the body. Police and an ambulance arrived to aid the snowmobile victim.

After the police left, and as Hans and Carmen were attempting to finish the job, two little girls began walking around the quarry. Abruptly, the two men decided to leave and come back the next morning. The following morning, Zagaria and Hans returned to the quarry, wired the manhole covers to the body, and returned it to the water. This time the body sank.

"DAVID" MURDER

Carmen said that another murder was committed earlier, in November of 1979, but he did not know the victim's full name. His first name was David. Sinito called Zagaria and informed him that one of his drug suppliers, David, was in Cleveland with a kilo of cocaine for sale. On the following day, Sinito and Carmen went to David's hotel room, where Sinito made the introductions. Zagaria agreed to buy the cocaine in two installments. Because the first shipment was of very poor quality, Zagaria and Graewe decided they would rip David off on the second installment. After Zagaria bought the cocaine from David for $57,800, David left for New York and, after a short stopover, he returned to Florida.

When David called to say he was returning to Cleveland with the second cocaine shipment, Hans and Carmen decided to put their plan into motion. Zagaria told Kevin McTaggart of their plan to steal the cocaine from David. Carmen invited Kevin to join them.

But when Hans learned all the details of the plan, including the fact that McTaggart was going to participate, he was infuriated with Zagaria because he didn't want to split any of the proceeds from the rip-off. Zagaria estimated that a three-way split would result in each of them receiving between $18,000 and $19,000.

Later that same night, between 10:30 and 11:00, David arrived at the Golden Anchor. After a brief conversation, Zagaria said he would meet David the next morning to purchase the cocaine. Before his meeting with David, Zagaria met with Graewe and McTaggart at a coffee shop to discuss the details of what they would do about stealing the cocaine from David.

At that point, no definite plans had yet been made to kill David. Zagaria then telephoned David at his hotel and asked that he come to the fish store immediately with his "gift." When David entered the building he was carrying an entire kilo of cocaine. Quietly awaiting his arrival were Fritz and Hans Graewe, Kevin McTaggart, and Carmen Zagaria.

Carmen tested a sample of the cocaine and felt it was of low quality, probably 50 percent purity. With David out of earshot, Zagaria asked Fritz, Kevin, and Hans what they thought should be done. Fritz spoke first: "Let me choke him with a coat hanger." Kevin was more practical and said, "Regardless of its quality, the coke can still be sold for a profit." Hans offered, "Let me just take him down to my farm and blast him."

By the end of their brief discussion, one thing was clear: They would take David to Hans's farm, where he would be murdered. Zagaria would tell him that Hans had a likely buyer for the cocaine near his farm in Guernsey County. When told of this potential new buyer, David said that to show good faith he would come down on the price of the cocaine.

After David agreed to sell his cocaine to Hans's contact, Carmen suggested he take Fritz with him in his vehicle as he followed Hans's Volkswagen van to the farm. At about noon, Hans drove off in his Volkswagen bus, with Kevin, Fritz, and David following behind him in David's car.

McTaggart drove David's car while David sat in the front passenger seat and Fritz sat in the back. Carmen, meanwhile, remained behind at the fish store.

The next day, Kevin McTaggart told Zagaria the details of how he, Fritz, and Hans killed David. Apparently, after they reached a dirt road located near Hans Graewe's farm in Guernsey County, Hans stopped his bus and told those in the other in the car that they should not drive any further because he did not want them to see where his drug buyer lived. While David was in the front passenger seat of his own car, Fritz suddenly placed a wire coat hanger around his neck and began choking him.

As David began kicking and struggling violently with Fritz, Kevin started to punch him. The hanger ultimately broke and McTaggart and Graewe ended up attempting to kick and strangle David to death on the dirt road outside the vehicle. Fritz had placed a dog leash around the semi-conscious man and choked him until he thought David was dead. Fritz suggested they run over David's head to make sure he was finished, but Kevin decided against it since it would be "too messy and he's dead anyway." Instead, the two men picked up the limp body, placed it inside the trunk of his vehicle, and drove it to Hans's farm nearby.

Upon arriving at Graewe's farm, Kevin and Fritz heard David moaning in the trunk of the car and realized that they had not killed him. McTaggart became very frightened. He quickly ran to Hans's farmhouse and, in front of Graewe's wife, Debbie, blurted out, "He's still alive!" Debbie Graewe asked, "Who's alive?" At this point it was about 4:00 P.M.

Hans became infuriated with Kevin and told his wife to get the kids and go for a ride. Confused, Debbie got their children in the car and left. Hans retrieved his .22 caliber nine-shot weapon, which he called his "nine iron," and ordered McTaggart to back David's car, with David still alive in the trunk, into Graewe's garage.

Hans handed the .22 revolver to Kevin and when the trunk lid was open, Kevin fired one shot through David's cheek and into his mouth. In close succession, he fired two more shots point-blank into David's head. Hans then grabbed the gun from Kevin and fired the remaining shots through David's heart.

According to McTaggart, all nine rounds from the .22 remained in David's body. The decision was made to dump the corpse in a remote area on a next-door neighbor's property. McTaggart told Zagaria that they drove his car up an old logging road on the neighbor's property and found a suitable location at the base of a hill. Hans followed with a backhoe and dug a four-foot hole.

David's corpse, clothed only in undershorts, was then thrown into the hole. Earlier, while going through his wallet, they found an identification card that indicated that David was Jewish. Because of this, Hans decided to smash David's skull with the backhoe shovel.

When the backhoe shovel was brought down, it struck the side of the hole and the backhoe almost tipped over with Hans at the controls. McTaggart laughed and suggested that Hans just fill the hole up and not mess around anymore.

Graewe placed four feet of dirt on the corpse, adding an additional two or three feet to the top to match the slope of the hill. David's car was then driven back to Hans's garage, where Fritz washed out the trunk to remove any traces of blood. During the entire episode, according to McTaggart, Hans was very upset with both Kevin and Fritz because of their poor performance in David's murder.

Meanwhile, Debbie returned to the house with the children and fixed lunch for everyone. Hans told her that they had shot Jimmy Coppola's dog and buried it, explaining the need to wash out the trunk of the car and use the backhoe.

McTaggart told Zagaria that Hans had taken David's suitcase and hidden it somewhere in the barn. Hans burned all of David's possessions, including his identification papers. Fritz, meanwhile, wiped down David's car of all fingerprints. According to McTaggart, the gun used to kill David was disposed of. The car was driven to Akron and left in a motel parking lot.

The day after McTaggart described the murder to Zagaria, Hans returned to Cleveland and laughingly began to tell Carmen his own version of the details. When Zagaria stopped him by saying he already knew the details, Graewe flew into a rage. "I wanted to tell you myself! That goddam Kevin! But I've been waiting so long to kill a Jew. I'm glad Hitler left some for me."

McTaggart's payoff on his split of the profits for the sale of David's cocaine was $4,000, plus an expensive wristwatch. But he owed Zagaria

$3,400, which was subtracted from his $4,000 portion of the split. Zagaria paid him the remaining $600 in twenty-dollar bills. Fritz's portion of the profits from the sale of David's kilo of cocaine was paid to him in both marijuana and cash. Hans was paid in hundred-dollar bills.

Carmen Zagaria's full cooperation with us now made the case against Angelo Lonardo and the others almost foolproof. Carmen had personal meetings with Lonardo, who had recently become boss when James Licavoli went to prison on the RICO-murder case. Using Carmen's information, we now began to secure search warrants to corroborate all the details he provided us.

Carmen Zagaria pleaded guilty to the entire indictment and his sentencing was delayed until he completed his testimony.

WE FINALLY CONVICT THE LEADERS

On October 27, 1982, we drove Zagaria to the Jacquay Road quarry located some twenty miles west of Cleveland. This quarry was as murky as one could imagine. The water was very oily, indicating that this was probably a place where cars were dumped for insurance purposes. Carmen showed us where Joseph Giamo's body had been thrown.

Special Agent Tom Kimmel, through his contacts with the U.S. Navy, made arrangements for the U.S. Navy diving team from Norfolk, Virginia, to fly into Cleveland that night to assist us in the search for Giamo's body. The following morning, divers from the FBI, the U.S. Navy diving team, and the Lorain County Sheriff's Department began the search for Giamo. The job was extremely dangerous. Under the murky water, hundreds of cars were stacked on top of each other and could topple with the slightest bump. On the first morning, one of the Navy divers became entangled in a wire screen. He was trapped for about a half hour before being rescued by others on the team. At 11:30 A.M. on October 29, we recovered the first body—that of Joseph G. Giamo. As Zagaria told us it would be, it was weighted down with several manhole covers. The two-bladed ax and sledgehammer were also recovered that day.

We then went to the LaGrange quarry and Zagaria pointed out to us the area where Keith Ritson's body, attached to the dolly, had been thrown into the water. Although we were getting a search warrant for the quarry, in order to expedite matters, we contacted LaGrange officials for permission to search the quarry. The mayor was reluctant and initially would not give us the authority to conduct the search until it was pointed out to him that this quarry was the principal source of drinking water for LaGrange residents.

This quarry was similar to the Jacquay quarry, although the water was not as dirty. On the second day of diving, we recovered Keith Ritson's body. The body was pretty well decomposed and smelled foul. I was amazed at the coroner. After the divers pulled Ritson out of the water, he walked up to the remains and began a preliminary examination. The stench was so strong that virtually all of us were gagging, but it didn't bother him. He told me later that because of his work he had long ago lost all sense of smell.

Another interesting development occurred prior to the trial in this case. The trial attorney was to be Strike Force Attorney Donna Congeni. Her brother, a Westlake, Ohio, dentist, received a threatening telephone call, which he correctly interpreted as an effort to intimidate Donna. The caller said that he would cut the brother's head off while he was still alive if Donna didn't drop the case. The brother immediately called Donna, who in turn called me. Within a half hour we placed a tracer and tap on his telephone. Then the extortionist made a critical mistake: He telephoned again and made another threat, but this time we were there listening. The threatening call was made from the home of Michael Ferrara, who lived in Westlake, a western Cleveland suburb. We secured an arrest warrant and a team of FBI agents went to his home, where he was arrested, handcuffed, and brought to the FBI office. Ferrara denied making the two telephone calls. Meanwhile, we received allegations that he was an associate of Joe Gallo. Ferrara was tried for obstruction of justice before U.S. District Court Judge John Manos. On June 21, 1983, after deliberating for less than an hour, the federal jury convicted Ferrara of having made the two calls. Judge Manos immediately remanded Ferrara to jail, allowing for no bond. Manos later sentenced Ferrara to prison.

The trial of Angelo Lonardo, Thomas Sinito, Joseph Gallo, Hartmut "Hans" Graewe, Fritz Graewe, and Kevin McTaggart for the RICO-murder and RICO-narcotics charges began in U.S. District Court, Cleveland, on November 15, 1982, before Judge John M. Manos. After opening statements, U.S. Strike Force Attorney Donna M. Congeni brought Jimmy Coppola to the stand as her first witness. He provided excellent, detailed testimony concerning how the drug ring began its association with the Cleveland LCN family. He also told about the various Florida trips to purchase drugs and described several of the murders that followed. He was on the stand for an entire day and the defense did not touch him. Then Donna's second witness, Carmen Zagaria, followed. Under direct examination he quietly described the operations of the narcotics ring and the details concerning the seven killings. Members of the jury gasped a few times when he described how each of the murders occurred. Zagaria quoted Hans Graewe after Hans had killed and cut up Billy Bostic in the basement of Zagaria's fish store: "They can get you for murder, but they can only get me for malpractice! I served my internship in your basement." Zagaria testified that when Hans returned from the basement he had a bucket, and that Hans grabbed his hand and shoved it into the bucket. When he felt a thick wetness, Zagaria looked down and saw Bostic's head and hands were in the bucket. Hans said, "Shake hands with your friend before he leaves," or words to that effect.

Zagaria was on the stand for four days. Leonard Yelsky, Lonardo's attorney, then began his cross-examination. After recalling the gruesome nature of the murders, Yelsky asked Zagaria, "Is it true that you are a murderer?" Zagaria replied, "Yes, I am." Yelsky continued by asking, "Is it true that you are an arsonist?" Again, Zagaria replied, "Yes, I am." Yelsky then asked Zagaria, "Is it true that you set fires to homes with little kids in them?" Zagaria hastily and angrily replied, with indignation, "What do you think I am, an animal?" This broke up the jury and the entire courtroom exploded with laughter.

We used a number of other relocated witnesses, including Linda Potter, Greg Hoven, and Don Newman, to make our case against Lonardo. This was Donna's first major trial and it went smoothly. She did a fabulous job.

I attended many of the trial sessions and was present when Zagaria provided his testimony. I made it a point to engage Lonardo in conversation during the court breaks and, as usual, he was very respectful and gentlemanly in my presence. He sat away from all the other defendants, attempting to appear independent of them. He was also a killer, but he was from the old school.

Donna made her closing arguments on January 19, 1983, and the case went to the jury. Five days later, on January 24, at around 4:35 P.M., I received a telephone call from Dean Winslow, who said that the jury was coming back with a verdict. We rushed over to the courthouse and entered the courtroom just as the jury members were taking their seats. When the first verdict was read, I knew we won: La Cosa Nostra boss Angelo A. Lonardo—guilty on all counts; Joseph C. Gallo—guilty on all counts; Thomas Sinito—guilty on all counts; Hartmut "Hans" Graewe—guilty on all counts; Frederick "Fritz" Graewe—guilty on all counts; and Kevin McTaggart—guilty on all counts. Judge Manos ordered that they all be remanded to jail and set the sentencing for April 8. I was elated! We had finally brought the Cleveland LCN family to its knees.

On April 8, 1983, all the subjects appeared before Judge Manos for sentencing. He sentenced Angelo Lonardo, Tommy Sinito, Joe Gallo, Hartmut "Hans" Graewe, and Kevin McTaggart to life terms plus 105 years, with the terms to run consecutively. Frederick "Fritz" Graewe was sentenced to forty-two years in prison. Lonardo, Sinito, Gallo, Hans Graewe, and Kevin McTaggart would be spending the rest of their lives behind bars. Fritz Graewe would not be eligible for release until he was seventy-two years old. The sentences meted out by Judge Manos were reassuring and instructive to the American people that there was justice in the United States.

Carmen Zagaria was already in the Witness Security Program. He was given a new identity and is now living somewhere in North America or Europe.

Using the forfeiture provisions of the RICO statute, we seized a total of over $1,500,000 in cash, cars, and narcotics from the subjects.

The evidence gathered in this case was also presented to the Cuyahoga County grand jury by Assistant County Prosecutor Tom Buford, who subsequently convicted twenty of the drug ring underlings on related murder and narcotics charges.

Several weeks after his incarceration, Hans Graewe called the FBI office and asked to speak to Dean Winslow. When Dean went to see him, Hans was very meek and he had lost about twenty pounds. He told Dean that he would now cooperate and he wanted to be an informant. Dean brought the news to me and we had a good laugh. I told Dean that he should take a big jar of vaseline to Hans with the advice that he would need it at the U.S. Penitentiary in Marion, Illinois, where he would be spending the rest of his life.

In October 1984 Patrick M. McLaughlin was appointed U.S. attorney for the Northern District of Ohio. Pat had previously been chief of the Civil Division, so I knew him and already had great respect for him. Several days after he was sworn in, Pat called and requested a full briefing on the organized-crime situation in northern Ohio. I was only too glad to oblige.

I asked my chief assistant, ASAC Dick Schwein, to meet with OC Supervisor Bob Friedrick and prepare the briefing material. Several days later Pat, along with two strike force attorneys, Steve Jigger and Steve Olah, came to my office. We gave them a thorough briefing on the current situation in Cleveland. We had some mopping up to do. After the Zagaria and Sinito drug rings were broken, we began to receive information that vicious drug rings, primarily from Jamaica, were moving in to fill the vacuum.

Almost immediately, Pat McLaughlin created the Caribbean Task Force, which I completely supported. It became a model of a successful multiagency enforcement operation in which local, state, and federal law officials actively contribute. The task force was modeled after the task forces we formed to investigate the Greene and Nardi gangland murders and the Zagaria murder/drug operations. And the Caribbean Task Force was just as successful.

The task force consisted of FBI agents, DEA agents, ATF agents, IRS agents, INS agents, U.S. Customs agents, the Cleveland Heights Police Department, the Cleveland Police Homicide and Narcotics Units, the

Cuyahoga County Prosecutor's Office, the Shaker Heights Police Department, the Ohio Bureau of Criminal Investigation (BCI), assistant U.S. attorneys, and the U.S. postal inspectors. The overall supervision of the task force was the responsibility of the U.S. attorney.

The results of the task force investigation were impressive. During the first year, there were thirty-two state prosecutions ranging from minor felony weapon violations to aggravated murder. There were also nineteen separate federal indictments charging a total of thirty-nine defendants with federal narcotics, weapons, and immigration violations.

Subsequent to the demise of Zagaria's drug ring, Tony Delmonti, a non-LCN member, used his close relationship and friendship with LCN member Joseph "Joe Loose" Iacobacci to organize and manage a major cocaine distribution ring operating in the eastern suburbs of Cuyahoga County and the western portions of Lake County. Delmonti's use of intimidation and threats of violence, as well as his relationship with Iacobacci, made the investigation into the operation extremely difficult. A court-ordered wiretap was installed on Delmonti's home telephone, which enabled us to crack the organization and obtain indictments against Delmonti, Iacobacci, and eight other individuals. All ten individuals were convicted, with Iacobacci and Delmonti receiving sentences of twelve years in prison and $200,000 fines.

Pat McLaughlin's successful prosecution of Iacobacci, the last "made" member of the Cleveland LCN family still in Cleveland and not imprisoned or cooperating with the government through the Witness Security Program, was hailed as a first, in that an entire LCN family had been taken off the streets. The only remaining member was John "Peanuts" Tronolone, the consigliere and a Miami resident, who refused to come to Cleveland. Tronolone was soon arrested by Miami FBI agents and convicted on charges relating to the "fencing" of stolen diamonds. He died while awaiting trial.

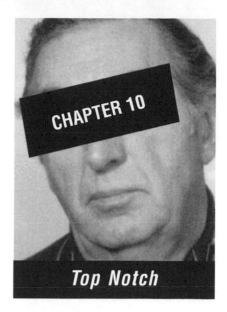

Top Notch

ANGELO LONARDO FLIPS

After Angelo Lonardo's conviction, he was immediately taken into custody and transferred to the U.S. Penitentiary at Springfield, Missouri. During the trial breaks, Lonardo was the only defendant who would routinely come up to me and engage in conversation. He would also do the same thing with case agents Bob Friedrick, Dean Winslow, John Summer, and Tom Kimmel.

Approximately three months after Lonardo's incarceration, Bob and I were attending an organized-crime conference in Chicago and we talked about Lonardo and the possibility of turning him. Lonardo was seventy-six years old and quite ill. In fact, he had a motion before Judge John M. Manos, requesting that he be released on medical bond. I told Bob that after the conference, he should swing down to the federal medical facility at Springfield, Missouri, where Angelo was being held. He could pop in and see Angelo, planting a seed with him to make him think about "flipping." I opened a potential informant file on Lonardo, code-named "Top Notch."

Bob went to see Lonardo, who agreed to see him in the visiting area. Bob told Lonardo that we understood he was having problems with his son, who was on cocaine, and Bob offered our assistance. He also suggested

275

to Lonardo that he look to the future and that if he ever decided he wanted to cooperate, he should give us a call. But he should do it quickly.

Lonardo took Bob's business card, and about a month later he called Bob and requested another visit. Bob came to me and told me about Angelo's telephone call. This was a very exciting development, since Lonardo was now the boss of the Cleveland LCN family, having succeeded Licavoli upon his imprisonment. (Lonardo's succession occurred right after Licavoli went to prison and before Lonardo himself was incarcerated.) I instructed Bob to go back to Springfield and visit with Lonardo to see what he had in mind. I cautioned that before we could even think about recommending some deal, Lonardo had to be fully debriefed about his activities in the LCN, his knowledge of other LCN bosses, and about the Commission.

Bob traveled with Agent Jerry Personen to Springfield, where they met with Lonardo. Lonardo said he was considering "flipping" and he wanted to know if anything could be done about the life plus 103-year consecutive sentence he had received. They told him that they would find this out and that before any deal could be even considered he would have to be debriefed fully so that a proper decision could be made concerning the extent of his cooperation and the value of his information. Lonardo said that if something could be done about his sentence he would agree to the debriefing.

He told the agents, however, that he was extremely fearful that if his potential cooperation was known to U.S. Attorney Bill Petro or the strike force, his life might be in jeopardy. He said he would not agree to be debriefed if these officials had to be told. He did not believe Petro was dishonest, but he knew Petro was very gregarious, knew a lot of people, and talked a lot. He was afraid that Petro would make an innocent remark to someone that would let the cat out of the bag.

Lonardo later told me that he did not trust the strike force because he knew that one of the Justice Department Organized Crime Section senior officials, who had previously been assigned to Cleveland, was associated with the on-again, off-again girlfriend of his capo, Tommy Sinito. The girlfriend was the former wife of Carmen Milano, the Los Angeles LCN underboss. He gave me the names of the official and the girlfriend, which I later furnished to FBI headquarters and the U.S. Department of Justice.

The girlfriend was a barmaid at a nearby tavern frequented by strike force attorneys, AUSAs, and Cleveland FBI agents. I knew the woman and did not consider her a bad person. Many of us had heard of this very close and personal friendship before, but I did not know if it could be verified. I also knew this official and I knew nothing to indicate that he was leaking information. In fact, he was aware of much of what we were doing in Cleveland and, other than Rabinowitz, there had been no leaks.

Incidently, Lonardo was right about Bill Petro. Soon thereafter, he was fired and criminally charged for innocently leaking information about a pending grand jury indictment in a federal copyright case.

Lonardo said he did not feel comfortable sitting down with us if anyone else knew about his possible cooperation. Angelo said he would not agree to the debriefing unless we could assure him that we would accept his wishes. We were in a real bind. We had to debrief Lonardo and we couldn't advise the Justice Department Organized Crime Section or the U.S. attorney's office.

Upon their return, Bob and Jerry reported the conversation with Lonardo to me. I called Sean McWeeney, chief of the FBI Organized Crime Section, and, later, Floyd Clarke, deputy assistant director of the FBI Criminal Division, and explained to them our contact with Lonardo. I pointed out that the case had already been adjudicated and was a closed case. Since the case was closed, I felt comfortable going to see Judge Manos, the trial judge, to determine from him if he still had control of the sentence and if he would consider any reduction if we could get Lonardo's cooperation.

They both agreed, and the following day I met Judge Manos for lunch. I briefed the judge concerning Lonardo's contact and told him that as a sitting La Cosa Nostra family boss, Lonardo would be the most important witness ever to enter the Witness Security Program if he actually told it all.

Judge Manos told me he would definitely consider reducing Lonardo's sentence based on a recommendation from the FBI. I thanked the judge and told him that I would get back to him after we debriefed Lonardo. Lonardo had a pending request to be released from prison on medical bond. The purpose of this type of release is to allow the prisoner the opportunity to receive specialized medical attention from his personal physician. If Lonardo was released on this bond, he could operate as an informant for a period of time before we had to divulge that he had "flipped." Jerry Personen went to see Lonardo and told him that a deal could be worked out if his total cooperation was obtained. Lonardo said that if he could be released from prison on medical bond, he would operate as an informant and at the end of our investigation he would testify at all proceedings.

Lonardo said that he would conduct all of his activities wired up and he would allow microphones in his residence and automobile, and wiretaps on all his telephones. He said he would provide us with sufficient information so that court-authorized intercepts and microphones could be obtained.

Jerry reported back to me on the third contact with Lonardo and I was elated. This was an outstanding opportunity. We still had Jackie Presser operating as an informant so it would be easy to initiate a meeting of the Commission in New York.

Lonardo said he would be willing to attend a Commission meeting with a body wire and, in all likelihood, he would have prior knowledge of the location of this meeting so it was possible that we could secure court-authorized electronic surveillance of the meeting. He told us he was willing to have new LCN members initiated under hidden closed-circuit television surveillance. The possibilities were endless and we were extremely excited.

Sean McWeeney arranged through the Department of Justice's witness protection people to have Lonardo transferred from Springfield to the U.S. Penitentiary in Lewisburg, Pennsylvania, with the plan for us to take custody of Lonardo en route for a week's debriefing.

In late fall of 1983, Cleveland FBI agents took Angelo Lonardo into custody, checked into an out-of-the-way Kentucky motel, and Jerry Personen and other 9 Squad agents began the debriefing. I flew to this small Kentucky city and spent a full three days with the debriefing agents listening to what Lonardo had to say and participating in the debriefing.

* * *

The information Lonardo had was at the highest level. When Licavoli was sent to prison, Lonardo immediately succeeded him as acting boss of the

Cleveland family. As an LCN boss, and earlier as an underboss, Lonardo had dealt directly with the Commission and the detailed information that he provided was amazing. He said that his father, Joseph Lonardo, was the first boss of the Cleveland LCN family. Joseph's power base came primarily from his control of the sugar trade in Cleveland during the early Prohibition era, a necessary commodity in the bootleg booze business.

Angelo said that his father was challenged by another faction of the crime family headed by Joe Porrello. Joe Porrello ordered the murder of Joseph Lonardo in October 1927, by Porrello henchman Sam Todaro. Angelo's uncle, John Lonardo, was with Joseph and was also killed.

After Joseph Lonardo's murder, Joe Porrello became boss of the Cleveland crime family. A gang war ensued for the next several years, resulting in the murders of another uncle, Frank Lonardo, and many of the seven Porrello brothers.

Angelo said that he and his cousin, Dominick Sospirato, murdered Sam Todaro on June 11, 1929, to avenge his father's death. Joe Porrello was murdered on July 5, 1930.

In 1930 Frank Milano became boss of the Cleveland crime family. Raymond Porrello and Rosario Porrello were killed on February 25, 1932, in a cigar store on the East Side of Cleveland. Angelo said that all of the Porrello murders were committed by loyalists to his father.

In the early 1930s Angelo Lonardo was proposed for membership in the Cleveland crime family by Albert "Big Al" Polizzi, who was an LCN member closely aligned with Milano. However, the newly formed Commission had "closed the books" of membership and it was not possible for him to be initiated into the family. Angelo said that he was finally made a member of the crime family in the late 1940s.

In the mid-1930s, Frank Milano moved to Mexico but still controlled Cleveland organized-crime operations and remained as boss of the family. In the early 1940s, Milano decided to become a permanent resident of Mexico and stepped down as boss. He promoted "Big Al" Polizzi to replace him as boss of the Cleveland family. Polizzi was boss of the Cleveland LCN family until the late 1940s, when he decided to retire in Florida. At this point, around 1949, Polizzi named John Scalish as boss.

When Scalish inherited the family, there were approximately fifty to sixty members. Scalish was very complacent and he made few if any additional members during his reign as boss. He believed that there were no trustworthy candidates for induction into the Cleveland family and he feared that if he chose individuals he could not trust, his comfortable lifestyle would be threatened.

Scalish's underboss was Tony Milano and the consigliere was John DeMarco. Lonardo furnished us with a list of all of the members of the Cleveland LCN family, both present and past. He also identified all of the past and present underbosses, consiglieri, and capos. He said that Scalish, in addition to being complacent as a boss, also was not familiar with the names and activities of his peers in other families throughout the country.

When Scalish had to travel to other cities, he would always consult with Lonardo to find out who the boss was in a particular area. In early 1976 Scalish was told by his physicians that he was in dire need of heart bypass surgery. Scalish was told that if he did not have the surgery his death was imminent. In May 1976 Scalish agreed to the surgery but died during the procedure. That evening, family members and the active remnants of the Cleveland family met at Scalish's residence.

When Lonardo arrived, after he paid his respects to the widow (who was his mother-in-law), he went down to the game room in the basement where he found James Licavoli and Milton "Maishe" Rockman, who was also married to one of Scalish's daughters. Rockman told Licavoli and Lonardo that prior to his surgery, Scalish told him that he wanted Licavoli to be his successor if he were to die during the course of the operation.

Licavoli said he did not want the job and that it was common knowledge that Angelo Lonardo was the most qualified to become boss. Licavoli told Lonardo and Rockman that Lonardo had contacts, was a better speaker, and better understood the requirements of being boss.

Lonardo was surprised by Scalish's choice but he attempted to persuade Licavoli to assume the position based on Scalish's wishes. Licavoli reluctantly agreed to become boss.

Several days later, Lonardo and Licavoli met with Tony Milano, who was then the family underboss. They told him that Licavoli was the new boss and related the story that Rockman had told them. Based on Milano's advanced age and the fact that he wanted an active underboss, Licavoli also respectfully asked Milano to step down.

Lonardo told us that Milano appeared very surprised and said that he had believed Lonardo would succeed Scalish. We had heard this story before from our informants. Lonardo told us that he was often suspicious as to Rockman's story about talking to Scalish just before the surgery. He said he believed that Rockman may have lied to get Licavoli made boss, knowing that Licavoli would be much easier to control in certain areas of the family activities than Lonardo would have been. Lonardo said that Licavoli was ignorant of certain matters of protocol required by his new position. He had to be told that he had to travel to New York to meet with the boss of the Genovese family to report he was the new boss of the Cleveland family.

Licavoli named his cousin, Leo Moceri, as the new underboss and Tony Delsanter as consigliere. Approximately two weeks later, Licavoli and Moceri traveled to New York, where they attempted to meet with Funzi Tieri, who was then the boss of the Genovese family.

Tieri was sick so they instead met with Anthony "Fat Tony" Salerno, the underboss of the Genovese family. The boss of the Genovese family represented the Cleveland family on the LCN Commission, so it was necessary to meet with Tieri or Salerno.★

Not long after Licavoli's elevation, the power struggle began between the John Nardi–Danny Green faction and the Licavoli faction. The first victim in this power struggle was Leo Moceri, who Lonardo believed was killed by Keith Ritson and Hans Graewe. When Moceri disappeared, Licavoli named Lonardo as his new underboss. Shortly thereafter, Tony Delsanter died of natural causes and John "Peanuts" Tronolone was made consigliere.

★It is noted that former Cleveland LCN boss John Scalish was a member of the Commission and represented the Cleveland organized crime family on the Commission. When Scalish died and he was replaced by James Licavoli, for some reason Licavoli did not become a member of the Commission and the Commission designated Salerno to represent Cleveland.

Lonardo and Licavoli later traveled to New York, where they met with Salerno, who by this time was boss of the Genovese family after Funzi Tieri's death. They secured his permission to make ten new members in the Cleveland family. Sometime in 1977 Anthony Liberatore and John Calandra were made members of the family. Lonardo said that murder usually was a prerequisite for becoming a member but in the case of Calandra and Liberatore this was not one of the facts they considered.

The induction ceremony for Calandra and Liberatore took place in the basement of the Roman Gardens Restaurant in the Murray Hill section of Cleveland. Licavoli and Lonardo were initially present for the ceremony. "Jimmy the Weasel" Fratianno was eating dinner upstairs and eventually wandered downstairs, unannounced and uninvited. He was, nonetheless, asked to remain. Lonardo and Licavoli had both forgotten how to conduct the LCN initiation ceremony and they asked Fratianno for assistance. Fratianno repeated the LCN oath to Calandra and Liberatore. Both Calandra and Liberatore had their fingers pricked by Licavoli to draw a small amount of blood. Lonardo explained to them the rules of the LCN—no one leaves the family alive, they should never talk to the FBI, they were expected to refrain from the use and/or sale of narcotics (what a joke that was!), they could never become involved in prostitution, and they could never become involved with another member's wife. They were instructed that they should keep Licavoli and/or Lonardo aware of all family matters and never "do anything" without first getting permission.

In the summer of 1979 Joseph Gallo and Thomas Sinito were also made members of the Cleveland family. Their induction ceremony took place in the back room of the Italian-American Brotherhood Club on Mayfield Road in the Murray Hill district. Present during this ceremony were Licavoli, Lonardo, and Charlie Casara, an old, retired member of the Cleveland family. Lonardo joked that this time he and Licavoli remembered the oath and the ceremony.

In early 1983 Lonardo presided over another induction ceremony wherein Russell Papalardo and Joseph "Joe Loose" Iacobacci Jr. were made members of the Cleveland LCN family. They were recommended for membership by both Joe Gallo and Tommy Sinito. At the time of these inductions Lonardo was told that Iacobacci had committed the Joe Bonarrigo murder. He told us that Bonarrigo and Curly Montana were responsible for the murder of John Nardi. A third individual, whose identity was not known to Lonardo, was also involved in the hit.

Patsy Feruccio of Canton, Ohio, and James Prato, of Youngstown, Ohio, were members of the John LaRocco (Pittsburgh) family of La Cosa Nostra. Lonardo told us that the Cleveland family's interests in Youngstown were represented by Ron Carabbia and his brothers, Charlie and Orlando "Orlie" Carabbia.

The Carabbias received 25 percent of the profits made in various vending businesses in the greater Youngstown area. Licavoli and Lonardo received 25 percent of the profits, and the Youngstown faction of the Pittsburgh LCN family, James Prato and Joseph Naples, received the other 50 percent.

Lonardo met with Naples and Prato on a monthly basis at a restaurant in Mayfield Heights, Ohio, to pick up the 25 percent. This monthly figure was usually about $10,000. Lombardo said that several years earlier, Prato and Naples became very upset with Charlie Carabbia. They determined that Carabbia had approximately fifty more slot machines in service than he admitted to and they were convinced he was skimming the profits from both the Cleveland and Pittsburgh families.

After Ronnie Carabbia was convicted in the Greene murder case and sentenced to prison, Lonardo met with Prato, Naples, and Pat Feruccio regarding Charlie Carabbia. At this meeting, Lonardo and Licavoli were told that Naples, Prato, and Feruccio were going to kill Charlie Carabbia because he continued to cheat them with his machines.

Lonardo and Licavoli interceded for Charlie and subsequently Licavoli went to the Cuyahoga County Jail, where he met with Ronnie Carabbia. He explained the situation to Ronnie in the hopes that he could straighten his brother out.

Lonardo subsequently was taken to Pittsburgh by Patsy Feruccio, where he met with Pittsburgh LCN underboss Kelly Mannarino. Mannarino turned over $23,000, which represented the Cleveland family's portion of the vending and gambling money from the Youngstown area for a period of about three months.

John LaRocco, whom Lonardo described as the boss of the Pittsburgh family, came to the house and they began discussing Charlie Carabbia. LaRocco wanted Carabbia killed, and he repeated the same reasons as those stated by Prato and Naples. According to Lonardo, Licavoli had met with Ron Carabbia and the matter was going to be taken care of.

Lonardo later met with Naples and Prato and told them the matter had been resolved with Charlie and they consented to allow him to live on the condition that he made no further problems for them. Naples and Prato requested and received permission from Lonardo and Licavoli to kill Carabbia if he did not live up to his side of the agreement and continued to steal from them.

Lonardo heard that Carabbia was continuing his skimming activities and about a month later he heard that Carabbia had been reported missing. His abandoned car was found on the streets of Cleveland.

About two weeks later, Lonardo and Licavoli met with Pat Feruccio, Jimmy Prato, and Joey Naples at a restaurant in Boston Heights, Ohio. During this meeting, Prato and Naples said Charlie Carabbia had been murdered and they apologized to Lonardo and Licavoli for leaving Charlie Carabbia's car in the Cleveland area. Naples and Prato told Lonardo that whoever drove the car there "didn't know where he was," or words to that effect. Prato and Naples said they had learned Charlie Carabbia was planning to kill them and that was the reason he was murdered.

THE CLEVELAND FAMILY AND THE TEAMSTERS

Lonardo told us that all matters involving the eastern seaboard docks and waterfronts were handled by the Gambino family in New York. Lonardo also said that the LCN controlled the Teamsters Union. He pointed out in connection with the last Teamsters presidential election, the Cleveland family supported Jackie Presser, who was at the time Teamsters international vice president. Rockman had a meeting with Nick Civella, the boss of the Kansas City family, who was supporting Roy Williams as president.

Rockman suggested that Williams, if elected, could step down as head of the Central States Pension Fund and allow Jackie Presser to become responsible for the pension fund. They now were on the same page.

As a result of this agreement, the Cleveland family agreed to support Williams's presidential bid. In order to ·solicit support for Williams, Lonardo and Licavoli went to Chicago to see Jackie Cerone's son, an attorney, and requested a meeting with his father. The meeting was set up. Rockman and Lonardo later drove to Chicago in Rockman's black Cadillac Fleetwood, where they went to the prearranged meeting at the law offices of Cerone's son.

They met with Jackie Cerone Jr. for lunch and he explained that the meeting was set up for three or three-thirty at a hotel near his law office. After lunch, the three of them walked to the hotel, where they saw Chicago LCN members Jackie Cerone Sr. and Joseph "Joey" Aiuppa, the Chicago LCN family boss, sitting in the lobby.

Lonardo said that Rockman and Lonardo joined them and they were told Cerone and Aiuppa had a meeting scheduled with a Teamsters official prior to meeting with the two Clevelanders. They apologized to Rockman and Lonardo for making them wait. When this Teamsters official, Dominic (last name unknown), showed up at the hotel, he went with Cerone and Aiuppa to a hotel room on an upper floor. Ten or fifteen minutes later, the Teamsters official came down and told Lonardo and Rockman to proceed to a particular hotel room, where Cerone and Aiuppa were waiting. They went to the room and when they entered, they explained they were soliciting support for Roy Williams in his quest for the Teamster presidency. Aiuppa said that he already knew, since he had heard from Kansas City that the Cleveland family was now supporting Williams for the Teamsters presidency. He explained that they wanted Williams to get the job since he was "Nick Civella's man." Several days after the meeting, Rockman received a telephone call from Joey Aiuppa, who told him that Chicago would support Roy Williams for president.

About a week later, Lonardo and Rockman flew to New York, where they met with "Fat Tony" Salerno at a card room he frequented on 116th Street in Harlem. Lonardo and Rockman explained Nick Civella's plan for the Teamsters presidency, as well as the future employment of Jackie Presser as head of the Central States Pension Fund. They asked if Salerno would support Williams and attempt to line up delegates for him. Salerno agreed and said he could line up the delegates through LCN member Tony Provenzano's brother, who was a Teamsters official in New Jersey.

Subsequently, through their Teamsters contacts, the Kansas City, Chicago, Cleveland, and New York families lined up delegates supporting Williams and he was elected president of the Teamsters Union. However, Williams reneged and did not name Jackie Presser as head of the pension fund, as promised.

Lonardo complained to Civella, who indicated that he was upset and embarrassed because of his inability to control the new Teamsters president. Roy Williams was later convicted in federal court in Chicago on labor-related charges and forced to step down as president of the Teamsters.

Lonardo and Rockman then made a move to elect Jackie Presser president of the Teamsters. They had several meetings with Jackie Cerone in Miami, Florida, and Chicago. They later went to New York, where they met with Salerno.

Salerno said he was very concerned since there was an article in a Cleveland newspaper indicating Jackie Presser was an FBI informant. Lonardo and Rockman told Salerno that they did not believe Presser to be an informant.

Lonardo told us that Salerno later contacted him and said that he would support Presser for president of the Teamsters. Salerno had contacted his attorney, Roy Cohen, about the news articles indicating Presser was an informant. Cohen said he represented the owner of the Cleveland *Plain Dealer* and said he would find out about the news article. Salerno then set up a meeting between Cohen and Rockman. Rockman later told Lonardo that he had met with Cohen and indicated he wanted the *Plain Dealer* to print a front-page retraction of the information concerning Jackie Presser being an FBI informant.

Cohen said he would talk to his client concerning the retraction. Later, Rockman learned that the retraction was to be printed and he passed this information to Lonardo. The retraction did appear in the Cleveland paper. Lonardo said that he and Licavoli did not really trust Presser but Rockman convinced them that he was not an FBI informant and was the man for the Teamsters job.

LAS VEGAS SKIMMING OPERATION

Lonardo was questioned by agents concerning La Cosa Nostra's control of casinos in Las Vegas. Lonardo said that shortly after World War II, Wilbur Clark began building what was to be the Desert Inn Hotel and Casino. During construction, he ran out of funds and was temporarily unable to complete the project. Clark made contact with a Cleveland native, Norman Khoury, who owned a number of bars in Cleveland. According to Lonardo, Khoury agreed to provide the funds to complete the project in return for receiving an ownership percentage in the casino. The deal fell through when Khoury insisted that the casino be called Khoury's Desert Inn. Clark refused and began making other efforts to secure financing.

Maurice Kleinman, Moe Dalitz, Sammy Tucker, and Lou Rothkopf, who were members of what Lonardo called the "old Jewish boys in the old Murray Hill gang," were previously involved with the Cleveland LCN family in the ownership of various gambling ventures, including the Beverly Hills Supper Club near Covington, Kentucky. When they operated the supper club, it had casino-type gambling. The supper club was eventually put out of business by George Ratterman, the former Cleveland Browns quarterback who became sheriff in Covington.

When the gambling club was closed, their interest in the Beverly Hills Supper Club was sold. Shortly after the supper club was closed, the "Jewish boys" entered into an agreement with Wilbur Clark in Las Vegas. They agreed to provide the necessary capital to complete construction of the Desert Inn Hotel and Casino and become partners with Clark in this venture. They went to Cleveland LCN boss Al Polizzi and offered him a hidden share in the Desert Inn, provided the Cleveland family supplied part of the needed capital.

Under this proposal, Polizzi and the Cleveland family would become silent partners in the Desert Inn Hotel and Casino, while Clark and the "Jewish boys" would be listed as the actual owners of the casino licenses. Polizzi turned the deal down. He was worried that the gambling licenses would not be issued after he provided all the capital. Nonetheless, the Desert Inn was built and became licensed. A few years later, the "Jewish boys" gave Polizzi and the Cleveland family a secret ownership percentage of the Desert Inn.

In exchange for this percentage, the Cleveland LCN family was to provide protection for the casino. The "Jewish boys" felt it was better to give a percentage of hidden ownership to the Cleveland family than a percentage to another family whose members would attempt to muscle in at a later date. Thereafter, Polizzi, his underbosses, consiglieri, and capos began splitting up monthly skim proceeds from the Desert Inn and they shared some of this money with other Cleveland LCN members.

This monthly distribution from the Desert Inn continued until Howard Hughes purchased the hotel and casino from Clark. The "Jewish boys" later obtained an interest in the Stardust Casino and they gave the Chicago family a percentage of that operation. Lonardo said that there was later a disagreement with the Chicago LCN family when they claimed the "Jewish boys" had reneged on their promises.

Lonardo said he traveled to Chicago in the early 1960s to meet with Tony Accardo and Jackie Cerone concerning the Stardust. Lonardo believed that Maurice Kleinman and Moe Dalitz were present at this sit-down. Lonardo said that Kleinman and Dalitz were refusing to pay the Cleveland family its share of the skim. It was agreed that the Chicago LCN family would get the percentage that Kleinman and Dalitz had offered earlier. As a result of participating in this sit-down and for backing the Chicago family, the Cleveland family also obtained a hidden ownership percentage of the Stardust Casino and began receiving the monthly skimmed funds. In the early years of this skimming operation, Mob courier George Gordon would travel to Cleveland to deliver the Cleveland family's share of the Stardust and Desert Inn skimming proceeds. Gordon delivered the money to John Scalish, who in turn would split it with Frank Milano, Al Polizzi, Frank Brancato, Dominic Sospirato, Maishe

Rockman, John DeMarco, and Angelo Lonardo. Scalish, Lonardo, and Rockman got the largest share of the casino money, about $10,000 each month. Everyone else was given between $1,000 and $2,000.

This routine continued until the Stardust and Desert Inn casinos were sold. Lonardo said that Kleinman and Dalitz sold their interest in the two casinos because Maurice Kleinman wanted to retire.

In later years, when California promoter Allan Glick was trying to purchase the Stardust and Fremont casinos, Nick Civella approached Maishe Rockman and asked him for assistance in obtaining a Central States Teamsters Pension Fund loan in connection with Glick's casinos. Civella told Rockman that he already had Roy Williams in his pocket and wanted Maishe Rockman to approach Bill Presser, a Teamsters official he knew to be close to Rockman. With the support of both Williams and Bill Presser, the approval of a Teamsters Pension Fund loan was likely.

Rockman briefed John Scalish, who initially did not want to assist Civella in obtaining the loan for Allan Glick. Scalish was already rich and he didn't stick his neck out. Rockman told Lonardo that he finally convinced Scalish to approve the Cleveland family's participation. Through Bill Presser, Rockman was able to assist Glick in getting the Central States Teamsters Pension Fund loan. As a result, Cleveland was given 10 percent of the casino's skim profits.

The Kansas City, Milwaukee, and Chicago families were also given equal percentages of the skim profits based on their support of the pension fund loan to Glick. Shortly after the loan was approved, the skim began. It was divided up equally between the LCN bosses in Chicago, Kansas City, Milwaukee, and Cleveland.

Lonardo said that casino executive Carl Thomas handled the actual skimming operation in Las Vegas. He and other executives under his direction would daily take money out of the cash boxes in the counting rooms before the counting began.

On average, they would skim about $250,000 per month. After taking their percentage, the executives provided about $160,000 per month to the LCN. Kansas City obtained all the skim money directly from the casino and divided it up among themselves, Chicago, Milwaukee, and Cleveland.

Cleveland's share of the skim money would be taken by courier from Kansas City to Chicago.

After being told that he could pick the money up, Rockman would drive to Chicago and get Cleveland's share of the skim money from Nick Civella's nephew, Frank Chivolla, a Chicago policeman. Rockman would return to Cleveland, where he and Scalish would divide up the skim money to various "made" guys. Those individuals who received the money from the skim were Scalish, Rockman, Lonardo, Licavoli, and Dominic Sospirato. Lonardo got approximately $2,000 per month and Sospirato was given $1,000 per month. Lonardo was unaware of what the others were getting specifically. Rockman had secret compartments in each of his automobiles, which he used to hide the money on his trips. He also had an extra twenty-gallon gas tank installed in his cars, which he used for his cross-country trips.

The original deal was for the Cleveland family to receive 10 percent of the actual ownership of the casino. However, this never materialized and the crime family also did not receive any hidden ownership. They were just given a percentage of the skim money through an agreement they worked out with the Chicago, Kansas City, and Milwaukee crime families.

After Scalish died, Lonardo learned through Rockman that each month Cleveland received $40,000 for its share of the skim. Licavoli, Rockman, Tony Delsanter, Dominic Sospirato, Leo Moceri, and Lonardo all received shares of the skim.

Lonardo made two separate trips to Chicago with Rockman to pick up the skim. On the first trip he traveled in Rockman's Cadillac Fleetwood and they went to a fancy downtown restaurant. Rockman telephoned Chivolla from the restaurant. Chivolla arrived shortly thereafter and Rockman introduced Lonardo to Chivolla. After eating a sandwich, Chivolla went to his car and brought back the skim money. On the second trip to Chicago, Lonardo and Rockman drove a borrowed Cadillac Seville. On this trip, they met with Chivolla and his son. Chivolla gave Rockman the skim money, which was all wrapped up.

After the Cleveland family ran into trouble in connection with the Danny Greene murder, the skim money was used for lawyers' expenses.

After the Danny Greene trials were over, Rockman told Lonardo that he had suspended the distribution of the skim and stashed $250,000, which was available for expenses. Lonardo said that during one of these trials, he gave some of the skim money to one of the defense attorneys for his fee.

***

Lonardo continued to provide very detailed information during this debriefing with regard to the Las Vegas skimming and all other activities of the Cleveland LCN family.

He provided details previously unknown to us concerning some of the gangland murders. I questioned him concerning the Rabinowitz leak in the Cleveland FBI office. He said that he did not recall the exact time frame but he did remember attending a meeting with Maishe Rockman and James Licavoli at Rockman's house in Beechwood, Ohio. During this meeting, Licavoli produced a copy of what appeared to be an informant list, which Licavoli said was given to him by Tony Liberatore. Lonardo recalled that Rockman also had a copy of this same list during the meeting. The list appeared to have been handwritten and was apparently a copy of an original. Licavoli indicated to Lonardo that he had given an undisclosed amount of money to Liberatore to give to Liberatore's source inside the FBI as payment for the retrieval of the classified information. Lonardo looked at the list and was amazed at some of the names on the list. He was shocked and actually did not believe that the list was authentic. He believed that the list was either a fake or Liberatore had added a lot of names to the list in an attempt to discredit some of his enemies.

During the meeting at Rockman's, it was decided that the copies of the list should be destroyed and Licavoli instructed that Liberatore be told to stop any further attempts to obtain information from his contact in the FBI. Licavoli said that he was fearful that the FBI would discover the leak and would then launch a massive investigation to identify the leaker. He said that if Liberatore's FBI source was discovered, she would undoubtedly confess and he, Rockman, and Liberatore would all be implicated in the conspiracy.

Both copies of the list were burned in Rockman's incinerator. To the best of Lonardo's recollection, John Calandra, Butchie Cisternino, Ronnie Carabbia, Tony Liberatore, Rockman, Licavoli and he had all seen a copy of the informant list at one time or another. As a result of this meeting Rockman later told Liberatore that he was to refrain from any further attempt to obtain information from his source in the FBI.

Lonardo said it became apparent that Liberatore continued his attempts to obtain further information in an effort to enhance his status within certain organized-crime circles.

After the arrests of Licavoli, Lonardo, and the other defendants for the Nardi and Greene murders, Lonardo heard that Liberatore was still talking to his FBI source. He also learned that Liberatore had met Jackie Cerone in Chicago and made an attempt to pose as "the man in charge" of LCN affairs in Cleveland. He now believed Liberatore was a treacherous guy who would do anything to advance himself in La Cosa Nostra.

Lonardo and Licavoli learned of Liberatore's trip from Jackie Cerone's son, who added that his father had given Liberatore the "cold shoulder." Lonardo also found out that Liberatore made a trip to New Jersey, where he met with a member of the DeCavalcante family. The purpose of his trip was to build himself up in an attempt to get support to take over the Cleveland family.

★★★

The debriefing of Angelo Lonardo continued for six days. I remained for three days and was consistently amazed at the detail of Lonardo's information.

He was willing to do anything required of him as an informant and at the conclusion when the government required his testimony he said he would provide honest testimony in all matters. In exchange, he wanted to go into the Witness Security Program and have his consecutive sentences of life plus 103 years commuted to time served. I told him that I was impressed with the information he had and with what he could do to convict others. I told him I would support his sentence reduction and his relocation.

I was really elated at this development. Lonardo would make an excellent witness. He was humble, soft-spoken, and very distinguished looking.

His violent days were over. The Commission case was being developed in New York and Lonardo would make a dynamite witness, since he actually participated as a boss and underboss in contacts and meetings with other Commission members.

Another case we were developing, code-named "Strawman," needed a strong witness such as Lonardo. We had begun this investigation several years before when we learned about the LCN skimming from Jackie Presser at the Teamsters. At the time of the Lonardo debriefing, we had an active and important organized-crime investigation underway. Lonardo would make an outstanding witness against bosses in Chicago, Kansas City, and Milwaukee. As he told us, he actually participated in setting up the Las Vegas skimming operation and had personally met with the bosses of all these families in connection with the skimming activity.

I flew back to Cleveland in the FBI plane and the first thing I did when I hit the ground was call my friend Floyd Clarke, who was the deputy assistant director of the Criminal Investigative Division. I briefed him on my conversations with Lonardo. Floyd was also familiar with what was happening in New York in connection with the Commission case, as well as the Strawman investigation, and he was also very excited about bringing Lonardo on board. I told Floyd that Judge Manos was willing to release Lonardo on medical bond based on the request that was currently pending.

WASHINGTON DISPUTE

Several days later, I received a telephone call from Sean McWeeney, who told me that he believed we should now brief the Department of Justice Organized Crime Section and the strike force since we had kept our word to Lonardo that the strike force would not be made aware of his cooperation until after the debriefing. I agreed, since we would need the support and participation of Section Chief David Margolis and the Cleveland Strike Force.

Sean requested that I come to Washington and personally brief Margolis on the Lonardo matter, which was code-named "Top Notch." I asked why he could not make the presentation himself, since he was the chief of the FBI Organized Crime Section. Sean replied that he thought it best that I go since I had actually participated in the Lonardo debriefing.

Bob Friedrick and I flew to Washington the next day, November 29, 1983, and, with McWeeney, we went to Margolis's conference room. In addition to Margolis, strike force attorneys from Milwaukee, Kansas City, and Chicago, as well as Steve Olah and Steve Jigger from the Cleveland Strike Force, were present.

At the beginning of the meeting, Margolis indicated he was outraged at me for not telling him about Lonardo's possible cooperation before and he told me that he was extremely disappointed that I had not told Olah in advance of our contacts with Lonardo.

I explained to him that Lonardo would not agree to submit to the initial interview unless we assured him that the strike force and the U.S. attorney would not be made aware of his possible cooperation. I told him that the debriefing was very successful and we were now in a position to advise everyone of the results of the debriefing and what we recommended be done. I told Margolis that if he wanted I would explain in more detail after the meeting about what Lonardo said and why he did not trust the strike force and the U.S. attorney. Margolis declined and asked me to proceed. He said that I could explain Lonardo's reasons later.

I then gave a detailed briefing to the assembled attorneys concerning the information Lonardo had provided. I explained to them that we wanted to use Lonardo as an informant for several months before he surfaced as a witness. I also told them that he had agreed to attend the Commission meeting wired up, induct new members under closed-circuit television surveillance, and basically put his entire life in our hands for this period until he entered the witness relocation program. Lonardo would be the highest-ranking La Cosa Nostra figure ever to "flip" and he was totally cooperative.

Olah asked how Lonardo could help in Cleveland. I said that he wouldn't be much help in our area but he would instead be of tremendous assistance to the efforts in Kansas City, Milwaukee, Chicago, New York, Las Vegas, Los Angeles, and San Francisco.

At the conclusion of the briefing, Bob and I met with Margolis privately and I asked him if he would support our efforts. I also told him what Lonardo had told me about why he did not trust the strike force. Margolis said that he liked the idea and he would support our efforts to use Lonardo as an informant and later as a witness. For the next several weeks, I waited for an official response from Margolis so that we could proceed with our plan.

I was on the telephone with McWeeney and Clarke every day. Frequent inquiries were made to Margolis but he would say only that the matter was still being considered in the department.

In the meantime, Judge Manos was sitting on Lonardo's request for the medical bond. He called me several times, inquiring as to what was happening in the department. I explained that I had made inquiries but was told that the matter was still being considered.

Eventually, when we received no news from Washington, the judge had to rule on motion and he denied Lonardo's request for medical bond. We had lost that opportunity. Another month went by with no word from the department on our request.

On the afternoon of December 21, 1983, I was on leave and at home. I received a telephone call from "Buck" Revell, who was now the assistant director of the FBI Criminal Investigative Division. Revell, who was not one of my closest friends, told me that I had to travel to Washington immediately in connection with a very urgent matter that had come up.

I asked Revell what this was all about. He said, "You'll find out when you get here." I told Revell that I would not be available to come to Washington until the following day, December 22. I told him I would fly in that morning. The next day, I went to Washington and reported to Revell's office. Revell told me in his usual pompous style that some very serious allegations had been made against me and that I was going to be interviewed by the assistant director of the Inspection Division and one of his aides and that I should "tell the truth."

I sarcastically told Revell, "I always tell the truth to FBI headquarters," left his office, and went to the Inspection Division. There, I was met by Dick Sonnichsen and Bob Ivey, who were both acquaintances of mine and good guys. But they were professionals and they had a job to do—this was not a friendly situation.

They told me that the Department of Justice had requested that the FBI conduct an Office of Professional Responsibility administrative inquiry concerning my meetings with Judge Manos. They told me that the FBI had been advised by the department that these contacts had possibly jeopardized the investigation. I was dumbstruck and couldn't believe what I was hearing.

This was Margolis's response to our meeting. Not only had he not approved our request to use Lonardo but now was attempting to get even with me for not cutting his office in earlier in the game.

Sonnichsen and Ivy grilled me for eight and a half hours on my conversations with Judge Manos—what I had said, what he had said—attempting to get me to recall exact phrases. It was ridiculous. They wanted me to stay over until the following day and I refused, telling them that I wanted to get out of Washington that day, even if I had to hitchhike back to Cleveland.

I gave them a sworn, signed statement detailing my conversations with the judge. They could not explain to me what I possibly could have done to cause this administrative inquiry.

Several months later, I received a communication from the Justice Department stating that the department approved our using Lonardo as an informant; however, I was advised that Lonardo must move to Florida, where he would be controlled by the Miami FBI Division. When Bob Friedrick told Lonardo about this, Lonardo was flabbergasted, saying that if he got out of prison and went to Miami he would be killed; he was now the boss of the family and if he left town with all the trouble they had in Cleveland, they would all surmise that something was wrong—La Cosa Nostra would no longer trust him. The plan proposed by the Department of Justice was totally ridiculous.

When I told the officials at FBI headquarters that Lonardo could not move to Miami, they told me that the Cleveland office should discontinue any further contact with Lonardo. I refused to follow these instructions. I told both Sean and Floyd that Lonardo frequently called Jerry Personen from the prison and that we would continue to accept his phone calls. I told Friedrick and Personen to maintain contact with Lonardo since he had told them he was still interested in testifying if his appeals were turned down.

I later learned from a friend at FBI headquarters that Revell had recommended I be censured and placed on probation for making contact with a U.S. district judge on a pending case when the U.S. attorney or a strike force attorney was not present. This was a little "no-no" paragraph buried in the FBI manual. However, Revell ignored the fact that this was not a pending case—Lonardo had already been sentenced, he was serving his sentence, and our case was closed. If Director Webster acted on Revell's recommendation, my FBI career was over. When an SAC is placed on probation, the next move is to take his office away from him and "bust him" back to the street. This recommendation sat on Webster's desk for months, my FBI future hanging in the balance.

About three months later, I received a telephone call from Clyde Groover, who was the assistant director of the Administrative Division, which handled promotions, demotions, and all disciplinary actions. He told me that Judge Webster had disagreed with Revell's recommendation and had returned the administrative write-up to him with the comment that the recommendation was ridiculous and "the SAC did what he is supposed to do." I told Clyde that I thought the whole thing was really outrageous and he agreed. But we had lost a golden opportunity. We could have used Lonardo as an informant—he would have been awesome.

We continued to maintain contact with Lonardo for approximately a year until all his appeals were resolved. About a year later, when Lonardo learned that the U.S. Supreme Court refused to hear his appeal, he called Jerry and said he was now ready to come into the fold—he would now testify. I wrote this up and sent it to FBI headquarters; the department responded by saying that Lonardo was too high up in the LCN and, since he was convicted for RICO-murder and RICO-narcotics, his crimes were too severe to consider using him as a witness. I later learned that Olah had recommended against Lonardo becoming a witness because he could not help Cleveland.

Lonardo could put the bosses in New York, Chicago, Kansas City, and

Milwaukee in prison, as well as the underbosses and consiglieri of all these families. He could cement the Commission case in New York and he would be dynamite in the Strawman case against the Chicago, Kansas City, and Milwaukee bosses and Maische Rockman for skimming in Las Vegas. This was the whole purpose of what we were trying to do—convict, flip, and work our way up in the chain. I talked to Sean McWeeney and Floyd Clarke and, after consulting with Margolis, they told me there was nothing further they could do to secure the department's approval to cut a deal with Lonardo and secure his cooperation.

In later conversations with my friend Tom Sheer, who was now assistant director in charge of the New York field division, I told him about Lonardo and the stonewalling efforts I was getting from Washington. Tom told me that New York could really use Lonardo in the Commission case and he asked me if I would agree to meet Manhattan U.S. Attorney Rudolph "Rudy" Giuliani. At the time, Giuliani and the New York FBI were deeply involved in a major effort to take down the five New York crime family bosses who were members of the Commission. I told him that I would be very happy to brief Giuliani, whom I highly respected. The meeting was arranged and Bob Friedrick and I flew to New York, where we met with Giuliani and his strike force staff. After we briefed them on the information provided by Lonardo, Giuliani picked up the telephone and called Attorney General William French Smith. He gave the attorney general a short briefing on Angelo Lonardo and requested that Lonardo be placed in the Witness Security Program. After this five-minute phone conversation, he thanked the attorney general and hung up the phone. He turned to me and said that the attorney general had approved Lonardo's entrance into the Witness Security Program. We now had Lonardo in the fold.

Rudy told me that Cleveland agents should take control of Lonardo and that I should send a teletype to FBI headquarters advising them that Lonardo was being placed in the Witness Security Program and that he would be testifying in New York at the Commission trial. I thanked Rudy, returned to Cleveland, and prepared the teletype with glee.

We secured an independent attorney for Lonardo and, now with the assistance of Washington, we cut the deal. We agreed to recommend a reduction in sentence if he cooperated fully and testified in all of the cases about which he was knowledgeable. I sent Cleveland agents to Springfield, Missouri, where Lonardo was confined to the Federal Medical Center for Prisoners because of a heart condition. They took Lonardo into our custody and transported him to an FBI safe house, where the debriefing continued for the next year.

Over the next five years Lonardo became the most important La Cosa Nostra witness ever to testify in the United States. He was a sitting boss and the highest-ranking member of La Cosa Nostra ever to testify. The Commission case in New York was the most important organized-crime prosecution ever undertaken. Giuliani had charged all five Commission members—the five New York bosses—and their top assistants with RICO-murder, loan-sharking, labor payoffs, and extortion. Angelo Lonardo and Jimmy "The Weasel" Fratianno became the star witnesses in the Commission case against Colombo family boss Carmen "Junior" Persico, Genovese family boss Anthony "Fat Tony" Salerno, Lucchese family boss Anthony "Tony Ducks" Corrallo, Bonanno family boss Phil Rastelli, Genovese family underboss Gennaro "Gerry Lang" Langella, Lucchese family underboss Salvatore "Tom Mix" Santoro, Lucchese consigliere Christopher "Christie Tick" Furnari, Bonanno family member Anthony "Bruno" Indelicato, and Colombo family member Ralph Scopo. Paul Castellano, the boss of the Gambino family, was originally a defendant, but he was murdered before the Commission trial began.

All of the Commission defendants were found guilty and each was sentenced to one hundred years in prison.

In 1986 Angelo Lonardo was the principal and "star" witness in the casino-skimming case code-named "Strawman." The trial was held in Kansas City. The defendants were Chicago family boss Joseph "Doves" Aiuppa, Milwaukee family boss Frank Balistrieri, Kansas City family boss Carl J. Civella, Chicago family underboss John P. "Jackie" Cerone, Chicago family capo Joseph "Joey the Clown" Lombardo, Chicago family capo Angelo LaPietra, Kansas City family underboss Carl A. DeLuna, Cleveland family financial wizard Milton P. "Maishe" Rockman, and three others.

All the defendants were convicted. Aiuppa and Cerone were given twenty-eight years in federal prison. DeLuna was also convicted for skimming at the Tropicana Casino and given thirty years imprisonment. Rockman was given twenty-four years. Lombardo and LaPietra were given sixteen years, while Balistrieri, who entered a guilty plea during the trial, was given ten years. Civella was given sixteen years. The remainder of the defendants were given prison terms ranging from five to ten years. Lonardo also testified several times before the United States Senate Rackets Committee and he appeared in several other federal prosecutions involving lower-ranking LCN figures and LCN associates.

On November 23, 1985, Licavoli learned for the first time that his replacement as boss, Angelo Lonardo, had "flipped" and gone into the Witness Security Program. Upon hearing this news, Licavoli had a massive heart attack and died. His lawyer, James Willis, commented after his death, "Nothing fazed him. Some people don't cry. He was one of those people who don't cry. I saw him about a month ago and he appeared to be in great health and he was quite optimistic that he was going to get a reduction in his sentence."

After completing his testimony, Lonardo was resentenced to five years probation. Upon Lonardo's entry into the Witness Security Program, the only remaining active member of the Cleveland La Cosa Nostra family was Consigliere John "Peanuts" Tronolone, who lived in Miami, Florida. By default, Tronolone became boss of the family, a boss of one.

During the entire period Lonardo was being debriefed and providing testimony, he was guarded twenty-four hours a day by Cleveland FBI agents, and I visited with him frequently.

We would cook delicious pasta and he would talk about old times in La Cosa Nostra. He was an outstanding witness and one of the few classy individuals I ever met in La Cosa Nostra. And he put a lot of La Cosa Nostra bosses in jail.

CHAPTER 11

Jackie Presser—
Code-Named ALPRO

For better or worse, the name Jackie Presser is synonymous with the Teamsters Union. But who was he and why did he become so important to the FBI? A bit of background is necessary in order to explain. Jackie Presser was the son of William Presser, a former International Brotherhood of Teamsters (IBT) official who initially began working with former Cleveland LCN boss John Scalish and Milton "Maishe" Rockman to infiltrate the gaming industry in Las Vegas. William Presser arranged for a Mob front, Alan Glick, to receive a $51-million loan from the Teamster's Central State Pension Fund to purchase the Freemont and Stardust casinos in Las Vegas. In return for arranging this loan, the Cleveland LCN family received what they thought was a hidden percentage of ownership in the casinos. Again, they did not receive the hidden ownership interest, but they did receive a percentage of the skim based on an agreement between the Chicago, Milwaukee, and Kansas City crime families. With his father's help, Jackie joined the IBT and, with Mob help, quickly rose in the ranks. In 1976 Jackie was an international vice president in the IBT. On April 20, 1983, Jackie became president of the IBT.

Since the days of Jimmy Hoffa and William Presser, the IBT had always been "mobbed up." Hoffa was replaced by Frank Fitzsimmons with the backing of LCN families in Cleveland, New York, New Jersey, and

Chicago. On May 6, 1981, Fitzsimmons died, and nine days later, the IBT Executive Board met in Las Vegas and elected Roy Williams president. LCN member Anthony "Tony Pro" Provenzano made the motion to elect Williams and Jackie Presser seconded the motion. Jackie was a key man in the LCN/IBT dance.

When I first reported to Cleveland in 1976 as assistant special agent in charge (ASAC), and during my first briefing by SAC Roy McKinnon, I was told that Jackie Presser was then a highly placed informant for the FBI, who was code-named "The Tailor." Because of the association of his true name to "Tailor" we changed the code name to "ALPRO" to further protect his identity. Jackie was extremely close to Maishe Rockman, the brother-in-law of LCN boss John Scalish and also of Angelo Lonardo.

Presser was considered one of the best organized-crime informants in the FBI. He was furnishing information of the highest quality concerning LCN control over the teamsters union and LCN infiltration of the gaming industry in Las Vegas.

Presser's status as an informant was a closely guarded secret disclosed only on a strict need-to-know basis. Marty McCann, one of the best informant agents in the FBI, had secured Presser's cooperation in the mid-1970s and was in contact with Jackie on a daily basis. Marty later told me that Presser was assisting the FBI primarily because he wanted to clean up the Presser name. I didn't doubt that. By talking to us, Jackie was certainly putting his life on the line.

When Jackie first agreed to cooperate with the FBI, he insisted that no file be maintained on him in Cleveland and that the knowledge of his existence as an informant be strictly controlled within the FBI. He insisted on getting assurances of confidentially from top FBI officials. Presser had met with then Cleveland SAC Roy McKinnon and Assistant FBI Director Fred Fehl, who assured him that his cooperation would be kept confidential provided he was completely truthful.

Arrangements were worked out between Fehl and McKinnon that no informant file would be maintained in Cleveland and that this file would be kept under the highest security by the chief of the FBI Organized Crime Section, who would personally supervise Presser's informant status.

McCann was instructed to personally forward his reports directly to the FBI Organized Crime Section chief, who would then disseminate the information from Presser to relevant FBI field divisions without any reference to Cleveland. If Cleveland was in the picture, someone could figure out that Presser was the informant.

Immediately before I came to Cleveland, my last assignment was chief of the FBI Intelligence Unit in the Organized Crime Section at FBI headquarters, which is the unit that supervises and coordinates organized-crime informants, and I had never before heard that Jackie was on our side.

Marty McCann showed me the unofficial informant folder on Jackie, which contained all the information that Jackie had provided since he was developed. I was shocked. I had seen this information before, being sent out to the field by my previous boss, Organized Crime Section Chief Jack Keith, as coming from an "FBI headquarters source." I remembered asking Jack who the hell this person was. He said to me that this could not be disclosed without the personal authority of the FBI director. After I reviewed Marty's folder, which he kept in a locked safe cabinet, I told him, based on my immediate prior assignment, that I was aware of all of the organized-crime information being received by the FBI nationwide and there was no question in my mind that Presser was at that time the most important organized-crime informant in the FBI.

He was providing information originating from the Commission, which he received from LCN boss John Scalish and Maishe Rockman, who dealt directly with Anthony "Fat Tony" Salerno. He was providing very detailed information concerning LCN infiltration of Las Vegas and Atlantic City from Mob leaders currently in the Teamsters.

The information was being used by offices in these areas to secure Title III wiretaps and hidden microphones. His development as an informant by McCann was a major coup for federal law enforcement. Of course, during the time I was ASAC in Cleveland, Marty and his successor, Pat Foran, kept the SACs—first Roy McKinnon and later Stan Czarnecki—and me fully apprised of the important information that Jackie was giving.

Marty retired in 1977 and Pat Foran took over as the "handling agent" for Presser. Pat was one of the finest agents I have known and the brains behind our successes in the Nardi and Greene murder investigations. As was the case with Marty McCann, Pat was a great informant handler. Shortly after I left Cleveland as ASAC in 1979, Pat was transferred to the Organized Crime Section, and Bob Friedrick replaced him as supervisor and took over as Presser contacting agent.

In 1981 the Cleveland *Plain Dealer* ran a story claiming that Jackie Presser was an FBI informant. Fortunately, we learned that the Mob did not believe the story. And, as Angelo Lonardo related, the *Plain Dealer* later printed a retraction. This story and some that followed caused a lot of discussion and speculation in the federal law enforcement community that Jackie was an informant. We didn't as a policy comment on informants and the Mob did not believe the rumors, so Jackie was secure for the time being.

On May 25, 1983, my labor supervisor, Rick Lind, called and said that Strike Force Attorney Steve Olah wanted to see me. Rick's function as the organized crime/labor supervisor was to supervise any labor cases related to organized crime, as well as to coordinate any other labor investigation we initiated. I told Rick to bring Olah in. He came to my office, accompanied by Rick, Labor Department SAC Donald Wheeler, and Labor Investigator Jim Thomas.

I had never met Wheeler, but I knew Jim Thomas and considered him a friend. Olah told me that in 1982 he had launched a federal grand jury investigation into possible criminal violations on the part of Jackie Presser involving members of Teamsters Local 507 and that he wanted to brief me on the matter.

Olah said the case was being handled by Assistant Strike Force Attorney Steve Jigger. I had heard from the handling agents that Presser had told them he was under Labor Department investigation, but this was the first official notification that I received. Presser was still furnishing extremely valuable information on a national basis and he was still regarded as a very important informant. Olah said that the strike force was assisted in this investigation by Department of Labor investigators Jim Thomas and Red Simmons.

Wheeler said that the investigation involved Presser and an alleged "ghost employee," Harold Friedman. Olah said that he anticipated indicting

Presser and Friedman during the summer or early fall of 1983. Jackie Presser was then secretary treasurer of Teamsters Local 507 and an international vice president of the International Brotherhood of Teamsters.

Wheeler advised that he would appreciate getting "criminal case histories" from us, meaning criminal arrest information. I told him that we would certainly comply with this request and, in his presence, I told Rick to give him any assistance he requested. At no time during this conference did they inquire about any possible relationship the FBI had with Presser and I did not volunteer this information. I was surprised that they did not ask the question, since it had already been extensively reported in the press that Presser was believed to be an FBI informant. I made the assumption that they already knew he was an informant, that they didn't care, and that they didn't ask because they didn't officially want to know. If they had asked, I lacked the authority to disclose this information. I had specific instructions from FBI headquarters that "under no circumstances should the existence of this source be discussed outside the FBI." I believed they failed to ask the question because they believed knowledge of his being an informant would possibly curtail their investigation.

Wheeler followed up this conference with a letter dated June 30, 1983, in which he thanked me for our cooperation and he asked for criminal case histories on Presser and six other individuals. I instructed Rick Lind to check the criminal histories and furnish them to Jim Thomas, as Wheeler requested. Lind was also aware by that time that Jackie was an informant and I told him that we had to be very conscious not to do anything that could be interpreted as interfering with the Department of Labor investigation.

During the strike force/Labor Department investigation, the FBI was kept completely in the dark concerning what was being developed by the labor investigators and the grand jury until that May meeting, more than a year after the investigation was initiated. That was as it should have been. There was no "need" for us to know about the investigation. Presser was not indicted in the summer or fall of 1983, so I believed that the investigation had not progressed as Olah had expected. I knew that in the past they had conducted at least two investigations of Presser, which had not resulted in any charges. Neither Olah nor Wheeler ever contacted me again about Presser.

PRESSER IS EXPOSED

The next time Presser came onto my radar screen was because the Los Angeles *Times* began reporting that the investigation of Presser was continuing and that the case involved "ghost employees" Presser had allegedly placed on the Teamsters payroll.* The *Times* was receiving and printing detailed information concerning this federal grand jury investigation and some of the stories indicated that Jackie was an FBI informant.

I knew that FBI headquarters had already officially advised the Department of Justice that Jackie was a valuable, highly placed informant, so I believed that these leaks were coming from Justice. I wrote an official communication to the FBI director requesting that a leak investigation be conducted.

On July 3, 1984, Department of Justice Attorney and Organized Crime Assistant Section Chief Paul Coffey came to Cleveland accompanied by FBI Assistant Organized Crime Chief Jim Moody. Olah and Jigger met with them at a private home, where they interviewed retired Supervisor Marty McCann, Supervisor Bob Friedrick, and former SACs Fred Fehl and Roy McKinnon about the FBI's relationship with Jackie Presser.

I was not aware of this meeting at the time and I was not invited to attend. I believe that the departmental attorneys issued some instructions that the meeting not be disclosed to anyone, including me. I have been told that this was an informal meeting and that only Coffey took notes. The contacting agents confirmed that Presser was an informant and that they were aware that Presser had placed the three ghost employees on the payroll. At that time, the FBI had general guidelines pertaining to the handling

---

*The term "ghost employees" refers to employees who receive pay for work not done. It is a common "shakedown" or extortion practice in organized-crime-controlled unions for criminal associates to be put on company payrolls where they are given paychecks, but they never show up at the work site.

of FBI informants. Under these guidelines, organized-crime squad supervisors could authorize the participation of an FBI informant in nonviolent criminal activity, if that activity materially furthered an FBI investigation. The hiring of the ghost employees occurred during the heat of the Cleveland gang war in the 1970s.

One of those allegedly placed on the payroll by Presser was Jack Nardi, the son of John Nardi. It was certainly in the FBI's best interest for Presser to stay close to John Nardi. The others were allegedly placed on the payroll based on instructions to Presser from Maishe Rockman and it was certainly important for Presser to stay close to Rockman.

I later learned that on July 3, 1984, after receiving the results of the Cleveland interviews, Assistant Director Oliver "Buck" Revell, who was the assistant director responsible for the organized-crime program at FBI headquarters, met with Assistant Attorney General Steve Trott about the Presser case. Revell told Trott that it was his considered opinion that if the handling agents knew of the ghost employees, there was no case against Presser because there would be no criminal intent. But based on the many subsequent newspaper articles quoting confidential "official government sources," I learned that the strike force investigation of Presser was continuing.

By 1984 Presser had become president of the Teamsters International. Because of his position with the Teamsters, FBI headquarters instructed that Cleveland no longer contact Presser as an informant and instructed that the contacting agent only accept information voluntarily provided by him. The instructions indicated Presser should be given no instructions or assignments.

On June 11, 1985, John Climaco, attorney for Jackie Presser, met with Department of Justice officials in Washington and revealed information that he had just received from Presser, indicating his "handling agents" had given him the authority to hire the ghost employees. Of course, they already knew this.

On June 20, 1985, Coffey and Moody made another secret trip to Cleveland and again spoke with McCann, Foran, and Friedrick about the Presser case. He took signed sworn statements from them all. At this meeting, the contacting agents again confirmed that they knew about the ghost employees and that they had been authorized.

On July 24, 1985, an article datelined Washington appeared in the Cleveland *Plain Dealer* headlined "U.S. Drops Investigation of Presser":

> The government has decided to drop its 32 month investigation of Teamsters President Jackie Presser, the *Los Angeles Times* reported last night. . . . Presser's alleged status as a source of information for the FBI was a key impediment to prosecution, sources said. It was learned yesterday that high Department of Justice officials have ordered a new inquiry into why the FBI did not tell the department for nearly two years that Presser had acted as an informant. . . . The Strike Force here wanted Presser, the man said to be the organizational talent, the inside man at Teamsters Local 507. Despite its recommendation to the Justice Department six months ago for prosecution of Presser, higher-ups in the department decided yesterday not to pursue an indictment. That decision, according to sources, was made primarily due to Presser's supplying of sensitive information to the FBI.

Later that day I received a telephone call from Ed Hegarty, who was now SAC in Chicago. He told me that Chicago FBI agents had just received reliable intelligence information that, because of all of the news coverage concerning Presser's allegedly being an FBI informant, Presser was in mortal danger. Joe Aiuppa, the Chicago LCN boss, now believed Jackie Presser was an informant and he wanted Presser killed—only the Commission stood in the way. I sent a teletype to FBI headquarters and followed up with a telephone call to Buck Revell, who was now executive assistant director, the number three person in the FBI. After I apprised him of the facts, Buck said that he had already sent a recommendation to Director Webster that a criminal investigation be conducted of the department as to who had leaked this sensitive information to the press.

We agreed that Jackie Presser was now in danger. Buck suggested, and I agreed, that Presser be immediately contacted and advised of what we had learned—and that he should strongly consider going public with his cooperation with the FBI over the years. We agreed that if he did not want to go into the Witness Security Program, which was likely, we would provide a full FBI security detail on an interim basis until permanent arrangements could be worked out with the Department of Justice.

I furnished these instructions to Organized Crime Supervisor Robert Friedrick and he immediately hopped on a plane to meet with Presser in Washington. Friedrick later called me from Washington and said that Jackie was not concerned and he believed he could take care of himself. Jackie was a tough guy and, in my opinion, a courageous guy. From what Friedrick said, Jackie never complained about being exposed as an FBI informant.

On July 30, 1985, NBC News quoted an unidentified source that Jackie Presser was regarded as one of the best informants the FBI used. On August 4, 1985, the *Chicago Tribune* reported that Jackie Presser was an FBI informant and interviewed him concerning his relationship with the FBI. Jackie refused to comment, but his lawyer, John Climaco, emphatically and repeatedly denied that he was an informant.

To the best of my knowledge no leak investigation was ever conducted by the Department of Justice or the FBI, but in September 1985 they did mount a massive federal grand jury investigation in Cleveland and Washington centered on why we did not inform the Department of Justice earlier as to Presser's status as an informant and to the validity of the FBI claims that agents had authorized the ghost employees.

Articles appeared in the newspaper on almost a daily basis quoting "informed sources" that Presser was an informant and that the FBI was protecting Presser from prosecution. One story quoted an unnamed "confidential government source" that this federal grand jury investigation was "bigger that Watergate." This, of course, occurred after Presser threw Teamsters support to President Ronald Reagan. I think that the strike force believed that this was a conspiracy beginning with McCann, Foran, and Friedrick, going to me, to Buck Revell, to Director Webster, to Attorney General Meese, and to President Reagan, all to protect Presser from prosecution. This, of course, was ridiculous.

I was one of the first agents to appear before the federal grand jury in September. I was questioned by attorneys from the Public Integrity Section. I do not have a transcript of my testimony, but this is my recollection on how it went. The questioning of me focused on a claim that I telephoned Steve Olah during the time that the Department of Labor investigators were executing a search warrant at Teamster Local 507. I was asked if I had called Olah when I learned of this search and I told the grand jury that I had not. I was then asked if I had ranted and raved at Olah during this conversation and said that he should have told the FBI about the raid. I told them that I had not called Olah that day and I had not complained about anything. I told them that this conversation did not take place.

One of the attorneys then asked me if Olah had asked me if Presser was an informant and if I had told Olah that he was not an informant. I said that this conversation never took place and I did not tell Olah that Presser was not an informant.

Several days later, I was recalled by the grand jury. The same Department of Justice OPR attorneys began the questioning. I was directed to a specific day in 1982 and a specific time of that day. I don't remember the exact day and time, but it was the day that Local 507 was raided by the Department of Labor. I was asked if I had called Olah that afternoon during the raid. I said that I certainly had not. I was then asked if I had berated Olah about not being advised of the Labor Department raid. I said that I did not call him and I did not berate him. I was then asked if, during that conversation, Olah asked me if Presser was an FBI informant and I said that he was not. I told the grand jury that this conversation did not take place and that none of this was true; that if someone had testified to this, the person was lying.

I knew from the tone and nature of the questions that I was now being targeted for criminal perjury charges.

I immediately checked my calendar, which is a daily record of my activities kept by my secretary. I had been ordered to bring this to the grand jury. I was relieved to see that on this particular day in 1982, I was in the presence of two federal judges for the entire day and I would have had no way to learn of the Labor Department raid and no opportunity to place a telephone call to Olah.

On that day, based on a request from Cleveland U.S. District Judge John M. Manos, I had accompanied him and Chief U.S. District Judge Frank Battisti to Akron, Ohio, for a judicial function.

I picked up the judges in the morning, took them to Akron, and attended the function with them, and we had a late lunch. I returned to Cleveland later in the day, dropped them off at their residences, and did not go into the FBI office that day. I didn't get home until after 6:00 P.M. and I did not even know about the Labor Department search. When I explained what I had done on that day, the questioning came to an abrupt halt and I was excused by the grand jury.

If I had not been lucky enough to have a solid record of my activities for that day—a perfect alibi, if you will—there is no question in my mind that I would have been facing criminal perjury charges. If the person who gave this fraudulent story to the grand jury had picked any other day, I would have been indicted and fired from the FBI.

The news stories based on government leaks continued on a daily basis. One news report, again from the *Los Angeles Times*, reported:

Expressing concern that failure to indict Presser could tarnish the integrity of the Justice Department and the Reagan administration, the prosecutors raised the possibility that FBI agents might have overstepped their authority if they promised the union boss immunity from prosecution. And citing intelligence reports that Presser's influence was waning, they dismissed as "specious" the FBI's contention that the government could use him to clean up the mob influenced Teamsters Union.

This highly confidential memorandum was written last January [1985] and spelled out in detail the evidence amassed against Presser during an almost three year investigation. It also outlined the charges prosecutors wished to bring against Presser. . . . In the memorandum, strike force officials Steven P. Olah and Stephen H. Jigger took issue with what later became the basis for Margolis' decision, the disclosure that Presser had served as an FBI informant. . . . Olah and Jigger contend in the memo that the FBI failed to inform them that Presser was a government informant when their investigation first became public on Nov. 10, 1982. On that date, a search warrant for the headquarters of Presser's hometown local, Local 507, was unsealed in Cleveland. According to the memo, it revealed the broad contours of the investigation. . . . In addition, the memo charges Joseph Griffin, Special Agent in Charge of the FBI's Cleveland Field office at the time, specifically denied that Presser was an FBI informant when Olah raised the question immediately after the search took place.

From my experience, I know that the document quoted in this *Los Angeles Times* article was what is called a prosecution memo or "pros memo," which is a highly confidential document prepared by the prosecutors (strike force attorneys in this case) that is submitted to the Department of Justice in Washington for approval of a planned federal grand jury indictment. The release of this highly sensitive document is a violation of Department of Justice regulations and a violation of federal law.

FRIEDRICK UNDER FIRE

On August 9, 1985, an agent in the FBI's Office of Professional Responsibility (OPR) contacted one of my ASACs, Philip Urick, and instructed him to have Bob Friedrick report to Washington on August 12 for a further interview on the Presser matter. The agent was unable to furnish Urick any information as to why they wanted to see Friedrick. Friedrick was in New England on vacation, but Urick was able to locate him and he was advised to report to Washington as indicated. I was also on annual leave and did not learn about this until the next week.

According to court records, Friedrick reported to FBI headquarters as ordered and went to the office FBI OPR Unit Chief Larry C. Upchurch. Upchurch and another agent presented to him the FBI Standard Form FD-645, which was the "Warning and Assurance to Employee Required to Provide Information," which he signed. This form basically tells the employee that he has to answer the questions under penalty of termination and that the answers to the questions cannot be used against him in a court of law. Friedrick was told that it had been decided he would not be prosecuted in the Presser case, but he had an obligation to be truthful in his statement. Agent Theodore Jackson arrived shortly thereafter and the interview began. The interview was completed for the day at about 1:54 P.M. and Friedrick returned the following day to complete the interview.

When Friedrick returned to Cleveland, I called him into my office and asked what was going on. He said that it was about the Presser case, but he had been instructed by Justice Department officials not to talk to anyone about the matter, including me. I told him that as his SAC, I needed to know what was going on and he again told me that he had specific instructions from OPR officials not to discuss this matter with me.

Court records indicate that in the following five months, Friedrick was interviewed at least ten more times about the Presser authorizations by two FBI OPR investigators and three different Department of Justice attorneys. Friedrick was never advised that he did not have to submit to interview. In fact, he was told that he had to submit to these interviews, otherwise he would be fired. It subsequently came out in testimony before the U.S. District Court in Washington that during one of the interviews, the FBI interviewer pulled out the Miranda form (the advice of constitutional rights form) for Friedrick to see, but he was waved off by one of the Justice Department attorneys participating in the interview.

Court records indicate that Justice Department attorneys alleged that during one of these interviews Friedrick said he "lied" when he said that he had authorized one of the ghost employees. They also alleged that Friedrick met privately with Presser's attorney, John Climaco, prior to Climaco's meeting with the Department of Justice attorneys on June 11, 1985.

On May 16, 1986, Jackie Presser was indicted by the federal grand jury in Cleveland for embezzling money from Teamsters Local 507. The charges related to the alleged ghost employees who were on the Local 507 payroll. The charges were filed when Presser was in Las Vegas preparing for the annual International Brotherhood of Teamsters convention. Presser returned to Cleveland, appeared for arraignment, and was released on $50,000 bond.

Later, Marty McCann and Pat Foran, who actually gave federal approval of the ghost employees, were waiting to testify as defense witnesses at his trial. Unfortunately, Jackie Presser died in 1988 while awaiting trial, still president of the Teamsters.

On May 16, 1986, Bob Friedrick was also indicted by the federal grand jury in Washington, D.C., and charged with five counts of violation of Title

1001, furnishing false information. Court records indicate that this indictment includes comparisons of statements made by Friedrick during some ten interviews by the multiple FBI OPR investigators and attorneys over a two-year period. Friedrick had to spend a week in jail before he was released on bond. Shortly thereafter, he was fired by Director Webster. Friedrick would later be eligible to have a civil service hearing to get his job back.

On December 5, 1986, Washington, D.C., U.S. District Judge George H. Revercomb threw out all of the evidence against Friedrick and dismissed the case against him. He ruled from the bench and it was reported in the press that departmental attorneys Richard M. Rogers and Robert R. Chapman had "tricked" Friedrick into believing that he had to answer their questions on the many dates that they had interviewed him. They had skipped a basic investigative step when interviewing a suspect, something that the newest beat cop knows—that is, advising him of his constitutional rights as an American citizen. These guys are supposed to be top lawyers. They must have known at the time Friedrick was indicted that they could not convict him.

During the hearings that led to the dismissal of the indictment against Friedrick, U.S. Attorney Pat McLaughlin testified that during the period Friedrick was being interviewed by OPR attorneys, Friedrick came to his office and requested a personal meeting. Pat testified that Friedrick asked for his legal advice. Pat testified that he told Friedrick that as U.S. attorney, he could not give him any advice because he, Friedrick, was under OPR investigation. Pat testified that Friedrick was confused about his status, about whether he had been given immunity, and he wondered if he should hire an attorney. Pat told him that as a U.S. citizen, he had the right to counsel and, under the circumstances, he should hire an attorney. Bob then hired former U.S. Attorney Bill Beyer, but it was too late to avoid the indictment and firing. Bill is a great attorney, but he could not turn back time. They had already "tricked" Friedrick.

Friedrick was not convicted of anything. However, if he did in fact lie to the OPR people, he made a terrible mistake. The truthful statements given by McCann and Foran were put in doubt, which permitted the strike force to proceed with charges against Presser, forcing the Justice Department to publicly identify Presser as an FBI informant. This was perhaps a case where an agent got too close to his informant, thereby placing them both in jeopardy. In truth, he was a first-office agent with only seven years experience, although he was forty-two years old. We may have been partly responsible for what happened. With his limited experience, he was given a tremendous responsibility when he was assigned to handle Presser. Maybe he was given this assignment too early in his career. Informants are the most important assets we have, but they are dangerous to handle.

No matter what Frederick told the attorneys, Presser would still have been exposed as an informant. His life was placed in jeopardy because of the numerous Department of Justice and/or Department of Labor leaks after the first indictment was not returned.

The strike force and OPR never challenged the statements of McCann and Foran in a forthright manner. The OPR sent Foran and McCann "target letters" indicating they were targets of a federal grand jury. As often happens, the grand jury cleared them of any suspicion, but after the grand jury was ended, no public announcement was made clearing their names.

This case was a true tragedy. Friedrick was a war hero—he had a wonderful background with many accomplishments in the FBI. As you know, he was one of the case agents in the Nardi and Greene murder investigations and was the principal factor in the turning of Angelo Lonardo. He had a very promising future in the FBI.

McKinnon and I testified for Friedrick at his subsequent civil service hearing when he attempted to be reinstated, but to no avail. No FBI agent can function when he has been charged in federal court with lying. His credibility as an agent had been destroyed.

Marty McCann retired in 1977 after a distinguished twenty-five-year FBI career. He personally solved countless important cases when he was an FBI agent and supervisor, including the 1969 murder of United Mining Workers official Joseph A. Yablonski and his family. He was an outstanding agent and supervisor. During this ordeal, he was working in the private sector and then, almost ten years after his retirement, TV cameras were camped on a daily basis outside his house, hounding him and his family. This was terrible.

Pat Foran was assistant special agent in charge of the Las Vegas office of the FBI when this investigation was initiated by the strike force. Of course, he was previously the Organized Crime Supervisor in Cleveland and the moving force behind the Nardi and Greene murder investigations. He was one of the most brilliant young leaders we had in the bureau. Before his retirement in 2000, he had become the FBI personnel officer, one of the highest positions in the FBI. But the FBI suffered because he did not become an SAC. Some of the problems the FBI is having today can be traced to the bureau not having adequate depth of experienced leadership in the SAC ranks.

Shortly thereafter, and as a result of the turmoil caused by the Cleveland Strike Force leadership and their cohorts in Washington, U.S. Attorney Pat McLaughlin joined Los Angeles U.S. Attorney Rob Bonner in the fight among the nation's U.S. attorneys to persuade Attorney General Edwin Meese to merge the strike forces into the U.S. Attorney's Office. In areas where there were outstanding U.S. attorneys and weak leadership in the strike force, problems always followed. That was my experience in Buffalo and Cleveland. The strike force had great prosecutors, but because of the way the cases were managed by the leadership, we always had a long backlog of cases awaiting trial. In Buffalo and Cleveland, it was not unusual for a case to come to trial three or four years after the initial arrest. My counterparts in Chicago and Pittsburgh told me they had the same experiences. The U.S. attorney is responsible to the local citizens, not to some bureaucrat in Washington. Meese was under severe attack from the left wing of the Democratic party, so he took no action. When Dick Thornburgh became attorney general, one of his first acts was to merge the strike forces into the U.S. Attorney's Office.

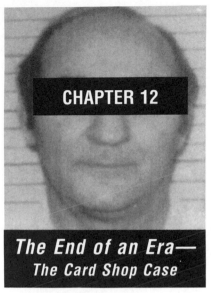

CHAPTER 12

The End of an Era—
The Card Shop Case

Upon my return to Cleveland in 1981, Dave Drab from the 9 Squad was working a case code-named "Whipsaw," which was an effort to trace illegal funds from gambling sources to James Licavoli and, later, his successor, Angelo Lonardo. Licavoli's headquarters was the Card Shop, a shabby storefront room on Mayfield Road in the Murray Hill section of Cleveland.

On January 8, 1982, Dave secured court authorization to install a microphone in the shop. We set up a discreet surveillance on Mayfield Road to determine the best time to make the entry. We found that there was a squad of young wannabe hoods that patroled the neighborhood for Licavoli throughout each night. This was going to be another tough entry.

On one occasion, while we were watching, these young toughs spotted an African American innocently driving down Mayfield Road and they jumped in front of his car, pulling him from the car and assaulting him. When we saw this situation start to develop, a call to the local police and their quick response probably saved the poor guy's life.

On January 11, 1982, at 3:10 A.M., when Mayfield Road was clear, I led a team of FBI agents, including Dave Drab, other 9 Squad agents, and our technical agents, into the Card Shop. We were trying to determine where to place the bug, and then we spotted a sign on one of the corner tables that said "VIP." That was Licavoli's table, so we placed the microphone right over the corner seat at this table. The installation took about an hour and when we were told by the outside agents that Mayfield Road was again clear, we quickly exited and walked to our waiting panel truck.

We began listening on January 11 and continued until March 14. During these three months we learned that the funds for all of Licavoli's gambling and bookmaking activities were being handled by Sam Perconti, a non-LCN member, but a close and trusted associate of Licavoli. Licavoli had three principal bookmakers, George Argie, Billy Dileno, and Anthony Spagnola. There was also a location called Pineway Trails, which was an illegal casino operation in the suburbs of Cleveland. These men represented what remained of the Cleveland LCN family. None of them were "made" members of the family, but they acted on behalf of Licavoli and Lonardo.

This investigation would last for six years, with the strike force leadership dragging its feet at every turn. During the intervening period, we would conduct ten raids of the bookmaking offices and Pineway Trails, and in each of these raids, we obtained voluminous records of the enterprise.

Based on an examination of the seized records, the interviews of hundreds of the bookmaking customers and game participants, Drab was successful in establishing that Licavoli was involved in a massive loan-sharking, bookmaking, and money-laundering operation which was being undertaken by non-LCN-member functionaries. After Licavoli and Lonardo were convicted in the other cases, we continued the investigation.

All this information was presented to the federal grand jury and on January 8, 1988, the grand jury returned an indictment charging William E. Dileno, Martin "Mutt" DeFabio, Gary P. "Midget" Compola, John C. Trunzo, George J. Argie, Joseph A. Spaganlo, Salvatore R. Perconti, and Zoltan P. "Zolty" Kalman with violation of the RICO statute and the illegal gambling business statute. We had previously seized $32,056 from the bookmakers and $76,729 from the loan sharks.

Later that day, at about 3:30, we raided the Card Shop and arrested all of the indicted subjects. Under the recovery provisions of the RICO law, we seized the Card Shop. The Card Shop, which had been Cleveland LCN headquarters since Licavoli took over as boss in 1976, was now the property of the people of the United States. Dave posted the notification of the seizure and the press arrived. I told the reporters that day it was the end of an era. And it was.

All of these men were later tried in federal court by U.S. Attorney Pat McLaughlin and his staff. They were convicted on all counts. The star witness at their trial was their former boss, Angelo Lonardo. He knew what each man did for LCN and he testified completely. The boss was now testifying against the soldiers.

On August 23, 1989, all of these subjects appeared for sentencing before U.S. District Judge Alice M. Batchelder. Billy Dileno was given five years in prison and fined $15,000. Joseph "Spaggs" Spaganlo was sentenced to three years and fined $10,000. John Trunzo, age sixty, was given three years probation and fined $10,000. Gary P. Compola, age forty-five, was sentenced to two years in prison and fined $5,000. Salvatore R. "Bones" Perconti, age fifty-two, was given two years and fined $2,000. Zoltan "Zolty" Kalman, age forty-five, was given one year in prison and fined $2,000. Earlier in the year, when he saw the overwhelming evidence, Martin N. "Mutt" DeFabio had entered a guilty plea and he was sentenced to six years in prison.

Subsequent to the turning of Angelo Lonardo and death of James Licavoli, our informants reported that John "Peanuts" Tronolone, a resident of Miami, Florida, had been named by the Commission as the boss of the Cleveland family. Tronolone was formerly with the Magaddino family, but had switched to the Cleveland family in the 1960s. Tronolone was the only Cleveland family member left standing.

Tronolone never returned to Cleveland. Unfortunately for him, he did not have the normal LCN "insulation," the levels between the actual criminal activity and the boss. Several months after he was made boss, he began dealing with a burglar to purchase stolen diamonds. The burglar was actually a Florida police officer, who promptly arrested him. Tronolone was subsequently convicted on criminal receiving charges and sentenced to nine years in prison.

Based in part on information provided by Angelo Lonardo and Jackie

Presser, then New York U.S. Attorney Rudolph W. Guiliani secured a federal indictment against Genovese family boss Anthony "Fat Tony" Salerno; Genovese capos Matthew "Matty the Horse" Ianniello, Vincent "Fat Vinnie" DiNapoli, Guiseppe "Pepe" Sabato, and Vincent "Fish" Cafaro; Louis Di Napoli, Carmine Della Cava, Thomas Cafaro, Alphonese Mosca, Neil Migliore, Milton "Maische" Rockman, and John "Peanuts" Tronolone. This indictment charged, among other things, that these individuals, representing La Cosa Nostra, controlled the International Brotherhood of the Teamsters (IBT) and were responsible for selecting Roy Williams and Jackie Presser as presidents of the IBT. Angelo Lonardo was the star witness at this trial, which lasted about a year. Former Teamsters President Roy Williams, serving a ten-year prison term for conspiring to bribe Nevada U.S. Senator Howard Cannon, also "flipped" and testified at this trial. Midway through the case, Vincent "Fish" Cafaro decided he wanted to become an informant, so he "flipped" and also testified.

On May 4, 1988, the jury found all of these defendants guilty with the exception of Rockman and Tronolone, who were acquitted. Rockman was already in prison as a result of the conviction in Kansas City and Tronolone was out on bond in regard to the Florida conviction.

On June 2, 1991, Tronolone, the lonely LCN boss, died in a Miami Beach hospital after suffering a heart attack.

Epilogue

After the Card Shop investigation was completed, I believed my work in Cleveland had reached its end. We had taken on the Mob in Cleveland and won. I knew that my time for a transfer was coming up—I had been in Cleveland for more than seven years, about two years longer than the normal tour of an SAC.

In July 1988 my friend John Glover, who was a top aide to FBI Director William Sessions, called to tell me that the director was transferring me to Kansas City as SAC. At the time I was the senior field commander in the FBI—I had been in this position longer than any other SAC. A number of the other experienced SACs had retired when the new director, Bill Sessions, began moving his favorites into place.

When I told my wife, Jan, about the transfer, she told me that she would not make another move and that if I went to Kansas City, I was on my own. I couldn't blame her. We had moved eight times during my FBI career and during most of these moves, she was by herself for long periods of time, sometimes more than a year at a stretch, while we tried to sell our previous house.

That same day, I received a call from an acquaintance of mine who had just been appointed executive vice president/general counsel for a major drug company in Chicago. He asked me if I knew of an SAC who would be retiring soon who could come to his firm and set up a security department. I said, "I have been thinking about going, so if you want me, I'll take the job." I telephoned John and told him that I was not taking the Kansas City job and that I was going to retire. He couldn't believe it, since I was only forty-eight years old. Several weeks later, I met Judge Sessions at our annual SAC conference and he attempted to talk me into staying, telling me that he would cancel the transfer. By this time, I had already made the commitment in Chicago, so I told him my decision was final.

I had fulfilled my ambitions in the FBI. From the beginning, I had wanted to be a force against organized crime in the United States, to help America defeat this cancer among us. The Cleveland LCN family had been virtually destroyed and I did not believe I could do much in Kansas City that had not already been done. With the conviction of the Kansas City LCN leadership in the Strawman case, it was my understanding that this family was also on its last legs. It was time for me to move on to other challenges.

On September 1, 1988, after thirty-one years, I retired from the FBI. My wife and I had some issues that we could not resolve, so we divorced. I took the job in Chicago as corporate security director for the drug company. I didn't like the job, especially when I found that they didn't really want a security department. Instead, I *was* the security department. I had been on my own too long to work for someone else, so I left in 1990 to establish my own investigative firm, Griffin Security Research, Inc. I was also appointed the regional supervisor of the Motion Picture Association of America (MPAA), supervising former FBI agents in Illinois, Ohio, Michigan, Kentucky, Wisconsin, and Minneapolis in the MPAA antipiracy investigations. This was a great job and a lot of fun. We identified video stores and manufacturers who were dealing in counterfeit video cassettes, secured federal court orders to seize the counterfeit videos, and, with deputy U.S. marshals, raided the stores and factories and seized all the bad tapes. It was almost like being back in the bureau.

My new wife, Martha, whom I married in 1990, was suffering from breast cancer and, tragically, she passed away from this disease in August 1993, at the age of thirty-eight. This was a very sad period in my life, but I buried myself in my work and continued my private investigative efforts for several Chicago law firms and for the MPAA. Being alone was new to me and not a pleasant experience. I am an oil painter, and I found myself waking during the night, going to my easel, and painting until dawn.

THE MOB AND LIUNA

In November 1994 I received a call from an old bureau friend, Doug Gow, who had just taken over as the inspector general of the Laborers' International Union of North America (LIUNA). This union was founded in 1903 and currently consists of over 750,000 members in the United States and Canada. Unfortunately, over the years, in many of the larger cities, La Cosa Nostra has taken over locals and in many areas it completely controls the union's activities. The LIUNA had been under investigation for many years and the federal government was now threatening to place the union in trusteeship. In order to avoid this, the union entered into a consent decree with the government. This consent decree required the union to adapt a constitution and a code of conduct forbidding union members to be members of organized crime or associates of organized-crime figures. It also required that the union put in place an independent structure to deal with allegations of corruption. The union first hired Peter F. Vaira, a former organized-crime strike force chief who was also a U.S. attorney, as the independent hearing officer (the judge over any charges brought against LIUNA members). Also hired were the following: Robert D. Luskin, a former Justice Department organized-crime prosecutor, as the independent general counsel; Doug Gow, a former associate director of the FBI, as inspector general; and Dwight Bostwick, a former assistant U.S. attorney, to work with Gow's staff to present the evidence in future hearings before Vaira. I knew all of these men with the exception of Dwight, and I highly respected all of them. Based on these appointments, I knew that the union was serious about getting rid of the Mob. It had hired people who knew organized crime for these key independent positions. This was a winning team and I wanted to be on it. J. Edgar Hoover once commented, "There is no such thing as a former FBI agent." He was so right.

Doug asked me to become an inspector on his staff and wanted me to coordinate the LIUNA inspector general's investigations in the Midwest. I jumped at the chance. The Chicago LIUNA was totally controlled by the Chicago LCN family and I knew that the FBI had been unsuccessful in its efforts to get the Buffalo LCN family out of Buffalo's Local 210. I had worked on that some thirty years before and the Mob still controlled Local 210.

At about this same time a friend, Lee Flosi, who was a former FBI organized crime supervisor in Chicago, called me and inquired if we might merge our private investigative businesses. He was slated to spend the next three years in Rome on a religious mission and he wanted a business to come back to. Lee had been the FBI legal attaché in Rome during the famous Pizza Connection case, relating to the Sicilian heroin-smuggling ring that was uncovered by FBI agents in New York and successfully prosecuted by Rudy Giuliani's office in the fall of 1986.

The Justice Department had filed a civil lawsuit against the Hotel Employees and Restaurant Employees International Union (HERIU) under the RICO Act on September 5, 1995, alleging theft of union funds, bribery, extortion, and breaches of union members' rights. Simultaneously with LIUNA, HERIU and the Justice Department had entered into a consent decree that established a process for cleansing the union of corrupt practices and criminal linkages.

Former Strike Force Attorney Kurt W. Mullenberg had been appointed as monitor of HERIU and was given the task of conducting the internal investigations. Lee Flosi had received a contract from Kurt to conduct all of the Chicago investigations. Edward Hanley had been president of HERIU for the past twenty-five years and he was believed to be "mobbed up." After several weeks of conversations, Lee and I merged our companies and founded a new investigative company, Quest Consultants International, Ltd. We brought Jack O'Rourke and Bob Scigalski, who had recently retired from the FBI, into the business as well.

Jack is an expert organized-crime agent who is renowned for his expertise in developing and handling informants. He still has a number of sources within organized crime whom he can contact to get current LCN information.

Bob is a former FBI supervisor who was one of the first FBI profilers. He is also an expert organized-crime specialist. We all became LIUNA inspectors and HERIU inspectors together and entered the battle, now as civilians.

My first assignment for Doug Gow was in my old stomping ground—Cleveland, Ohio. The LIUNA inspector general had received allegations that Zip Liberatore, the business manager of one of the Cleveland locals and the nephew of Anthony Liberatore, was involved in several corrupt practices, including skimming money from training fund contributions and receiving kickbacks from employers. I was sent to investigate these allegations, and I teamed up with Inspector John Billi, another former FBI agent.

At the conclusion of the investigation, the independent hearing officer removed Zip Liberatore from this position and he was thrown out of the LIUNA, forever barred from a LIUNA membership. However, Zip was not charged with any criminal violations. That was up to law enforcement.

THE MOB AND LIUNA IN BUFFALO

My second assignment as an inspector for LIUNA was Local 210 in Buffalo. When I returned to Buffalo in 1995 to begin the work of cleaning up Local 210, it was surreal. The sons of the guys that we put in jail in the 1960s were now running the Buffalo LCN family and Local 210.

Joe Todaro Jr. was a former Local 210 business agent who had recently resigned. My old nemesis, Daniel G. Sansanese, had two sons, Daniel Sansanese Jr. and Victor Sansanese. Daniel was now the secretary treasurer of Local 210. Victor Sansanese was the director of training. Sam Pieri's brother, Joseph Pieri, had two sons, John and Joey Pieri, who were in their early forties. They were now business agents of Local 210.

Harold Boreanaz was a famous defense attorney who represented many of the LCN guys in the 1960s and now his son, Robert, was representing Local 210 and the pension fund.

I thought about it and I realized that this was human nature—the sons are exposed to their father's occupation and many times follow in their footsteps. One of my sons went to the U.S. Air Force Academy and, after five-year tour as an air force officer, he became an FBI agent. So be it. The apple falls close to the tree.

In Buffalo I teamed up with three other former FBI agents: former Buffalo SAC Phil Smith, John Billi, and Tommy McDonnell, and we began assembling information to prove that the leadership of Local 210 were members of the LCN or associated with organized crime. We first had to establish through our testimony and exhibits that La Cosa Nostra actually existed in Buffalo, and then we had to prove that the current officers were members or associates of La Cosa Nostra. Phil, Tom, John, and I were qualified as an organized-crime experts by Vaira.

We located and interviewed Tom's former informant, Fred Saia, who was then in the Witness Security Program, as well as Ron Fino, a former informant who was developed by Ron Hadinger in the 1960s, also in the Witness Security Program. I had already interviewed Angelo Lonardo about Local 210 and I contacted another former informant who was still alive in Buffalo.

We learned that during the past sixty-five years, Local 210 had never had a contested election. During this period, when it was necessary to replace a union officer, the new officer would be appointed by the union's executive board, and in the next election the new officer would run unopposed. After we had assembled our evidence, Gow and Luskin filed charges against Local 210 and twenty-eight Local 210 officers and members who were believed to be members or associates of the LCN.

The hearings regarding these charges began before Independent Hearing Officer Peter Vaira in February 1996. I was permitted to testify about information I had received from my LCN member informants thirty years ago—it was amazing! I could remember the details of these guys activities in the 1960s, but sometimes I couldn't remember what I had for dinner the previous night.

When I was testifying, the attorneys for one of the officers asked me if I could remember anything that his client did that was illegal. I remembered an incident that had occurred in the late 1960s; no prosecution resulted because the witness refused to come forward. As I was testifying,

I watched the officer, and when he heard my response to his lawyer's question, his eyes lit up and he smiled. He had forgotten the incident himself.

We presented charts showing what occurred when the leadership of the Buffalo LCN family changed—the leadership of Local 210 would change in tandem with the LCN family. Local 210 was a mirror of the organized-crime family.

At the conclusion of the hearings, Independent Hearing Officer Vaira, with the later concurrence of LIUNA Appellate Officer W. Neil Eggleston, ruled that La Cosa Nostra had until that time controlled Local 210. He found that Frank "Butchie" Bifulco, Salvatore "Sam" Cardinale, John Catanzaro, Leonard Falzone, Sam "The Farmer" Frangiamore, Peter Gerace, Bart Mazzara, Robert Panaro, Donald "Turtle" Panepinto, John A. Pieri, Joseph R. Pieri, Charles Pusateri, Joseph Rosato, Danny Sansanese Jr., Victor Sansanese, Louis Sicurella, Vincent "Jimmy" Sicurella, and Joseph A. Todaro Jr. were members of organized crime. He found that the other ten LIUNA members charged were organized-crime associates. He barred them all from any future union position and barred them forever from LIUNA.

Local 210 was placed in trusteeship and later Buffalo Organized Crime Supervisor Jack McDonald was appointed by U.S. District Court Richard Arcara to be court liaison officer for Local 210, overseeing the trustee for the court.

On January 12 and 13, 2001, Local 210 held its first contested election and a slate of actual laborers became officers of Local 210. For the first time in history, the twelve-hundred-member Local 210 was in the hands of the workers it represents.

THE MOB AND LIUNA IN CHICAGO

When I returned to Chicago, my partners—now also LIUNA inspectors—were well on their way gathering evidence concerning the Chicago District Council of LIUNA and a number of other locals that we believed were controlled by the Chicago LCN family.

We also began an intensive investigation of Edward Hanley, the presi-

dent of HERIU. Through the use of several of Jack O'Rourke's informants, extensive physical surveillance, and countless interviews of union
associates, we gathered sufficient information for Kurt Mullenberg to permanently remove Hanley from the union.

Our first LIUNA target in Chicago was John Serpico. He was the
business manager for Local 8, a union that consisted mostly of Hispanic
women, many of whom could not speak English. Serpico was also an
international vice president in LIUNA. We developed information that he
was being groomed by the Chicago family to replace Arthur Coia as president of LIUNA. After our investigation, Serpico was dismissed from the
union and forever barred from membership in LIUNA. Local 8 was placed
in trusteeship.

We also investigated the Chicago District Council, which had also
never had a contested election in its history. We found that the leadership
of the council changed in unison with the changes in the leadership of the
Chicago family. Another mirror.

At the beginning of our investigation, the LIUNA Chicago District
Council consisted of John Matassa, Frank Caruso, Joe Lombardo, and
Bruno Caruso. The FBI identified John Matassa as the LCN capo in charge
of Chicago's North Side organized crime and Frank Caruso as the LCN
capo running Chicago's Chinatown.

Lee Flosi attempted to interview Frank Caruso early on in our investigation. The LIUNA constitution and code of conduct require LIUNA
officials and union members to answer any inquiries by the inspector general's office. The officials have to talk to us or they can be barred from the
union. They are not permitted to "lawyer up." When Lee tried to talk to
Frank Caruso, he abruptly resigned from the District Council and moved
over to become deputy director of one of the LIUNA funds.

At the conclusion of the Quest investigation, hearings were heard
before Independent Hearing Officer Peter Vaira. We all testified as expert
organized-crime witnesses and we also used a number of witnesses who
are now in the Witness Security Program. These are people who were
informants and witnesses for Jack, Bob, and Lee when they were FBI
agents. We also used my friend Ron Fino and Fred Saia.

At the conclusion of the hearing, Vaira ruled that the Chicago District Council was actually operated by the Chicago LCN family. He dismissed all the council members and the council was placed in trusteeship. Attorney Robert Bloch was named trustee by LIUNA and recently former Assistant U.S. Attorney Steve Miller was named monitor of the council, overseeing Bloch's trusteeship. Quest continues to work closely with Bloch and Miller.

We uncovered corruption in our investigation of Local 225 and, after hearings before Vaira, Local 225 was placed in trusteeship and the business manager, John Galioto, was kicked out of LIUNA and forever barred from membership.

The business manager of Local 2 was John Matassa. This local represents the deep tunnel workers in Chicago. At the conclusion of our investigation, Luskin and Gow filed charges against Matassa, charging he was a member of the "Chicago Outfit." After extensive hearings, Varia ruled that Matassa was an organized-crime member. Varia placed the local in trusteeship and permanently removed Matassa from LIUNA. Varia appointed Dave Shippers, a former chief of the Chicago strike force and majority counsel on the U.S. congressional impeachment committee, as the trustee of Local 2.

Another local that was controlled by organized crime was Local 5, whose business manager was Frank Zeuberis. A hearing was held at the conclusion of our investigation, and Vaira threw Zeuberis out of LIUNA permanently. The evidence we developed was turned over to local prosecutors and Zeuberis was subsequently charged criminally for defrauding Local 5.

Our sources reported that two additional Chicago locals were dominated by the Chicago LCN family: Local 1006, whose business manager was Leo Caruso, and Local 1001, whose business manager was Bruno Caruso. Local 1001 represents the workers in the Chicago Department of Streets and Sanitation.

At the conclusion of the Quest investigation these locals, charges were filed by the LIUNA general executive board attorney charging Frank Caruso, Bruno Caruso, Leo Caruso, and James DiForti with membership in the Chicago LCN family and knowing association with the Chicago

Outfit. Frank and Bruno Caruso are the sons of Frank "Skids" Caruso, who, according to the FBI, was an LCN capo who ran the "26th Street Crew" from the 1950s until his death in 1980. Leo is Skids's nephew.

DiForti died during the hearings. After the hearings, which lasted several months, Vaira issued his order on January 11, 2001. In this 123-page legal decision, Varia found that Frank Caruso, Bruno Caruso, and Leo Caruso were closely associated with the Chicago LCN family, commonly referred to as the Chicago Outfit. Vaira stated, "There is a preponderance of the evidence that the Carusos were deeply involved with organized crime figures in a substantial manner." According to Vaira, "The totality of the circumstances of this record presents a closely intertwined body of corroborative evidence that proves by a preponderance of the evidence that Frank Caruso, Leo Caruso, and Bruno Caruso were trusted associates of the Chicago Outfit." Later in the ruling, Vaira stated, "There is a preponderance of the evidence that the Chicago Outfit dictated the selection and promotion of officers and trustees of major LIUNA locals and the Chicago District Council. Frank Caruso, Bruno Caruso, and Leo Caruso participated with organized crime leaders to manipulate the election machinery of the Chicago District Council and their local unions to completely rig the succession and transfer of officers and trustees to the dictates of organized crime."

Vaira permanently revoked Frank Caruso's membership in LIUNA and permanently barred him from holding an office in or being employed by Local 1001 and/or the Chicago District Council, and from being an officer or being employed by any LIUNA-affiliated entity or fund. Bruno and Leo Caruso got the same medicine. They were all kicked out of LIUNA. They appealed and their appeal was denied. They are out of LIUNA for life. This was an administrative hearing and no criminal charges were filed against any of the officers.

Our investigation into the Chicago LCN control over other LIUNA is continuing. But I think that we have made great progress in cleaning up LIUNA in Chicago so far.

Two of my old friends, Tom Kelly, the former deputy administrator of the Drug Administration and a former FBI SAC, and Tom Sheer, the former assistant director of the New York FBI office, have rececntly joined Quest as senior corporate consultant and senior investigative consultant, respectively. Here in Chicago, we are continuing our work for LIUNA, where much remains to be done.

I am now president and CEO of Quest Consultants International, Ltd. Fortunately, Quest has been quite successful, developing into an outstanding investigative firm with many law firm and Fortune 500 clients. We are continuing to grow, with associated offices throughout the United States. I recently opened a branch office in Palm Beach, Florida. We have also developed investigative assets throughout the world. This is the only investigative firm of any size in the United States that is comprised exclusively of former FBI agents.

In 1996 I attended an FBI party where I met a wonderful woman who was then working as the FBI nurse in Chicago. Sandy and I fell in love and we were married on Valentines Day, February 14, 1999. We are very happy and our respective children (eight) and grandchildren (six) are like brothers and sisters with each other.

***

In this story, I have discussed many cases. Some we won, some we lost. Ultimately, we were successful in eradicating the Mob in Cleveland, but don't think for a minute that we have won the war against La Cosa Nostra. Not by a long shot. We have made great strides, but in many cities, such as Chicago and New York, the Mob remains strong. In many of our cities, the Mob has successfully infiltrated legitimate businesses, so their presence is not so obvious. Unless federal and local law enforcement authorities are vigilant and continue their coordinated efforts against this "cancer from within," the Mob will remain strong, and they will return to the cities in which we have beaten them back.

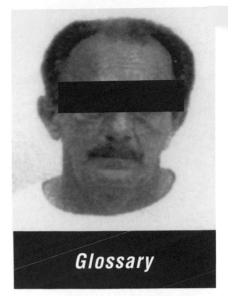

Glossary

Assistant Director (AD) – The number three official at FBI headquarters. The AD reports to the FBI director through the associate director. The AD is responsible for the operations of individual divisions at FBI headquarters.

Assistant Special Agent in Charge (ASAC) – The number two official of an FBI field division. Most FBI field divisions have more than one ASAC, who is responsible for overseeing the operations of the investigative squads assigned to him or her.

Associate Director – The number two official of the FBI. The associate director is most active as the day-to-day coordinator of the activities of the various divisions at FBI headquarters, and represents the FBI director when he is out of the country.

Boss (Capo di Famiglia) – The head of a La Cosa Nostra family. Directives flow down from the boss; profits flow up to the boss.

Bureau Supervisor – The official at FBI headquarters who is responsible for coordinating specific investigative programs. The supervisor is usually responsible for program coordination in specific geographical areas.

Capo (Caporegima, Capodecima) – The head of a crew; reports to the boss and the underboss.

Capo di Tutti Copi ("Boss of All Bosses") – This is a very old concept in La Cosa Nostra. There has not been a capo di tutti capi for many years.

Commission – The national LCN body created in 1931 to oversee organized-crime activities throughout the United States and Canada. The original Commission consisted of the bosses of the five New York City families, as well as the bosses of the Buffalo, Cleveland, and Chicago families. At various times, it has also included the bosses of the Philadelphia and Detroit families. The Commission plays a coordinating and mediating role among the families.

Consigliere (Advisor, Counselor) – Generally an older family member who advises the boss and serves as a buffer between the soldiers and the boss.

Crew – A group of soldiers under the direction of a capo. The size of the crew depends upon the size of the crime family.

Family (La Famiglia) – An individual unit of La Cosa Nostra, comprised of a boss, an underboss, a consigliere, several capos and crews of soldiers, and associates. The territorial jurisdiction of the family is determined and assigned by the Commission. The twenty-four identified La Cosa Nostra families derive their names from either their location or the name of one of the earlier bosses.

Initiation Ceremony – A ceremony in which new members are "made." In this ceremony, a handgun and a knife or dagger is placed on the table in front of the initiate, who holds hands with the boss and other LCN members present. The boss says, "This represents that you live by the gun and the knife and you die by the gun and the knife." The initiate is asked to cup his hands and the boss places a Roman Catholic holy card in his hands and lights the paper. The initiate is told to repeat the words, "This is the way I will burn if I betray the secret of La Cosa Nostra." The initiate recites an oath of allegiance to the crime family over his blood family, his religion, and his country. He is told that to violate any member's wife means death without trial. The initiate's trigger finger is then pricked by the boss, who squeezes the finger until it bleeds and then says, "This blood means that we are now one family."

La Cosa Nostra (LCN) – The national organized-crime operation. La Cosa Nostra was formed in 1931 when the Sicilian Mafia families merged with the Italian Camorra organized-crime families in the United States. La Cosa Nostra translates as "this thing of ours" or "our thing." This organization is uniquely North American. In some cities it is known by other names; in Buffalo it is known as the Arm, and in Chicago it is called the Outfit.

LCN Associate – Individuals who are not made members, but whose criminal activities are directed by or dependent upon the LCN.

Omerta – The rule of silence. After induction into the LCN, death is the penalty for breaking Omerta (for example, by talking to law enforcement or becoming a witness).

Resident Agency (RA) – Satellite FBI office located in a smaller city within an FBI field division. The RA is headed by a supervisory senior resident agent who reports directly to the special agent in charge of the division.

Soldier ("Made" Member) – One who has been proposed for membership, gone through the initiation ceremony, and become a member of La Cosa Nostra.

Special Agent (SA) – Special agents who are assigned to the various investigative squads in an FBI field office. Street agents are the backbone of the FBI, working on the front lines to gather evidence and make cases.

Special Agent in Charge (SAC) – The FBI field commander who heads up one of the fifty-seven field divisions located throughout the United States. All FBI field offices are headed by an SAC, except the largest offices in New York City, Los Angeles, and Washington, D.C., which are headed by an assistant director in charge (ADIC). The SACs and ADICs report directly to the FBI director.

Support Employees – The second most important element in the FBI; support employees operate computers, type reports, answer telephones, maintain files, and conduct other clerical activities so the street agents can concentrate on developing cases.

Underboss – The second in command in an LCN crime family.